DATE DUE

DEMCO 38-296

Specialty **Occupational Outlook:**

Trade & Technical

Highlights

Specialty Occupational Outlook: Trade and Technical (SOO:TT) extends the coverage of the premier career guidance publication, the U.S. Department of Labor's *Occupational Outlook Handbook (OOH)* by 150 selected occupations. Students, first-time job seekers, career changers, counselors, librarians, and other researchers will use these newly compiled profiles to explore such trade and technical occupations as:

- Arborists
- Border patrol officers
- Dietetic technicians
- Bicycle repairers
- Physical therapy assistants and aides
- Legal secretaries
- Smokejumpers
- Psychiatric technicians

- Avionics technicians
- Caterers
- Fish and game wardens
- Corporate travel specialists
- Manicurists
- Solar energy system installers
- Operating engineers
- Veterinary technicians

SOO:TT is also a companion to *Specialty Occupational Outlook: Professions (SOOP)*, which extends the *OOH*'s coverage of administrative, managerial, and professional specialty careers.

New information in a familiar format

SOO:TT presents detailed information on each career under standard *OOH* headings, including:

- Nature of the Work
- Working Conditions
- Employment
- Training, Other Qualifications, and Advancement
- Job Outlook
- Earnings
- Related Occupations
- Sources of Additional Information

Additional features enhance use

- The **At a Glance** fact box at the beginning of each profile highlights key information for easy browsing.

- A combined index of careers quickly directs users to managerial, professional specialty, technical, and trade occupations covered in *SOO:TT, SOOP* and *OOH*.

- The *Dictionary of Occupational Titles (DOT)* index helps career counselors and others locate *DOT* numbers and standard occupational category (SOC) numbers that correspond to occupations covered in *SOO:TT*.

ISSN 1083-4680

Specialty
Occupational
Outlook:

Trade &
Technical

Joyce Jakubiak

Editor

Gale Research

An ITP Information/Reference Group Company

Changing the Way the World Learns

NEW YORK • LONDON • BONN • BOSTON • DETROIT
MADRID • MELBOURNE • MEXICO CITY • PARIS
SINGAPORE • TOKYO • TORONTO • WASHINGTON
ALBANY NY • BELMONT CA • CINCINNATI OH

Editor: Joyce Jakubiak
Contributing Editor: Sara T. Bernstein
y: Theresa J. MacFarlane, Susan Martin, and Tara Sheets

Research Manager: Victoria B. Cariappa
Research Associate: Donna Melnychenko

Production Director: Mary Beth Trimper
Production Assistant: Shanna Heilveil
Art Director: Cynthia Baldwin
Graphic Designer: Pamela A.E. Galbreath
Graphic Services Supervisor: Barbara J. Yarrow

∞™ The paper used in this publication meets the minimum requirements of American National Standard for Information Sciences--Permanence Paper for Printed Library Materials, ANSI Z39.48-1984.

♻ This book is printed on recycled paper that meets Environmental Protection Agency standards.

Copyright © 1996
— Gale Research Inc. —
835 Penobscot Bldg.
Detroit, MI 48226-4094

ISBN 0-8103-9645-9
ISSN 1083-4680

Printed in the United States of America

I(T)P™ Gale Research Inc., an International Thomson Publishing Company.
ITP logo is a trademark under license.

10 9 8 7 6 5 4 3 2 1

Contents

Occupational Coverage

Technicians and Related Support Occupations

Health Technologists and Technicians

Technicians, Except Health

Marketing and Sales Occupations

Administrative Support Occupations, Including Clerical

Service Occupations

Protective Service Occupations

Transportation and Material Moving Occupations

Handlers, Equipment Cleaners, Helpers, and Laborers

Acknowledgments

Specialty Occupational Outlook: Trade and Technical was compiled in consultation with librarians and career experts from across the United States. The following individuals have earned special thanks for their participation throughout the development of the project:

Patrick J. Brunet
Library Manager
Western Wisconsin Technical College
Wisconsin

Christine C. Godin
Public Services Librarian
Johnson County Community College
Kansas

Lynn C. Hattendorf
Associate Professor and Reference Librarian
University of Illinois at Chicago

Michael R. Lavin
Business and Management Subject Specialist
Lockwood Memorial Library
State University of New York at Buffalo

Dale Luchsinger
Director of Library and Media Services
Athens Area Technical Institute
Georgia

The editor would also like to thank the following writers, who contributed material for inclusion in *SOO:TT*: David P. Bianco, Kimberly B. Faulkner, and Michael P. Smith.

Introduction

Specialty Occupational Outlook: Trade and Technical (SOO:TT) expands the career guidance provided by the U.S. Department of Labor's *Occupational Outlook Handbook (OOH)* by profiling 150 additional job titles. Careers covered in *SOO:TT* are those that typically require less than two years of post-secondary education. Occupations were chosen by career librarians and counselors based on popularity, growth potential, and technological advances. By combining authoritative data from government sources, professional associations, and original research, Gale editors have strived to match *OOH* data quality and format to create a useful companion publication.

Arrangement

The order of the 150 profiles contained in *SOO:TT* reflects the general arrangement of the *OOH*. Occupations are covered in 10 areas:

■ Technicians and Related Support Occupations
■ Marketing and Sales Occupations
■ Administrative Support Occupations
■ Service Occupations
■ Agriculture, Forestry, and Related Occupations
■ Mechanics, Installers, and Repairers
■ Construction Trades and Extractive Occupations
■ Production Occupations
■ Transportation and Material Moving Occupations
■ Handlers, Equipment Cleaners, Helpers, and Laborers

SOO:TT is also a companion to *Specialty Occupational Outlook: Professions (SOOP)* (Gale Research Inc.), which contains 150 selected career profiles organized under the first three *OOH* headings:

■ Executive, Administrative, and Managerial Occupations
■ Professional Specialty Occupations
■ Technicians and Related Support Occupations

Some occupations covered in *SOO:TT* and *SOO:P* are mentioned briefly in *OOH* in the context of another essay. *SOO:TT* and *SOO:P* expand this brief coverage into full-length profiles for users who need more detailed information on these job titles. Together, *SOO:TT* and *SOO:P* extend *OOH* coverage by 300 occupations, representing all job categories.

Content

As in the *OOH*, career profiles are organized into eight sections describing different aspects of each occupation. Brief descriptions of each of these sections are provided below.

• **Nature of the Work**. Each profile begins with an explanation of professional duties and responsibilities. This section answers such questions as, "What do these professionals do all day? What equipment do they use on the job?" It also lists specializations available within the field and the effects technological advances may have on job performance. This detailed information about the daily responsibilities of each occupation was compiled using literature from professional associations and agencies, and the U.S. Bureau of Labor Statistics' *Dictionary of Occupational Titles*, as well as published accounts from practicing professionals.

• **Working Conditions**. While many occupations have regular working hours and pleasant surroundings, working conditions do vary. This section describes work hours, stress levels, the physical work environment, and safety conditions specific to a particular job title. It also informs users if a particular job requires irregular hours or frequent overtime, has a high rate of on-the-job injuries, or if the job is performed in hazardous or unpleasant surroundings. Information for this section was compiled using literature provided by professional associations and agencies, published accounts from practicing professionals, and the U.S. Department of Labor's *Selected Characteristics of Occupations Defined in the Revised Dictionary of Occupational Titles*.

• **Employment**. This section provides detailed information on who employs these professionals, how many people in the United States are employed in this profession, and in which areas of the country jobs are available. Where data for a specific occupation is not available, statistics for the broad occupational category that encompasses that career are provided. Information in this section was compiled using literature provided by professional associations and agencies, U.S. Bureau of Labor Statistics' publications *Career Guide to Industries, The American Work Force: 1992-2005, Occupational Projections and Training Data*, and published accounts from practicing professionals.

• **Training, Other Qualifications, and Advancement**. Preparation for most trade and technical positions may require a high school diploma, on-the-job training, a program certificate, an associate degree, and/or licensing or certification. This section describes what type of specific training is necessary, what courses should be taken, and if a degree is necessary. Testing, licensing, and certification data is provided, as well as details about continuing education requirements. This section also describes the advancement process--what tasks are performed at the entry level and what advancement opportunities are available.

In addition to formal preparation requirements, this section also describes personal abilities and qualities that will help ensure success in this career. Information in this section was compiled using literature provided by professional associations and agencies, published accounts from practicing professionals, the *Professional and Occupational Licensing Directory*, published by Gale Research Inc., and the Bureau of Labor Statistics' *Occupational Projections and Training Data*.

• **Job Outlook**. Many factors, such as changing technology, government spending, and shifting demographics, affect future employment in a specific field. This section identifies the growth rate for a specific occupation and which factors affect this growth. It also describes the competition for job openings and job security while employed. Where specific data is not available, statistics for the broad occupational category that encompasses that career are provided. Information in this section was compiled using literature provided by professional associations and agencies, published accounts from practicing professionals, and Bureau of Labor Statistics' publications *Career Guide to Industries, The American Work Force: 1992-2005*, and *Occupational Projections and Training Data*.

• **Earnings**. Workers may be paid hourly wages or an annual salary. This section provides average wages and salaries for individuals in specific occupations. National figures are usually provided, but regional figures may also be included. Entry-level wages, average wages, and wages for experienced workers are also provided when available. For some occupations, information about benefits such as health insurance, vacation, and sick leave is also included. Information in this section was compiled using literature provided by professional associations and agencies, published accounts from practicing professionals, *American Salaries and Wages Survey*, published by Gale Research Inc., and the Bureau of Labor Statistics' *Career Guide to Industries*.

• **Related Occupations**. This section lists occupations with similar functions or educational requirements or for individuals with similar interests. Information in this section was compiled using literature provided by professional associations and agencies, published accounts from practicing professionals, and Bureau of Labor Statistics' publications *Career Guide to Industries* and *Dictionary of Occupational Titles*.

• **Sources of Additional Information**. Associations, unions, and federal agencies are all excellent sources of career information. Organizations that have general career information or specific information regarding areas such as licensing or certification are listed at the end of each entry. Information in this section was compiled using literature provided by professional associations and agencies, the *Encyclopedia of Associations*, published by Gale Research

Inc., and the Bureau of Labor Statistics' *Career Guide to Industries.*

At a Glance Fact Box

The **At a Glance** fact box contains a concise summary of basic information from each entry, including:

- *Dictionary of Occupational Titles (DOT)* reference number
- Preferred level of completed education
- Average salary
- Useful information about the occupation, such as employment trends, training requirements, and industry outlook.

For some occupations, the average salary is listed as "varies." Salaries for these occupations vary too widely to list an accurate average salary figure and users are encouraged to read the entire profile for detailed information.

Indexes Enhance Use

SOO:TT's combined job title index helps users quickly locate trade and technical careers covered in *SOO:TT* as well as all occupations covered in *SOO:P* and *OOH*. This allows the use of only one index to locate over 500 occupations. Page numbers from the 1994-95 edition of *OOH* are cited.

SOO:TT also includes an index that lists *D.O.T.* numbers for each occupation covered in *SOO:TT*. These numbers correspond to entries in the 1991 *Dictionary of Occupational Titles*, Revised Fourth Edition. Also listed are standard occupational classification (SOC) codes corresponding to the job categories cited in the 1980 *Standard Occupational Classification Manual.*

Comments and Suggestions Welcome

Users can make important contributions to future editions of *SOO:TT* by passing along comments and suggestions regarding the format, coverage, and usefulness of this publication. Please address remarks to:

Specialty Occupational Outlook: Trade and Technical
Gale Research Inc.
835 Penobscot Bldg.
Detroit, MI 48226-4094
Phone: (313) 961-2242
(800) 877-GALE
Fax: (313) 961-6083

Specialty
Occupational Outlook:

Trade & Technical

Technicians and Related Support Occupations

Health Technologists and Technicians

DIALYSIS TECHNICIANS

At a Glance

- **D.O.T.:** 078.362-014

- **Preferred Education:** On-the-job training

- **Average Salary:** $18,000 to $45,000

- **Did You Know?** With additional training, dialysis technicians can advance to become biomedical equipment technicians.

Nature of the Work

More than 100,000 people in the United States receive dialysis treatments for kidney problems an average of three times per week. These treatments are given by dialysis technicians, who are also known as *renal dialysis technicians* or *hemodialysis technicians*.

Dialysis technicians connect patients to a dialysis machine, which performs the kidneys' function of filtering out impurities, poisons, wastes, and excess fluid from the patient's blood. The patient's blood is circulated through the machine, cleaned of impurities, and returned to the patient's body.

Before administering treatments, dialysis technicians set up the dialysis machine. This involves positioning the machine properly, attaching and installing tubing, preparing the fluid delivery system, connecting the machine and its pumps, and assembling the appropriate supplies and equipment. If necessary, they test the machine, calibrate and check its alarms, and set its monitors.

Dialysis technicians then prepare patients for treatment. They record the patient's weight, blood pressure, pulse, temperature, and respiratory rate. They try to keep the patient calm, explaining the procedure and how the machine works.

They examine the patient's access sites, where tubes from the dialysis machine are to be inserted. They clean areas of insertion using an antiseptic solution.

Dialysis technicians start the treatment by inserting tubes into the access sites, usually located in the patient's forearm or a catheter site, to start the blood flowing through the dialysis machine. If necessary, they make adjustments to the machine's settings and to the chemical dosages being used. During treatment, dialysis technicians monitor blood-flow rates, making sure pressures are within established limits. They monitor and record the patient's vital signs, checking for any adverse reactions to the treatment.

During treatment, dialysis technicians also make sure the dialysis machine is working properly. They must respond to any alarms that go off and make the necessary adjustments. Throughout the treatment dialysis technicians must follow established standardized procedures and techniques. They must be prepared to respond to any emergency. In some cases they may have to perform cardiopulmonary resuscitation (CPR) or administer oxygen.

After the treatment is over, dialysis technicians again record the patient's weight, blood pressure, pulse, temperature, and respiratory rate. They clean and dress the access sites. They also clean the machine, dispose of any used supplies, and perform any necessary repairs to the machine.

Some patients are able to conduct their own dialysis treatments. In this case dialysis technicians must teach patients about dialysis and how to conduct the treatments. They must show patients how to recognize and deal with problems such as contaminated equipment, bacterial infection, and malfunctioning machines. They may also show family members how to assist the patient during treatment.

In some situations dialysis technicians may have expanded duties. These might include conducting research on how to improve treatments using different equipment. They may be involved with biochemical analyses. Other duties may include supervision and training.

Working Conditions

Dialysis technicians always work under the supervision of nurses and physicians. Treatments may be given in the units where dialysis technicians are employed, or they may be given in patients' homes. In some cases dialysis technicians have to travel locally to patients' homes to give them treatments.

Dialysis technicians typically work standard 40-hour

weeks. They may have to work unusual hours, though, to accommodate the schedules of patients who work during the day.

Their work is not physically demanding and is usually conducted under quiet conditions in a clean environment. They may have to give treatments to critically ill patients, which can be upsetting.

Employment

Most dialysis technicians are employed in the dialysis units of hospitals. Others may work in outpatient clinics, nonprofit centers, or for private companies that operate dialysis units. The Department of Veterans Affairs hires dialysis technicians to work in VA hospitals.

In the health services industry, one out of two health service jobs were in hospitals in 1992. Jobs in health services are found throughout the U.S., but large states such as California, New York, Florida, Texas, and Pennsylvania provide a substantial number of jobs.

Training, Other Qualifications, and Advancement

Dialysis technicians are high school graduates with one to two years of training that is usually learned on the job. Appropriate high school classes include biology, chemistry, science, mathematics, communications, and health-related subjects.

Most dialysis technicians learn the techniques of dialysis treatment through on-the-job training. There are very few formal training courses offered in colleges and universities. On-the-job training typically consists of classroom instruction, demonstrations, and independent study. Students progress through a series of tasks until they achieve proficiency. They learn about anatomy, physiology, kidney disease, medical terminology, infectious diseases, microbiology, and related medical topics. In addition they are given specialized instruction in dialysis therapy, procedures, and equipment.

Dialysis technicians may obtain certification from the Board of Nephrology Examiners. Applicants for certification must be high school graduates. They must be employed in a recognized dialysis facility and have at least one year of experience. To obtain certification applicants must pass a certification examination covering topics such as anatomy, physiology, dialysis, treatments and technology related to renal failure, and general medical knowledge.

Dialysis technicians are genuinely interested in helping people with their physical problems. They must have good communication and language skills to be able to put patients at ease, communicate with members of the dialysis team, and to read scientific books, technical manuals, and journals. They must have good observation and recording skills. Other important qualities include patience and the ability to remain calm during medical emergencies.

Dialysis technicians can advance to supervisory positions, especially if they are employed in large dialysis units. They may be promoted to chief technician. With additional education or training, they may advance to become biomedical equipment technicians or nurses.

Job Outlook

According to the Bureau of Labor Statistics, the health technicians and technologists occupational category that includes dialysis technicians is expected to increase by nearly 44 percent between 1992 and 2005, which is faster than the average for all occupations.

The growing number of people receiving dialysis treatments will support the need for dialysis technicians, who provide most of that treatment. Factors that may temper employment growth for dialysis technicians include people on home dialysis and an increase in the number of kidney transplants, which eliminates the need for dialysis.

Earnings

Salaries for dialysis technicians vary depending on experience and proficiency. According to the National Association of Nephrology Technologists, annual salaries range from $18,000 to $45,000. Most dialysis technicians work for hospitals or other institutions that provide full benefits, including medical insurance, paid vacations and holidays, and sick leave.

Related Occupations

Occupations in medical and dental technology are concerned with the application of technical knowledge to examine and treat patients, or for research. Other occupations in this category include medical technologists, cardiopulmonary technologists, cytotechnologists, dental hygienists, nuclear medicine technologists, EKG technicians, radiation-therapy technologists, perfusionists, MRI technicians, CT scan technicians, cardiac catheterization technicians, angiographers, and ultrasound technicians.

There are many related occupations in therapy and rehabilitation, including recreational therapists, dental hygienists, psychiatric technicians, orthoptists, occupational therapists and occupational therapy assistants, physical therapists and physical therapy assistants, respiratory therapists, hypnotherapists, art and music therapists, radiologic technologists, and athletic trainers.

Sources of Additional Information

For additional information contact:

- Board of Nephrology Examiners--Nursing and Technology, PO Box 44085, Madison, WI 53719. Phone: (913)541-9077.

- National Association of Nephrology Technologists, 60 Revere Dr., Ste. 500, Northbrook, IL 60062. Phone: (513)223-9765.

- National Kidney Foundation, 30 E. 33rd St., Ste. 1100, New York, NY 10016. Phone: (212)889-2210.

- American Hospital Association, 1 N. Franklin, Ste. 27, Chicago, IL 60611. Phone: (312)422-3000.

- National Health Council, 1730 M St. NW, Ste. 500, Washington, DC 20036. Phone: (202)785-3910.

DIETETIC TECHNICIANS

At a Glance

- **D.O.T.:** 077.124-010

- **Preferred Education:** Associate degree

- **Average Salary:** $12,500 to $18,700

- **Did You Know?** Dietetic technicians usually start out as assistants to professional dietitians or food service directors.

Nature of the Work

Diet and nutrition are recognized as important elements in maintaining health and wellness. Dietetic technicians work independently or under the direction of professional dietitians in many different employment settings involving health care and food service. Their responsibilities may range from seeing that dietary programs for hospital patients are properly implemented by food service personnel to gathering data about individual nutrition needs.

The specific duties of dietetic technicians depend on the nature of their employment. In health care settings such as hospitals, hospices, and nursing homes, dietetic technicians generally work under the supervision of a registered dietitian. They are concerned with the nutrition of individual patients, each of whom may require a different nutrition program. In such cases dietetic technicians provide dietitians with the support necessary to properly implement and monitor individual nutrition programs.

The duties of dietetic technicians involved in nutrition care include interviewing patients about their eating habits and food preferences. They may consult with patients and their families about food selection, preparation, and menu planning. Based on this information, dietitians develop nutrition programs that are monitored by dietetic technicians. In some cases dietetic technicians submit menu recommendation for patients and help patients select their own menus.

Dietetic technicians may also be involved with patient education. They may teach patients and their families about nutrition. They may work in community programs where they are expected to teach families how to purchase food and prepare nutritional meals. Once patients are discharged, dietetic technicians may keep in touch with them to monitor their diets.

Dietetic technicians may work independently in food service management. Their duties may include supervision of food preparation in institutional kitchens. They may supervise individuals who serve food to patients in their rooms or in lunchrooms. They may be responsible for making up work schedules for food service personnel. They may also train individuals working in the food service department. Other areas of responsibility for dietetic technicians may include cost control, safety, food sanitation, food storage, and procuring and receiving supplies and equipment.

In some cases, dietetic technicians may have to fulfill nutrition-related clerical duties if there are no diet clerks on staff. Clerical duties involve recording and processing information regarding food portions, diet orders, and menus for different departments of a hospital or other healthcare institution. Information on new diets and changes must be recorded and processed. They may verbally inform food service personnel about such matters as meal changes, complaints, and patient discharges.

Working Conditions

Wherever dietetic technicians work, conditions are usually clean, well-lighted, and well-equipped. In most institutions they work standard eight-hour shifts. They must be fast and accurate to finish their work in time. While their work is not physically demanding, dietetic technicians may have to stand for long periods of time during food preparation. Food preparation also requires frequent reaching and handling.

Employment

Dietetic technicians work in various settings. These include clinical settings such as hospitals, clinics, HMOs, nursing homes, retirement centers, hospices, home health care programs, and research facilities. Dietetic technicians working in food service management are employed by institutions such as schools, day care centers, correctional facilities, restaurants, corporations, hospitals, and long-term care facilities.

Other employment opportunities for dietetic technicians are in community health programs and public agencies. Health clubs, weight management clinics, and community wellness centers also employ dietetic technicians. They may also work for food companies, food vendors, and food distributors.

Training, Other Qualifications, and Advancement

The basic educational requirement for dietetic technicians is a two-year associate degree. There are more than 70 two-year programs accredited by the American Dietetic Association (ADA). Accredited programs combine academic study with 450 hours of supervised practical experience.

The ADA also offers a "Dietetic Technician, Registered" credential, which allows dietetic technicians to use the initials, DTR. The DTR credential indicates that the dietetic technician holds at least an associate degree, has completed an approved dietetics program and supervised practice, and has passed the Registration Examination for Dietetic Technicians. To keep their credential, DTRs must complete 50 hours of continuing education every five years.

Dietetic technicians usually start out as assistants to professional dietitians or food service directors. They may advance to supervisory or management positions in food service. With a bachelor's degree and additional training, they are eligible to become registered dietitians.

Job Outlook

A number of factors indicate a strong demand for dietetic technicians in the future. An aging population and a growing emphasis on health and nutrition contribute to a demand for the services of dietetic technicians and others in the nutrition field. Employment in the health services industry as a whole is projected to increase 43 percent through the year 2005, about twice as fast as the average for all industries. According to the Bureau of Labor Statistics, employment of the related occupation of food service managers will increase by 43.5 percent between 1992 and 2005.

Earnings

According to *American Salaries and Wages Survey*, average salaries for dietetic technicians ranged from approximately $12,480 to $18,720 per year in 1993. Higher-level earnings ranged from about $15,912 to $30,680 per year.

Related Occupations

Other occupations concerned with the application of the principles of nutrition include several different types of dietitians such as research dietitians, community dietitians, clinical dietitians, consulting dietitians, and teaching dietitians.

Related food service occupations include kitchen supervisors, hospital food service workers, food service supervisors, industrial cafeteria managers, and kitchen-food assemblers.

Sources of Additional Information

- American Dietetic Association, 216 W. Jackson Blvd., Ste. 800, Chicago, IL 60606. Phone: (312)899-0040.

- National Health Council, 1730 M St. NW, Ste. 500, Washington, DC 20036. Phone: (202)785-3910.

- American Institute of Nutrition, 9650 Rockville Pike, Bethesda, MD 20814. Phone: (301)530-7050.

PSYCHIATRIC TECHNICIANS

At a Glance

- **D.O.T.:** 079.374-026

- **Preferred Education:** Associate degree

- **Average Salary:** $13,800 to $17,000

- **Did You Know?** Psychiatric hospitals and mental health clinics are the major employers of psychiatric technicians.

Nature of the Work

Working under the supervision of doctors, nurses, or mental health professionals, psychiatric technicians perform a range of duties involving emotionally disturbed, mentally ill, or mentally impaired patients in psychiatric hospitals or mental health clinics. Their duties may include participating in rehabilitation and treatment programs, observing and reporting on patients' behavior patterns, interviewing and counseling patients, contacting and conferring with patients' families, issuing medication, and maintaining records.

Psychiatric technicians also perform routine nursing tasks. They may take patients' temperatures, record pulse and respiration rates, and monitor and record other aspects of their patients' physical condition. They administer oral medication and give hypodermic injections, following a physician's prescription and established hospital procedures. Psychiatric technicians also help patients with their personal hygiene, including bathing and keeping their clothing, beds, and living areas clean.

Psychiatric technicians take part in patients' rehabilitation and treatment programs. They may be involved in planning as well as implementing such programs. They may lead individual or group therapy sessions. They may interview patients and gather information about them that serves as a basis for planning programs for each patient and monitoring their progress. They may administer psychological tests.

In hospitals, psychiatric technicians sometimes work in admitting units where they are responsible for admitting, screening, evaluating, and discharging patients. They may put patients in touch with community mental health services and make referrals. They may contact patients' families to set up conferences.

Psychiatric technicians are sometimes available to help their patients after they have left the hospital or institution. They may visit discharged patients at home. They may help patients with individual concerns, such as finding employment or housing, or help them with their personal finances. Psychiatric technicians sometimes help their patients locate services, agencies, and mental health professionals that are available to serve them.

There are some opportunities for psychiatric technicians to specialize by working with certain types of patients. Typical areas of specialization include working with mentally disturbed children, participating in alcohol and substance abuse programs, and working in community mental health.

Community mental health involves working with patients who are not hospitalized. Specialized problem areas in community mental health include alcohol and substance abuse, parenting, aging, and interpersonal relationships.

Working Conditions

Psychiatric technicians interact with a wide range of individuals. They are supervised by doctors, nurses, and mental health professionals. They spend a lot of time talking and listening to their patients. They may have to work closely with patients who are depressed, suicidal, violent, or otherwise difficult to handle.

Most healthcare institutions where psychiatric technicians work are clean and well lighted, although conditions may be moderately noisy.

Psychiatric technicians typically work a standard five-day, 40-hour week. They may occasionally have to work evenings, weekends, and holidays.

Employment

According to the Bureau of Labor Statistics, there were approximately 72,000 psychiatric technicians employed in 1992. Psychiatric hospitals and mental health clinics are the major employers of psychiatric technicians. Other places of employment include general hospitals, social service agencies, schools for the mentally impaired, and other facilities that provide psychiatric services.

Training, Other Qualifications, and Advancement

Psychiatric technicians are usually high school graduates with a two-year associate degree in a related field such as mental health, social services, or human services. While entrance requirements to these two-year programs vary from school to school, appropriate high school courses include biology, psychology, sociology, and English.

Two-year degree programs typically include general study, mental health subjects, and practical training. They cover subjects such as human development, abnormal psychology, mental illness, anatomy, physiology, basic nursing, and medical science. Social science courses provide an understanding of family and community structures. Practical training covers interviewing skills, psychological testing, crisis intervention, child guidance, group counseling, family therapy, and behavior modification.

A few states require psychiatric technicians to be licensed. While requirements vary from state to state, they typically include at least two years of appropriate training and a licensing examination.

Psychiatric technicians are people who are genuinely interested in helping others with their mental, social, and physical problems. They must have good communication skills and a stable personality to help patients with a wide range of psychological and behavioral problems. They must be good listeners and observers. Other necessary qualities include patience, understanding, a sense of responsibility, and the ability to remain calm under trying circumstances.

Psychiatric technicians can advance in their careers by gaining more experience, education, and training. They may be promoted to positions of greater responsibility in the institutions where they are employed.

Job Outlook

Employment of psychiatric technicians is projected to increase from 72,000 in 1992 to 90,000 in 2005. This 26 percent increase is somewhat higher than the average for all occupations.

Several factors will support the increased need for psychiatric technicians. It is expected that more community mental health clinics will be created to treat patients who are released from hospitals and other institutions after a short period of institutionalization. There will be an increased need for psychiatric technicians in public schools as schools provide more education for mentally and emotionally impaired children. Psychiatric technicians also help reduce overall health care costs by performing tasks that were once assigned to higher-paid professionals.

Earnings

According to *American Salaries and Wages Survey*, entry-level salaries for psychiatric technicians were approximately $12,500 in 1992. Experienced technicians earned between $13,800 and $17,000. Higher-paid technicians earned $25,000 or more.

Related Occupations

There are many related occupations in therapy and rehabilitation, including recreational therapists, dental hygienists, dialysis technicians, orthoptists, occupational therapists and occupational therapy assistants, physical therapists and physical therapy assistants, respiratory therapists, hypnotherapists, art and music therapists, radiologic technologists, and athletic trainers.

Sources of Additional Information

- American Association of Psychiatric Technicians, 2030 E. Broadway Blvd., Ste. 218, PO Box 13912, Tucson, AZ 85732. Phone: (602)321-2075.

- American Psychiatric Association, 1400 K St. NW, Washington, DC 20005. Phone: (202)682-6000.

- National Mental Health Association, 1021 Prince St., Alexandria, VA 22314-2971.

RESPIRATORY THERAPY TECHNICIANS

At a Glance

- **D.O.T.:** 076.361-014

- **Preferred Education:** High school diploma and certified vocational training

- **Average Salary:** $20,500 (entry level)

- **Did You Know?** In 1992, there were 187 accredited programs for respiratory therapy technicians.

Nature of the Work

Breathing is a person's most immediate need. A person can survive without food for weeks, without water for days, but a person deprived of air will die within minutes. Respiratory therapy technicians are trained to evaluate, treat, and care for patients with breathing disorders.

Many people have impaired or non-functioning lungs caused by either a serious illness or an accident. Respiratory therapy technicians treat various types of patients, including premature infants with under-developed lungs; people with chronic lung problems, such as asthma or emphysema; and victims of lung disease, stroke, heart failure, drowning, or shock.

Respiratory therapy technicians work under a physician's supervision in a variety of healthcare settings and assist in the diagnosis, treatment, and management of breathing-impaired patients.

Respiratory therapy technicians can be members of hospital response teams that tend to patient emergencies. They are present during high-risk deliveries, where it is possible that a premature baby will have breathing complications. They help administer life-saving oxygen to heart attack, stroke, or traumatized accident victims who have lost the ability to breathe on their own.

Respiratory therapy technicians provide temporary relief to asthmatic patients and patients with emphysema. They are responsible for the ongoing monitoring and treatment of patients with cardiopulmonary disease. To help patients who have chronic lung problems, respiratory therapy technicians are involved in rehabilitation activities. Many patients with lung problems may never regain their total lung function. Respiratory therapy technicians help these people rehabilitate their pulmonary systems to their fullest capacity.

Monitoring patients who are using oxygen or ventilators is a routine part of the work day. Respiratory therapy technicians constantly check equipment to make certain that it is functioning properly and that there are no complications. If equipment readings are abnormal, or if a patient is having trouble breathing, adjustments are made. Respiratory therapy technicians alert the physician and regulate equipment according to the physician's orders. In the area of diagnosis, respiratory therapy technicians measure the capacity of a patient's lungs to determine if there is impaired function. They draw blood and have samples analyzed to determine the levels of oxygen, carbon dioxide, and other gases. Results are given to the physician. Whether or not lung deficiencies exist can be assessed by comparing these measurements with normal readings for a person of the same age, gender, weight, and height. The physician can then decide the best course of treatment for the patient.

Once a disorder is diagnosed, respiratory therapy technicians are responsible for treating patients and providing therapy that will help them recover their lung function. They do this by using various types of equipment that stimulate breathing or administers oxygen. The three most common treatments are the administration of oxygen or oxygen mixtures, chest physiotherapy, or the administration of aerosol medications.

Respiratory therapy technicians teach patients and their families how to use and maintain breathing equipment in their homes. They may make routine visits to make certain a patient is properly using and maintaining breathing equipment.

Respiratory therapy technicians may also direct smoking cessation programs to prevent the onset of lung disease.

Working Conditions

Most respiratory therapy technicians are employed by hospitals, which operate 24 hours a day, seven days a week. Thus, respiratory therapy technicians may work a shift at any time during the day or week, including nights, weekends, and holidays. Respiratory therapy technicians are under a certain amount of stress due to the critical nature of their work. They must also adhere to established safety procedures.

Employment

According to the American Association for Respiratory Care, there are approximately 100,000 respiratory care practitioners employed in the United States. About 80,000 work in hospitals; 20,000 work for nursing facilities, rehabilitation facilities, and home healthcare companies.

Training, Other Qualifications, and Advancement

Most states require that respiratory therapy technicians become certified before practicing. To become certified, candidates undergo a 12- to 18-month training program. Accredited programs are available at vocational/technical schools and community colleges. According to the Department of Labor, there were 187 preparation programs for respiratory therapy technicians that were accredited by the American Medical Associations' Committee on Allied Health Education and Accreditation in 1992. Students are taught human anatomy and physiology, physics, chemistry, microbiology, and math. Much of their training involves treatment administration, breathing equipment operation, and sterilization procedures.

Graduates are awarded certificates of completion. Once this certificate is granted, they can take the entry-level examination for a Certified Respiratory Therapy Technician (CRTT). If they pass the exam and meet other specific requirements, they are awarded the CRTT credential.

Respiratory therapy technicians must be sensitive to the needs of physically impaired patients. They must carefully follow instructions and be able to pay strict attention to detail. They must also be able to work well as a team member.

With additional education, training and certification, respiratory therapy technicians may advance to become respiratory therapists. Respiratory therapist programs generally last two to four years and lead to the designation of Registered Respiratory Therapist (RRT). Respiratory therapists may care for patients who are in critical condition or specialize in an area of respiratory care, such as neonatal care. Further education can lead to supervisory or management positions.

Job Outlook

According to the U.S. Bureau of Labor Statistics, job openings for respiratory care practitioners will increase 52 percent by the year 2005, much faster than average for all occupations. The need for respiratory therapy technicians will be brought on by an aging population and expected increases in cardiopulmonary disease, the increasing number of AIDS patients with lung disease, and treatment advances for premature babies, accident victims, and heart attack victims.

Earnings

Earnings for respiratory therapy technicians vary by employer, geographic region, and experience. According to the American Association for Respiratory Care, starting salaries for certified respiratory therapy technicians average $20,500 per year. Respiratory technicians earn somewhat less than respiratory therapists, whose median earnings were $32,084 in 1992, according to the Bureau of Labor Statistics. According to *American Salaries and Wages Survey*, respiratory therapists earned an average salary of $30,264 per year in 1993. Full-time respiratory therapists and technicians receive benefits such as paid vacations, health and life insurance, and retirement plans.

Related Occupations

Other occupations similar to respiratory therapist technicians include respiratory therapists, dialysis technicians, registered nurses, occupational therapists, physical therapists, and radiation therapy technologists.

Sources of Additional Information

For more information on a career as a respiratory therapist technician, contact:

- American Association for Respiratory Care, 11030 Ables Ln., Dallas, TX 75229-4593.

- The National Board for Respiratory Care, Inc., 8310 Nieman Rd., Lenexa, KS 66214.

- Joint Review Committee for Respiratory Therapy Education, 1701 W. Euless Blvd., Ste. 300, Euless, TX 76040.

SPECIAL PROCEDURES TECHNOLOGISTS

At a Glance

- **D.O.T.:** 078.362-046; 078.362-050; 078.362-054; 078.362-058

- **Preferred Education:** Two-year radiography program

- **Average Salary:** $23,000 to $34,000

- **Did You Know?** Most medical special procedure technologists learn their skills in two-year radiography programs offered by hospitals, colleges and universities, and vocational-technical institutes.

Nature of the Work

Physicians commonly use x-rays to diagnose broken bones. For special procedures, however, hospitals, clinics, and other medical facilities use even more advanced technologies to produce images or "pictures" of the interior of the body. These diagnostic imaging techniques include radiography, magnetic resonance imaging, and computed tomography. Special procedures technologists operate and monitor diagnostic imaging equipment during the examination of patients.

Angiogram radiographers operate diagnostic imaging equipment that generates images of a patient's blood vessels. They position the patient for examination, often using head or shoulder braces to hold the patient in place. To perform an angiogram, a contrast media, which is a substance opaque to radiation, must be injected into blood vessels. Angiogram radiographers operate an instrument called a fluoroscope to help physicians inject this substance. The fluoroscope helps physicians see into the blood vessel so they can guide a long, flexible tube called a catheter through the blood vessel to the desired area of the body.

Angiogram radiographers use an automatic injector to inject the substance through the catheter into the patient's blood vessel. They monitor the blood vessel on a video display and adjust the density and contrast to get the best image. If a film of the angiogram is needed, angiogram radiographers deliver the film to a darkroom for development. They review the finished images for accuracy and quality.

Cardiac catheterization radiographers perform many of the same duties as angiogram radiographers. Their equipment, however, produces enhanced images of a patient's heart and cardiovascular system. Physicians use these images to perform cardiac catheterizations. During cardiac catheterizations, physicians instill enzymes or insert a small balloon into a patient's blood vessel to remove a blockage.

CT scan technologists operate computer tomography scanners that produce cross-sectional images of a patient's body. Physicians use these radiographs to view body tissue in isolated planes or sections. CT technologists use supportive devices to position and immobilize the patient on the examining table. They administer the contrast media orally or help the physician inject it into the patient. They also enter data into the computer, such as the type of scan requested, slice thickness, and scan time.

CT technologists scan the patient's body with the CT scanner. To ensure patient safety and comfort, they talk to the patient over an intercom system and observe the patient through windows in the control room. CT technologists view images of the organs or tissue on the video display screen to make sure they meet quality standards. Once the images are correct, technologists start the camera that produces the radiographs.

Another special procedure performed by technologists is magnetic resonance imaging. MRI equipment uses powerful magnets to produce cross-sectional photographs of a patient's body for diagnostic purposes. *MRI technologists* talk to patients to explain MRI procedures. They position the patient on the examining table and place a receiver or coil, such as a head coil or knee coil, near the area of interest. They also demonstrate the intercom system that allows patients and technologists to communicate during the procedure. MRI technologists enter commands into the computer. They observe the patient through a window or on a television monitor. They view the images of the patient's body on a video display screen and activate a camera to photograph the images.

Working Conditions

Medical special procedure technologists typically work a standard 40-hour week. Some, however, may work evening or night shifts in hospitals. They generally work under the direct supervision of a physician, radiologist, or surgeon. Most work in clean, sanitary, well-lit areas in hospitals or diagnostic clinics. Some technologists travel in mobile vans equipped with MRI equipment to rural communities. Technologists follow rigid safety procedures to minimize the hazards of working with radiation.

Employment

In 1992, there were about 14,200 medical special procedure technologists employed in the United States. Most worked in hospitals, health maintenance organizations, outpatient health facilities, and diagnostic imaging centers, universities, and private practices.

Training, Other Qualifications, and Advancement

Most medical special procedure technologists learn their skills in two-year radiography programs offered by hospitals, colleges and universities, and vocational-technical institutes. Some colleges and universities offer bachelor's degrees in radiologic technologies. One-year certificate programs are available for individuals from other health occupations such as medical technologists and registered nurses who want to change careers.

Radiography programs require a high school diploma. These programs include classroom and laboratory sessions, and supervised experience in a clinical setting. Classroom instruction typically includes courses on patient care, radiation safety and protection, medical terminology, anatomy, principles and techniques of diagnostic imaging, and instrumentation and procedures. Graduates of a radiography program can apply for certification with the American Registry of Radiologic Technologists. Certification requires passing a comprehensive test. Many employers prefer to hire certified technologists. Some states also require radiographers to be licensed.

Technologists become medical special procedure technologists with additional training and experience. Experienced special procedure technologists may be promoted to supervisor, chief radiologic technologist, and department administrator or director. Other career paths include education, research administration, commercial applications, or sales and marketing.

Job Outlook

Employment of medical special procedure technologists is expected to grow faster than the average for all occupations through the year 2005. Physicians are increasing their use of cardiac catheterization, magnetic resonance imaging, and computed tomography to diagnose heart disease, cancer, and other diseases. Also, the growing and aging population in the

United States, which has a high risk of such diseases, should result in a growing demand for diagnostic imaging services.

Earnings

The earnings of medical special procedures technologists depend upon their education, experience, area of specialization, and geographic location. The U.S. Bureau of Labor Statistics reported that the median annual earnings for radiologic technologists, which includes special procedures technologists, was $28,236 in 1992. The middle 50 percent earned between $22,932 and $33,748 per year; 10 percent earned less than $19,708; and 10 percent earned more than $40,456. Depending on the employer, technologists receive such benefits as paid vacations, sick leave, health and life insurance, retirement benefits, and tuition reimbursement.

Related Occupations

Other workers who operate sophisticated equipment to help physicians, dentists, and other health practitioners diagnose and treat patients include nuclear medicine technologists, perfusionists, respiratory therapists, clinical laboratory technologists, and electroencephalographic technologists.

Sources of Additional Information

- American Registry of Radiologic Technologists, 1255 Northland Dr., St. Paul, MN 55120. Phone: (612)687-0048.
- American Society of Radiologic Technologists, 15000 Central Ave. SE, Albuquerque, NM 87123. Phone: (505)298-4500.
- Society for Magnetic Resonance Imaging, 2118 Milvia St., Ste. 201, Berkeley, CA 94704. Phone: (510)841-1899.

ULTRASOUND TECHNOLOGISTS

At a Glance

- **D.O.T.:** 078.364-010
- **Preferred Education:** Two-year program
- **Average Salary:** $30,000 to $35,000
- **Did You Know?** The demand for ultrasound technologists is expected to outpace the supply of qualified candidates.

Nature of the Work

Ultrasound is a high frequency sound wave that is used to create two-dimensional pictures of a person's internal body parts. These pictures are examined by physicians to diagnose abnormalities, injuries, and diseases. The individuals who operate ultrasound machines and perform sonographic examinations are ultrasound technologists. They are also known as diagnostic medical sonographers, or simply as sonographers.

Ultrasound is one of several diagnostic imaging techniques used in healthcare today. Diagnostic imaging provides physicians with visual representations of a patient's body parts, including bones, organs, tissue, arteries, and blood vessels.

Ultrasound technologists perform sonographic examinations using ultrasound equipment that sends high frequency sound waves into specific areas of the patient's body. The equipment collects the reflected sound waves to form an image that can be viewed on a screen. When conducting an examination, technologists watch the screen to make sure the image is suitable for diagnostic purposes. They record the image on a printout strip, film, videotape, magnetic tape, or computer disk. The images are then interpreted by a licensed physician.

Ultrasound technologists work closely with their patients. They explain the procedure to them and position them for testing. In performing sonographic examinations, ultrasound technologists closely follow instructions received from physicians. They may discuss results with their supervisor or a physician.

Ultrasound technologists and other diagnostic imaging technologists are part of a healthcare team. In addition to performing sonographic examinations, they are also responsible for maintaining accurate records, adjusting and maintaining their equipment, reviewing patient history, and recording data for interpretation by supervising physicians.

Working Conditions

Ultrasound technologists work under conditions similar to those of other diagnostic imaging technologists. They interact frequently with patients, supervisors, physicians, and other members of the healthcare team. Working closely with patients may expose them to communicable diseases. Their work is not physically demanding, but they may be on their feet for long periods of time. They may also have to turn or lift disabled patients.

Ultrasound technologists usually give sonographic examinations under quiet, clean, well-lighted conditions typical of a laboratory or healthcare institution. They generally work standard 40-hour weeks, with occasional overtime.

Employment

There were approximately 16,000 ultrasound technologists employed in 1992. They work in hospitals, diagnostic imaging centers and clinics, physicians' offices, and industry, such as equipment manufacturers.

Training, Other Qualifications, and Advancement

Ultrasound technologists generally have two to four years of specific vocational preparation that includes some formal

training. They are high school graduates who have completed training programs that last from one to four years, with two years being the most common. These programs are offered by hospitals, community colleges, and universities. Depending on their length, the programs lead to a certificate, associate degree, or bachelor's degree. One-year certificate programs are usually taken by individuals with previous experience in a related healthcare field who have already completed a two-year program in another specialty. There are approximately 80 programs in the United States that provide sonography education. Approximately 52 of the programs are accredited by the Committee on Allied Health Education and Accreditation (CAHEA) of the American Medical Association. Admission requirements to these programs vary, but typically they require either two years of college or previous experience in a related allied health field. Appropriate pre-admission courses of study include science and mathematics. English and communication courses are also recommended.

Formal training in sonography includes classroom instruction, laboratory sessions, and supervised experience in a hospital ultrasound department. Typical areas of study include ultrasound physics and instrumentation, equipment standards, biologic effects, physiology and pathophysiology, general anatomy, cross sectional anatomy, patient care, clinical medicine, ultrasound applications and limitations, related diagnostic procedures, image evaluation, and administration.

Ultrasound technologists are not licensed in any state except Utah. Technologists may become registered with the American Registry of Diagnostic Medical Sonographers, which certifies their competence. Registered technologists must have graduated from a CAHEA-approved program or have met other prerequisites and have passed an examination.

Ultrasound technologists are people with an interest in using scientific research findings to solve medical problems. They must have the mechanical ability to operate laboratory equipment to perform tests and examinations. They must have highly developed reasoning skills to collect data, establish facts, and draw valid conclusions. They must be able to interpret technical instructions.

Since they work closely with patients, ultrasound technologists must be caring and compassionate. They must have good communication skills to effectively deal with patients and other healthcare professionals. Good vision is required to determine precise differences in shape, color, and texture.

Ultrasound technologists can advance with experience and training. They may learn other specialties in diagnostic imaging. In large imaging departments they may be promoted to supervisor, administrator, or director. Some technologists choose to become instructors or take jobs as sales representatives with equipment manufacturers.

Job Outlook

While the Bureau of Labor Statistics does not publish separate employment projections for ultrasound technologists, the category of radiologic technologists and technicians is one of the fastest growing occupational categories. According to the BLS, employment of radiologic technologists and technicians, including ultrasound technologists, is expected to increase by nearly 63 percent between 1992 and 2005.

The demand for ultrasound technologists is expected to outpace the supply of qualified candidates. This demand will be supported by the increased use of ultrasound for diagnosis, especially in cardiology and obstetrics/gynecology. In addition, the rapid growth of healthcare facilities, such as offices and clinics of physicians, that employ ultrasound technologists will create more opportunities for employment. New applications of ultrasound technology, in addition to those currently in use, are also expected in the future.

Earnings

Earnings depend on such factors as geographic location, education and experience, and type of employer. The national average for experienced ultrasound technologists typically ranges from $30,000 to $35,000. Entry-level salaries range from $20,000 to $27,000 depending on the factors cited above. Most ultrasound technologists are employed in hospitals or clinics that provide benefits such as health insurance, paid vacations and holidays, and sick leave.

Related Occupations

Closely related diagnostic imaging occupations include radiographers, radiation therapists, and nuclear medicine technologists. Related occupations involving medical technology include cardiovascular technologists and technicians, perfusionists, respiratory therapists, clinical laboratory technologists, and electroencephalographic (EEG)

technicians. Other occupations for health technologists and technicians include dental technicians, emergency medical technicians, dispensing opticians, surgical technologists, licensed practical nurses, and medical records technicians.

Individuals primarily interested in laboratory technology might consider careers as laboratory technicians and testers, pharmacists and pharmacist assistants, fingerprint classifiers, metallurgical technicians, spectroscopists, criminalists, and forensics ballistics experts.

Sources of Additional Information

* American Registry of Diagnostic Medical Sonographers, 2368 Victory Pky., Ste. 510, Cincinnati, OH 45206-2810. Phone: (513)281-7111.

* Society of Diagnostic Medical Sonographers, 12770 Coit Rd., Ste. 508, Dallas, TX 75251. Phone: (214)239-7367.

* American Registry of Radiologic Technologists, 1255 Northland Dr., St. Paul, MN 55120. Phone: (612)687-0048.

* American Society of Radiologic Technologists, 15000 Central Ave. SE, Albuquerque, NM 87123-3909. Phone: (505)298-4500.

* American Medical Association, Division of Allied Health Education and Accreditation, 515 N. State St., Chicago, IL 60610. Phone: (312)464-5000.

* National Health Council, 1730 M St. NW, Ste. 500, Washington, DC 20036. Phone: (202)785-3910.

Technicians, Except Health

AGRICULTURAL AIRCRAFT PILOTS

At a Glance

- **D.O.T.:** 196.263-010

- **Preferred Education:** Flight training program and commercial pilot's license.

- **Average Salary:** $17,000

- **Did You Know?** Work is seasonal for agricultural aircraft pilots, ranging from six to nine months in the southern states to two months in the north.

Nature of the Work

Agricultural aircraft pilots fly specially designed airplanes and helicopters to apply herbicides, insecticides, and fertilizers on crops, orchards, and other areas. They also spread seeds for reforestation and assist in firefighting efforts by dumping fire retardants.

Like other pilots, agricultural pilots test their aircraft to make sure the engines and other systems are functioning properly prior to a flight. Their flights generally involve flying at low levels in regular patterns over a designated area. They observe flags or markers to make sure they cover an entire field evenly. Since they fly at low levels, agricultural pilots must be familiar with obstacles or hazards, such as trees, powerlines, fences, and hills. They acquaint themselves with the area by studying maps and making test flights. They must be aware of weather and wind conditions and be able to recognize the possible danger of chemicals drifting to other fields or near livestock. Some agricultural pilots may also perform aerial surveys of cattle and crops.

Working Conditions

Agricultural pilots generally fly during the early morning and early evening when the air is still. Takeoffs are often made from country roads and open fields. Work is seasonal, ranging from six to nine months in the southern states to two months in the north. Agricultural pilots usually own their own aircraft.

Pilots must wear protective clothing and masks to protect themselves from poisonous liquids and chemicals.

Employment

According to the Federal Aviation Administration (FAA), approximately 3,300 agricultural operators in the United States employ more than 25,000 people and operate some 9,000 aircraft. Agricultural pilots are in demand mostly in California and southern states where the crop-growing season is longest. Many pilots travel north as the season progresses. Others work in the northeastern and western states with extensive forest areas.

Training, Other Qualifications, and Advancement

Agricultural aircraft pilots must complete a flight training program and earn a commercial pilot's license. To do this, they must be at least 18 years old and have at least 500 hours of accident-free, precision, low-level flying experience. A Class II Medical Certificate is also required.

In general, candidates for aircraft pilot positions must be in good health and pass a strict physical examination. They must have 20/20 vision with or without glasses, good hearing, and no physical handicaps that could impair performance. They must also pass a written test covering safety, navigation techniques, and FAA regulations. (For more information on the qualifications of aircraft pilots, see the *Occupational Outlook Handbook*.)

Organizations other than airlines generally require less flying experience. A commercial pilot's license is a minimum requirement, and employers of agricultural aircraft pilots prefer applicants with specialized flight training in agricultural applications.

Advancement for all types of pilots is generally limited to other flying jobs. Many pilots start as flight instructors while they gain flying experience. Other jobs may involve flying charter flights or working for small air transportation firms.

Job Outlook

Employment for all pilots is expected to grow 30 percent between 1992 and the year 2005. However, the U.S. Department of Labor expects considerable competition for jobs. One reason is the increasing number of pilots leaving the Armed Forces and looking for jobs in the civilian sector. This situation will be compounded by the large number of airline pilots who lost their jobs due to restructuring in the industry.

Earnings

According to the FAA, the average mid-range salary for agricultural pilots is $17,000. Some pilots also receive a percentage of the fees charged by their employer. By earning wages in the off-season through other commercial flying jobs, agricultural pilots can earn as much as $30,000 to $35,000 per year.

Related Occupations

Other commercial pilot occupations include patrol pilots, ferry pilots, helicopter pilots, aerial survey pilots, photography pilots, advertising pilots, sightseeing pilots, and ambulance pilots.

Sources of Additional Information

For more information on careers in aviation, contact:

- Federal Aviation Administration, Office of Public Affairs, Aviation Education Program, Washington, DC 20591. Phone: (202)267-3471.

- Future Aviation Professionals of America, 4959 Massachusetts Blvd., Atlanta, GA 30337. Phone: (800)538-5627.

ARCHITECTURAL DRAFTERS

At a Glance

- **D.O.T.:** 001.261-010

- **Preferred Education:** Associate degree

- **Average Salary:** $27,400

- **Did You Know?** It is estimated that almost all drafters will use CAD (computer aided drafting) systems regularly by the year 2005.

Nature of the Work

Architectural drafters prepare the detailed drawings used in the construction of buildings ranging from skyscrapers to residential houses. These drawings show the exact dimensions of the buildings, as well as the specific materials to be used, procedures to be followed, and other information needed to complete the construction. Architectural drafters base their drawings, often called blueprints or layouts, on sketches and notes provided by architects, engineers, and designers.

Some architectural drafters create their drawings at a large, slanted table called a drawing board. They use pens, pencils, compasses, t-squares, dividers, protractors, triangles, and other drafting tools to prepare the drawing manually. Many architectural drafters, however, are abandoning this traditional method for computer-aided drafting (CAD) systems. CAD systems allow drafters to create drawings on a computer video screen. When the drawing is completed, it can be stored electronically so that revisions can be made easily. The drawings are printed on paper with a plotter.

By the year 2005, it is estimated that almost all drafters will use CAD systems regularly. CAD operators will still need the knowledge and skill of traditional drafters, however, as well as computer skills. Many architectural firms, particularly those that produce one-of-a-kind drawings, will continue to rely on manual drafting.

Most architectural firms and companies maintain several levels of drafters. *Senior drafters*, or chief drafters, are responsible for turning the ideas of architects and engineers into final construction drawings. They assign projects to drafters in their departments and work directly with architects and engineers. Drafters usually have several years of experience and help senior drafters prepare detailed drawings. *Junior drafters* typically work under the supervision of senior drafters. These workers complete simple drawings and perform other routine drafting tasks. *Checkers* are senior drafters who carefully check drawings for mistakes. *Tracers* correct mistakes found by the checkers and then trace the completed drawings onto transparent paper for reproduction.

Small drafting or engineering firms may not have all these levels. Some workers may perform most or all duties. Large firms may have several workers at each level. Architectural drafters may specialize in one type of building, such as office buildings or residential properties. Others may specialize in certain construction materials such as concrete or stone.

Working Conditions

Architectural drafters work in clean, comfortable offices. They ordinarily work 40 hours per week. Drafters spend most of their time sitting at drawing boards or computer terminals doing detailed work. This can cause eyestrain or back discomfort. Drafters who spend a great deal of time using a computer keyboard risk repetitive motion injuries, such as carpal tunnel syndrome.

Employment

More than 104,000 drafters worked for architectural and engineering firms in 1992. These firms designed construction projects or performed other engineering work on a contract basis for companies in other parts of the economy.

Training, Other Qualifications, and Advancement

Technical institutes, vocational-technical schools, junior and community colleges, and extension divisions of universities all provide training in architectural drafting. These public and private schools generally offer two-year programs. Most require a high school diploma or its equivalent for admission. Four-year colleges usually do not offer drafting training. However, some graduates of associate degree programs continue their education in a related field at four-year colleges.

A typical two-year architectural drafting program may include courses in mathematics, English, technical report writing, architectural drawing, and computer-aided drafting. Technical institutes usually offer more intensive technical training but less theory and general education courses than junior and community colleges. However, courses taken at community or junior colleges may be more likely to transfer to four-year colleges.

Graduates of two-year architectural drafting programs usually enter the workforce as junior drafters. They do routine work under close supervision until they gain enough experience to perform more complex work. They may advance to senior drafter, designer, or supervisor. With additional education, architectural drafters may become engineers or architects.

Job Outlook

Job opportunities for drafters, including architectural drafters, are expected to grow 11 percent between the years 1992 and 2005. This is slower than the average for all occupations. While industrial growth and increasingly complex architectural designs will increase the demand for drafters, some of this demand will be offset by greater use of CAD equipment. According to the U.S. Department of Labor, those with at least two years of training in a technically strong drafting program and experience with CAD systems will have the best opportunities.

Earnings

According to the U.S. Bureau of Labor Statistics, median annual earnings for drafters who worked year round, full time were approximately $27,400 in 1992. The middle 50 percent earned between $20,600 and $35,100 annually; 10 percent earned more than $43,500; and 10 percent earned less than $15,900.

Related Occupations

Architectural drafters prepare or analyze detailed drawings and make precise calculations and measurements. Other workers with similar duties include aeronautical drafters, electrical drafters, electronic drafters, civil drafters, and mechanical drafters.

Sources of Additional Information

State employment services offices can provide information about job opportunities for drafters. For additional information on careers in architecture, contact:

- American Institute of Architects, 1735 New York Ave. NW, Washington, DC 20006. Phone: (202)626-7300.

- National Institute for Architectural Education, 30 W. 22nd St., New York, NY 10010. Phone: (212)924-7000.

AUDIO AND VIDEO OPERATORS

At a Glance

- **D.O.T.:** 194.262-010 and 194.282-010

- **Preferred Education:** 2 or more years of technical training

- **Average Salary:** $22,000

- **Did You Know?** Post-secondary two-year programs in broadcast technology typically include courses in electronics, communications, transmitting equipment, engineering mathematics, technical drawing, and technical writing.

Nature of the Work

Audio and video operators provide technical support for radio and television programming. Audio operators, also known as *audio* or *sound engineers*, are in charge of the equipment that regulates the quality and level of audio signal. They set up or direct other workers to place microphones in various studio locations to ensure the quality of sound reproduction. During broadcasts, they monitor sound quality through headphones or loudspeakers and adjust control-panel dials. They mix different audio sources together, including microphones, audio tape machines, and video tape machines to produce the final program audio.

It is the responsibility of audio operators to have the necessary tapes, records, and theme music available for broadcast according to schedule. They obtain these items from the station library and play or cue prerecorded messages and music according to program schedules.

They may operate recording machines to reproduce music and audio for specific programs. They may operate CD players, turntables, and tape recorders for disc jockeys during their programs. They may direct the adjustment of curtains, blinds, and other materials affecting acoustics in the studio.

When there are broadcasts from outside the studio, audio operators may travel to the location to set up special sound equipment and monitor the sound quality of the broadcast. They may travel to on-the-spot interviews, sporting events, and the sites of other news reports. Other duties may include repairing and maintaining the station's sound equipment.

Video operators work at the video console in the station's control room to regulate the quality, brightness, and contrast of television pictures during transmission. They watch video monitors, setting switches and observing dials on the console to control different aspects of the picture being transmitted.

They may switch from one camera to another or from a live broadcast to film. They monitor on-air programs, such as news broadcasts, to ensure their technical quality. They also preview upcoming programs, checking the signal and making sure the program will be ready for transmission at the scheduled time.

Working Conditions

Since most radio and television stations broadcast 24 hours a day, audio and video operators may be required to work different shifts as well as weekends and holidays. They typically work 40 hours a week but may have to work overtime occasionally to meet broadcast deadlines.

Most radio and television stations provide pleasant indoor surroundings for audio and video operators. Audio operators occasionally have to travel to outside locations and set up audio equipment for news reports or sporting events.

Employment

According to the Bureau of Labor Statistics, there were approximately 25,000 broadcast technicians including audio and video operators working for radio and television stations in 1992. Audio and video operators also work in noncommercial television stations operated by school systems, universities, and public broadcasting companies as well as at corporations that have their own multimedia systems or closed-circuit television systems. Video and production houses employ audio and video operators to assist in the production of local television advertisements or programming.

Although audio and video operators work at television stations located in cities throughout the country, television positions tend to be concentrated in cities such as New York, Los Angeles, Chicago, and Washington, DC, where most television programming originates. Radio stations, on the other hand, are widely scattered in small towns and cities as well as in large metropolitan areas.

Training, Other Qualifications, and Advancement

Audio and video operators are usually high school graduates who have completed two-year associate degree programs in broadcast technology, radio and television production, engineering, or electronics at technical schools, community colleges, or four-year universities. A bachelor's or a master's degree are usually needed for supervisory or administrative positions.

High school courses in mathematics, physics, and electronics are recommended. Post-secondary two-year programs in broadcast technology typically include courses in electronics, communications, transmitting equipment, engineering mathematics, technical drawing, and technical writing. After gaining on-the-job experience, audio and video operators may seek to become certified as broadcast technicians by the Society of Broadcast Engineers.

Audio and video operators need to have mechanical abilities and an aptitude for working with electrical, mechanical, audio, and video systems. Some manual dexterity is needed. Video operators need good vision, including being able to work with objects close at hand and adjusting their field of vision easily. Audio and video operators often have to make quick, split-second decisions, and must be able to act quickly and reliably.

Audio and video operators can advance in several ways. Many begin at smaller stations and advance to larger ones with wider audiences. Some may advance to supervisory positions such as engineering supervisors, while others gain experience by learning to operate different types of technical equipment.

Job Outlook

Competition for entry level positions in broadcasting is expected to be strong, since there are generally more qualified applicants than openings. Additional employment opportunities will occur in nonbroadcast industries that utilize audio and video operators in their production facilities. According to the Bureau of Labor Statistics, overall employment of broadcast technicians in radio and television will decline slightly between 1992 and 2005, primarily because of technological advances that reduce the number of employees needed.

Earnings

Audio and video operators generally earn more if they work for television stations rather than radio stations. Higher paying positions are found at commercial stations in large cities. Public and educational stations tend to pay less than commercial stations, and stations in large markets pay better than those in small ones.

Broadcast technicians had median earnings of $22,725 at radio stations and $22,136 at television stations in 1992, according to a survey conducted by the National Association of Broadcasters and the Broadcast Cable Financial Management Association. Salaries at radio stations ranged from $13,250 in the smallest markets to $28,500 in the largest markets. In television, salaries for broadcast technicians ranged from $15,500 to $37,282.

Related Occupations

Other types of broadcast technicians in radio and television include transmitter operators, maintenance technicians, recording engineers, videotape operators, light technicians, and field technicians. Supervisory positions include chief engineers, transmission engineers, and broadcast field supervisors.

Other occupations that involve electronics and technical equipment include drafters, engineering and science technicians, surveyors, air traffic controllers, radiologic technologists, respiratory therapy workers, and medical laboratory technicians.

Occupations that involve working with audio equipment include audiovisual technicians, communications equipment mechanics, disc jockeys, electrical and electronics engineers, electronics technicians, and sound technicians.

Sources of Additional Information

For more information on careers in the broadcast industry, contact:

- Broadcast Education Association, 1771 N St. NW, Washington, DC 20036-2891. Phone: (202)429-5355.

- National Association of Broadcast Employees and

Technicians, 501 Third St. NW, 8th Fl., Washington, DC 20001. Phone: (202)434-1254.

* National Association of Broadcasters, Employment Clearinghouse, 1771 N St. NW, Washington, DC 20036. Phone: (202)429-5300.

* Society of Broadcast Engineers, 8445 Keystone Crossing, Ste. 140, Indianapolis, IN 46240. Phone: (317)253-1640.

AUDIOVISUAL TECHNICIANS

At a Glance

- **D.O.T.:** 960.382-010

- **Preferred Education:** High school diploma

- **Average Salary:** $13,000 to $17,500 (entry level)

- **Did You Know?** Audiovisual technicians must adhere to strict schedules, solve problems quickly and effectively, and work well under pressure.

Nature of the Work

Audiovisual materials and equipment, which combine sound with visual images, are increasingly being used to supplement educational instruction. Audiovisuals illustrate, enhance, or clarify the impact of a presentation. Audiovisual technicians set up, operate, and maintain audiovisual materials and equipment for educational institutions, public service institutions, and businesses.

Video cassette tapes, audio cassette tapes, films, compact discs, laser discs, records, slides, floppy disks, and overhead transparencies are examples of audiovisual materials. Video cassette recorders, television monitors, microphones, amplifiers, cameras, lights, loud speakers, film projectors, slide projectors, video cameras, overhead projectors, and computers are examples of audiovisual equipment. Audiovisual technicians know how to make all of these items function.

Before a presentation, audiovisual technicians install, position, and connect equipment. They test the set-up to make certain that it is working correctly. Audiovisual technicians often operate the equipment after setting it up. They may coordinate equipment operation with the presentation, according to cues or script notations. For example, a technician may use a video camera to film a ceremony, operate a slide projector so that it is in sequence with a lecture, or provide background music or sound effects during a presentation.

Audiovisual technicians maintain, adjust, and make minor repairs to equipment. This may entail programming a video cassette recorder, installing a new lamp in a movie projector or new batteries in a camera, or replacing a blown fuse in a sound system. Technicians notify the maintenance staff or another authority when a major repair needs to be made.

Audiovisual technicians are responsible for their media department's inventory. They order, rent or borrow materials or equipment that is not on hand. They keep records of all materials and equipment, whether part of their department's permanent media library or rented from outside sources.

Outside resources must be requested in advance, checked in, and returned after use. It is essential that accurate records are kept and that the location of all equipment is known at all times. After a presentation, audiovisual technicians pack up and store their own department's equipment, and pack and return rented or borrowed items.

Audiovisual technicians who work in elementary and secondary schools order audiovisual materials, such as films, video tapes, and audio tapes pertaining to various subjects. Technicians must set up the equipment, such as film projectors or VCRs, in the classroom. In some school districts, audiovisual technicians transport shared equipment and materials between different locations.

Those who work for colleges and universities perform similar duties as those who work in schools, ordering audiovisual materials and setting up and maintaining equipment. However, their duties are usually on a much larger scale. These technicians also set up microphones and loud speakers for lecturers in auditoriums or lecture halls. Similarly, public service institutions such as libraries, museums and zoos often present historical or cultural films and lectures to visitors.

In business settings, audiovisual technicians create and present information and training programs for employees and clients. Audiovisual technicians who work for large companies may travel to different locations to help present programs, including conventions, trade shows, and employee training sessions at various sites.

Working Conditions

Audiovisual technicians typically work about 40 hours per week. Overtime may be necessary during busy periods, especially for those who work for large corporate training or media centers that serve several clients at various locations. Work on evenings and weekends is not uncommon.

Audiovisual technicians usually work in safe and clean environments, such as schools, libraries, conference centers, museums, and business offices. Audiovisual technicians often work under pressure due to hectic schedules and the need to please clients with prompt service and functioning equipment.

Employment

Audiovisual technicians are employed by school systems, college and university media centers, corporate or business media centers, industrial training centers, advertising agencies, marketing education centers, governmental agencies, military agencies, and businesses that provide audiovisual equipment and services.

Training, Other Qualifications, and Advancement

Many employers prefer that audiovisual technicians have

a high school diploma and two years of technical training in audiovisual or media technology from a technical school or community college. Most employers allow new hires an orientation or probationary period so that they may familiarize themselves with the employer's equipment and services.

Audiovisual technicians must adhere to strict schedules, solve problems quickly and effectively, and work well under pressure. They should also be able to work well independently and on a team.

Audiovisual technicians do not have licensing requirements. They may find it to their benefit to become certified with the Institute for Certification of Engineering Technicians.

Job Outlook

Audiovisuals are experiencing increased use in schools and in the workplace. Advances in audiovisual technology are constantly being made, and the complexity of audiovisual equipment can be intimidating to the untrained. These trends suggest that there will be a continuing need for capable audiovisual technicians.

Earnings

According to *American Salaries and Wages Survey*, audiovisual technicians typically earn between $5 and $10 per hour. Experienced technicians typically average about $34,000 per year. Full-time audiovisual technicians receive benefits that include paid vacations and holidays, health and life insurance, and retirement plans.

Related Occupations

Other occupations concerned with operating motion-picture projectors and related equipment include motion picture projectionists and chief projectionists.

Occupations with responsibilities similar to those of audiovisual technicians include audio-control technicians, communications equipment mechanics, recording industry workers, sound recording technicians, studio technicians, and video technicians. Occupations that involve reproduction include film laboratory technicians, color-printer operators, silk screen printers, and microfilm processors.

Sources of Additional Information

For more information on a career as an audiovisual technician,contact:

- Association of Audio-Visual Technicians, PO Box 101264, Denver, CO 80210. Phone: (303)698-1820.

- Association for Informational Media and Equipment, PO Box 9212, Green Bay, WI 54308-9212. Phone: (414)465-8090.

- Electronic Industries Association, 2500 Wilson Blvd., Arlington, VA 22201. Phone: (703)907-7500.

- Society for Technical Communications, 901 N. Stuart St., Ste. 904, Arlington, VA 22203. Phone: (703)522-4114.

BIOLOGICAL TECHNICIANS

At a Glance

- **Preferred Education:** Associate degree

- **Average Salary:** $25,300

- **Did You Know?** Most biological technicians work for agencies within the federal government, colleges and universities, hospitals, medical laboratories, pharmaceutical companies, and police crime labs.

Nature of the Work

Helping to find cures for deadly diseases or examining evidence in criminal investigations are examples of the varied responsibilities of biological technicians. Biological technicians work with biologists to study living organisms. They set up, operate, and maintain laboratory equipment, monitor experiments, analyze data, and record and interpret findings.

Biological technicians analyze organic substances such as blood, body tissues, drugs, and food. They may work with laboratory animals, insects, or microscopic organisms. They use a variety of laboratory procedures and equipment, such as microscopes and scales. To guarantee the reliability of experiments, biological technicians carefully control the conditions under which experiments are conducted.

In medical and pharmaceutical laboratories, biological technicians assist scientists in finding causes and cures for diseases, or medications for ailments. They play an important role in both the research and development of new medicines.

In police laboratories, biological technicians assist in examining blood and other bodily fluids, body tissues, hair, skin cells, samples to test for specific characteristics, as well as non-human substances, as evidence in criminal investigations.

Biological technicians also work in the areas of food science, plant science, horticulture, natural resources conservation, forestry, and animal breeding. Some biological technicians are involved in biotechnology research. Biotechnology entails modifying organisms, usually to serve a medical or agricultural purpose.

Biological technicians help research scientists with procedures in gene splicing, recombinant DNA, and cloning, and apply these techniques in product development.

Working Conditions

Like other science technicians, biological technicians work about 40 hours per week, five days a week. Most work indoors, typically in a laboratory that is well lit and ventilated. Biological technicians may work with disease-causing organisms or radioactive agents, but risks are minimized if safety procedures are followed. Long periods of time at a microscope may cause eyestrain. Those who work with live animals may have to contend with the controversy of protecting animals from harm versus possible medical gains based on animal experimentation.

Employment

According to the U.S. Bureau of Labor Statistics, there were about 244,000 science technicians employed in 1992. This figure includes biological technicians. Most biological technicians work for agencies within the federal government, colleges and universities, hospitals, medical laboratories, pharmaceutical companies, and police crime labs.

Training, Other Qualifications, and Advancement

Employers prefer that biological technicians have at least two years of specialized education. Many community colleges offer two-year associate degree programs in biological technology. Some of these programs are designed to transfer credits to a four-year college or university. Some biological technicians qualify with Armed Forces training.

High school courses in biology, chemistry, geometry, and statistics are good preparation for students. Biological technicians also need to be able to read and write detailed technical reports. Some companies offer formal on-the-job training to graduate biological technicians.

Biological technicians usually start as trainees performing routine tasks under the direct supervision of a scientist or experienced technician. As they gain experience, they handle more responsibilities under less strict supervision.

Experienced biological technicians may advance to become supervisors. More advanced or professional work will require additional education.

Job Outlook

According to the U.S. Bureau of Labor Statistics, job opportunities for biological technicians are expected to grow 25 percent, as fast as average for all occupations, through the year 2005. The continued growth of scientific research and development, especially advances in biotechnology, should stimulate demand for biological technicians.

Despite job growth, most openings will occur from the need to replace biological technicians who retire or transfer to other occupations.

Earnings

According to the U.S. Department of Labor, in 1992 the median annual earnings of biological technicians were about $25,300. The average annual salary for all biological technicians employed by the federal government was $24,828 in 1993. Entry-level positions usually started between $14,600 and $18,340, depending on education and experience.

According to *American Salaries and Wages Survey*, biological technicians earned an average of $9.45 to $13.52 per hour in 1993. Biological technicians usually receive benefits such as paid vacations and holidays, health and life insurance, and retirement plans.

Related Occupations

Other science technician occupations include chemical technicians, medical technicians, agricultural technicians, nuclear technicians, petroleum technicians, weather technicians, and oceanography technicians.

Sources of Additional Information

For more information on a career as a biological technician, contact:

- American Institute of Biological Sciences, 730 11th St. NW, Washington, DC 20001-4521. Phone: (202)628-1500.

CHEMICAL TECHNICIANS

At a Glance

- **D.O.T.:** 022.261-010

- **Preferred Education:** Associate degree

- **Average Salary:** $25,300

- **Did You Know?** The day-to-day responsibilities of chemical technicians depend on education, technical skills, and job setting.

Nature of the Work

Whether developing a new lifesaving drug, improving the safety of automobiles, or just making fast food tastier, chemical technicians affect all parts of our lives.

Chemical technicians help chemists and chemical engineers investigate, invent, and improve products. Most work in laboratories, conducting research and development and testing materials for quality, performance, and composition. They conduct a variety of laboratory procedures from routine process control to complex research projects. For example, chemical technicians may test the chemical content of a plastic milk carton to determine its strength, stability, and impact on the environment. Others may collect and analyze clothing fibers for a criminal investigation.

The day-to-day responsibilities of chemical technicians depend on education, technical skills, and job requirements. Research and development technicians generally work in experimental laboratories, developing new or improved chemical compounds. Process control technicians work in manufacturing plants, monitoring product quality or developing new production techniques. Chemical technicians operate and maintain sophisticated instruments. Some design and build their own equipment. Many use computers during their experiments. They frequently train other workers. Chemical technicians document the results of their tests and experiments.

Working Conditions

Chemical technicians usually work indoors, most often in clean, well-lit laboratories. Most work regular hours. Some, however, may work irregular hours to monitor experiments. Chemical technicians may work with toxic chemicals. Therefore, they usually receive training to recognize and avoid potential hazards. Chemical technicians usually work as part of a team.

Employment

Science technicians, including chemical technicians, held about 244,000 jobs in 1992. The federal government employed 19,000 science technicians in 1992, only about 8 percent of the total. Most worked in the Departments of Defense, Agriculture, Interior, and Commerce.

Training, Other Qualifications, and Advancement

Most chemical technicians receive training through two-year degree programs offered by junior and community colleges, trade and technical schools, and some four-year colleges. These programs provide students with the necessary scientific knowledge and laboratory skills for an entry-level job. Technical institutes generally offer technician training but less theory and general education than junior or community colleges. Some schools allow students to work at a local company while attending classes.

Many companies provide on-the-job training for their chemical technicians. New hires often work with experienced technicians while they learn the duties and responsibilities of the job. Some training takes place in a classroom, or it may be individually paced, much like a correspondence course.

Appropriate high school courses for students interested in becoming chemical technicians include math, science, English, and computer courses. Since most chemical technicians work as part of a team, good oral and written communication skills are needed.

Chemical technicians usually begin their careers as trainees under the direct supervision of a scientist or experienced technician.

Job Outlook

According to the American Chemical Society, the employment outlook for chemical technicians has been, and continues to be, favorable. The need for technicians should grow as industry expands. Continuing automation, complex production methods, and the demand for new products will require trained technicians who are willing to keep up with advancements in technology.

The U.S. Bureau of Labor Statistics expects employment of science technicians to increase about 25 percent by the year 2005. Job growth for chemical technicians may be restrained by an expected slowdown in overall employment growth in the chemical industry. Still, job opportunities should be very good for well-trained graduates of chemical technician programs.

Many job openings will also arise from the need to replace technicians who retire or otherwise leave the work force.

Earnings

The U.S. Department of Labor reported that median earnings for all science technicians were about $25,300 in 1992. Ten percent earned over $42,400, while ten percent earned less than $14,400.

Related Occupations

Other technicians who apply scientific principles and theories to solve problems include agricultural technicians, biological technicians, nuclear technicians, petroleum technicians, engineering technicians, broadcast technicians, and drafters.

Sources of Additional Information

For more information on a career as a chemical technician, contact:

- American Chemical Society, 1155 16th St. NW, Washington, DC 20036. Phone: (202)872-4600.

CIVIL ENGINEERING TECHNICIANS

At a Glance

- **D.O.T.:** 005.261-014

- **Preferred Education:** Associate degree

- **Average Salary:** $17,000 to $35,000

- **Did You Know?** Civil engineering technicians may draft detailed drawings, such as those needed for highway plans, structural steel fabrication, and water control projects.

Nature of the Work

As the population continues to expand, so does the demand for new roads, highways, bridges, dams, sewer systems, and other works necessary for a growing civilization. Civil engineering technicians help civil engineers plan and build these projects.

During the planning stages of a project, civil engineering technicians may estimate costs, specify the required materials, or handle various surveying and designing assignments. For example, a civil engineering technician involved in designing a new roadway alongside a river may study the project's potential impact on the river and area wildlife. The technician may also estimate the amount of concrete, asphalt, and steel required to complete the road.

Civil engineering technicians often prepare reports detailing their tests and the results. They may draft detailed drawings, such as those needed for highway plans, structural steel fabrication, and water control projects.

Once construction begins, technicians help engineers by conducting work inspections and determining whether the project meets design specifications. They also keep track of costs and make sure each phase of construction is completed before the next phase begins.

Some civil engineering technicians specialize in specific types of projects, such as highways or waterways. Others may work for local governments and work on streets, sewers, and drainage systems.

Working Conditions

Most civil engineering technicians work 40 hours per week with extra pay for overtime. Technicians who work in construction or surveying may spend most of their time outdoors. Those who do drafting or design work, or materials testing generally work indoors. Civil engineering technicians usually work as part of a team.

Employment

Engineering technicians, including civil engineering technicians, held about 695,000 jobs in 1992. About 59,000 were employed by the federal government. State governments employed about 30,000; local governments employed about 28,000. More than 25 percent of all engineering technicians worked in service industries or business services companies that do engineering work on contract for government, manufacturing, and other organizations.

Training, Other Qualifications, and Advancement

Individuals interested in becoming civil engineering technicians can receive training through technical institutes, junior and community colleges, extension divisions of colleges and universities, vocational-technical schools, and the Armed Forces.

Technical institutes and junior and community colleges offer two-year associate degree programs. There may be little difference between programs at technical institutes and community colleges. However, technical institutes generally offer more technical training and less theory and general education than junior and community colleges. Vocational-technical schools often serve local students and emphasize training needed by local employers. These programs generally require a high school diploma or its equivalent for admission.

Many military training programs provide the skills needed for employment as a civil engineering technician. Additional on-the-job training may be required, depending on the military skills acquired and the type of job. Some correspondence schools offer programs for engineering technicians. All technicians receive some on-the-job training.

Civil engineering technicians usually work in teams and should be able to work well with others. As civil engineering technicians gain experience, they are usually given larger tasks with less supervision.

Job Outlook

According to the U.S. Department of Labor, well-qualified engineering technicians, including civil engineering technicians, should experience good employment opportunities through the year 2005. However, employment of civil engineering technicians is affected by local and national economic conditions. Many engineering technicians will also be needed to replace technicians who retire or leave the workforce for other reasons.

Earnings

Salaries for civil engineering technicians can vary according to region. For example, according to *American Salaries and Wages Survey*, the average salary for civil engineering technicians in Atlanta, Georgia was $17,108 in 1993. Civil engineering technicians in New York city averaged $20,488. In Oakland, California, technicians earned an average salary of $35,568. Starting salaries in the federal government were $14,600, $16,400, or $18,300, depending on education and experience.

Related Occupations

Other engineering technician occupations include electronics engineering technicians, industrial engineering technicians, mechanical engineering technicians, and chemical engineering technicians. Similar occupations also include science technicians, drafters, surveyors, broadcast technicians, and health technologists and technicians.

Sources of Additional Information

- American Society of Civil Engineers, 1015 15th St. NW, Ste. 600, Washington, DC 20005. Phone: (202)789-2200.

ELECTRONICS ENGINEERING TECHNICIANS

At a Glance

- **D.O.T.:** 003.161-014

- **Preferred Education:** Associate degree

- **Average Salary:** $20,900 to $28,800

- **Did You Know?** Electronics engineering technicians who work in production or manufacturing jobs may be responsible for improving manufacturing efficiency or ensuring product quality.

Nature of the Work

The electronics industry is one of the largest industries in the economy, producing a wide range of products used by consumers and the military. These include computers, televisions, video cameras, radar, sonar, and missile guidance systems. Electronics are also making their way into other products as well, such as automobiles, toys, and appliances.

Electronics engineering technicians help develop, manufacture, and service these electronic devices.

Many technicians assist scientists and engineers in researching and developing new products. Their job responsibilities may include setting up equipment, conducting experiments, and recording the results. They also may build prototype versions of the newly designed equipment. These working models can be tested for performance and reliability. After the tests, technicians help make adjustments and improvements. Some electronic engineering technicians use computer-aided design systems to perform routine design work.

Electronics engineering technicians who work in production or manufacturing jobs may be responsible for improving manufacturing efficiency or ensuring product quality. Many in this field work directly for engineers. They may supervise other production workers.

Some electronics technicians work in the service area. They help customers install and maintain electronic devices. They also use measuring and diagnostic devices to test and repair equipment. Technicians often check newly installed equipment to evaluate system performance under actual operating conditions.

Working Conditions

Most electronics engineering technicians work standard 40-hour weeks in laboratories, offices, or industrial plants. However, technicians who service equipment that is used around the clock may be required to work evenings, nights, or weekends.

Those involved with research and development may work overtime to meet deadlines. Technicians almost always work in teams. Those who act as sales representatives or field technicians often deal directly with the public. Technicians who work in laboratories or factories and repairers who work in large shops meet the public much less often.

Employment

According to the Bureau of Labor Statistics, electrical and electronics technicians and technologists held approximately 72,000 jobs in 1992.

There are electronics manufacturing plants in almost all parts of the country. Some areas of the country, however, have a high concentration of electronics companies. The most prominent has been Silicon Valley, a concentration of integrated circuit and computer firms near San Jose, California. Other industry centers are in Texas, New York, Florida, and Massachusetts. American companies that develop and design electronics products in this country may manufacture them overseas.

The United States electronics industry had over 13,000 establishments in 1992. More than 70 percent of these had fewer than 50 employees. However, large firms employed almost three-quarters of the workforce.

Training, Other Qualifications, and Advancement

Individuals interested in becoming electronics engineering technicians can receive training through technical institutes, junior and community colleges, extension divisions of colleges and universities, vocational-technical schools, and the Armed Forces. Programs accredited by the Accreditation Board of Engineering and Technology provide a minimum level of competence in the mathematics, science, and technical courses required for this occupation.

Technical institutes and junior and community colleges offer two-year associate degree programs. There may be little difference between technical institute and community college programs. In general, however, technical institutes offer more technical training and less theory and general education than junior and community colleges. Vocational-technical schools often serve local students and emphasize training needed by local employers. These programs generally require a high school diploma or its equivalent for admission.

Many military training programs provide the skills needed for employment as an electronics engineering technician. Additional on-the-job training may be required, depending on the military skills acquired and the type of job. Some correspondence schools offer programs for electronics engineering technicians.

All technicians receive some on-the-job training, regardless of their formal education. Large companies usually have formal training programs that include home study courses and shop classes. Service technicians often learn the details of their jobs through informal training. Many join experienced workers as helpers.

Technicians must be able to use arithmetic, shop geometry, and algebra. Therefore, high school students interested in a career as an electronics engineering technician should take science and math courses. Many high schools also offer related technical or vocational courses.

Since electronics engineering technicians usually work in teams, they should be able to work well with others. Those in service should be able to deal effectively with customers. Experienced electronics engineering technicians may advance to supervisory positions or move into other production and inspection operations.

Job Outlook

According to the U.S. Department of Labor, well-qualified engineering technicians, including electronics engineering technicians, should experience good employment opportunities through the year 2005. Continued growth in the development of technical products should keep employment in this field increasing as fast as the average for all occupations. Employment in this area can be affected by local and national economic conditions. Many engineering technicians will also be needed to replace technicians who retire or leave the workforce for other reasons.

Earnings

Junior level engineering technicians earned a median salary of $20,900 in 1992, according to the U.S. Bureau of Labor Statistics. Those with more experience and the ability to work with little supervision earned about $28,800. Engineering technicians in supervisory or senior level positions earned approximately $41,400. In 1993, electronics technicians in management positions in the Federal Government earned an average salary of $42,436.

Related Occupations

Other engineering technicians include civil engineering technicians, industrial engineering technicians, mechanical engineering technicians, and chemical engineering technicians. Similar occupations also include science technicians, drafters, surveyors, broadcast technicians, and health technologists and technicians.

Sources of Additional Information

- International Society of Certified Electronics Technicians, 2708 W. Berry St., Fort Worth, TX 76109 Phone: (817)921-9101

- The Electronics Technicians Association, International, 602 N. Jackson, Greencastle, IN 46135. Phone: (317)653-8262.

HELICOPTER PILOTS

At a Glance

- **D.O.T.:** 196.263-038
- **Preferred Education:** Flying experience
- **Average Salary:** $20,000
- **Did You Know?** Learning to fly helicopters can be expensive, with lessons ranging from $130 to $200 per hour or more.

Nature of the Work

Helicopters can go where airplanes cannot. They can fly straight up and down, hover in one spot, and take off and land in very tight spaces. These advantages make helicopters the ideal aircraft for a wide variety of jobs, including pipeline and powerline patrol, logging, sightseeing, traffic reporting, law enforcement, emergency medical service, and others. Helicopter pilots are responsible for operating these aircraft.

Helicopter pilots prepare for each flight by following rules and regulations set by their employers and the Federal Aviation Administration (FAA). They use a checklist to inspect their helicopters for unsafe conditions, such as leaking fluids, broken controls or instruments, or low fuel. They carefully plan their flights with the use of aeronautical charts and navigation instruments. Once the flight begins, pilots monitor gauges and dials while manipulating the controls to fly the helicopter. They check landmarks and use compasses, maps, and directional equipment to navigate.

Many helicopter pilots use their helicopters to transport passengers and cargo. For example, helicopter pilots may fly workers and supplies to offshore oil rigs. In emergencies, helicopters may be used to fly accident victims to a hospital, or rescue people stranded by floods. Helicopters are also used to transport fire fighters and equipment to the scene of a forest fire.

Law enforcement agencies use helicopters to regulate traffic and pursue criminals. Some helicopter pilots use their helicopters to carry logs from forests to loading areas, or to lift heavy loads to the tops of buildings. Helicopters can also be used to spray insecticides or seeds on farmland, take aerial photographs, survey parcels of land, and carry hunters and fishers to remote sites.

Working Conditions

The working hours for helicopter pilots depend upon the job. Some work on rotating schedules with day and night shifts. Others may work regular 40 hour weeks. Although flights are usually short in duration, the job can be stressful. Pilots are responsible for passengers and the aircraft. Also, pilots are often required to do precision flying, hovering over a particular spot or landing in small areas. They typically fly near buildings, trees, power lines, and other obstacles.

Employment

Helicopters are used throughout the United States. Helicopter pilots are employed just about everywhere there are airports or heliports. Many pilots work for companies that charter their services. Others work for federal agencies, corporations, air taxi services, oil and gas companies, and flight training schools.

Training, Other Qualifications, and Advancement

There are no formal education requirements to become helicopter pilots. Individuals may learn to fly helicopters in the military or in civilian flying schools. Learning to fly helicopters can be expensive, with lessons ranging from $130 to $200 per hour or more. Flying lessons for high-end turbine helicopters start at $500 per hour. To receive a commercial helicopter pilot's license from the Federal Aviation Administration, pilots need at least 150 hours of flying time and a Class II medical certificate. Of the 150 hours, 100 must be in a powered aircraft; only 50 hours need to be in a helicopter. This means students can use lower-priced airplanes to fulfill a large part of the training requirements.

Entry-level jobs may be hard to find. Many employers require considerable flight experience, often 1,500 to 2,000 hours of flying time. Some helicopter pilots gain these additional hours by working as flight instructors. Other entry-level jobs involve pipeline and powerline inspection, aerial tours, and fish spotting. Advancement often depends on hours of flight time and experience with particular types of helicopters. Pilots typically begin by flying single-engine helicopters and advancing to larger aircraft. Pilots may be promoted to chief pilots or aviation department managers. Some may build their own businesses and employ other pilots.

Helicopter pilots should have maturity, good judgement, and the ability to perform under pressure. They may be required to pass drug and alcohol tests.

Job Outlook

According to the FAA, the short-term job outlook for helicopter pilots is mixed. One reason is military force reductions, which are forcing many military pilots to find jobs in the private sector. This is causing a glut of helicopter pilots in some areas. For the long-term, however, the FAA expects the need for helicopter pilots to grow as more pilots retire and the demand for their services expands.

Earnings

According to the FAA, the average mid-range salary for commercial pilots, which include helicopter pilots, is $20,000 per year. Earnings generally depend on a pilot's experience, aircraft, employer, location, and duties. Benefits also vary according to employer. Most pilots receive medical, dental, and life insurance.

Related Occupations

Other occupations concerned with piloting aircraft include flight instructors, corporate pilots, air taxi or charter pilots, airline pilots, test pilots, and agricultural pilots.

Sources of Additional Information

- Helicopter Association International, 1635 Prince St., Alexandria, VA 22314-2818. Phone: (703)683-4646.

- Federal Aviation Administration, 800 Independence Ave. SW, Washington, DC 20591.

LASER TECHNICIANS

At a Glance

- **D.O.T.:** 019.261-034

- **Preferred Education:** Associate degree

- **Average Salary:** $20,000 to $24,000

- **Did You Know?** High school students interested in becoming laser technicians should take courses in English, mathematics, physics, basic electronics, and computers.

Nature of the Work

Lasers are changing almost every aspect of our lives. Doctors now use lasers to perform difficult surgical procedures. Dentists use lasers to clean teeth. Manufacturers use lasers to cut, drill and weld materials. Lasers are used in the military for measuring and surveying as well as high speed photography and navigation. Lasers send our voices over fiber-optic telephone lines, play music on compact discs, and read information from bar code labels in the supermarket.

Laser technicians build, test, operate, and repair laser devices and equipment. A laser (light amplification by stimulated emission of radiation) is a powerful, narrow beam of intense light that provides pin-point accuracy, as lasers can affect specific targets without disturbing the surrounding areas. There are two main types of laser systems--*gas* and *solid state*. Gas laser systems are used primarily in industrial and medical settings. Solid-state lasers are primarily used with computers and telecommunication systems. Laser technicians need to understand the types of lasers as well as how lasers function.

In order to perform their jobs correctly, laser technicians must understand how laser light works. Laser light is monochromatic, meaning it consists of only one color in various frequencies. It travels only in one direction, which is why laser light can be used to send and receive information and to track and measure distances.

Ordinary light travels in all available directions, diffusing the light too much to be used for transmission to a specific target. This characteristic in laser light is called directionality. Finally, light waves in laser light travel in an uniform pattern, resulting in stronger and more powerful light beams.

Laser technicians use specific equipment to control laser light. In order to activate lasers, there must be an excitation mechanism, or a device that simulates the light energy (stimulated emission). There must also be a feedback mechanism, which keeps up the stimulation of the laser light. Finally, the output coupler transmits the correct percentage of laser light from the laser device to the target.

Some laser technicians work as part of a team under the supervision of engineers and scientists. These teams conduct laboratory experiments using laser technology. Laser technicians review the experiment instructions, such as the layout, blueprints, and sketches. Then they work with the engineers to make sure the lasers are used properly by helping to interpret the various elements of production, including the dimensions and functional requirements of mirrors, waveplates, and lasers. Other laser technicians work alone or with salespeople, installing equipment at customer sites.

Laser technicians frequently build and test laser devices. They install and align optical parts such as mirrors and waveplates, using precision instruments. They operate controls on vacuum pumps and gas transfer equipment to fill the laser device with gases.

Laser technicians assemble the laser device's chassis and connect controls such as valves, regulators, dials, and switches. They also set up precision electronic and optical equipment to test the laser device.

After the experiments are completed, laser technicians analyze test data and report the results to the engineers and scientists. Laser technicians may also prepare and write technical reports suggesting solutions to technical problems.

Working Conditions

Most laser technicians work regular hours in modern

offices and laboratories. These worksites are generally quiet, clean and air-conditioned. Some technicians work in noisy manufacturing plants or construction sites. There is some overtime and weekend work. Technicians involved in sales may need to travel.

Laser technicians often work in teams with engineers and scientists. Those who install laser equipment at customer sites may work alone. Laser technicians perform exacting work and must pay great attention to detail. They frequently handle small components and should enjoy working with their hands. Working with lasers can be dangerous. Lasers can cause severe injuries to the eye and, in extreme cases, laser injuries can be fatal. Laser technicians, therefore, must wear safety goggles and be extremely careful.

Employment

Engineering technicians, the category that includes laser technicians, held approximately 695,000 jobs in 1992. About 40 percent of engineering technicians worked for manufacturing companies. These include electronic and industrial machinery companies, and computer and office equipment companies. Over 25 percent of engineering technicians worked for service companies. The U.S. military employs some enlisted personnel for laser installation and repair.

Training, Other Qualifications, and Advancement

Many community colleges and technical schools offer two-year programs in laser technology. These programs include comprehensive technical and scientific coursework. First-year courses include mathematics, physics, drafting, and drawing. Second-year students study lasers, geometrical optics, and technical report writing. Students also receive "hands-on" experience with lasers during laboratory study.

High school students interested in becoming laser technicians should take courses in English, mathematics, physics, basic electronics, and computers. Laser technicians do not need great physical strength, but students interested in a career in laser technology should have good manual dexterity and excellent eye-hand coordination.

(For more information on qualifications for engineering technicians, see the *Occupational Outlook Handbook*.)

Job Outlook

Engineering technicians, including laser technicians, can expect good employment opportunities through the year 2005. The number of engineering technicians is expected to grow 19 percent, which is as fast as the average for all occupations, during that period. Many jobs will come from companies in the defense industry and other companies updating their manufacturing facilities. Additional job openings will become available as technicians retire or leave the workforce for other reasons.

Earnings

The average salary for laser technicians nationwide ranges from $20,000 to $24,000 per year. Starting annual salaries

range from $14,000 to $17,500. Experienced laser technicians can earn up to $30,000 per year. Laser technicians in supervising, sales and private consulting work can earn up to $38,000 per year.

Related Occupations

Occupations similar to laser technicians include civil engineering technicians, electronics engineering technicians, industrial engineering technicians, mechanical engineering technicians, chemical engineering technicians, and science technicians.

Sources of Additional Information

- Optical Society of America, 2010 Massachusetts Ave. NW, Washington, DC 20036. Phone: (202)223-8130.

- Laser Institute of America, 12424 Research Parkway, Ste. 130, Orlando, FL 32826. Phone: (407)380-1553.

- Junior Engineering Technical Society, 1420 King St., Ste. 405, Alexandria, VA 22314. Phone: (703)548-5387.

LIGHTING TECHNICIANS

At a Glance

- **D.O.T.:** 962.362-014 and 962.381-014

- **Preferred Education:** Two to four years experience

- **Average Salary:** Varies

- **Did You Know?** Employment for lighting technicians can be somewhat irregular. Motion picture and theatrical lighting technicians are usually employed for specific productions.

Nature of the Work

Motion pictures, videos, television programs, and stage plays all require the services of lighting technicians to help capture moods and create special effects. Lighting technicians are part of the production crew that is responsible for making the actions, words, ideas, and settings of a script come to life in front of a camera or audience.

Motion picture and television lighting technicians are also known as *gaffers*. They set up and operate electrical lighting equipment for motion picture or television productions. They work under the direction of a director of photography or lighting director. They must be able to provide appropriate lighting for film as well as video and be familiar with lighting techniques for single camera as well as multicamera shooting. They work closely with camera operators to create the desired effects. They may be required to provide lighting for soundstages, studio lots, and a variety of locations.

Specific duties of lighting technicians may include laying down electrical cables from portable generators to provide power for lighting sets and locations. They set up lights ranging in size from 500 to 10,000 watts. Television lights are typically in the 2,000 to 10,000 watt range and can get very hot. Lighting technicians rig and light the set according to directions received from the director of photography or lighting director. Rigging the set includes setting up the necessary pedestals and scaffolding to hold the lights.

Gaffers or chief lighting technicians may direct assistant lighting technicians to perform these tasks. Gaffers may decide what types of lights to use and how to set them up in order to achieve the effects desired by the director of photography or lighting director.

Lighting technicians use light meters during setup and production to determine that the correct light intensity is maintained during a scene. Lighting technicians sometimes have to handle hot lamps using protective gloves. They may also adjust and repair lights and scaffolding using small power and hand tools. They make minor repairs and replace broken cables, plugs, and fuses as needed.

Theatrical lighting technicians work under different conditions, but the nature of their work is similar to that of motion picture and television lighting technicians. They work under the direction of a lighting designer. Each play typically has one lighting designer. Theatrical lighting technicians must be on hand during every production to operate spotlights and colored lights according to cue sheets and scripts.

Working Conditions

Working conditions for lighting technicians vary depending on the type of production they are employed on and whether they are working in motion pictures, television, or theater. Motion picture and television lighting technicians work inside on soundstages and outside on studio lots or other locations. They must be prepared to work under many different conditions. They may have to rig sets before production and take them down afterward. Theatrical lighting technicians always work indoors and usually only have one set-up and take-down per production.

Lighting technicians need to be in good physical condition. They may have to lift heavy cables and wires as well as large lamps and equipment. They are frequently climbing ladders, stooping, bending, and walking. They are often on their feet for long periods of time. They must be able to work at heights of approximately 60 feet above the ground on hydraulic lifts or scaffolding.

Lighting technicians are subject to physical hazards such as back strain from improper lifting, electrical shocks, and burns from hot lamps. Motion picture and television lighting technicians often work long, irregular hours in order to accommodate shooting schedules. Theatrical lighting technicians work with the same play until its run is over.

Lighting technicians employed in the theatrical, television, and motion picture centers of New York and Los Angeles usually belong to a union, the International Alliance of Theatrical Stage Employees and Moving Picture Machine Operators of the U.S. and Canada (IATSE).

Employment

Lighting technicians are employed in the motion picture, television, and performing arts industries. Major employers are the movie production studios located in Los Angeles, television production studios located in New York and Los Angeles, and theaters and performing arts groups located in New York and elsewhere.

Employment can be somewhat irregular. Motion picture and theatrical lighting technicians are usually employed for a specific production. When the production of a film or play is completed, they must seek employment on another production. Studios and theaters typically have a list of IATSE members who are available for employment, and they are contacted before new applicants are hired.

According to the Bureau of Labor Statistics, there were approximately 6,000 precision production, craft, and repair personnel including lighting technicians employed in the motion picture industry in 1992.

Training, Other Qualifications, and Advancement

Individuals often learn about lighting by working on different productions as assistants. They may also learn lighting techniques by working on amateur productions in high school or college. Lighting technicians in the theater usually have one or two years of on-the-job experience. Motion picture and television lighting technicians generally have more preparation, sometimes up to four years.

Individuals can prepare for careers as lighting technicians by studying subjects such as electronics and electricity, television production, set design, and photography. Courses in motion picture and television production as well as theatrical production are offered at many two- and four-year colleges and vocational schools.

Lighting technicians enjoy applying mechanical principles to practical situations. They generally have an aptitude for electronics or electrical work. They must have good vision and not be affected by color blindness. It is important for lighting technicians to be able to get along with people and work well with others. The productions they work on require the cooperation of many different talented professionals.

The motion picture, television, and theatrical industries all offer lighting technicians opportunities for advancement. Those in motion pictures can progress to higher levels, such as lamp operator, rigger, chief rigging electrician, assistant chief lighting technician, and chief lighting technician or gaffer. Gaffers can advance in motion pictures and television to become directors of photography or lighting directors.

With additional education and training, lighting technicians may become studio engineers in television production. Theatrical lighting technicians can advance to become lighting designers. With additional experience and skills, lighting technicians may advance to work on larger, more complex productions.

Job Outlook

The Bureau of Labor Statistics projects that employment of precision production, craft, and repair personnel, including lighting technicians, will increase by more than 56 percent between 1992 and 2005 in the motion picture industry. While production of feature films for theatrical release is projected to decline, there is an increasing demand for motion pictures from network and cable television.

Competition for openings is expected to remain strong. There are relatively few openings that occur as a result of lighting technicians leaving the occupation.

Earnings

Earnings for lighting technicians depend a great deal on experience, where employed, and size of production. Limited earnings data is available, and annual earnings are difficult to calculate because of periods of unemployment between productions. The hourly union scale for IATSE members was $15.63 in 1988 for entry-level workers and $17.76 for experienced or journey workers in motion pictures. Lighting technicians are classified as journey workers after completing 230 days of work with one or more producers. Recent union scale for theatrical lighting technicians and other production workers ranged from $15 to $20 per hour in New York and Los Angeles. Standard benefits for union members include health and life insurance, pension plans, and vacation and holiday pay.

Related Occupations

Related occupations include electrical technicians, cable pullers, antenna installers, field technicians, photographic equipment technicians, and stage technicians. Related engineering occupations in television include studio engineers, master control engineers, videotape engineers, and maintenance engineers.

Sources of Additional Information

For more information on a career as a lighting technician, contact:

- Broadcast Education Association, 1771 N St. NW, Washington, DC 20036-2891. Phone: (202)429-5355.

- International Alliance of Theatrical Stage Employees and Moving Picture Machine Operators of the U.S. and Canada (IATSE), 1515 Broadway, Ste. 601, New York, NY 10036. Phone: (212)730-1770.

- International Association of Lighting Designers, 18 E. 16th St., Ste. 208, New York, NY 10003. Phone: (212)206-1281.

- International Brotherhood of Electrical Workers, 1125 15th St. NW, Washington, DC 20005. Phone: (202)833-7000.

- National Association of Broadcast Employees and Technicians, 501 3rd St. NW, 8th Fl., Washington, DC 20001. Phone: (202)434-1254.

STAGE TECHNICIANS

At a Glance

- **D.O.T.:** 962.261-014, 962.684-014 and 962.687-022

- **Preferred Education:** Specialized training

- **Average Salary:** Varies

- **Did You Know?** The best paid stage technicians work in New York or Los Angeles.

Nature of the Work

Theatrical productions, concerts, and other types of stage productions require the services of stage technicians. Stage technicians also work on television, motion picture, and video productions. They perform tasks such as installing lights and sound equipment, moving props and scenery, and building sets. They may build temporary stages for theatrical and musical events held in parks, arenas, stadiums, and other locations. They may operate light and sound equipment and pull ropes and cables to raise curtains and move stage scenery during rehearsals and performances. (For more information on *lighting technicians*, see separate profile.)

Also known as *grips*, stage technicians combine the skills of electricians and carpenters with a knowledge of stage design and theatrical production. In some productions stage technicians specialize in certain tasks and may be designated as electricians, carpenters, lighting technicians, sound technicians, and set builders, among other specialties. If they belong to a union, as most stage technicians working in New York and Los Angeles do, they may be subject to strict union rules limiting the type of work they are allowed to do.

Stage technicians form a tightly knit crew that does all the work necessary to prepare a stage for actual performances. Depending on their specialties, they may work under the direction of stage managers, lighting directors or designers, audio engineers, or set designers. When setting up a production, stage technicians read stage layout specifications and blueprints and follow the directions of the stage manager regarding type and location of sets, props, scenery, lighting, and sound equipment.

Stage technicians install and set up lighting, sound equipment, and scenery. They rig sets by setting up the necessary scaffolding and pedestals that will hold lights and other equipment. They often work in high exposed places, crawling on high beams and narrow catwalks. They may lay down electrical cables from portable generators or other power sources to provide power for lighting the stage.

Stage productions usually require an array of sound equipment, including microphones, speakers, amplifiers, and sound boards. Stage technicians set up the sound equipment and lay down cables and electrical wiring using an electrician's hand and power tools. They must follow applicable electrical codes when wiring lighting and sound equipment. They often work under the direction of audio engineers when setting up sound systems.

Stage technicians assemble all of the props supplied by the production company and construct additional props, scenery, or stages as needed using a carpenter's hand and power tools. They attach braces to support the scenery, and attach cables to scenery, curtains, and other equipment to move it or hold it in place. They climb ladders or scaffolding to run the cables through a ceiling grid. During rehearsals and performances they may operate curtains and move scenery using these cables.

Working Conditions

The work of grips and stage technicians can be physically demanding. They frequently have to move or lift objects weighing 50 pounds or more and occasionally as much as 100 pounds or more. Noise conditions range from moderately noisy to loud, due primarily to the use of power tools.

Stage technicians frequently work in high, exposed places such as scaffolding, ladders, and catwalks. They spend a lot of time climbing, balancing, stooping, and crouching. They are subject to physical injuries related to working in high places as well as working with electrical wires and cables, power tools, and heavy equipment. Depending upon the nature of the production, stage technicians may work indoors or outdoors.

Employment

Stage technicians work for community theaters, college and university playhouses, and corporate video production studios in addition to commercial theaters, television stations, and motion picture and film studios. While the highest concentration of employers is in New York and Los Angeles, there are employment opportunities for stage technicians in cities located throughout the country.

According to the Bureau of Labor Statistics, there were approximately 6,000 precision production, craft, and repair personnel including stage technicians employed in the motion picture industry in 1992.

Training, Other Qualifications, and Advancement

Stage technicians are usually high school graduates. They can learn the basics of the job in six months to one year, but more advanced stage technician work may require two or more years of specialized training. Two-year programs in theatrical or motion picture production are available at many community colleges and at four-year colleges and universities. Students in these programs learn mechanical, technical, and artistic skills, including carpentry, electrical work, photography, and how to use computerized equipment.

Stage technicians may obtain their basic training from experienced stage technicians. Some work on local or amateur theatrical productions. Others work on college productions in film or theater. Stage technicians should take general studies courses, including English and mathematics. For more advanced work, they should learn carpentry and electronics.

Most employers in New York and Los Angeles require

that stage technicians belong to a union such as the International Alliance of Theatrical Stage Employees and Moving Picture Machine Operators of the U.S. and Canada (IATSE) or the National Association of Broadcast Employees and Technicians. Employers in smaller markets generally do not require union membership.

Stage technicians enjoy applying mechanical principles to practical situations. They must have manual dexterity and mechanical skills to work with different hand and power tools. They must be in good physical condition to meet the demands of their work, including lifting and climbing. They must be comfortable working at heights well above the ground. Advanced stage technicians must be able to follow complex directions and communicate with their fellow workers.

Stage technicians generally advance by gaining more experience and skills. They can advance to work on bigger productions or in larger facilities. With specialized training, they can become property managers, electricians, carpenters, production assistants, and set designers.

Job Outlook

Within the motion picture industry, employment of precision production, craft, and repair personnel, including stage technicians, will increase by more than 56 percent between 1992 and 2005. Employment opportunities in theaters and other facilities tend to vary with overall economic conditions, the number of productions scheduled, and public and private funding.

Employment opportunities are expected to be good for stage technicians in the growing video production industry, including cable television, music videos, and corporate videos. The trend is for corporations to have their own in-house video production departments, requiring the skills of stage technicians.

Earnings

Limited earnings data is available for stage technicians. Since this occupational category covers many different functions, there can be a considerable range in salaries. In New York, for example, theatrical stage technicians can earn between $30 and $150 per hour.

The best paid stage technicians work in New York or Los Angeles. Union scale is generally higher than for non-union workers. Union contracts typically provide for standard benefits, including health insurance, paid vacations, and pension plans.

Related Occupations

Related occupations in theatrical production include stage directors, costume designers, makeup artists, set designers, property designers, carpenters, lighting designers, sound designers, electricians, and technical directors.

Other occupations involving mechanical crafts include house repairers, television and radio repairers, automatic door mechanics, electronic equipment repairers, and used car renovators.

Sources of Additional Information

- Broadcast Education Association, 1771 N St. NW, Washington, DC 20036-2891. Phone: (202)429-5355.

- International Alliance of Theatrical Stage Employees and Moving Picture Machine Operators of the U.S. and Canada (IATSE), 1515 Broadway, Ste. 601, New York, NY 10036. Phone: (212)730-1770.

- International Brotherhood of Electrical Workers, 1125 15th St. NW, Washington, DC 20005. Phone: (202)833-7000.

- National Association of Broadcast Employees and Technicians, 501 3rd St. NW, 8th Fl., Washington, DC 20001. Phone: (202)434-1254.

SURVEYING TECHNICIANS

At a Glance

- **D.O.T.:** 869.567-010, 018.167-034

- **Preferred Education:** High school diploma and specialized training

- **Average Salary:** $9 to $14 per hour

- **Did You Know?** Survey technicians should enjoy working outdoors in a variety of locations.

Nature of the Work

Throughout history, property boundaries have been important to mankind. Today boundary lines are more elaborate than ever. From large masses of land and sea to highways, airports, and housing developments to drainage ditches, power lines, and private residential lots, border lines are drawn and recorded. Surveying technicians help establish, describe, and document geographic areas.

Surveying technicians assist professional surveyors, civil engineers, and map makers. Surveying technicians are typically the first workers to be involved in a task that calls for precise plotting. Surveying technicians help determine the exact location and boundaries for public and private land and water, lots, highways, pipelines, railways, power lines, airports, mines, new communities, housing developments, roads, bridges, dams, buildings, and other structures.

When helping to survey land, technicians measure property boundaries, read surveying instruments and maps, and interpret land deeds. To measure property boundaries, surveying technicians use modern, highly sensitive surveying instruments, including theodolites (which measure vertical and horizontal angles of land or buildings), electronic measuring equipment, measuring tape and chains, alidades (telescopic surveying instruments), levels, transits, and plane tables. Surveying technicians set up, adjust, operate and take readings from these instruments.

When measuring, they hold levels, stadia rods, or range poles at designated points so that the theodolite can be focused on the correct site, similar to the way an object is viewed through a camera lens. In like manner, surveying technicians may measure the distance between survey points using a measuring tape or surveyor's chain. Surveying technicians understand the science and math involved in measuring and recording boundary lines. As readings are taken, surveying technicians keep careful notes so that their reports will be accurate. They mark points of measurement with elevation, station number, or another identifying mark.

Survey technicians also help prepare legal documents, such as deeds and leases. The records technicians keep from surveying an area are used for devising deeds and leases. One of the main reasons for surveying is so that boundary lines can be recorded into legal documents. Surveying technicians also check that existing deeds are accurate.

There are several kinds of surveying technicians. *Geodetic surveying technicians* help measure large masses of land, sea, and space. Their measurements take the curvature of the earth and its geophysical characteristics into account. Measurement information of this type is useful in preparing maps, determining national boundaries, and establishing major points of reference for smaller land surveys.

Topographical surveys establish the way land is formed. They show features such as mountains, lakes, rivers, forests, roads, farms, buildings, and other landmarks. Surveying technicians who help perform topographical surveys take aerial and land photographs with special cameras that can capture large areas of land. This process is known as photogrammetry. The photographs permit accurate measurements of terrain and surface features to be made.

They are useful in preparing topographical maps, measuring farm land, and planning highways, railway lines, and other large engineering projects. *Hydrographic surveying technicians* help survey harbors, rivers, and other bodies of water. These surveys are useful for designing navigation systems, as well as planning and building breakwaters, bridges, dams, levees, and piers. This data is also used to prepare nautical maps and determine property boundaries.

Most surveying technicians are employed in the construction industry. Their responsibilities are needed throughout a construction project. Surveying technicians help keep a project's progress within engineering specifications for size, height, depth, level, and shape.

Surveying technicians also work for mining companies. They help establish the boundaries of mining claims and indicate terrain features that attest the presence of valuable natural resources.

Surveying technicians often supervise assistants during routine surveying.

Working Conditions

Surveying technicians work about 40 hours each week. Overtime may be necessary during peak work periods, which is during the summer in northern climates. Surveying technicians work outdoors and are exposed to all types of weather conditions. They also work in a variety of settings. They are at risk of being struck by a vehicle or flying debris when working near traffic. They are at risk of natural aggravations, such as insects, snakes and poison ivy when working in uncleared land. In construction or mining areas, surveying technicians must wear hard hats, steel-toed shoes and other protective clothing. Surveying technicians walk across all types of terrain, carrying their equipment.

Employment

Surveying technicians are employed by surveying firms that focus on one or more types of surveying (i.e. geodetic, topographical, hydrographic), construction companies, mining companies, and exploration companies. Most surveying technicians work in construction.

Training, Other Qualifications, and Advancement

A high school diploma is required to become a surveying technician. Courses in algebra, geometry, trigonometry, English, science, computer science, mechanical drawing, and drafting are very helpful. Two-year programs in surveying offered by a community college or vocational/technical school is highly recommended. These programs offer intensive training in surveying and mapping and include summer field study.

Surveying firms usually provide on-the-job training to new hires. To be hired by the federal government, applicants must first pass civil service exams. Some surveying technicians begin as survey helpers. Surveying technicians should be able to travel on foot across all types of terrain. They should have the physical strength to carry surveying equipment.

Experienced surveying technicians can advance to become licensed land surveyors if they pass the required examination.

Job Outlook

Employment in the construction industry is expected to grow 26 percent through the year 2005, about as fast as average for all industries. This statistic translates into employment growth for surveying technicians. The continuing development of suburban areas will yield the planning of new streets, homes, utility lines, and shopping centers, all of which will require property and boundary line surveys, thus contributing to the need for surveying technicians. Urban redevelopment and highway improvement are other factors that will provide employment opportunities. Despite job growth, most job opportunities will result from the need to replace workers who leave the trade.

Earnings

Surveying technicians' earnings vary by employer, geographic location, and experience. According to *American Salaries and Wages Survey*, surveying technicians earned an average of $9 to $14.11 per hour. Overall wages range from $6.50 to $24.04 per hour.

Full-time surveying technicians usually receive benefits that include paid vacation time, health and life insurance, and retirement plans.

Related Occupations

Other occupations similar to surveying technicians include land surveyors, topographic computators, field-map editors, geodetic surveyors, mapping supervisors, and photogrammetric engineers.

Sources of Additional Information

For more information on a career as a surveying technician, contact:

- American Congress on Surveying and Mapping, 5410 Grosvenor Ln., Bethesda, MD 20814-2122. Phone: (301)493-0200.

- Accreditation Board for Engineering and Technology, 111 Market Pl., Ste. 1050, Baltimore, MD 21202. Phone: (410)347-7700.

Marketing and Sales Occupations

ADVERTISING SALES REPRESENTATIVES

At a Glance

- **D.O.T.:** 254.357-014

- **Preferred Education:** On-the-job training

- **Average Salary:** $26,000

- **Did You Know?** Earnings of advertising sales representatives generally depend on the circulation size of the publication and an individual's education and previous experience.

Nature of the Work

Magazines and newspapers rely on advertising as a major source of revenue. For newspapers, advertising provides more than $32 billion annually; for magazines, it accounts for almost half of the industry's total revenue. Individuals who sell advertising for newspapers and magazines are known as advertising sales representatives. They work closely with established clients as well as potential advertisers.

In larger publications, advertising sales representatives are usually part of a sales team that includes marketing, research, and promotional support. Research provides important information about the publication's readership for advertisers who are interested in reaching a particular segment of the population. The overall sales strategy may be determined by the publication's marketing director, who establishes the image of the publication and how it is positioned in the marketplace.

With the appropriate background information, advertising sales representatives must convince advertisers of the benefits of advertising in their publication. Their sales presentations usually include information about the publication's readership, including such data as age, income, education, and other demographics. Advertising sales representatives must also explain the publication's advertising rate structure, based on the size and frequency of an advertisement, as well as the value of an ad relative to the audience being reached. They must help clients obtain maximum value for their money.

Advertising sales representatives may specialize in selling classified or retail ads. Usually the size of the publication determines how much the advertising sales representatives can specialize. Advertising sales representatives who work for very large publications may specialize to the extent of servicing only a few major clients. Those who work for smaller publications generally have a wider range of responsibilities.

In addition, advertising sales representatives may call on prospective advertisers at their place of business. This is called "outside sales." Outside sales also includes calling on existing accounts to maintain a relationship with clients and to make sure they renew their advertising. The amount of traveling involved in outside sales depends on the size of the publication and the location of the advertisers.

"Inside sales" involves contacting advertisers from the publication's office. Inside sales are conducted primarily over the telephone, although there may be some meetings in the office with clients. Inside advertising sales representatives make telephone calls to prospective advertisers based on lists that have been compiled from sources such as business directories, advertisers in other publications, and leads provided by associates.

In addition to selling space in their publication, advertising sales representatives also work with advertisers to use that space effectively. They may help clients visualize potential advertisements and provide creative input. They may write sample headlines for advertisers and create sample layouts.

Working Conditions

Selling advertising can be stressful. Advertising sales representatives must balance the needs of their clients with the requirements of their publication. They are often required to work long hours and are under pressure to meet publication deadlines.

Advertising sales representatives work under moderately noisy conditions typical of a busy office. They may have to travel to meet with established clients and potential advertisers. Much of their time is spent interacting with others.

Employment

Newspapers and magazines are the primary employers of print advertising sales representatives. In addition, specialized agencies that "rep" for several publications employ advertising sales representatives. According to the *Occupational Outlook Quarterly*, there were approximately 166,000 individuals employed in advertising and related sales occupations in 1994.

Training, Other Qualifications, and Advancement

Advertising sales representatives generally have one to two years of training that is usually learned on the job. A college degree is desirable, but most newspapers and magazines will hire a high school graduate with a proven sales record.

Appropriate college courses include journalism, business, economics, communications, and marketing. A good background in English, graphic arts, sociology, and sales is also helpful. Internships can provide valuable experience in advertising sales.

Advertising sales representatives need accurate typing skills and the ability to handle word processing software in order to fulfill the requirements of an inside sales position. Selling over the telephone requires good diction and communication skills. Advertising sales representatives must be compatible with different types of people. When calling on clients, they must be tactful and project a desire to help.

Advertising sales representatives at most publications have a distinct career path leading to management should they choose to follow it. They may specialize in retail or classified advertising and advance to management positions in those departments.

Job Outlook

The Bureau of Labor Statistics projects that employment of advertising sales representatives will grow at about the same rate as the average for all occupations between 1992 and 2005. More employment opportunities will occur as a result of people leaving those sales positions that require the least specialized training.

Earnings

Earnings of advertising sales representatives generally depend on the circulation size of the publication and an individual's education and previous experience. Large city newspapers, for example, generally offer higher salaries than suburban or rural newspapers.

According to the Bureau of Labor Statistics, the median annual income for full-time advertising sales representatives was more than $26,000 in 1992. Magazine advertising sales representatives averaged nearly $32,000 in 1991.

Advertising sales representatives are typically paid a base salary plus commission. Their commission is based on the amount of advertising they sell. In addition many publications offer incentives and bonuses to motivate individuals to generate more sales.

Related Occupations

Related occupations that require selling skills and a knowledge of the service being sold include broadcast advertising sales representatives, real estate agents, insurance agents, securities and financial services sales representatives, manufacturers' and wholesale sales representatives, travel agents, and a wide range of other service sales representatives.

Within magazine publishing, there are related sales support positions such a marketing assistants, research analysts, promotion assistants, and merchandising assistants.

Sources of Additional Information

- Magazine Publishers of America, 919 Third Ave., 22nd Fl., New York, NY 10022. Phone: (212)872-3700.

- Newspaper Association of America, The Newspaper Center, 11600 Sunrise Valley Dr., Reston, VA 22091. Phone: (703)648-1000.

APPAREL SALES WORKERS

At a Glance

- **D.O.T.:** 261.357-050 and -066

- **Preferred Education:** On-the-job training

- **Average Salary:** $13,625

- **Did You Know?** With a two-year associate degree in marketing or business, apparel sales workers can advance to such positions as buyers, merchandise managers, fashion coordinators, and even store managers.

Nature of the Work

When people shop for clothes, they often seek advice on current styles, fabrics, and accessories. They also need help finding merchandise and locating specific sizes. It is up to apparel sales workers to interest customers in a store's merchandise and assist them in making a purchase.

It is not always necessary for apparel sales workers to have an in-depth knowledge of the clothes they are selling. However, the more a salesperson has learned about the merchandise, the better they can help customers. Apparel sales workers should be prepared to offer advice regarding styles, fit, colors, fabric care and durability, and answer any other questions. They must also be able to tell customers about current promotions and discounts, return policies, and the availability of new merchandise.

In many cases, customers select the clothes they want to purchase, and sales workers need only ring up the sale on the cash register. Sales workers accept payment from customers in the form of cash, checks, or credit cards. They operate cash registers and give change and receipts to customers. They may be responsible for cash in the register. Their duties may include counting money and separating charge slips, coupons, and exchange vouchers. They may make cash deposits at their store's cash office.

An important part of apparel sales workers' duties is to keep the merchandise on the floor neat and orderly. After customers try on different clothes without purchasing them, it is necessary to refold the clothes so they can be put back on display. Apparel sales workers may check clothes that are arranged by size, such as men's suits and sport coats, to make sure they are in the proper order. They also check the racks to make sure a sufficient variety of sizes is available, bringing out new merchandise from storage as needed.

Apparel sales workers also handle merchandise exchanges and returns. In some stores they may assist customers by providing a gift box and wrapping gifts for them. Other duties may include arranging for delivery or mailing of a purchase, marking garments for alterations, writing sale prices on price tags, taking inventory, and preparing displays.

Apparel sales workers usually specialize in a certain type of clothing, such as men's and boys' clothing or women's apparel and accessories. Other areas of specialization include men's furnishings, shoes, women's hats and related accessories, women's fashion accessories, women's handbags, women's hosiery, women's lingerie, women's dresses, and women's sportswear.

Working Conditions

Apparel sales workers spend a lot of their time interacting with customers. Their work is not physically demanding, although they may have to stand for long periods of time. Depending on the size of the store, sales workers may be one of several salespeople in a busy department, or the only salesperson working in a relatively quiet store.

Apparel sales workers are usually expected to work during peak selling periods, including nights and weekends. It is not uncommon for them to work at least one day each weekend and have one day off during the week. During especially busy seasons, such as Christmas and back-to-school time, or during special sales, they may have to work longer hours than normal.

Employment

According to the Bureau of Labor Statistics, there were approximately 1.6 million retail salespersons employed in department, clothing, and variety stores in 1992. This group includes apparel sales workers.

In the apparel industry, many of the workers are young, with nearly one-third under 25 years of age in 1992. More than one-third were employed on a part-time basis. An estimated six out of every 10 jobs were in department stores.

Training, Other Qualifications, and Advancement

There are no formal training requirements for apparel sales workers. Some employers, especially chain and department stores, may require a high school diploma. Apparel sales workers can learn the basics in less than six months of on-the-job training. In small stores, training typically consists of an experienced employee or store manager showing a newly hired salesperson how to handle the cash register, fill out sales slips, and show customers around the store. They are given an introduction to the store's merchandise and its policies. As new employees gain experience, they receive additional advice and training on sales techniques and merchandise.

Training programs in larger stores are usually more formal and may last for several days. New salespeople are shown how to handle the register and make sales by cash, check, and credit card. They are instructed in the store's policies on returns and special orders. They may be given classroom instruction in customer service, security, and other store policies and procedures. They may be given information on how buyers and merchandise managers select and display the store's goods.

Apparel sales workers enjoy working with other people and the general public. They need to be friendly and courteous when dealing with customers. They must have good communication and language skills to be able to speak confidently and persuasively in front of others.

Opportunities for advancement depend on the employment situation and the individual's own objectives. In smaller apparel stores, advancement may be limited. Apparel sales workers may be promoted to assistant manager in such situations, or be considered for a manager's position should the store open a new location. They may use their sales experience to find a better position selling some other type of goods or services.

In other cases, such as in department and chain stores, an entry-level position in apparel sales may be the start of a career in fashion merchandising. With a two-year associate degree in marketing or business and experience in apparel sales, advancement is possible to positions such as buyer, merchandise manager, fashion coordinator, and even store manager.

Job Outlook

According to the Bureau of Labor Statistics, employment of retail salespeople in department, clothing, and variety stores is projected to increase by 15 percent between 1992 and 2005, somewhat less than the average for all occupations. This is a relatively large occupational category, however, and many openings are projected to result from high turnover. Many positions for apparel sales workers will be available for young workers, first-time job seekers, persons with limited job experience, senior citizens, and people with children seeking part-time work.

Earnings

The Bureau of Labor Statistics reports that the median earnings for apparel sales workers in 1993 were approximately $13,625, or about $262 per week. Within this field, men's and boys' apparel sales workers generally earned more than women's apparel and accessories sales workers. According to *American Salaries and Wages Survey*, men's furnishings sales workers in New York earned an average of $18,150 in 1991. Men's and boys clothing sales workers in New York earned an average of $14,250 in 1991, and women's apparel and accessories sales workers in New York earned an average of $13,150 in 1991.

While most stores offer discounts on store merchandise to their sales workers, only the larger apparel stores and department stores are likely to offer a full package of benefits such as health insurance, paid vacations, and sick leave.

Related Occupations

Related occupations in fashion merchandising include stock clerks, adjustment clerks, expeditors, buyers, merchandise managers, fashion coordinators, and department and store managers.

There are also many other occupations in retail sales, including the sale of motor vehicles and boats, televisions and appliances, furniture and home furnishings, hardware and building supplies, parts, and other commodities. Other occupations involving sales include manufacturers' and wholesale trade sales workers, service sales representatives, counter and rental clerks, real estate sales agents, wholesale and retail buyers, insurance sales workers, and cashiers.

Sources of Additional Information

- Apparel Retailers of America, 2011 Eye St. NW, Ste. 250, Washington, DC 20006. Phone: (202)347-1932.

- National Retail Federation, 325 7th St. NW, Ste. 1000, Washington, DC 20004-2802. Phone: (202)783-7971.

AUCTIONEERS

At a Glance

- **D.O.T.:** 294.257-010

- **Preferred Education:** Apprenticeship or auctioneer school

- **Average Salary:** $20,000

- **Did You Know?** According to the National Auctioneers Association, there were approximately 25,000 licensed auctioneers in the United States in 1994.

Nature of the Work

Antiques, personal property, real estate, livestock, industrial equipment, automobiles, art, and collectibles are just some of the items commonly sold at auctions. Auctioneers conduct these sales, selling items to the highest bidders. Their job involves meeting with sellers, receiving and appraising merchandise to be sold, organizing and cataloging items, and advertising the auction. Auctioneers may sell a wide variety of merchandise at the retail or wholesale level. Some auctioneers specialize in a single type of merchandise.

The auction method involves a specific way of marketing or selling goods to interested buyers. Auctions may be conducted before large crowds of two or three thousand people, or before only a handful of interested buyers. During an auction, specific items are offered for sale to a series of bidders, with title for the merchandise passing to the highest bidder. Auctions are regarded as providing an indication of the fair market value of the goods being sold, and bidders know that they have paid only slightly more for an item than the previous bidder.

Like other sales workers, auctioneers try to keep prospective buyers interested in the merchandise. When conducting an auction, auctioneers use specific bid calling techniques. The auctioneer's chant consists of announcing the last bid, asking for the next highest bid, and "fill words" to give bidders time to consider their next bid. The chant determines the tempo of the auction and generates interest among the audience. Auctioneers must speak clearly, with good diction, so that buyers can keep up with the pace of the auction. A public address system is often used to amplify the auctioneer's voice, which is one of the most distinctive aspects of an auction.

Conducting an auction is the most visible aspect of the work of auctioneers, but they also spend a lot of time preparing for an auction. Their job begins with receiving merchandise to be sold and meeting with sellers. Auctioneers determine the sellers' expectations and explain the services available. They also must make sure the auction will meet all legal requirements. This involves verifying title to the property being auctioned, notifying creditors of the auction if necessary, and complying with local licensing requirements.

After meeting with sellers, auctioneers appraise merchandise, usually setting a price range in which they believe the goods will sell. They may consult with the sellers to determine the price range and decide if a minimum bid, or reserve, is to be set. When a minimum bid is in effect, the merchandise will not be sold if there is no bid above the minimum. If no minimum bid is set for an item, then it is said to be an absolute sale. In larger auction houses, appraisals may be conducted by specialists who are experts in appraising certain categories of merchandise.

Once the merchandise for an auction has been appraised, auctioneers then organize the merchandise into the order it will be sold. In some cases several items may be sold together as lots. When organizing materials for auction, auctioneers take into account the price range and desirability of the items and arrange the sale to maximize interest among prospective buyers. In the case of collectibles, items are often organized according to other principles, such as chronologically, alphabetically by artist (in the case of paintings), or by author (in the case of rare books).

Auctioneers may also be involved in cataloging the merchandise to be sold. As with appraisals, cataloging in larger auction houses may be done by specialists who are not auctioneers. Catalogs are designed to provide prospective buyers with an opportunity to see what's being offered for sale and deciding in advance which items they are interested in. Catalogs include descriptions of the items along with any interesting facts concerning their history, ownership, and other significant data. Catalogs are frequently illustrated with photographs of the merchandise being sold. They also include the estimated price range within which the goods are expected to sell. When the bidding becomes more competitive, it is not uncommon for items to sell for much more than their estimates.

Catalogs that are sent through the mail to prospective buyers are one means of publicizing auctions. Auctioneers may also be responsible for writing advertisements and other promotional materials to help publicize auctions. Auctioneers may supervise clerks and assistants who handle a variety of related tasks. Additional duties may include training apprentice auctioneers.

Working Conditions

Auctioneers may work under a variety of conditions. Their working conditions are usually determined by the nature of the auctions they conduct and the type of merchandise being sold. Auctioneers may work indoors or outdoors, depending on what is being sold and where. Outdoor auctions usually take place as scheduled, regardless of weather conditions. Auctioneers often work odd hours in preparing for and conducting auctions.

Auctions can last for several hours, so some degree of physical stamina is required. Auctioneers must keep their vocal chords in top condition and practice breathing exercises for the long hours involved in conducting an auction. Throughout the sale auctioneers are like performers in front of an audience, trying to keep the audience's attention and generating interest in items being sold.

Auctioneers frequently travel to a variety of locations. Certain kinds of auctions are usually held in rural areas, while others typically take place in large cities.

Auctioneers interact with a wide range of people, including buyers, sellers, appraisers, catalogers, auction assistants and clerks, and other auctioneers. Their work allows them to become knowledgeable about a range of merchandise.

Employment

According to the National Auctioneers Association, there were approximately 25,000 licensed auctioneers in the United States in 1994. In addition, there are unlicensed auctioneers working in states that do not require auctioneers to be licensed.

Auctioneers may work part-time or full-time. They may be self-employed or work for an established auction firm. Whether they work in a rural area or a large city is largely determined by the type of goods they sell. Auctioneers who specialize in livestock or farm equipment would typically work in rural areas, while art auctioneers are employed in large cities. Most merchandise and personal property can be auctioned virtually anywhere in the United States.

Training, Other Qualifications, and Advancement

Individuals can learn to be auctioneers either by apprenticing with a practicing auctioneer or by attending an auctioneering school. Home study courses are also available. Topics covered include appraising, presentation, and voice training.

The National Auctioneers Association offers continuing education programs for auctioneers. Experienced auctioneers may also take advanced training courses at the Certified Auctioneers Institute located at Indiana University.

Some states require auctioneers to be licensed. Requirements vary from state to state and may include serving an apprenticeship, completing a course of study from an approved auctioneering school, passing an examination, and paying a license fee. Additional licensing requirements usually apply to real estate auctioneers. In addition, auctioneers must post liability or surety bonds.

Auctioneers should be effective, persuasive speakers with good diction and pronunciation skills. Like other salespeople, part of their persuasiveness stems from their personal manner and good humor. They must be alert and enjoy performing in front of an audience. They should enjoy communicating with people and have the stamina to conduct auctions lasting several hours.

Auctioneers generally advance in their careers by building a reputation and creating a demand for their services. They may also enhance their employment prospects by specializing in certain types of goods.

Job Outlook

While employment projections for auctioneers are not available from the Bureau of Labor Statistics, the general category of marketing and sales occupations is expected to increase by approximately 24 percent between 1990 and 2005. The employment outlook for auctioneers is also enhanced by the growing success of auctions in a variety of fields. The auction method is proving to be an effective sales and marketing tool for merchandise and property that had previously not been sold at auction. As a result, the demand for skilled, well-trained auctioneers is expected to be strong.

Earnings

Earnings for auctioneers varies with type of goods auctioned, geographic location, and nature of employment. Auctioneers usually work on commission, so auctioning real estate or antique furniture would result in higher wages than auctioning general merchandise at an estate sale, for example.

Part-time auctioneers can expect to earn about $10,000 per year, while $20,000 is an average annual salary for full-time auctioneers. Experienced auctioneers have been known to earn as much as $50,000 to $75,000 in a year.

Related Occupations

Related occupations in general sales include sales and manufacturing representatives, trade show exhibitors, leasing agents, product demonstrators, retail sales workers, real estate agents, insurance agents and brokers, and securities sales workers.

Retail and wholesale buyers also need to have product knowledge and sales skills similar to that of auctioneers. In addition there are a variety of miscellaneous sales occupations to be considered.

Sources of Additional Information

For additional information about auctioneering, contact:

- National Auctioneers Association, 8880 Ballentine, Overland Park, KS 66214. Phone: (913)541-8084.

For a list of auctioneer schools, consult the American Trade Schools Directory, *available in most libraries.*

AUTOMOBILE RENTAL CLERKS

At A Glance

- **D.O.T.:** 295.467-026

- **Preferred Education:** On-the-job training

- **Average Salary:** $252 per week

- **Did You Know?** Some large rental companies have formal classroom training programs where employees learn equipment operation and customer service techniques.

Nature of the Work

Each year, millions of Americans rent automobiles for their vacations, business trips, and other temporary transportation needs. These people rely on automobile rental clerks to make renting a car a trouble-free and efficient process.

Automobile rental clerks rent automobiles and other vehicles to customers. They help customers decide what type of automobile they need and for how long. They inform customers about the various options such as automatic transmission, power steering, and air-conditioning. Automobile rental clerks quote prices, which are generally based on the type of vehicle and length of time. These details are often handled over the telephone.

When a customer rents a car, automobile rental clerks take the customer's driver's license and credit card information, generally entering the information into a computer. They fill out the rental agreement and explain the rental policies and procedures.

When a vehicle is returned, rental clerks record the mileage and fuel level, and check for damage. They compute the rental charges, figuring in additional charges such as taxes, late fees and damage fees.

Working Conditions

Many car rental agencies are open 24 hours a day, seven days a week. Rental clerks generally work eight-hour shifts, which may include nights, weekends, and holidays. Many clerks work a 40-hour week. Others work part-time. Rental clerks spend much of their time on the telephone or assisting customers. They also work with computers and handle paper work such as rental contracts and claim forms.

Employment

Counter and rental clerks held about 242,000 jobs in 1992. A large number were employed by automobile and truck rental companies. These companies have operations all across the country. Many are located in airports, train stations, bus terminals, and hotels. Some car dealerships and service stations also rent vehicles.

Training, Other Qualifications, and Advancement

Many car rental agencies prefer workers with high school diplomas. Some clerks receive on-the-job training. They learn how to use the equipment and become familiar with the company's policies and procedures under the supervision of a more experienced worker. However, some large companies have formal classroom training programs where employees learn equipment operation and customer service techniques.

Automobile rental clerks should have patience, tact, and a friendly personality. Since much of the work is processed on computers, good typing skills are a benefit. Good oral and written communication skills are essential.

Working as an automobile rental clerk can be a stepping stone to more responsible positions. Clerks can be promoted to supervisors, assistant managers, or branch managers. Advancement into higher management positions may require a bachelor's degree.

Job Outlook

Employment of counter and rental clerks, which includes automobile rental clerks, is expected to increase faster than the average for all occupations through the year 2005. The U.S. Bureau of Labor Statistics estimates that 88,000 counter and retail clerk jobs will be created between 1992 and 2005. Most job openings will arise from the need to replace workers who leave the workforce or transfer to other occupations. There should be plenty of part-time employment opportunities.

Earnings

According to the U.S. Department of Labor, counter and rental clerks earned a median weekly income of $252 in 1992. The middle 50 percent earned between $201 and $383 per week. Counter and rental clerks typically start around the minimum wage, which was $4.25 an hour in 1992. In South Dakota, for example, the average wage offered to automobile rental clerks was $4.50 per hour in 1992.

Full-time counter and rental clerks often receive benefits such as health and life insurance, and paid vacation and sick leave. Benefits for part-time counter and rental clerks tend to be significantly less.

Related Occupations

Other workers who take orders and receive payments for services rendered include cashiers, retail sales workers, food counter clerks, postal service clerks, and bank tellers.

Sources of Additional Information

- American Car Rental Association, 1225 Eye St., NW, Ste. 500, Washington, DC 20005. Phone: (202)682-4778.

- National Vehicle Leasing Association, P.O. Box 281230, San Francisco, CA 94128-1230. Phone: (415)548-9135.

AUTOMOBILE SALESPEOPLE

At a Glance

- **D.O.T.:** 273.353-010

- **Preferred Education:** Sales experience and on-the-job training

- **Average Salary:** $25,000

- **Did You Know?** Automobile salespersons typically work under pressure to meet sales quotas and often work long hours, including some evenings and weekends.

Nature of the Work

Purchasing an automobile, whether new or used, can be a complicated process. Customers must decide what type of vehicle they want, what added features are necessary, and an appropriate price range. To help customers with this process, automobile salespeople provide detailed information and complete the sales transaction.

When prospective customers enter a showroom, salespeople generally talk with them to determine their interests. They find out what type of vehicle and features the customer is looking for. Using their extensive product knowledge, automobile salespersons suggest appropriate models. They take into account such factors as selling price, seating and cargo capacity, fuel economy, engine size, luxury items, and other product features. They may accompany customers on test drives to further acquaint them with a particular model's features and benefits.

Depending on a customer's level of interest, an automobile salesperson may close the sale. Automobile salespersons employ different sales techniques to convince customers to commit to a purchase. If it is clear that a customer is not yet ready to make a purchase, the salesperson may make arrangements for future contact.

Once a sale is made, automobile salespersons complete the necessary paperwork. They may consult with their sales manager to obtain approval of the terms of a particular sale. They explain financing options to the buyer along with any legal requirements concerning ownership that must be met. They may help customers obtain appropriate financing by contacting lenders for them. They may make arrangements for vehicles to be delivered or for new owners to take possession.

Automobile salespeople spend much of their time prospecting for new customers. Prospecting may involve making telephone calls, leaving business cards in conspicuous locations, and sending out direct mail packages. Automobile salespeople who work for auto brokers may not have the advantage of a showroom and must rely on their ability to describe different makes and models to prospective customers.

Salespeople may specialize in new or used cars, trucks, and other types of vehicles. While the nature of their work may vary depending on whether they work for a dealer or a broker and whether they are selling new or used vehicles, automobile salespersons must be persuasive and knowledgeable in order to convince prospective customers that a certain vehicle is right for them.

Working Conditions

There is a high turnover among automobile salespersons, because they frequently leave one dealership for another with a higher sales volume. They typically work under pressure to meet sales quotas and often work long hours, including some evenings and weekends. The competitive nature of the business adds to the stress felt by most automobile salespersons.

Automobile salespersons may spend most of their time in comfortable, well-lighted showrooms. However, their individual offices are usually small with few comforts. Those who work for brokers may only have a desk and a telephone from which to conduct their business.

Like other retail sales workers, automobile salespersons spend a lot of time talking and listening to the general public. They also interact frequently with other salespersons and individuals in other departments of the dealership. They frequently use the telephone to contact prospective customers.

Employment

There were approximately 197,000 retail salespersons employed in motor vehicle dealerships in 1992. The average dealership employed eight new- and used-vehicle salespersons. Vehicle sales relate directly to the number of people in an area, so there are more employment opportunities for automobile salespersons in densely populated areas than in rural areas.

In addition to working for dealerships, automobile salespersons may be employed by brokers who sell all types of cars and other vehicles from different manufacturers. Brokers themselves are self-employed automobile salespersons.

Training, Other Qualifications, and Advancement

Most dealerships require a high school diploma or equivalent for sales positions. High school adult education classes, technical institutes, community colleges, and universities offer courses covering most aspects of automobile sales. A college degree is desirable for those who hope to advance to a sales management or marketing position.

Automobile salespersons receive extensive on-the-job training. Their employer may provide them with several days of classroom training to acquaint them with sales and negotiation techniques and the models they will be selling. In the course of their work, automobile salespersons also attend sales meetings and receive periodic guidance from their sales managers.

Training modules for salespersons have been developed by NADA.

Automobile salespersons are generally well organized. They must be self-starters who can take the initiative. Excellent communication skills are required, as well as a neat appearance. They are usually genuinely interested in working with the public and communicating with people.

Automobile salespersons with several years of experience can advance to sales management positions. Many dealers look for college graduates to fill management positions. Salespersons can also advance by moving to a larger dealership and selling more vehicles.

Job Outlook

Employment of retail salespersons in motor vehicle dealerships is projected to increase by 22.6 percent between 1992 and 2005, according to the Bureau of Labor Statistics. Several demographic factors point to an increased demand for motor vehicles in the future. These include a growing population, rising personal incomes, and more households with two workers who each need their own vehicle.

Despite growth, much of which is due to high turnover, competition for sales positions will remain strong. There is a trend for dealerships to consolidate and offer vehicles from more than one manufacturer, a development that will tend to reduce overall employment in dealerships.

Earnings

The median weekly earnings for automobile salespersons was $479 in 1992, according to the Bureau of Labor Statistics, or an annual income of about $25,000. It's possible to earn quite a bit more, since most automobile salespersons are paid on commission or a combination of commission and salary.

Compensation programs vary from dealer to dealer, but most dealerships pay their salespersons bonuses. They also have special incentive programs that provide additional compensation when sales targets have been exceeded. Newly hired salespersons are usually given a modest salary until they have learned the basics.

Related Occupations

There is a wide range of specialized retail sales occupations to be considered. Occupations that require similar skills involving product knowledge and sales techniques include manufacturers' and wholesale trade sales workers, service sales representatives, real estate sales agents, wholesale and retail buyers, and insurance sales workers.

Sources of Additional Information

For more information on automobile sales and other careers in the automotive industry, contact:

• National Automobile Dealers Association, 8400 Westpark Dr., McLean, VA 22102. Phone: (703)821-7000.

BROADCAST TIME SALES REPRESENTATIVES

At a Glance

- **D.O.T.:** 259.357-018
- **Preferred Education:** Sales experience or college degree
- **Average Salary:** Usually based on commission
- **Did You Know?** Opportunities to learn the business of advertising sales include summer student internships offered by radio and television stations, broadcasting groups, and associated industries.

Nature of the Work

Whether in television or radio, selling advertising time in broadcast media involves similar rewards and responsibilities. In stations serving larger markets, sales staffs tend to be larger and individual tasks more specialized. In smaller markets advertising sales representatives tend to have a wider range of responsibilities.

Entry-level employees in advertising sales usually begin as sales assistants, although at smaller stations the entry-level sales position might have duties similar to those of an account executive. Sales assistants prepare presentations, compile ratings data, assist in processing sales orders, and update time availability information for use by account executives. They generally work closely with account executives and provide them with the necessary information for calling on and servicing accounts.

Entry-level sales representatives spend much of their time "cold calling" on prospective advertisers. These are generally small- and medium-size business owners in the area served by the station. Sales representatives are expected to research prospects and find out as much as possible about the business. They set up appointments with prospective advertisers and continue their fact-finding in face-to-face meetings. They continue to develop leads and find new prospects using sources such as newspaper ads, local directories, and word of mouth.

After making initial contact with a prospect, sales representatives begin to prepare an advertising plan that incorporates the prospect's marketing goals and other factors.

Sales representatives take into consideration such factors as their knowledge of the programs on their stations, the prospect's customer profile, the prospect's potential budget, and the cost and availability of specific time slots. Once a detailed plan has been developed, it is presented to the client for approval and, hopefully, a commitment to purchase advertising time with the station.

As sales representatives gain experience, they develop a list of clients to contact on a regular basis. In effect they become partners with their clients, helping them solve their marketing problems with effective advertising solutions. They provide clients with information about the station's commercial production and presentation capabilities. They may help clients create appropriate commercial messages and campaigns.

Experienced advertising sales representatives advance by being assigned to larger accounts. They may be assigned to work with advertising agencies who represent local and national accounts. They may be given a specific territory to work. They also handle duties associated with account servicing, including making changes in schedules, fine tuning commercials, and dealing with problems that may arise.

The major responsibilities of advertising sales representatives are similar at every level. They involve identifying prospective advertisers and helping them become satisfied clients. Advertising sales representatives must learn the marketing objectives of their clients and develop an appropriate advertising plan for them. They must convince clients of the value of advertising with their station and make sure that advertising plans are implemented in accordance with the client's wishes.

Working Conditions

Selling broadcast advertising is stressful and competitive. Advertising sales representatives are under pressure to meet sales goals and maintain a high sales volume. They often put in long hours and are under pressure to meet deadlines.

Advertising sales representatives work under moderately noisy conditions typical of a busy office. Some travel is usually required to meet with advertisers and prospects. Advertising sales positions also require constant communication with others.

Employment

The major employers of broadcast advertising sales representatives are television networks (including cable), local and cable television stations, radio networks, and local radio stations. These employers are located throughout the country, but the best opportunities are at stations in the top 100 markets located in major metropolitan areas. Large market stations may employ a sales staff of up to 25 people. Smaller market stations typically have a sales staff of two or three.

In radio there are more than 9,000 commercial stations that employ more than 65,000 sales personnel. Local television stations and cable companies employ advertising sales representatives to sell local advertising time. Approximately 75 percent of television network advertising sales takes place in New York City.

There are many employment opportunities for women in broadcast advertising sales, especially at television stations in the top 100 markets. While the national average of women in sales is approximately 28 percent, about half of all television salespeople in the top 100 markets are women.

Training, Other Qualifications, and Advancement

While a station may hire someone with a proven sales record for an entry-level position, most employers are looking for applicants with a college degree in subjects such as journalism, business, communications, or liberal arts. Specific sales training is then provided by the employer.

Opportunities to learn the business of advertising sales include summer student internships offered by radio and television stations, broadcasting groups, and associated industries. Educational seminars and career-enhancement programs for professional development are offered by different industry groups. The Radio Advertising Bureau administers a certification program that leads to the designation, Certified Radio Marketing Consultant (CRMC).

Advertising sales representatives and account executives must be well-organized in order to handle a complex schedule of appointments. They must have good reasoning skills and be able to analyze research data concerning a station's audience. Some creative ability may be needed to help clients conceptualize advertising messages.

Advertising sales representatives need personal qualities such as tact, poise, self-confidence, and the ability to handle rejection in order to succeed. Top-notch communication skills are required to convert prospects into clients and to keep clients satisfied. Attention to detail, the ability to work well with others, and computer and word processing skills are also essential.

Advertising sales offers a clear career path into management-level positions. Starting out as a sales assistant or account executive, advertising sales representatives can look forward to being promoted to positions such as local sales manager, national sales manager, and general sales manager. Top-level general manager positions at many radio and television stations are filled by former general sales managers.

Advertising sales representatives can also advance their careers by moving to stations located in larger markets. While a broader range of experience can be gained in smaller market stations, substantial salary increases are to be found by working in the top 100 markets.

Job Outlook

The outlook for broadcast advertising sales representatives is good. Specifically, sales employment opportunities at radio stations and networks can be expected to parallel the continued growth of radio's share of total advertising in the United States. In television, employment opportunities will result in part from the average 21 percent annual turnover in television advertising sales positions.

In addition, competition between television stations and networks will increase as cable television becomes more widespread, resulting in more advertising sales positions. More entry-level opportunities will occur in smaller markets, where the turnover rates are highest.

Competition is expected to be strong, however, for all types of entry-level positions in the broadcast industry due to the number of jobseekers the industry attracts. Most entry level positions will likely be at smaller stations; most stations in large metropolitan areas usually seek experienced personnel.

Earnings

Broadcast advertising sales representatives may earn a straight salary, a combination of salary and commission, or straight commission. In television nearly nine out of 10 stations use a straight commission system to compensate advertising sales representatives.

Incentive and bonus plans can add additional income for advertising sales representatives who meet or exceed sales targets. In addition salespeople are compensated for job-related expenses.

The size of the market served and the geographical location of a station are major determinants of salary ranges in both radio and television advertising sales.

According to the National Association of Broadcasters, annual earnings in 1992 for radio advertising sales representatives ranged from $17,825 in the smallest markets to $49,349 in the largest markets. Annual earnings for local radio sales managers ranged from $23,975 to $86,230. Entry-level salaries for television salespeople ranged from $30,000 for the top 100 markets to $19,000 for smaller markets in 1991.

Related Occupations

Related occupations that require selling skills and a knowledge of the service being sold include advertising account executives, newspaper and magazine advertising sales representatives, real estate agents, insurance agents, securities and financial services sales representatives, manufacturers' and wholesale sales representatives, and travel.

Sources of Additional Information

For more information on careers in the broadcast industry, contact:

- National Association of Broadcasters, 1771 N St. NW, Washington, DC 20036. Phone: (202)429-5300.

- National Cable Television Association, 1724 Massachusetts Ave. NW, Washington, DC 20036. Phone: (202)775-3550.

- Radio Advertising Bureau, 304 Park Ave. S., New York, NY 10010. Phone: (212)387-2100.

For additional information on careers in advertising, contact:

- American Association of Advertising Agencies, 666 Third Ave., New York, NY 10017-4056.

CIRCULATION SALES REPRESENTATIVES

At a Glance

- **D.O.T.:** 299.167-010

- **Preferred Education:** Sales experience

- **Average Salary:** $19,000 to $23,000 entry level

- **Did You Know?** Since more than 75 percent of all daily newspapers are home delivered, circulation personnel are frequently involved in the newspaper distribution process.

Nature of the Work

Circulation sales representatives are involved in the marketing, sales, and promotion of newspapers and magazines. They perform a variety of functions related to building the circulation of newspapers or magazines through subscriptions and single-copy sales. In smaller markets, circulation sales representatives may have responsibilities similar to those of a circulation supervisor or circulation director. Circulation sales representatives are known by a variety of titles, and the nature of their work depends on whether they are employed by a newspaper or magazine publisher.

In the newspaper industry, entry-level circulation personnel are typically called district sales managers. Their job involves marketing and promotion as well as the sale and distribution of newspapers. They develop marketing programs based on research and corporate objectives. They have access to lifestyle and demographic analyses and are able to determine a newspaper's sales potential within a specific geographical area. Based on their analysis of the research, district sales managers recommend outlets and locations for newsstands, racks, and carrier routes. They schedule the distribution and delivery of the newspaper, regulating the size of orders from distributors to maximize sales and minimize returns of unsold newspapers.

District sales managers provide support and guidance to the individuals who sell newspapers to the public, including dealers and carriers. They may conduct sales training programs for dealers and carriers and help initiate sales promotion programs. They monitor dealer sales and inspect carrier routes to ensure prompt and regular delivery of newspapers. They keep dealers and carriers informed of new circulation policies and programs.

Since more than 75 percent of all daily newspapers are home delivered, circulation personnel are frequently involved in the newspaper distribution process. They generate computerized instructions, which are included with every bundle of newspapers picked up at the loading dock. They instruct drivers, dealers, and carriers in sales techniques and keep them informed of special sales promotions and offers by writing promotional bulletins. They may arrange for the sale of newspapers at special events and the sale of special editions when there are important news developments.

Circulation sales representatives are also involved in

generating sales through marketing programs. Traditionally, newspaper sales were generated at the carrier level by calling on private residences and businesses. Newspapers still conduct sales incentive programs for carriers to increase sales. Modern circulation techniques now include telemarketing, sampling, direct mail, advertising, and reader involvement programs.

Circulation sales representatives may be involved in developing, monitoring, and supervising such programs. They may work with outside freelancers on direct mail or advertising programs. In larger markets, the development of sales and promotion strategies is typically handled by circulation supervisors.

Entry-level positions in magazine circulation are usually called circulation analysts or assistants. Circulation analysts prepare a variety of reports, sales forecasts, and computer models. They work primarily with numbers and support such functions as budgeting and planning. Circulation assistants may perform similar work but generally have more contact with outside vendors and freelancers. They may work on promotional or marketing programs and help produce direct mail packages or television commercials.

Like newspapers, magazines are sold through subscriptions and single-copy sales. However, magazine circulation personnel are not concerned with such logistical matters as carriers and delivery routes. Direct mail programs are more significant in magazine circulation than with newspapers. They are used to sell new subscriptions as well as renewals.

In selling magazines through direct mail, circulation personnel are responsible for the package, the offer, and the lists to be used. They may work with outside freelancers, including writers and graphic artists, to create direct mail packages. Specific duties may include selecting and testing mailing lists, coordinating production and mailing of direct mail packages, and analyzing subscription renewal orders.

Single copy sales are also important to magazine circulation. Circulation sales representatives generally work with distributors to determine how many copies should be sent to each location. They obtain authorizations from each retailer to allow the magazine to be sold there. They conduct special sales promotion programs to provide for the proper display of the magazine at retail outlets.

Additional duties of magazine circulation sales representatives may include analyzing data and preparing reports on promotion efforts, monitoring promotion expenses and results, analyzing and testing various pricing strategies, developing computerized circulation models, and tracking performance of competitive publications.

Some circulation sales representatives specialize in fulfillment. Subscription fulfillment may be a function of another department or an outside vendor. Circulation sales representatives maintain communications with whoever is responsible for subscription fulfillment. They make sure that fulfillment reports are produced as needed. They schedule and monitor renewal and invoice mailings. They may handle subscriber complaints. They may analyze billing procedures to determine which are the most effective.

Working Conditions

Like other positions in newspaper and magazine publishing, circulation sales representatives work under time pressure from publication deadlines. The ability to establish and meet schedules is important. Circulation sales representatives may have to work long hours occasionally to handle unexpected crises. Often their work is not routine, and they must be flexible to handle new challenges and demands. In some cases their work takes them out of the office.

Circulation sales representatives generally have to manage or handle several projects simultaneously. They interact frequently with other departments in the company, including editorial, research, and production. In larger markets, they may work in large departments and be part of a team effort.

Employment

Circulation sales representatives are employed by magazine and newspaper publishers. There are generally more newspapers serving larger markets, such as cities and metropolitan areas. Magazines are published throughout the country, with a concentration in large cities such as New York, Chicago, Atlanta, and Los Angeles.

Training, Other Qualifications, and Advancement

Circulation sales representatives generally have one to two years of on-the-job training. For advancement to supervisory and management circulation positions, a college degree is usually necessary. Appropriate college majors include business, journalism, and marketing. Prior knowledge of the principles of direct marketing and advertising is helpful.

Good writing skills are needed to prepare reports and write interoffice communications. A mastery of the principles of high school math, including statistics, is needed to work with research data and circulation figures. Circulation sales representatives generally know how to use computers, including word processing and spreadsheets. Good interpersonal skills help circulation sales representatives communicate with other newspaper and magazine employees, work as part of a team, and deal with outside vendors, distributors, and carriers.

Circulation sales representatives are generally high-energy individuals who enjoy the freedom to work independently, assume responsibility, and take risks. There is ample opportunity for innovation in circulation departments. The challenges of the job require a positive mental attitude, attention to detail, good organization, and the ability to set priorities. Self-confidence can help individuals accept constructive criticism as they learn from their mistakes.

Circulation sales representatives can advance by being promoted within their organization or by going to work for a larger newspaper or magazine publisher. In the newspaper industry, district sales managers can advance to circulation supervisor and circulation director. Circulation directors may advance to higher executive positions, including president, within the publishing company. Similar career paths exist in magazine publishing.

Job Outlook

According to the Bureau of Labor Statistics, employment of marketing and sales personnel in the printing and publishing industry will increase by only 7 percent between 1992 and 2005.

In major metropolitan areas, many large newspapers are replacing their district sales managers with independent home delivery agents, so there is a reduced demand for that type of position at metropolitan daily newspapers.

However, the role of circulation is recognized as critical to the success of a newspaper or magazine. Competition among newspapers and magazines remains strong, and publishers realize that a healthy circulation base is needed to attract advertisers. Publishers are allocating more money and resources into circulation in an effort to win the competitive battle. In magazine publishing, rising costs combined with flat or soft advertising revenues have caused publishers to look for more revenue from circulation.

Earnings

Earnings for circulation sales representatives depend on size and type of employer and geographic location. Large circulation newspapers pay more than smaller market publications. Educational background and previous work experience also affect earnings. According to *American Salaries and Wages Survey*, circulation sales representatives in the West earned an average salary of $19,136 in 1993-94.

At a major daily newspaper in one of the top 20 markets, circulation sales representatives can expect to start at about $23,000 for an entry-level position. District sales managers at major daily newspapers start at $30,000 or more, and with an advanced degree may start at upwards of $35,000. Circulation employees with three to five years of experience and good performance records commonly earn between $40,000 and $50,000 in major markets.

Related Occupations

Related sales and promotion occupations include advertising managers, media directors, account executives, promotion managers, and advertising agency managers.

Sources of Additional Information

- Circulation Council of the Direct Marketing Association, 11 W. 42nd St., New York, NY 10036. Phone: (212)768-7277.

For more information about careers in newspaper circulation, contact:

- Newspaper Association of America Foundation, The Newspaper Center, 11600 Sunrise Valley Dr., Reston, VA 22091-1412. Phone: (703)648-1000.

For more information about careers in magazine circulation, contact:

- Magazine Publishers of America, 919 Third Ave., 22nd Fl., New York, NY 10022. Phone: (212)872-3700.

CORPORATE TRAVEL SPECIALISTS

At a Glance

- **D.O.T.:** 252.152-010
- **Preferred Education:** Travel agent experience
- **Average Salary:** $16,461 to $32,896
- **Did You Know?** A growing number of companies have contracts with large travel agencies specializing in business travel.

Nature of the Work

Escalating travel expenses and complicated business itineraries are prompting many companies to hire corporate travel specialists. These travel specialists control expenses by handling all travel arrangements for a single company. Corporate travel specialists perform many of the same duties as leisure travel agents, such as gathering information on air fares, reserving hotel rooms, and arranging for rental cars.

Corporate travel specialists may work individually or as part of a corporate travel department. Like other travel agents, corporate travel specialists consult a variety of published and computerized sources of information on airline departure and arrival times, fares, car rental rates, and hotel ratings and facilities.

Corporate travel specialists must keep travel costs to a minimum and can often negotiate with hotels and car rental companies for special corporate rates. Corporate travel specialists may formulate a travel budget, which can amount to several million dollars, and establish company travel policies. They may also establish a budget for employee expenses, arrange for credit cards, and secure passports.

Some corporate travel specialists plan conferences and large meetings. They may schedule the event, pick a location with the required facilities, and make travel arrangements. In choosing a location, travel specialists consider the hotel's location, parking facilities, special group rates for guest rooms, number and size of meeting rooms, and availability of recreational and entertainment facilities. They often use a checklist to make sure meeting rooms have adequate facilities. The checklist includes such information as the seating plan, acoustics, lighting, and audio-visual equipment.

Other responsibilities of corporate travel specialists may include planning complicated itineraries, relocating personnel, administering corporate aircraft and automobiles, coordinating transportation to and from training programs, and organizing group vacations or recreational trips for employees.

Working Conditions

Corporate travel specialists work in modern offices equipped with computers. They frequently negotiate with hotel and airline representatives and communicate with fellow company employees. Corporate travel specialists are often under pressure to make arrangements on short notice. They typically work hours comparable to those of other company employees.

Employment

Corporate travel specialists are generally employed by large companies with travel budgets, which are typically located in metropolitan areas. A growing number of companies, however, have contracts with outside travel agencies specializing in business travel. These agencies may establish an office on the company's premises and handle all travel arrangements.

Training, Other Qualifications, and Advancement

Many corporate travel agents have had previous experience working for a private travel agency. Others have been promoted from within the company, as they saw the need for handling travel services and established their company's first travel department.

Increasingly, however, formal education is becoming more important for travel agents. Formal or specialized training in travel and tourism is offered through vocational schools, community colleges, adult education centers, and colleges. Full-time programs can last three to 12 weeks and may be taught during the evenings or on weekends.

The American Society of Travel Agents and the Institute of Certified Travel Agents offer home study courses. The National Business Travel Association offers a Certified Travel Executive program, geared toward enhancing the skills of business travel managers. A few colleges offer a bachelor's and a master's degree in travel and tourism.

Since there are generally few senior positions within a corporate travel department, corporate travel specialists tend to advance by moving to a higher position in the travel department of another company. Some corporate travel specialists are promoted to supervisory or management positions in other departments.

Corporate travel specialists need good communication, organizational and administrative skills. They must be detail-oriented and be able to quickly analyze financial information. Tact, good negotiating skills, and a sharp business sense are also beneficial. In addition, it is important for corporate travel specialists to stay abreast of changing technologies, requirements, and fares in the travel industry by reading current literature.

Job Outlook

According to the Bureau of Labor Statistics, employment of all travel agents is expected to increase much faster than the average for all occupations through the year 2005. Business-related travel in particular is projected to increase as business activity becomes globally oriented. These factors, combined with efforts to reduce corporate travel costs, provide a favorable outlook for corporate travel specialists. As companies streamline processes, however, technology is lessening the need for travel agents to some extent. In some companies, employees book routine business trips by filling out forms on their personal computers.

Earnings

In 1993, corporate travel agents had annual salaries ranging from $12,776 to $30,069. Salaries for managers ranged from $16,461 to $32,896. Corporate travel specialists employed by a company receive the same benefits as other employees. However, they do not receive the reduced-rate travel privileges offered to travel agency employees.

Related Occupations

Other workers with responsibilities similar to corporate travel specialists include leisure travel agents, secretaries, tour guides, airline reservation agents, rental car agents, and travel counselors.

Sources of Additional Information

- National Association of Business Travel Agents, 3255 Wilshire Blvd., Ste. 1514, Los Angeles, CA 90010 Phone: (213)382-3335.

- National Business Travel Association, 1650 King St., No. 301, Alexandria, VA 22314 Phone: (703)684-0836

- American Society of Travel Agents, 1101 King St., Alexandria, VA 22314 Phone: (703)739-2782.

HOTEL SERVICES SALES REPRESENTATIVES

At a Glance

- **D.O.T.:** 259.157-014

- **Preferred Education:** Sales experience

- **Average Salary:** Varies.

- **Did You Know?** To promote their facilities, lodging chains often employ salesworkers in regional offices located in major cities.

Nature of the Work

Conventions, business meetings, conferences, training classes, trade shows, wedding receptions, and other social gatherings are major sources of revenue for hotels. To encourage groups to use their facilities and services for special events, many hotels employ sales representatives.

Hotel sales representatives contact government, business, and social groups to solicit special event business for the hotel. They generally begin the sales process by developing a list of prospective customers. To create interest in the hotel, sales representatives may mail brochures to the prospects on their lists. They contact the leader of each group, either by phone or in person, to analyze the group's requirements. During the phone call or meeting, sales representatives learn as much about the event as possible. This includes the date of the event, the number of people expected to attend, the need for additional services such as food, refreshments, and audio-visual equipment, and the budget.

Using this information, sales representatives prepare a contract and obtain the proper customer signatures.

Selling the hotel's services is only part of the job, however. Once the customer agrees to the terms, sales representatives work with the hotel staff to organize the event. They may arrange for any necessary transportation and make sure that the correct number of guest and meeting rooms are reserved. They also may coordinate details such as food service and decorations. On the day of the event, sales representatives may serve as advisors to minimize confusion and resolve problems, such as providing additional equipment or meeting space.

Sales representatives follow up with customers after events to make sure the service was satisfactory and thank them for using the hotel. If there were problems, sales representatives work with hotel department managers to correct the problems and avoid future complaints.

Working Conditions

Hotel services sales representatives spend much of their time calling prospective customers to interest them in the hotel's services. Depending on the position, some travel may be required. Like most sales positions, stress is a large part of the job. Hotels generally set quotas and have sales contests. There often is considerable pressure on sales representatives to meet sales quotas by the end of every sales period.

Employment

According to the U.S. Department of Labor, the hotel and motel industry employed about 13,000 salesworkers in 1992. Employment in the hotel and motel industry is concentrated in densely populated and resort areas. Lodging chains employ salesworkers in regional offices located in major cities to promote their facilities. Many of the hotel and motel industry's workers are young. The industry provides many people with their first jobs.

Training, Other Qualifications, and Advancement

While many hotels seek graduates from college hotel administration programs, they may hire sale representatives with a high school diploma if they have a proven sales record. Summer internship programs are one way workers can gain sales experience. Many hotel sales departments hire summer interns to work on a variety of activities such as market research, account management, and other sales projects. The American Hotel & Motel Association's Education Institute offers home-study courses for individuals interested in marketing and sales careers.

Many hotels conduct sales training programs for their

sales representatives. A typical training program will cover the history of the hotel, its services, and basic sales techniques. Sales representatives also may attend training seminars to learn about new services and to update their sales skills. These sessions may include motivational or sensitivity training to make the sales representative more effective in communicating with people.

The ability to communicate is the most important skill hotel sales representatives can develop. Effective salesworkers need to demonstrate other important attributes, some of which include self-confidence, high self-esteem, aggressiveness, reliability, and empathy. Sales representatives also should be self-starters who can work under pressure to meet sales goals.

Hotel sales representatives who have good sales records and leadership ability may advance to upper management positions. These may include general manager, food and beverage manager, front office manager, or sales manager.

Job Outlook

Employment growth of hotel marketing and sales workers is expected to be faster than the industry average. The U.S. Bureau of Labor Statistics predicts employment of hotel salesworkers to grow more than 25 percent between 1992 and 2005. Job growth in the hotel and motel industry will reflect rising personal income, continued growth of two-income families, continued low-cost air fares, emphasis on leisure-time activities, and growth of foreign tourism in the United States. In addition, many openings will be created by job turnover, which is relatively high in this industry.

Earnings

Earnings of hotel sales representatives generally depend on performance. Sales representatives work on different types of compensation plans. Some get a straight salary; others are paid on a commission basis. A commission is a percentage of the dollar value of a sale. Most sales representatives receive a combination of salary and commissions. In addition, some companies offer bonuses, including vacation time, trips, and prizes, for sales that exceed assigned quotas. Some hotels offer profit-sharing plans, tuition reimbursement, and other benefits to their employees.

The U.S. Department of Labor reports that the median annual income for representatives selling business services was nearly $30,000 in 1992.

Related Occupations

Hotel sales representatives must have sales ability and knowledge of the service they sell. Workers in other occupations who require these skills include travel agents, education courses sales representatives, advertising sales representatives, group-sales representatives, dancing instructions sales representatives, and television cable service sales representatives.

Sources of Additional Information

• Hospitality Sales and Marketing Association

International, 1300 L St. NW, Ste. 800, Washington, DC 20005. Phone: (202)789-0089.

- American Hotel and Motel Association, 1201 New York Ave. NW, Ste. 600, Washington, DC 20005. Phone: (202)289-3100.

MERCHANDISE DISPLAY WORKERS

At a Glance

- **D.O.T.:** 298.081-010

- **Preferred Education:** High school diploma or associate degree

- **Average Salary:** $5.69 to $12.64 per hour

- **Did You Know?** Courses in art, fashion design, interior decorating, advertising, industrial design, merchandising, and related subjects are helpful for merchandise display workers.

Nature of the Work

Every day millions of shoppers are drawn into retail stores to admire tastefully arranged furniture sets, the clothes of stylishly outfitted mannequins, and an unlimited variety of attractively displayed merchandise available for purchase. Attractively displaying merchandise takes the creative talent of merchandise display workers. Merchandise display workers carefully arrange merchandise of all types in windows, showcases, and on the sales floor of retail stores to attract customers' attention.

A merchandise display worker first consults with the store's display director or advertising or sales manager to determine which merchandise is to be featured in the display. A display worker may also meet with directors and managers to develop display ideas and schedule construction of the display. Sometimes displays are designed with a theme, while others are designed from the display worker's imagination. The end product must usually meet a manager's approval before it is shown to the public.

Depending upon the complexity of the display, a display worker may construct background settings with carpeting, lighting, and wallpaper. Display workers sometimes use power and hand tools to build or assemble props; they may also need the assistance of carpenters, painters, or store maintenance workers to complete a background setting or move heavy objects, such as furniture.

Merchandise display workers decide how the backdrops, props, furniture, mannequins, accessories, and merchandise are arranged in the display. They dress mannequins, deciding what clothing and accessories will make up the total ensemble. To make a complete display, merchandise display workers may have to use merchandise or equipment from other departments

or stores. For instance, a furniture store showcasing a child's bedroom may feature toys in the display to make the setting more realistic and appealing. A display worker also places price tags and descriptive information in the display.

As new merchandise comes into the store, old displays must be dismantled by display workers. They pack and store reusable items and maintain a record of these items for future use.

Working Conditions

Merchandise display workers work in clean, well-lighted, air conditioned retail stores. They do, however, often have to set up displays in cramped spaces, climb ladders, lift objects weighing up to 50 pounds, and use power tools and other hardware. They must also do a lot of standing, stooping, bending, kneeling, and crawling.

Their work week is typically 35 to 40 hours. Working evenings, weekends, and overtime is not uncommon when displays must be set up during nonbusiness hours or for holidays and special sales events. The Christmas season is particularly busy for merchandise display workers because of the substantial increase in retail sales.

Travel may be necessary, although it is usually limited to a regional area, as a display worker may work for a chain of retail outlets or need to set up displays at trade shows or other events.

Employment

According to the U.S. Bureau of Labor Statistics, display workers are part of the 104,000 workers in the retail sales industry that are not salespersons, cashiers, or supervisors. Display workers are employed by department stores, clothing stores, furniture stores, specialty stores, and other retail outlets.

Most display workers work in urban areas, and the best opportunities are usually found in large metropolitan regions. Some merchandise display workers are self-employed freelancers who are contracted by retail stores.

Training, Other Qualifications, and Advancement

Employers prefer that display workers have at least a high school diploma. Some desire a two-year college degree. Courses in art, fashion design, interior decorating, advertising, industrial design, merchandising, and related subjects are helpful, although not always necessary.

Merchandise display workers need to be artistic, creative, fashionable, and imaginative. Technically, they must have the ability to work easily and skillfully with their hands, the ability to coordinate colors, shades and shapes, and know how to skillfully integrate merchandise and other fixtures.

Display workers receive most of their training on the job. They may advance to become display managers or promotion directors. Some display workers become self-employed. Talent, experience, and education are factors in advancement opportunities.

Job Outlook

According to the U.S. Bureau of Labor Statistics, employment opportunities in retail stores are projected to increase only 12 percent by the year 2005. However, strong competition among retailers is expected to continue, emphasizing the importance of attracting customers.

Overall, many employment opportunities in the industry are the result of the high turnover rate. Job opportunities in retail stores are generally good for young workers and first-time job-seekers.

Earnings

Earnings for display workers depend on the geographic location of the employer, the size of the employer, and the display worker's experience. Pay is higher in urban areas, and larger retail establishments generally pay more than smaller ones.

According to *American Salaries and Wages Survey*, wages for merchandise display workers may start as low as $4.25 per hour for a beginning display worker in a low-population state such as Nebraska and be as high as $21.16 per hour for an experienced display worker in the Northeast. Average wages are $5.69 to $12.64 per hour.

College experience may also increase earnings. Freelancers' earning potential depends on the number of clients and the amount of time worked, as well as their personal talent and reputation.

Most employers offer merchandise display workers discounts on merchandise. Larger companies may provide full-time merchandise display workers benefits that include paid vacations, sick leave, health and life insurance, and retirement plans.

Related Occupations

Other occupations similar to merchandise display workers include commercial decorators, interior decorators, floral designers, commercial artists, fashion artists, and graphic designers.

Sources of Additional Information

For additional information on a career as a merchandise display worker, contact:

- Apparel Retailers of America, 2011 Eye St. NW, Ste. 250, Washington, DC 20006.

- National Association of Display Industries, 355 Lexington Ave., New York, NY 10017. Phone: (212)661-4261.

- National Retail Federation, 325 7th St. NW, Ste. 1000, Washington, DC 20004. Phone: (202)783-7971.

PERSONAL COMPUTER SALESPEOPLE

At a Glance

- **D.O.T.:** 275.257-010

- **Preferred Education:** Sales experience or college degree

- **Average Salary:** Varies

- **Did You Know?** More than three-quarters of those currently involved in computer sales, both retail and corporate, are college graduates.

Nature of the Work

Personal computers have created a worldwide technology revolution. Once found only in large businesses and government agencies, computers can now be found in small businesses and homes all across the country. Many of these personal computers are purchased through retail operations that employ personal computer salespeople.

Retail personal computer salespeople help customers purchase the appropriate computer equipment for their needs. By talking with customers, they find out how the customer will use the computer and what functions are important. Computer salespeople then describe the various brands and models, demonstrate their use, and explain the different types of software and accessories available.

Beyond selling personal computers to new users, personal computer salespeople help customers upgrade to more sophisticated systems. They help customers select the right peripherals and add-ons, which may include monitors, printers, modems, surge protectors, and computer furniture.

To do their jobs properly, salespeople must have a thorough knowledge of personal computer equipment and software. Like all salespeople, computer salespeople must use their skills to convince prospective customers of the value of their products and services. They do this by emphasizing a computer's features, such as flexibility, cost, capacity, and performance.

Customer service is an important part of the salesperson's job. They must be able to answer customer questions and handle complaints. If a customer requests a specific product that is not in stock, salespeople may call other stores to locate the item. They may also special order products as a service to customers.

Working Conditions

Retail personal computer salespeople work in a store environment that may sell only computers or be a small department within a larger store. Most retail salespersons work evenings and weekends. During Christmas and other peak periods, retail salespersons can expect to work longer than normal hours. They spend much of their time on their feet. Some computer retailers employ an outside sales force to make sales calls at customer locations.

Employment

According to the Bureau of Labor Statistics, there are more than 59,000 marketing and salespersons employed in the computer industry in 1992. Those working in retail are employed by computer stores, office equipment stores, department stores, and furniture and appliance dealers. These stores are located all across the country, primarily in or near metropolitan areas.

Training, Other Qualifications, and Advancement

Many employers in retail computer sales will hire salespersons with only a high school diploma. As the computer industry matures, however, more employers will look for college graduates who have a specialized knowledge of computers. More than three-quarters of those currently involved in computer sales, both retail and corporate, are college graduates. High school students can prepare for a career in computer sales by taking courses in English, mathematics, and computers. College students may want to pursue a degree in computer science.

Retail computer salespersons need to know more than computers and their capabilities; they also need to know how to sell. Success in sales requires ambition and perseverance. Good salespeople must understand their customers and keep abreast of recent developments in computer technology. Many employers and computer vendors offer sales and product training courses and seminars. These training programs generally last several days. Retail workers also attend sales meetings to learn about new products and applications.

Although a college degree is not a requirement, it may be necessary to advance to higher paying positions. Successful retail salespersons may become outside salespersons, store managers, or district managers. Others may be hired by computer vendors to sell to corporate customers. Some computer retailers open their own computer stores.

Job Outlook

The Bureau of Labor Statistics expects employment in the computer and data processing services industry to more than double by the year 2005. This is mainly due to the development and expansion of the personal computer. As prices for computers continue to fall, personal computers will become more widespread. This will contribute to the need for knowledgeable salesworkers to help customers select and operate their computers.

Earnings

Earnings for retail personal computer salespersons generally depend on performance. Retail workers in general often receive commissions and bonuses in addition to an hourly wage. A recent survey shows that computer salespeople earn on the average about 10 percent commission on sales. Salespeople can also earn special bonuses, often called SPIFFS, for selling certain products. Benefits may be limited in smaller stores, but larger retailers usually offer such

benefits as health insurance, paid vacations and sick days. Some retailers allow their employees to purchase their store's merchandise at discounted prices.

Related Occupations

Retail personal computer salespersons use sales techniques and their knowledge of merchandise to help customers and encourage purchases. These skills are also used by manufacturers' and wholesale trade sales workers, service sales representatives, counter and rental clerks, real estate sales agents, insurance sales workers, and cashiers.

Sources of Additional Information

- American Society of Computer Dealers, P.O. Box 100, Ho Ho Kus, NJ. 07423. Phone: (201)444-5006.

- Computing Technology Industry Association, 450 E. 22nd St., Ste. 230, Lombard, IL. 60148. Phone: (708)268-1818.

TELEMARKETING SALES REPRESENTATIVES

At a Glance

- **D.O.T.:** 299.357-014

- **Preferred Education:** On-the-job training

- **Average Salary:** $4.25 to $9.50 per hour

- **Did You Know?** Automated computer systems provide telemarketing sales representatives with a wealth of customer information that can be accessed before, during, and after a conversation.

Nature of the Work

Telemarketing is a strong direct response medium that is often used in conjunction with direct mail, television commercials, and print advertising. Used correctly, it can generate business and provide companies with an opportunity to engage in meaningful, mutually beneficial dialogues with their customers and prospects.

Telemarketing operations can have inbound and outbound components. With an outbound telemarketing program, telemarketing sales representatives (TSRs) make telephone sales calls to customers and prospects. In an inbound program, TSRs receive telephone calls--usually at an advertised 800 number--and take orders. Both types of programs have several different applications, and it is not uncommon for TSRs to be responsible for handling inbound as well as outbound programs.

TSRs may be involved in business-to-business marketing, or they may sell directly to consumers. When they are given a new sales account, TSRs learn as much as they can about the product or service they are selling. They are given lists from which to make telephone calls and information about the customers and prospects they will be speaking with. They keep records of their calls and make notes of pertinent data about their contacts.

TSRs usually work from a prepared script that has been written by one or more professional communicators. Although carefully structured, scripts provide TSRs with the flexibility to be interactive with their contacts. When following a telemarketing script, TSRs usually begin by identifying themselves and the reason for the call. They verify that they are speaking with the correct person and make the scripted offer. Also included in the script are answers to a variety of possible questions or objections that might occur during the conversation. During the course of a telemarketing program, scripts may be refined and adjusted as needed. Eventually TSRs memorize their scripts, although they usually have onscreen prompts available to them at their computer terminals.

In addition to making sales calls and taking orders over the telephone, TSRs may be involved in conducting market surveys and gathering data over the telephone. In some cases data obtained by TSRs can be followed up by sending appropriate prospects a direct mail offer or sales promotion. TSRs may also call to confirm orders that have been taken by field sales representatives. They may call to sell customers related products (cross-selling) or a more expensive product (up-selling).

The productivity of TSRs has increased over the years with the advent of new technologies. Automated computer systems provide TSRs with a wealth of customer information that they can access before, during, and after a conversation. TSRs may be able to call up on their computer screens specific product information, competitive product comparisons, and appropriate responses to objections while on the telephone.

The most technologically advanced telemarketing system now on the market is call predictive dialing. Without it TSRs spend approximately 12 to 18 minutes per hour actually speaking to customers or prospects. With predictive dialing, TSRs can spend closer to 40 minutes per hour talking to customers. Predictive dialing saves time through automatic dialing, call recognition, and call transfers to TSRs. Busy signals, answering machines, and no-answers are routed for future dialing. Only "live" prospects are transferred to TSRs, who are waiting for the calls at their computer terminals.

TSRs follow similar procedures when handling inbound calls. They usually have a script that provides them with appropriate responses to different types of inquiries. They follow specific procedures for taking orders and may be instructed to offer callers related merchandise. They are able to check on the availability of specific merchandise using computer terminals. They are aware of current advertising and marketing programs and may provide callers with information about special offers and discounts. In some cases they may gather data from callers for use in evaluating specific marketing programs.

Working Conditions

TSRs generally work in a well-lighted and ventilated area that has been set aside for telemarketing. In a telemarketing agency, TSRs may work in a room with 50 or more TSRs. In some companies the telemarketing department may consist of only a few TSRs. Some independent contractors work out of their own homes.

TSRs spend most of their time on the telephone or at their computer terminals. The work is sedentary and not physically demanding. It may be stressful, however, since TSRs may be expected to make a certain number of calls per hour as well as meet sales quotas. In addition, their performance is constantly monitored by their supervisors, who usually have the ability to listen in on their sales calls.

TSRs may work odd hours. Outbound calls to consumers are usually made between five and ten o'clock at night on weekdays and during the day on Saturday. Weekday mornings have the highest rate of business-to-business telemarketing calls.

Employment

TSRs are employed in a wide range of businesses that sell to other businesses as well as to consumers. Publishers, home improvement contractors, and financial institutions are some of the major industries employing TSRs. Catalog marketers may have their own in-house telemarketing departments to handle incoming calls. In addition TSRs may work for specialized telemarketing agencies who contract out their services to different businesses.

Part-time TSRs may be college students, homemakers, and office workers with a second job. Full-time TSRs are usually interested in a sales career.

Training, Other Qualifications, and Advancement

Most companies and agencies that hire TSRs are looking for high school graduates with some sales experience. Some companies may requires a college degree. Appropriate background subjects include speech, drama, English, marketing, sales, and general business.

TSRs typically receive extensive on-the-job training from their supervisors or special telemarketing trainers. In-house training programs usually provide new hires with an orientation to the company or agency's business, structure, and objectives.

Trainees receive an introduction to the products or services being sold. They are schooled in selling skills, using such techniques as role playing and interactive tutorials. They are introduced to telemarketing applications and may be given an opportunity to practice specific applications. As TSRs take on new accounts and get new scripts to learn, they are given additional product training and time for script rehearsal.

TSRs must have good communication skills, including a clear, pleasant, and articulate manner of speaking. They should be able to project enthusiasm, friendliness, and other positive personality traits over the telephone. They must be persistent and able to bounce back from rejection. The flexibility to adapt to different selling situations is needed, as are good organizational skills.

TSRs employed by telemarketing agencies have a clear path for career advancement. With additional training, they may advance in a well-staffed agency to become telemarketing trainers, supervisors, telemarketing center managers, account or customer service representatives, and marketing representatives who try to land new accounts for the agency. TSRs may also advance by joining larger agencies or companies with bigger telemarketing departments.

Job Outlook

Although the Bureau of Labor Statistics does not make projections specifically for telemarketing sales representatives, several factors point to a growing demand for TSRs. More and more businesses are viewing telemarketing as a cost-effective alternative to personal sales calls.

New communication technologies have made TSRs more productive, with the result that more businesses will utilize their services.

In addition, many openings will occur as a result of the high turnover of entry-level TSRs, who tend to leave after a short period of time if they are not suited for the job.

Earnings

According to *American Salaries and Wages Survey*, TSRs typically earn between minimum wage and $9.50 per hour. Some companies and agencies pay bonuses and commissions to TSRs in addition to a base salary.

Annual earnings of full-time TSRs range from $15,000 to $50,000, with higher-end salaries earned by those working on commission or salary plus commission.

Related Occupations

Occupations with similar responsibilities to those of telemarketers include outside sales representatives and inside sales representatives in different service industries, travel agents, securities and financial service sales representatives, retail sales workers, real estate agents and brokers, insurance agents and brokers, and manufacturers' and wholesale sales representatives.

Sources of Additional Information

For more information on telemarketing and other careers in marketing, contact:

* Direct Marketing Association, 1120 Avenue of the Americas, New York, NY 10036-6700. Phone: (212) 768-7277.

* American Telemarketing Association, 444 N. Larchmont Blvd., Ste. 200, Los Angeles, CA 90004. Phone: (213)463-2330.

* American Marketing Association, 250 S. Wacker Dr., Ste. 200, Chicago, IL 60606. Phone: (312)648-0536.

WEDDING CONSULTANTS

At a Glance

* **D.O.T.:** 299.357-018

* **Preferred Education:** On-the-job training

* **Average Salary:** Varies

* **Did You Know?** The average cost of a modern wedding ranges from $8,000 to $25,000.

Nature of the Work

For many couples, their wedding day is one of the most important days of their lives--and one of the most complicated. To handle the numerous details of a successful event, many brides and grooms hire wedding consultants. These professionals handle every aspect of a wedding, from ordering flowers to locating a caterer.

Wedding consultants, also known as bridal consultants, generally meet with engaged couples and their families to discuss wedding details and develop a budget. After getting an idea of the type of wedding planned, wedding consultants then negotiate with bakers, limousine services, photographers, musicians, printers, and caterers. Often, consultants recommend vendors to their clients who then make the final decision. Depending on the type of business, however, wedding consultants may be responsible for hiring all the vendors.

Wedding consultants sometimes assist brides in selecting and fitting their wedding gown; if employed by a bridal shop, wedding consultants may even sell gowns. Wedding consultants also help the mothers and bridesmaids choose their gowns and dresses and advise the groom, the fathers, and the male attendants on the proper formal wear.

One of the major services provided by wedding consultants is guiding couples through the intricacies of wedding etiquette, such as seating arrangements and financial obligations. They also help select appropriate stationery and give advice on when to mail the invitations.

At the wedding rehearsal, wedding consultants help orchestrate the ceremony and answer questions. On the day of the wedding, they handle all the details of the ceremony. They make sure everyone knows the location of the ceremony and is in the right place at the right time. They make sure the flowers and other decorations are in place.

Wedding consultants sometimes make hotel reservations for out-of-town guests. They may even help plan a couple's honeymoon, arranging for hotels and transportation. After the wedding, they follow up with the vendors and make payment arrangements.

Wedding consultants who own their own businesses may spend up to half their time completing marketing tasks, such as identifying potential clients and advertising.

Working Conditions

Many wedding consultants have offices in their own homes and travel to their clients' homes for planning sessions. Others work in business offices that may be located near other wedding services such as photographers or bridal shops. In the office, wedding consultants frequently contact vendors via telephone to make wedding arrangements and use computers to process business transactions. The rest of their time is spent meeting with customers, shopping with them or for them, visiting potential wedding and reception locations, and meeting with vendors.

Wedding consultants often set their own hours, but usually conduct a certain amount of business in the evenings and on weekends, when many weddings take place. They must be able to handle the pressure of organizing and directing large events.

Employment

There are no exact figures on the number of wedding consultants in the United States, but the Association of Bridal Consultants lists more than 1,200 members. Wedding consultants may have their own business with one or two employees or be employed by a bridal store. Wedding consultants work primarily in affluent suburban areas, where people are more likely to hire consultants.

Training, Other Qualifications, and Advancement

There are no formal educational requirements for wedding consultants. Many begin by assisting another consultant and learning the profession on the job. Others may begin by specializing in one specific area, such as floral design or catering, and eventually offer all services.

Wedding consultants should have strong leadership abilities and be able to give directions to others. They must also have style, poise, and excellent manners. They must be well organized and have the ability to work under pressure. They should have time management skills and be able to work within a budget. A good sense of humor and an even temperament can be strong assets.

The Association of Bridal Consultants offers certificate courses for wedding planners, which cover such areas as counseling and consulting, etiquette, receptions, and sales. The National Bridal Service also offers a program for wedding consultants, who may eventually receive the title of Certified Wedding Specialist.

Job Outlook

With today's trends moving toward larger, more traditional weddings, the job outlook for wedding consultants is positive. Also, with many women working full-time, professional wedding consultants are needed to save time coordinating formal weddings. Trends toward increased mobility also affect the employment outlook for wedding consultants, who may be hired to plan weddings for out-of-town couples.

Earnings

Annual income for wedding consultants varies depending on whether they are full-time and the size of the weddings they plan. Most wedding consultants charge a flat fee, which includes consultations with clients and planning and coordinating the event. Others charge by the hour, or a percentage of the total wedding cost, typically between 10 and 15 percent. With the average cost of a modern wedding ranging between $8,000 and $25,000, wedding consultants can earn between $1,200 and $3,750 per wedding.

Related Occupations

Other occupations that involve negotiating and selling skills are retail sales people, travel agents, sales agents for business services, and customer service representatives.

Sources of Additional Information

Fore more information on becoming a wedding consultant, contact:

- American Society of Wedding Professionals, 268 Griggs Ave., Teaneck, NJ 07666. Phone: (201)836-8895.

- Association of Bridal Consultants, 200 Chestnutland Rd., New Milford, CT 06776-2521. Phone: (203)355-0464.

- National Bridal Service, 3122 W. Cary St., Richmond, VA 23221. Phone: (804)355-6945.

Administrative Support Occupations, Including Clerical

ADVERTISING TRAFFIC COORDINATORS

At a Glance

- **D.O.T.:** 221.367-078

- **Preferred Education:** One to two years postsecondary education

- **Average Salary:** $18,000 to $25,000

- **Did You Know?** There are nearly 21,000 advertising establishments in the United States.

Nature of the Work

Schedules and deadlines play an important role in the smooth operation of advertising agencies. It is the responsibility of traffic coordinators to organize the workflow to make sure that ads are produced on time.

Traffic coordinators work with account executives, graphic artists, copywriters, and production managers to keep track of each client's job. When account executives bring in new work for the agency, traffic coordinators schedule production so that jobs--such as magazine ads, commercials, or brochures--will be completed by specified dates.

Traffic coordinators enter project data into computers and provide schedules to the agency's creative and production departments, making sure they are aware of their deadlines. They may consult with artists and writers to make sure they have all the materials they need to do their jobs. Once the creative aspect of a job has been completed, traffic coordinators may arrange to obtain the necessary approvals from creative directors and account executives. They may consult with production managers to review jobs in process and discuss any problems or delays that might affect the schedule. They may review production costs and compare them with a client's budget.

Traffic coordinators may sometimes work directly with outside vendors, including freelance artists and copywriters, printers, photographers, and other suppliers. They must make sure that all suppliers are aware of their schedules and deadlines. They must be prepared to work with outside vendors to resolve any problems or delays that might arise.

Working Conditions

Traffic coordinators generally work in comfortable offices equipped with computers. They spend much of their time communicating with others and must occasionally work long hours during busy periods. Like others who work in advertising agencies, traffic coordinators are under a certain amount of stress due to the fast-paced nature of the industry.

Employment

There are nearly 21,000 advertising establishments in the United States. Seven out of ten of these are known as advertising agencies, which provide a full range of services. Approximately three out of 10 specialize in particular markets, such as outdoor advertising, or ads placed on buses or in airports. While advertising agencies are located throughout the country, the best opportunities are in major cities, such as New York, Chicago, and Los Angeles. Agencies in metropolitan areas tend to have larger staffs and offer more employment opportunities. According to the Bureau of Labor Statistics, there were approximately 7,000 clerical supervisors and managers employed in advertising in 1992.

Training, Other Qualifications, and Advancement

Entry-level traffic coordinators are typically high school graduates who have some education beyond high school. While a college degree is not required, it is useful for individuals seeking to advance to other positions within an advertising agency. Since jobs at advertising agencies are highly desirable, having a degree in advertising, general business, or communications can be very helpful.

Traffic coordinators generally have good organizational skills and must be detail-oriented. They must be able to work well with others and be part of a team.

Traffic is an area that can lead to other positions within an advertising agency. It provides an opportunity for individuals to learn many aspects of the business, and they come into contact with most of the other departments within an agency. In larger agencies traffic clerks can advance to become traffic managers.

Job Outlook

Employment in the advertising industry is projected to grow 27 percent from 1992 to 2005. Competition for jobs, however, will remain strong due to the number of people attracted to the industry. The number of clerical supervisors and managers is expected to increase approximately 32 percent through the year 2005.

Earnings

Earnings of traffic coordinators depend on geographic location and the size of the agency where employed. Entry-level traffic coordinators can expect to earn between $18,000 and $25,000 at an advertising agency, with traffic managers earning an average of $30,000 annually.

Related Occupations

Related clerical occupations involving coordinating and scheduling include broadcast traffic clerks, reservation clerks, personnel schedulers, airline crew schedulers, booking clerks, travel counselors, dispatchers, police clerks, expediters, and transportation agents. Occupations more involved with record preparation and maintenance include medical record clerks, stenographers, insurance agent licensing clerks, motion picture continuity clerks, and construction clerks.

Sources of Additional Information

- *Standard Directory of Advertising Agencies*, available in most large libraries.

- American Advertising Federation, 1101 Vermont Ave. NW, Ste. 500, Washington, DC 20005. Phone: (202)898-0089.

- American Association of Advertising Agencies, 666 Third Ave., 13th Fl., New York, NY 10017. Phone: (212)682-2500.

AIR FREIGHT AGENTS

At a Glance

- **D.O.T.:** 248.367-018
- **Preferred Education:** On-the-job training
- **Average Salary:** $416 per week
- **Did You Know?** Air freight agents may handle all types of cargo, including "special" items, such as live animals, human remains, and hazardous materials.

Nature of the Work

Every day thousands of items are shipped by air, the fastest mode of transportation available. Customers entrust air freight agents to see that their valuables are sent quickly and securely.

Air freight agents, also known as *cargo agents*, route inbound and outbound air freight shipments to their destinations. Depending on the size of the air freight agency, an air freight agent may either have a variety of duties or be specialized. Air freight agents can work at the freight office's front counter to assist customers and receive shipment; control shipping and receiving at the dispatch desk; load freight in the warehouse area; or use transport vehicles to run freight to aircrafts. Large air freight operations may have air freight agents who only answer the telephones to quote rates and answer other questions, or agents who only enter data into the computer system.

In general, when a customer brings a shipment to the freight office, an air freight agent weighs, measures, and tags it, fills out the appropriate forms, and determines the shipping cost and the destination flight plan. The air freight agent uses a computer system, rate books, and calculators to determine cost. The flight plan is also usually determined with the help of a computer system. Customers pay at the counter in cash, by credit card, by billing, or a COD (cash-on-delivery) collection is arranged.

To efficiently route and sort freight, air freight agents must memorize the city codes of common destination cities because these codes appear on all identifying tags and paperwork. An air freight agent may handle any type of cargo item imaginable, including items considered "special." Special items include live animals, human remains, cremated human remains, and hazardous materials such as corrosive, poisonous, explosive, and radioactive materials. Special freight typically goes through a more formalized process than regular shipments.

Air freight agents assemble cargo according to destination. They deliver shipments to the appropriate gates, verify incoming flights in case there is a gate change and a special shipment has to be moved to another gate, and ensure that the receiving air freight station is capable of handling the incoming shipment. Air freight agents who handle special items meet the incoming flight and run the item immediately over to the connection gate. They inform shippers of delays in the departure of shipment.

Air freight agents arrange for freight pick-up or delivery. They unload inbound freight and notify consignees (receivers) of the arrival of their shipment and arrange for pick-up or delivery.

Air freight agents load shipments into the cargo bins of aircrafts. After flights have departed, freight runners retrieve empty carts or return the freight that hasn't been shipped to the holding yard. Freight runners are assigned tug vehicles and are responsible for their fueling and basic maintenance.

Working Conditions

Air freight agents typically work 40 hours a week. Large air freight facilities are often open 24 hours-a-day, so many air freight agents work day and night shifts, including weekends and occasional holidays.

Air freight agents often lift, carry, and handle very heavy and bulky objects, and perform the majority of their jobs while standing. Air freight agents may be subjected to loud aircraft engine noise and must wear earplugs when driving on airport grounds. They must also wear uniforms and steel-toed shoes.

Employment

According to the U.S. Bureau of Labor Statistics, 824,000 people were employed in traffic, shipping, and receiving occupations in 1992. This figure includes air freight agents. Air freight agents usually work within or near the edge of an airport. They are employed by airline air freight departments.

Training, Other Qualifications, and Advancement

Most employers require that air freight agents have a high school diploma or equivalent. Air freight agents must be able to read and write proficiently. They must have good spelling and basic math skills for filling out freight logs, air bills, and other forms. They should also know how to take measurements and be able to memorize codes. Accuracy and the ability to pay attention are necessary. Air freight agents must have a valid driver's license and an airport driver's license if driving on airport grounds.

The majority of an air freight agent's training is received on the job. Many aspects of freight handling are computerized, and air freight agents are trained to use computers.

Qualified air freight agents may advance to supervisory or management positions.

Job Outlook

Increasingly, individuals and businesses are demanding that goods be shipped in a timely fashion, and shipping by air is the fastest mode of transportation. Furthermore, shipping by air has become more affordable. These factors should lead to the need for more air freight agents. Automation, however, and other improvements in productivity that allow air freight agents to handle materials more efficiently may slightly reduce potential employment opportunities. Most job openings will come from retirement and employees transferring to other occupations.

Earnings

Earnings for air freight agents vary by employer, geographic location of employer, and the air freight agent's experience. According to *American Salaries and Wages Survey*, in 1991 cargo agents in New York earned an average salary of $416 per week. Full-time air freight agents receive benefits that include paid vacations, sick leave, health and life insurance, and a retirement plan.

Related Occupations

Other occupations in shipping, receiving, and stock checking include inventory clerks, shipping checkers, stock clerks, parts-order clerks, shipping and receiving clerks, and senior-commissary agents.

Sources of Additional Information

- Aviation Education Program, Federal Aviation Administration, U.S. Department of Transportation, Office of Public Affairs, 800 Independence Ave. SW, Washington, DC 20591.

BILINGUAL SECRETARIES

At a Glance

- **D.O.T.:** 201.362-030

- **Preferred Education:** Secretarial and foreign language skills

- **Average Salary:** $20,000 to $36,000

- **Did You Know?** The federal government is the largest single employer of Americans working abroad.

Nature of the Work

As U.S. companies become more involved in foreign trade, tourism, and international joint ventures, many employers need secretaries with both professional and foreign language skills.

Bilingual secretaries use their ability to speak one or more foreign languages while performing secretarial tasks. Like other secretaries, their duties include scheduling appointments, sorting and opening mail, answering telephones, organizing files, taking dictation, and typing documents. They increasingly use personal computers to run spreadsheet, word processing, and desktop publishing programs. Some secretaries arrange luncheon meetings, handle travel accommodations, and maintain confidential files.

Beyond traditional secretarial tasks, bilingual secretaries have specific duties that require the knowledge of foreign languages. They may take dictation in one language and translate it to another language in letter form. Bilingual secretaries also may take notes at meetings and then transcribe them into various languages. They frequently translate letters, documents, and records written in a foreign language into English. They may serve as translators during meetings.

Bilingual secretaries who work in foreign countries may be responsible for supervising other clerical workers. This may require giving instructions in a foreign language. Those in a specialized field, such as medicine, may need specific knowledge of technical terminology or procedures.

Working Conditions

Bilingual secretaries usually work 40 hours per week in well-lighted, climate-controlled offices. However, bilingual secretaries who must communicate with people in various time zones may work overtime. Like other secretaries, bilingual secretaries use personal computers, voice recorders, copiers, telephones, and fax machines to complete their assignments. Because bilingual secretaries perform a variety of tasks, the work is rarely monotonous; however, if they spend a lot of time typing on a word processor, they may encounter eyestrain, stress, or repetitive motion problems such as carpal tunnel syndrome.

Bilingual secretaries working in other countries may need to adjust to unfamiliar customs, foods, and living accommodations. Weather conditions in some countries may be extreme.

Employment

Bilingual secretaries work overseas for U.S. companies that range in size from large multinational companies to small trading companies. Others work for international agencies, nonprofit organizations, and the federal government. The federal government is the largest single employer of Americans working abroad. Over 100,000 federal civilian employees worked in other countries in 1994.

Not all bilingual secretaries work in foreign countries. Most federal workers with jobs related to international affairs are employed in this country. Some state and local governments also employ bilingual secretaries. Many bilingual secretaries work for U.S. companies that operate in communities where English is not the language most people speak. For example, secretaries who understand English and Spanish may work for companies with offices in southern California or south Texas. Hotels, travel agencies, import/export firms, airlines, and companies involved in foreign trade may need bilingual secretaries.

Training, Other Qualifications, and Advancement

Bilingual secretaries need both secretarial and foreign language skills. There are several ways to learn secretarial skills. Some high schools teach basic office practices, shorthand, typing, and word processing. Business schools, vocational-technical institutes, and community colleges offer one- to two-year programs in secretarial science. Many secretarial skills are learned on the job. For example, secretaries may attend classes to learn how to operate new word processing equipment, personal computers, or office automation software packages.

Foreign languages can be learned through a variety of sources. High schools, community colleges, junior colleges, and universities offer formal language study programs. Self study programs are also available. Language study should include grammar, composition, word study, and translation and conversation techniques. When learning a foreign language, it is best to use that language as often as possible. Students should read foreign language books and magazines, join a language club, and converse with others who speak the language they are learning. An understanding of the customs and culture of the country in which the language is spoken can be beneficial.

Like other secretaries, bilingual secretaries should have good work habits and good judgment. They should be able to follow instructions and work without direct supervision.

Bilingual secretaries must be well organized and willing to accept responsibility. A neat, well-groomed appearance is also necessary.

Bilingual secretaries typically advance by learning new skills and taking on more responsibility. Qualified bilingual secretaries may advance to other positions such as executive secretary, clerical supervisor, or office manager.

Job Outlook

With U.S. companies conducting business all over the world, there is an increasing need for secretaries and other clerical workers who speak at least one language in addition to English. The U.S. Department of Labor reports that opportunities will be greatest for those who have prepared themselves through education, experience, and travel.

World politics, business, immigration, entertainment, and science will affect the need for specific language skills. Major foreign languages over the next several years will include Japanese, Spanish, French, and German. The breakup of the Soviet Union will create interest in workers with the ability to speak Eastern European languages such as Lithuanian, Latvian, and Armenian. Companies engaged in business with Pacific Rim countries will need secretaries who speak Chinese and Korean, in addition to Japanese.

The federal agencies with the largest numbers of international opportunities are the Departments of State and Defense, the U.S. Agency for International Development, the United States Information Agency, the Peace Corps, and the Central Intelligence Agency. However, these agencies have a limited need for secretaries. Therefore, strong competition exists for available openings.

Earnings

Secretaries typically earn between $20,000 and $36,000 per year, depending on their skill, experience, and level of responsibility. According to the U.S. Bureau of Labor Statistics, the average annual salary for all secretaries was $26,700 in 1992. The average salary for secretaries employed by the federal government was about $24,000 in 1993.

Related Occupations

Other workers with similar responsibilities as secretaries include bookkeepers, receptionists, stenographers, personnel clerks, typists and word processors, legal assistants, medical assistants, and medical record technicians. Workers who use foreign language skills on the job include translators, interpreters, flight attendants, telephone operators, tariff clerks, tour operators, insurance agents, and teachers.

Sources of Additional Information

- Professional Secretaries International, 10502 NW. Ambassador Dr., Kansas City, MO 64195-0404 Phone: (816)891-6600

BROADCAST TRAFFIC COORDINATORS

At a Glance

- **D.O.T.:** 209.382-022

- **Preferred Education:** 1 to 2 years postsecondary education

- **Average Salary:** $446 to $494 per week

- **Did You Know?** Competition is expected to be strong for entry-level positions in the broadcasting industry.

Nature of the Work

Broadcast traffic coordinators at radio and television stations serve as the daily link between sales and programming. They compile a daily log, or broadcast schedule, of commercial and public service announcements (PSAs), accounting for each minute of programming.

In order to generate the daily broadcast log, traffic coordinators review orders received for commercials and PSAs. They enter data into a computer for each order, including sponsor identity, date, time, frequency of the announcement, and whether it will be a live or recorded announcement. If additional information is needed, traffic coordinators contact the appropriate staff member at the station.

Sometimes advertisers request specific times or dates for their announcements. Traffic coordinators revise their logs to accommodate such requests. If necessary, they will suggest alternate times and dates to avoid conflicts.

After recording all information, traffic coordinators compose the daily broadcast log and have it printed and distributed to the station's staff. At the end of the broadcast day, they review the log for any authorized changes that have been made during the day. The revised log then becomes a permanent record for the station.

Other duties of broadcast traffic coordinators include generating air-time availability reports for sales staff. They also review the content of commercial and public service announcements and test-run announcements to verify their running times. Traffic coordinators may also have to perform additional clerical duties, such as billing, typing correspondence, handling the reception desk, and filing.

Working Conditions

Like other administrative support workers, broadcast traffic coordinators at radio and television stations work in clean comfortable office surroundings. Although their work is not physically demanding, they must pay careful attention to detail in an environment that is often fast-paced and governed by strict time schedules. Much of the work of broadcast traffic coordinators is computerized. They spend a significant amount of time entering data into computers and producing reports. They also interact with other employees and advertising clients to confirm details.

Employment

According to the Bureau of Labor Statistics, there were 32,000 clerical and administrative support workers (not including secretaries) employed at radio and television stations in 1992. Broadcast traffic coordinators are employed by radio, television, and cable television stations. While these employers are located throughout the country, the best opportunities are in major metropolitan areas where there is a concentration of larger stations. Stations in these urban areas tend to have larger staffs and offer more employment opportunities.

Training, Other Qualifications, and Advancement

Entry-level traffic coordinators are typically high school graduates who have had some additional education at a community college, vocational, or trade school. Students should take courses in computer training, office skills, and basic broadcast operations. Internships are also a good way to gain experience.

While a college degree is not required, it is useful for individuals seeking to advance to other positions within a broadcast station. Since jobs at radio and television stations are highly desirable, having a degree in a subject such as advertising, general business, or communications can be very helpful.

Traffic coordinators must pay careful attention to details and have good organizational abilities. They must also have good computer skills and be able to work well with others.

Traffic is an area that can lead to other positions within a broadcast station. It provides an opportunity for individuals to learn many aspects of the business, as they come into contact with most of the other departments within a station.

Job Outlook

Competition is expected to be strong for entry-level positions in the broadcasting industry due to the number of jobseekers the industry attracts. Most entry level positions will likely be in smaller stations; most stations in large metropolitan areas usually seek highly-experienced personnel. Total employment in the broadcasting industry is expected to increase 11 percent through the year 2005, which is slower than the average for all industries.

Earnings

Earnings of broadcast traffic coordinators depend on geographic location and type of station. Television stations tend to pay more than radio stations, while stations in larger metropolitan areas tend to pay more than smaller stations. In 1993, nonsupervisory workers in radio and television broadcasting earned an average of $494 per week, while those in cable services earned $446 per week.

Related Occupations

Related clerical occupations involving coordinating and scheduling include reservation clerks, motion picture continuity clerks, airline crew schedulers, booking clerks, travel counselors, dispatchers, police clerks, expediters, and transportation agents.

Occupations primarily involved with record preparation and maintenance include medical record clerks, stenographers, insurance agent licensing clerks, construction clerks, government property clerks, shorthand reporters, airplane dispatch clerks, and order department supervisors.

Sources of Additional Information

- National Association of Broadcasters, 1771 N St. NW, Washington, DC 20036. Phone: (202)429-5300.

- National Cable Television Association, 1724 Massachusetts Ave. NW, Washington, DC 20036. Phone: (202)775-3550.

BUS DISPATCHERS

At a Glance

- **D.O.T.:** 913.167-010 and 913.167-014

- **Preferred Education:** On-the-job training

- **Average Salary:** $5.50 to $15.14 per hour

- **Did You Know?** Bus dispatchers may be on night, weekend, or holiday shifts to keep buses operating 24 hours per day.

Nature of the Work

Many people know that nothing can be more aggravating than a delayed bus. Bus dispatchers work to prevent this occurrence by making certain drivers are aware of schedules and that assistance is dispatched quickly during emergencies or traffic delays.

Bus dispatchers work for bus lines that provide long-distance service or public transit authorities that provide local bus service. Bus dispatchers make sure that local and long distance buses stay on schedule. They handle problems that may interrupt service and dispatch orders to restore service and schedules.

Interstate bus dispatchers dispatch interstate or long-distance buses according to schedule and a specific timetable. They announce incoming and outgoing buses over the public address system in the bus terminal. They arrange for extra buses and drivers in case of accidents or heavy traffic. They may supervise loading, unloading, and checking of baggage shipped by bus. They oversee bus drivers and attendants while the workers are at the terminal.

Local transit bus dispatchers supervise and coordinate activities of bus operators within a local transportation system.

They make sure buses are running according to schedule. They record the movement and location of buses and road crews to inform other departments or public regarding current schedules and routes. They receive telephone or radio reports of accidents, delays, equipment breakdowns, and other operating or maintenance problems. They report problems and dispatch orders to appropriate divisions to maintain or restore service and schedules. They dispatch extra vehicles and emergency crews to the scene of an accident or breakdown. They maintain a log of scheduled runs, the number of vehicles, vehicle numbers, and driver names.

Working Conditions

Bus dispatchers typically work 40 hours per week. Bus service is generally available 24 hours a day, seven days a week, so dispatchers may be on night, weekend, or holiday shifts. During emergency situations, dispatchers may have to work overtime.

Bus dispatchers work indoors inside the bus terminal. There is some pressure involved in keeping buses on schedule and handling unexpected circumstances.

Employment

According to the U.S Bureau of Labor Statistics, there were 146,000 dispatchers employed in 1992. This figure includes bus dispatchers, who are employed by public transit authorities, bus lines, and school systems.

Training, Other Qualifications, and Advancement

Employers prefer that bus dispatchers have a high school diploma. Employers usually provide on-the-job training. Bus dispatchers must be familiar with their terminal's procedures, the way their company operates, and with federal and state driving laws. Bus dispatchers should have good oral and written communication skills, be able to handle emergency situations calmly and efficiently, and have good organizational abilities.

Many bus dispatchers started as bus drivers or clerical workers who moved into a dispatch position. Experience and organizational skills, however, are still usually necessary before being placed in this position.

Bus dispatchers who demonstrate technical and leadership skills may advance to supervisory or management positions.

Job Outlook

According to the Bureau of Labor Statistics, job openings for bus dispatchers is expected to increase 23.3 percent by the year 2005, as fast as average for all occupations. Most job openings will be replacement positions.

Earnings

Bus dispatchers' earnings varies according to employer, geographic location, and experience. According to *American Salaries and Wages Survey*, bus dispatchers in Wisconsin earned an average hourly wage of $12.84 in 1992. In other states, earnings ranged from $5.50 to $15.14 per hour.

Bus dispatchers usually receive benefits that include paid vacations, health and life insurance, and retirement plans.

Related Occupations

Other occupations similar to bus dispatchers include taxicab dispatchers, train dispatchers, tow truck dispatchers, public safety dispatchers, and utilities service dispatchers.

Sources of Additional Information

- Associated Public Safety Communications Officers, 2040 S. Ridgewood, South Daytona, FL 32119-8437.

- International Municipal Signal Association, 165 E. Union St., Newark, NY 14513-1526.

- American Trucking Association, Inc., 2200 Mill Rd., Alexandria, VA 22314-4677.

- Service Employees International Union, AFL-CIO, 1313 L St. NW, Washington, DC 20005-4100.

- Communications Workers of America, 501 3rd St. NW, Washington, DC 20001-2797.

- American Train Dispatchers Association, 1401 S. Harlem Ave., Berwyn, IL 60402-1295.

EXECUTIVE SECRETARIES

At a Glance

- **D.O.T.:** 169.167-014

- **Preferred Education:** Associate or bachelor's degree

- **Average Salary:** $27,000 to $32,000

- **Did You Know?** The nature of executive secretaries' work may depend on the style of the executives they work for as well as their own individual initiative and level of responsibility.

Nature of the Work

Like other professional secretaries, executive secretaries perform a variety of administrative and clerical duties in an office setting. They generally work for high-level executives and perform fewer clerical tasks than lower level secretaries, whom they may supervise. Their duties may include handling correspondence, scheduling appointments, arranging meetings, organizing and maintaining files, taking dictation, making travel arrangements, meeting visitors, and providing information to callers.

The nature of executive secretaries' work may depend on the style of the executives they work for as well as their own individual initiative and level of responsibility. At one level, executive secretaries may handle correspondence by using standard form letters. At another level, they may receive general direction from executives and compose letters for them to sign. In some cases, executive secretaries may send out correspondence with their own signatures, after clarifying general policies with their bosses.

The work of executive secretaries may involve meeting visitors and interacting with business people from outside the company. They may arrange meetings by contacting other executives in the company and checking their schedules. When their boss is out of town or delayed, they may be relied upon to convey messages.

Executive secretaries are often called on to handle a variety of personal matters for the executives they work for. These may include handling matters related to an executive's outside business activities, such as their work with charities, nonprofit or business organizations, or corporate boards of directors.

Executive secretaries may also serve as administrative secretaries in a business or nonprofit organization. Their duties include keeping official corporation records and executing administrative policies. They may prepare memos for supervisory personnel outlining specific policies. They may direct the preparation of official records, including the recording of corporate stock issues and transfers and legal documents that must be filed with government agencies.

Working Conditions

Executive secretaries generally work with other professionals in a busy office with moderate noise levels. They frequently listen and speak to others in their office, ranging from business executives to lower level secretaries. They may supervise and train other secretaries. Executive secretaries generally work at least 40 hours per week and may be expected to work overtime as needed.

Employment

Executive secretaries are employed by business firms and nonprofit organizations of all types and sizes. While no figures are available for the number of executive secretaries who are employed, there were an estimated 2,810,000 secretaries, excluding medical and legal secretaries, employed in 1992.

Training, Other Qualifications, and Advancement

Executive secretaries generally have at least four years of education and training. They may obtain their basic secretarial skills in high school or through a secretarial or business program leading to an associate degree from a two-year community or junior college. Increasingly, depending on the employment setting, many executive secretaries have bachelor's degrees.

Executive secretaries must have strong clerical skills. They should be able to accurately type 65 to 80 words per minute and be able to take shorthand. They are usually expected to have a working knowledge of word processing, spreadsheet, and database management programs, with an ability to master the particular computer system used by their employer.

Employers look for good interpersonal skills in executive secretaries. Their work requires discretion and tact as they interact with people at all levels and handle the sensitive details of business and personal matters. Being well organized and attentive to detail are also important assets.

Executive secretaries keep up with changes in office technology by attending classes to learn new computer systems and software packages. These may be taken in a variety of settings, including at work, in adult education classes, or through other educational institutions.

Executive secretaries are usually the highest level of secretary in their organization. They may be given a broader range of responsibilities as they advance, including some managerial duties relating to human resources, public relations, or some other aspect of the business. In smaller firms, executive secretaries can advance to managerial positions, while in larger firms they would likely be competing with professionally trained managers for such positions. Their administrative skills and knowledge of business practices often allow them to transfer to other departments within an organization.

Job Outlook

Job opportunities for well-qualified and experienced secretaries should be plentiful, according to the Bureau of Labor Statistics. In addition, many of the specialized administrative duties of executive secretaries cannot be automated, as is the case with a growing number of basic clerical tasks. This will help maintain the demand for executive secretaries.

There are generally a very large number of job openings each year for secretaries in general due to the need to replace those who leave the labor force each year or transfer to other occupations. Actual new job growth for all secretaries, however, is expected to increase by only 4.3 percent between 1992 and 2005.

Earnings

According to the National Association of Executive Secretaries, the average salary for executive secretaries doubled between 1980 and 1990, ranging from $27,000 to $32,000 depending on skills. Salary levels vary significantly according to geographic region and type of business as well as with experience. Executive secretaries generally receive a complete benefits package, including paid vacations and medical insurance. In some cases they may receive management-level benefits, such as stock options or profit-sharing.

Related Occupations

Secretaries, legal secretaries, medical secretaries, and administrative assistants are occupations that have similar administrative and clerical duties as executive secretaries. Related occupations that require word processing skills include word processing trainers, supervisors, and managers within corporations as well as instructors and sales representatives for computer companies. Related occupations involving human resources skills include office managers, clerical supervisors, and personnel officers.

Sources of Additional Information

- National Association of Executive Secretaries, 900 S. Washington St., No. G-13, Falls Church, VA 22046. Phone: (703)237-8616.

- Professional Secretaries International, 10502 NW Ambassador Dr., PO Box 20404, Kansas City, MO 64195-0404. Phone: (816)891-6600.

FINANCIAL CUSTOMER SERVICES REPRESENTATIVES

At a Glance

- **D.O.T.:** 205.362-026

- **Preferred Education:** High school diploma

- **Average Salary:** $350 per week

- **Did You Know?** Customer service representatives gain much of their experience from previous positions as tellers or bank clerks.

Nature of the Work

At some time in their life, most Americans will open a savings or checking account. To do this, a person must first approach a financial customer services representative, who is trained to handle this and many other financial services.

When a customer opens a bank account, financial customer services representatives interview the customer to obtain information. They record the customer's name, address, employer information, and other pertinent data. Depending upon what the customer is seeking, customer service representatives explain the bank's account and investment services, such as savings and checking accounts, Individual Retirement Accounts, Certificates of Deposit, savings bonds, and securities. They help customers fill out the forms necessary to start any of these services. They give funds received from a customer to a teller for deposit and obtain the receipt for the customer.

Financial customer services representatives also assist individuals seeking loans such as personal, mortgage, auto, boat, or home equity loans. They provide customers with a loan application and may help customers complete the application. Customer services representatives also obtain credit records from credit reporting agencies to verify a customer's credit history.

Financial customer services representatives are often problem-solvers. They answer customers' questions and investigate and correct financial errors. They also execute wire fund transfers when a customer needs money quickly deposited to a distant location.

Financial customer services representatives also rent safe deposit boxes to customers who wish to store valuables and important documents. Similarly, they admit customers to the safe deposit vault.

Working Conditions

Financial customer services representatives usually work about 35 hours per week, although some work part-time. Overtime is not common.

Financial customer service representatives spend a good deal of time sitting at desks, dealing with customers in person or by phone. Every now and then customer service representatives must tactfully handle frustrated customers.

According to the U.S. Bureau of Labor Statistics, financial institutions are relatively safe places to work and have among the lowest rate of work-related injuries.

Employment

According to the U.S. Bureau of Labor Statistics, there were about 105,000 financial customer service representatives employed in 1992. Financial customer service representatives work for banks, credit unions, and savings and loan institutions located throughout the nation.

Training, Other Qualifications, and Advancement

Employers require that financial customer service representatives have at least a high school diploma. Financial customer service representatives often enter their occupation as a promotion from a teller position. Employers desire individuals who have good oral and written communication skills as well as basic math skills, and are comfortable handling large sums of money. Financial customer services representatives have frequent customer contact and must be able to solve problems.

Financial customer service representatives learn from both on-the-job training and formal classroom instruction. Much of their experience is gained from a previous teller or bank clerk position. Employers make sure that entry level customer service representatives are well acquainted with their job's procedures and regulations.

Many financial customer service representatives take advantage of training courses offered by the American Institute of Banking and the Institute of Financial Education. Some financial institutions help their employees prepare for their responsibilities by offering their own certified training programs.

With additional education, most likely a bachelor's degree or an M.B.A., experienced financial customer service representatives may advance to branch manager or another management-level position.

Job Outlook

According to the U.S. Bureau of Labor Statistics, job openings for financial customer service representatives will increase only 9.3 percent by the year 2005. Employment growth is rather slow due to bank mergers and electronic technology advances. Most job openings will result from the need to replace workers who transfer to other occupations.

Earnings

Earnings for financial customer service representatives vary by employer, geographic location, and experience. According to the Bureau of Labor Statistics, financial customer services representatives earned about $350 per week in 1992. According to *American Salaries and Wages Survey*, financial customer services representatives working in the Great Plains area earned an average of $6.80 to $7.22 per hour.

Full-time financial customer service representatives usually receive benefits such as paid vacations and holidays, health and life insurance, and a retirement plan.

Related Occupations

Other occupations similar to financial customer service representatives include bank tellers, bookkeeping clerks, accounting clerks, auditing clerks, credit clerks, employment clerks, survey workers, and medical services admitting officers.

Sources of Additional Information

For more information on a career as a financial customer service representative, contact:

● American Bankers Association Education Foundation, 1120 Connecticut Ave. NW, Washington, DC 20036.

HEALTH UNIT CLERKS

At a Glance

■ **D.O.T.:** 245.362-014

■ **Preferred Education:** High school diploma

■ **Average Salary:** $374 per week

■ **Did You Know?** According to the U.S. Bureau of Labor Statistics, job opportunities for health unit clerks are expected to grow 43 percent through the year 2005, nearly twice as fast the average for all occupations.

Nature of the Work

Imagine how long the wait at a doctor's office would be if the doctor personally answered every telephone call and organized every patient's medical record. To avoid inconceivable mayhem, hospitals and other health care facilities employ health unit clerks to handle clerical tasks and provide administrative support to professional health care providers. Health unit clerks play an important role in making sure patient care and facility administration runs smoothly.

A health unit clerk is often the first person a patient or visitor speaks with at a medical facility. It is the health unit clerk's duty to prepare and compile a patient's medical records by documenting the name, address, and other relevant information. Health unit clerks also register a patient's insurance information. They record the name of the attending physician and transfer information such as the patient's temperature, blood pressure, and pulse rate from a nurse's chart onto the patient's medical records. They also transfer the physician's orders and instructions, dietary requirements, and other medication information onto the patient's medical records. They are responsible for the organization and filing of all patient medical records.

Health unit clerks also direct visitors to patients' rooms. They answer telephone calls, schedule appointments and answer general questions. They take messages for patients and medical personnel. They distribute mail to staff, and mail and flowers to patients. They transport patients in wheelchairs to locations within facility.

Health unit clerks prepare records and notices to be sent to billing and insurance offices. They order supplies for the medical facility or unit and may also keep time card information of unit personnel.

Working Conditions

Full-time nonsupervisory workers in health services worked an average of 34.5 hours per week in 1993. Most health unit clerks work during the day, but some work night shifts. Weekend hours are common, and overtime and holiday hours are also possible. Some health unit clerks work part-time or as temporaries.

Health unit clerks work in clean, well lighted, air conditioned medical facilities. Health unit clerks usually sit behind a desk and are equipped with a computer and telephone. Patient records are easily accessible to their work station. They usually work with other health unit clerks.

Employment

According to the U.S. Bureau of Labor Statistics, there were 275,000 health unit clerks employed in the United States in 1992. Administrative support occupations are the third largest segment of all occupations within the health services industry. Health unit clerks are employed by hospitals of all sizes, medical clinics, physicians' offices, dental offices, and other health and allied service establishments, such as blood banks, family planning clinics, childbirth preparation clinics, rehabilitation centers, and drug treatment centers.

Full-time health unit clerks typically receive paid vacations, sick leave, health and life insurance, and retirement plans.

Training, Other Qualifications, and Advancement

Employers expect health unit clerks to have a high school diploma. Typing and general office skills are required, and word processing abilities are very important. Business skills such as typing and word processing can be learned in high school, in community college, or at a business school. Health

unit clerks must also have good oral and written communication skills.

Health unit clerks who demonstrate strong leadership and technical abilities may advance to supervisory positions. Advancement to professional occupations requires additional education.

Job Outlook

According to the U.S. Bureau of Labor Statistics, job opportunities for health unit clerks are expected to grow 43 percent through the year 2005, nearly twice as fast the average for all occupations.

Within the health services industry, employment growth will be slowest in the hospital segment, although the number of opportunities in hospitals will remain abundant.

Earnings

According to the Bureau of Labor Statistics, in 1993, full-time industry workers such as health unit clerks earned an average weekly salary of $374, or $10.83 per hour. Earnings are generally higher in large hospitals and group practices. Earnings also are affected by geographic location, with larger metropolitan areas paying higher wages.

Related Occupations

Other administrative and clerical occupations in medical services include medical-record clerks, animal-hospital clerks, blood bank clerks, diet clerks, hospital switchboard operators, billing clerks, and bookkeeping clerks.

Sources of Additional Information

• American Hospital Association, One N. Franklin, Chicago, IL 60606.

LEGAL SECRETARIES

At a Glance

■ **D.O.T.:** 201.362-010

■ **Preferred Education:** Specialized training

■ **Average Salary:** $15,000 to $38,000

■ **Did You Know?** Two levels of professional certification are available to legal secretaries from the National Association of Legal Secretaries (NALS).

Nature of the Work

Like other professional secretaries, legal secretaries perform a variety of administrative and clerical duties in an office setting. Their general secretarial duties may include scheduling appointments and court appearances, organizing and maintaining files, taking dictation or transcribing tapes, filling out forms, and providing information to callers.

In addition to general secretarial duties, legal secretaries specialize in preparing legal correspondence and documents relating to specific cases. They may prepare documents such as summonses, complaints, motions, and subpoenas using a typewriter, word processor, or personal computer, either by taking dictation or transcribing audio tapes. They may schedule and participate in client interviews, taking notes or transcribing conversations. In some cases, legal secretaries assist with legal research by reviewing legal journals and in other ways.

Other duties include composing and typing correspondence, recording and preparing minutes of meetings, preparing billing statements for services rendered, reading and routing incoming mail, and processing outgoing mail. Legal secretaries may also answer and screen telephone calls, take messages, and arrange conference calls.

Those who work in the court system for judges or state attorneys may assist in setting trial dates. They keep the judge's calendar or list of cases to be tried up to date, reviewing the appropriate legal documents and arranging for hearings or motions. They may be responsible for notifying attorneys of hearing dates and removing case files according to docket sheets for each hearing.

Working Conditions

The work of legal secretaries is conducted under conditions typical of a busy office with moderate noise levels. They frequently listen and speak to others in their office, including attorneys or judges, office managers, other legal secretaries, paralegals, and clerk typists, among others.

Legal secretaries may supervise clerk typists, messengers, and receptionists. They may report directly to an attorney or judge, or they may be supervised by an office manager or higher ranking legal secretary. In addition to full-time employment, legal secretaries are often employed on a part-time basis or as temporary help. Legal secretaries may be expected to take continuing education classes to keep up with changing office technologies.

Employment

There were an estimated 280,000 legal secretaries employed in 1992, out of a total of 3,324,000 secretarial jobs, according to the Bureau of Labor Statistics. Approximately 80 percent of legal secretaries are employed by law firms. The remaining 20 percent are evenly distributed among the court system, corporate legal departments, and government services. Local, state, and federal courts all employ legal secretaries. Most legal secretaries are women, with very few men entering the profession. Legal secretaries are employed throughout the country.

Training, Other Qualifications, and Advancement

Legal secretaries generally have one to two years of specific vocational preparation in addition to a high school education. They may receive their training in a number of ways. They may have an associate degree in a secretarial or business program from a two-year community or junior college, business school, or vocational-technical institution. They may receive their basic training in secretarial skills in a high school vocational educational program, then take specialized training programs for legal secretaries.

Once hired, legal secretaries are often required to take continuing education classes or receive additional instruction at the office. Equipment and software vendors often offer on-site training at the workplace. In addition to being able to handle word processing, legal secretaries may be required to learn the basics of online database searching to assist in legal research. They are generally required to have some knowledge of computer hardware and software.

Two levels of professional certification are available to legal secretaries from the National Association of Legal Secretaries (NALS). The designation of Accredited Legal Secretary (ALS) can be earned by individuals without experience as a legal secretary by passing the appropriate certification exam. Certification as a Professional Legal Secretary (PLS) is given after passing a two-day exam and having at least three years of experience. The NALS offers a variety of continuing education programs as well as providing for professional certification.

Shorthand skills are decreasing in importance as more attorneys and judges rely on legal secretaries to transcribe from taped dictations. Legal secretaries are expected to have good communication and interpersonal skills. They must be tactful in dealing with a variety of people, including judges, attorneys, clients, supervisors, colleagues, and other office workers. In addition, they must have a strong command of business English, knowledge of legal terminology, and familiarity with court rules and procedures.

Legal secretaries are usually well organized and enjoy performing clearly defined tasks. Their work requires careful attention to detail. They must be familiar with general office practices and be able to handle a variety of administrative duties. They should enjoy word processing and be able to operate personal computers.

Legal secretaries can advance to positions of more responsibility through promotions based on their performance in the office. Those who work in the court system can take examinations that enable them to advance to senior or supervisory positions.

Job Outlook

The Bureau of Labor Statistics projects that employment of legal secretaries will increase from 280,000 in 1992 to 439,00 in 2005, a relatively high degree of employment change. However, the number of annual job openings due to growth and replacement needs is expected to be 62,000, a relatively low figure. Some factors accounting for the low number of job openings in the field include increasing office automation and the number of years legal secretaries tend to stay in the profession. In some law offices, paralegals have taken over tasks formerly done by legal secretaries.

A strong demand for legal services will support growth

in employment of legal secretaries. Increased litigation, the regional expansion of law firms, and the increased scrutiny of legal billings all point to increased employment of legal secretaries. According to the NALS, there was a shortage of qualified legal secretaries as of late 1993.

Earnings

Legal secretaries who are employed full-time generally receive a straight salary or hourly wage. In addition, it is common for legal secretaries to receive a yearly bonus. According to *American Salaries and Wages Survey*, legal secretaries earned between $9,500 and $34,820 annually. Entry level salaries ranged from $9,500 to $25,980, while experienced legal secretaries earned between $20,200 and $34,820.

In 1991, the NALS reported a mean salary of $23,800 for its members, who include legal secretaries, legal assistants, and paralegals. A 1993 survey by the Institute on Law Firm Management (ILFM) revealed regional differences in salaries earned by legal secretaries. Salaries for legal secretaries with less than three years of experience ranged from $15,000 to $30,000, depending on region and whether the person worked for a law firm associate or partner. The highest paying region was the West Coast, and the lowest paying regions were the plains, mountain, and south central states. Salaries along the East Coast and in the Great Lakes states were generally higher than average. According to the ILFM survey, top salaries for legal secretaries with eight or more years of experience ranged from $27,000 to $38,000.

Related Occupations

Secretaries, executive secretaries, medical secretaries, and administrative assistants are occupations that have similar administrative and clerical duties as legal secretaries. Related occupations that require word processing skills include word processing trainers, supervisors, and managers within corporations as well as instructors and sales representatives for computer companies. Related occupations involving human resources skills include office managers, clerical supervisors, and personnel officers.

Other related occupations involving typing, recordkeeping, and paperwork include bookkeepers, receptionists, stenographers, personnel clerks, typists, legal assistants, paralegals, medical assistants, and medical record technicians.

Sources of Additional Information

For additional information contact:

- National Association of Legal Secretaries (International), 2250 E. 73rd St., Ste. 550, Tulsa, OK 74136-6864. Phone: (918)493-3540.

- Professional Secretaries International, 10502 NW Ambassador Dr., PO Box 20404, Kansas City, MO 64195-0404. Phone: (816)891-6600.

MEDICAL CLAIMS PROCESSORS

At a Glance

- **D.O.T.:** 241.362-010 and 205.367-018

- **Preferred Education:** On-the-job training

- **Average Salary:** $18,000

- **Did You Know?** Medical claims processors with at least two years of claims assistance experience or three years of general medical claims processing can apply for certification to the National Association of Claims Assistance Professionals.

Nature of the Work

As America's older population increases in size, so too too does the number of medical insurance claims, supplemental benefits payments, and Medicare and Medicaid beneficiaries. A growing number of senior citizens are eligible for Medicare coverage every day. Private insurance companies are providing more supplemental benefits to senior citizens through "Medigap" policies that cover the difference between what Medicare pays and the health care provider charges.

As a result, specialists in medical claims processing have become an important part of the health insurance industry. Self-employed medical claims processors even operate their own claims assistance agencies. Their clients include physicians and other health care providers as well as senior citizens and other individuals who require assistance with their medical insurance claims.

Self-employed medical claims processors are also known as claims assistance professionals. They provide individuals with a service that ensures their claims are handled in a timely fashion by insurers. Using their knowledge of health industry coding requirements, procedures, and insurance company jargon, they prepare medical claims for their clients. They also track health insurance payments received by consumers and file secondary insurance claims to other insurers, such as Medigap insurers or a spouse's insurer, as needed.

Claims assistance professionals monitor their clients' claims, payments, and benefits, making sure they do not overpay and that they receive the benefits they are entitled to. When claims are denied, they work with consumers to challenge denied claims. They also work with health care providers to provide the information required to obtain legitimate payments for consumers.

Some medical claims processors work in an electronic billing environment where forms and documents are transmitted electronically via fax or modem. Specialists in electronic claims provide a link between health care providers and health insurers. Using computers they convert patient billing information into electronically readable formats. Working independently or for a health care provider or facility, electronic claims specialists transmit patient billing information to the insurer or government payer. Their duties also include maintaining and upgrading software applications to comply with requirements set forth by clearinghouses and health care payers.

Other medical claims processors work as *claim clerks* for insurance companies. They review claim forms for completeness and obtain information from policyholders as needed. They prepare reports and update claim files. They either pass on claims for payment or route claims needing further investigation to their supervisors.

Working Conditions

Most medical claims processors work a standard 40-hour week in an office setting. Some medical claims processors may work evenings or weekends if they provide a 24-hour claim service to their clients.

The work of medical claims processors is sedentary in nature. They spend most of their time at computers creating and updating records. They also spent time communicating with clients to gather and clarify information.

Employment

There are several thousand medical claims processing services located throughout the United States that are operated by and also employ medical claims processors. Medical claims processors also work for insurance companies and health care providers such as hospitals, medical centers, clinics, and physicians' offices. According to the Bureau of Labor Statistics, overall employment of all types of insurance claim clerks was approximately 116,000 in 1992.

Training, Other Qualifications, and Advancement

Medical claims processors are generally high school graduates who have business arithmetic, typing, and computer skills. They can learn the basics of their work in three to six months of on-the-job training.

Medical claims processors with at least two years of claims assistance experience or three years of general medical claims processing can apply for certification to the National Association of Claims Assistance Professionals. In addition to meeting the experience requirement, certified Claims Assistance Professionals (CAPs) and certified Electronics Claims Professionals (ECMs) must also meet a minimum educational requirement of either a degree in an approved field, a current certification in an appropriate field, or a current insurance agent's or broker's license.

Medical claims processors must be able to work quickly and accurately and not mind the routine nature of medical claims processing. They must be able to analyze and classify documents according to established procedures. Good interpersonal skills are needed to communicate with clients and policyholders.

Medical claims processors can advance in their occupation by gaining experience and establishing their own medical claims assistance service. Those working for insurance companies can advance to positions such as claims manager, claims representative, or claims examiner.

Job Outlook

Accordng to the Bureau of Labor Statistics employment of all insurance claim clerks will increase faster than the average for all occupations between 1992 and 2005. In the health services industry, employment of adjusters, investigators, and collectors will increase by more than 50 percent between 1992 and 2005.

Earnings

According to the Bureau of Labor Statistics, insurance claims clerks had medial annual earnings of about $18,000 in 1992. According to *Small Business Profiles*, a medical claims processing service will make an average profit of $25,000 before taxes annually, and have the potential to make as much as $100,000 before taxes.

Related Occupations

Related occupations that involve record verfication and proofing include production proofreaders, insurance checkers, mail censors, credit authorizers, title searchers, meter readers, and script readers. Other related occupations include bill and debt collectors, customer complaint clerks, adjustment clerks, mortgage loan interviewers, welfare eligibility workers, claims examiners, insurance policy processing clerks, and insurance adjusters, examiners, and investigators.

Sources of Additional Information

- Health Insurance Association of America, 1025 Connecticut Ave. NW, Ste. 1200, Washington, DC 20036.

- Insurance Information Institute, 110 William St., New York, NY 10038. Phone: (212)669-9200.

- National Association of Claims Assistance Professionals, 4724 Florence Ave., Downers Grove, IL 60515.

MEDICAL SECRETARIES

At a Glance

- **D.O.T.:** 201.362-014

- **Preferred Education:** High school diploma

- **Average Salary:** $4.50 to $12 per hour

- **Did You Know?** The health services industry is the largest employer in the United States. Over the next 10 years, one out of every six jobs created will be in health care.

Nature of the Work

Without medical secretaries, a physician's office would

be very chaotic. Medical secretaries handle the multitude of administrative tasks related to healthcare so that physicians can devote their time to treating patients.

Using their knowledge of medical terminology and hospital, clinic, or laboratory procedures, medical secretaries compile patient histories, maintain medical charts, and handle correspondence. They also assist physicians with reports, speeches, articles, and conference proceedings.

A medical secretary is usually the first person a patient sees when visiting a doctor's office. When dealing with patients in person, medical secretaries note symptoms, take medical histories, and handle medical insurance. They make sure that patients who need immediate care are able to see a doctor as soon as possible. Medical secretaries also reassure waiting patients during appointment delays. When talking to patients on the telephone, medical secretaries schedule appointments, inquire about symptoms, or give test results.

Medical secretaries handle patient billing, maintain files, and order supplies. They compile documents using word processors, typewriters, and other office equipment. They may also take dictation and make business travel arrangements for physicians.

Working Conditions

Medical secretaries typically work 35 to 40 hours per week, although many work part-time. Their hours usually match that of doctors', especially in private offices, and may include evenings and weekends.

Medical secretaries work in comfortable offices and spend most of their time sitting at a desk. They may work alone or with other medical secretaries, depending on the size of the medical office. Medical secretaries have to deal with patients and visitors, and their schedules are often hectic.

Employment

According to the U.S. Bureau of Labor Statistics, there were 234,000 medical secretaries employed in 1992. Medical secretaries are employed by physicians' offices, hospitals, clinics, and other health care agencies.

Training, Other Qualifications, and Advancement

Employers require that a medical secretary have a high school diploma as well as typing and office skills. Most employers also require that medical secretaries be well-versed in computer skills, such as word processing, spreadsheets, and database management. Medical secretaries must also have good oral and written communication skills. Medical secretaries must know medical terminology and be familiar with hospital and laboratory procedures; this knowledge can be learned on the job or through courses at a community college or vocational school. Typing, word-processing, and other business skills can be learned in high school and at a business school or community college. Medical secretaries are continuously trained (usually at the employer's expense) to keep abreast of new office technology, personal computers,

and software packages. Medical secretaries with experience, demonstrated skills, and leadership abilities may advance to supervisory positions.

Job Outlook

According to the U.S. Bureau of Labor Statistics, job openings for medical secretaries are expected to increase 45.2 percent by the year 2005, much faster than average for all occupations. As the population grows, physicians will need well-qualified secretaries with medical knowledge and the ability to handle the increase in health insurance paperwork.

The health services industry is the largest employer in the United States. One out of every six new jobs created between 1992 and 2005 will be in health services.

Earnings

According to *American Salaries and Wages Survey*, medical secretaries earn anywhere from $4.50 to $12 per hour. Some states pay as high as $17 per hour. Earnings depend on the employer, geographic location of employer, and experience. Pay is usually higher in larger metropolitan areas. Full-time medical secretaries receive benefits such as paid vacations, sick leave, health and life insurance, and a retirement plan.

Related Occupations

Other occupations related to that of a medical secretary include legal secretary, medical transcriptionist, technical secretary, business secretary, social secretary, school secretary, and financial trust operations assistant.

Sources of Additional Information

- Professional Secretaries International, 10502 NW Ambassador Dr., Kansas City, MO 64195-0404. Phone: (816)891-6600.

MEDICAL TRANSCRIPTIONISTS

At a Glance

- **D.O.T.:** 203.582-058

- **Preferred Education:** One to two years

- **Average Salary:** $23,000 to $45,000

- **Did You Know?** Medical transcriptionists must possess a thorough knowledge of medical terminology and be familiar with a variety of medical documents.

Nature of the Work

Medical transcriptionists are specialized stenographers

or transcriptionists who provide written transcripts of notes dictated by physicians and other healthcare professionals. Medical transcriptionists listen to audiotapes containing physicians' comments on such matters as patient care, consultations, operations, medical histories, examinations, autopsies, and lab reports. They input the data into a computer to provide a permanent written record for physicians and hospitals. They may specialize in one or more medical fields, such as radiology, pathology, or emergency room medicine.

Medical transcriptionists do not simply transcribe a physician's comments word for word. Often they must edit the information to follow grammatical rules, spell out abbreviations, and translate complex medical terms. Medical transcriptionists must be able to recognize factual discrepancies in the data and make corrections accordingly. The data must be transcribed accurately without distorting its meaning. All terms must be spelled correctly, which may involve looking words up in specialized reference books.

Medical transcriptionists typically use word processing software on personal computers to input data. They also use a transcribing machine with headphones that allows them to control the audiotapes as they input the physician's spoken comments. They are usually responsible for keeping their equipment in working order and reporting the need for maintenance or replacement as it occurs.

Working Conditions

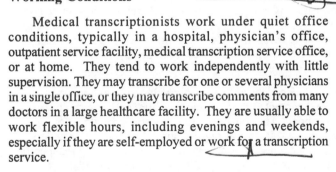

Medical transcriptionists work under quiet office conditions, typically in a hospital, physician's office, outpatient service facility, medical transcription service office, or at home. They tend to work independently with little supervision. They may transcribe for one or several physicians in a single office, or they may transcribe comments from many doctors in a large healthcare facility. They are usually able to work flexible hours, including evenings and weekends, especially if they are self-employed or work for a transcription service.

The job of medical transcriptionists may be stressful when material must be transcribed by a specified deadline. Medical transcriptionists are often under pressure to be accurate and fast. Their work requires intense mental and physical concentration as they listen to physicians through their headphones. Even though it is sedentary, the work can be physically demanding. Medical transcriptionists may be subject to ailments associated with repetitive motion and using video display terminals. In addition, medical transcriptionists may be required to sit in one position for long periods of time.

Employment

Medical transcriptionists may be self-employed or work for a medical transcription service. They also work for physicians, hospitals, insurance companies, and a variety of other healthcare institutions.

There were an estimated 29,000 medical transcriptionists in 1992, according to the U.S. Bureau of Labor Statistics. Approximately 9,100 were members of the American Association of Medical Transcriptionists.

Training, Other Qualifications, and Advancement

In addition to typing and transcription skills, medical transcriptionists must possess a thorough knowledge of medical terminology and be familiar with a variety of medical documents. They usually have at least six months of training in transcribing, which can be obtained while in high school or from a vocational-technical school. Medical transcriptionists must be fast and accurate typists.

Training in medical terminology is available in two-semester courses at vocational-technical schools or through two-year programs leading to an associate degree. Formal training programs for medical transcriptionists are also available through colleges and universities as well as through adult education programs. Among the subjects covered are medical terminology, anatomy and physiology, medical supplies and equipment, drugs, surgical procedures, medicolegal issues, and laboratory procedures and results.

Professional certification as a Certified Medical Transcriptionist (CMT) is available from the American Association of Medical Transcriptionists. Applicants must have at least three years of medical transcription experience and pass a certification examination.

Medical transcriptionists should enjoy compiling data for use in record processing. They are detail-oriented and able to operate transcription and word processing equipment, including computers. They must be able to format written reports using correct punctuation, grammar, and spelling. Good listening skills allow them to understand diverse accents and dialects and varying dictation styles.

Job Outlook

Strong growth in employment in the health services industry over the next decade indicates there will be a demand for medical transcriptionists. The need for health care documentation will increase, although demand may be moderated if more doctors and nurses resort to entering data directly into their computers instead of using audiotapes. According to the Bureau of Labor Statistics, employment of administrative support personnel, including medical transcriptionists, within the health services industry is expected to increase by 38 percent between 1990 and 2005.

One area of potential growth is in the area of independent medical transcription services and self-employed medical transcriptionists. Some estimates indicate the number of such services will double between 1992 and 2000.

Earnings

Earnings for medical transcriptionists vary with geographic location, education, and experience. Self-employed medical transcriptionists can earn between $23,000 and $45,000 annually, depending on their client base and location. According to *American Salaries and Wages Survey*, salaries for stenographers range from $8,000 to $28,000. Because of the additional training and education required, medical transcriptionists can expect to earn higher salaries than stenographers.

Related Occupations

Stenographers and court reporters are involved in work that is very similar to that of medical transcriptionists. Other related occupations that involve records and paperwork include bookkeepers, receptionists, secretaries, personnel clerks, administrative assistants, and medical assistants.

Sources of Additional Information

• American Association of Medical Transcriptionists, PO Box 576187, Modesto, CA 95357. Phone: (209)551-0883.

• American Health Information Management Association, 919 N. Michigan Ave., Ste. 1400, Chicago, IL 60690. Phone: (312)787-2672.

POLICE AIDES

At a Glance

■ **D.O.T.:** 243.362-014 and 375.362-010

■ **Preferred Education:** On-the-job training and civil service exam

■ **Average Salary:** Varies

■ **Did You Know?** Police aide positions are sometimes filled by high school graduates who are planning to pursue careers as police officers.

Nature of the Work

Police aides provide administrative support in city, county, and state police departments. Also known as *police clerks* or *police attendants*, they perform duties that do not require the skills of sworn police officers, thus freeing up police officers' time for other law enforcement assignments. The job responsibilities of police aides may include clerical duties as well as operating radio and telephone communications equipment. They may also assist in the booking and detention of suspects, work directly with the public, and help enforce security regulations in police buildings. In some cases, police aides wear special uniforms and work under the direction a police officers.

Police aides are usually assigned to compile daily duty rosters for police departments. They arrange schedules and record personnel information indicating days on, days off, and equipment assigned. They prepare daily schedules to ensure personnel are available for court appearances and otherwise make efficient use of personnel and equipment. Daily duty rosters are submitted to superiors for approval. Other scheduling duties may include arranging for training for police personnel, scheduling vacations, and recording daily work assignments.

Police aides are often assigned to personnel, property, or recordkeeping units. They may take shorthand, and maintain logs of police activities. They may fill out accident reports, arrest records, evidence cards, and attendance records and schedules. They also index, distribute, and file copies of forms and documents relating to crimes reported, persons arrested, traffic accidents and citations, property inventories, and calls for police service.

If their office is computerized, police aides may take reports written by police officers and enter specific data into computer terminals. They may post other information from forms and reports into computers. They also respond to requests from police officers for information. They may search their computer terminals for information such as outstanding warrants or prior arrest records.

Police aides may also respond to requests for information from police officers using radio and telephone communications equipment. These requests typically come from officers on patrol and involve such information as license and car registration checks, stolen vehicle identification, and fugitives wanted for questioning. Police aides enter the requests into computerized systems, retrieve the necessary data, and relay the information via the radio communication system.

Police aides may also perform clerical and other duties relating to the arrest and detention of suspects. They prepare arrest cards containing each suspect's name, address, criminal charge, and arresting officer. They may use rollers and ink pads to record suspects' fingerprints and take their photographs. Other duties may include searching suspects and issuing receipts for personal items. They may issue clothing to suspects and escort them to detention cells. They may also escort them to and from court, prepare and deliver meal trays to suspects in detention cells, and patrol detention areas to ensure security.

Police aides who are assigned to information units have direct contact with the general public, both in person and by telephone. They answer inquiries and provide information about local laws and regulations. They may refer callers to other agencies. They help people who are looking for specific records or have to fill out authorization and release forms. They may fingerprint applicants for special permits and conduct information searches for prior criminal records.

In some police departments police aides are responsible for enforcing security regulations. They are uniformed, armed, and specially trained for security duty. They patrol designated areas to maintain security, prevent loitering, and report suspicious behavior. They inspect packages and briefcases coming into police buildings and check visitors for proper authorization. They may maintain visitor logs.

Police aides sometimes perform parking and traffic control duty. This involves wearing distinctive uniforms and patrolling for parking violations or directing traffic at busy intersections. When on parking control duty police aides may ride scooters or three-wheel motorcycles.

Working Conditions

The work of police aides is sedentary and not physically demanding. They work under typical office conditions that are moderately noisy with adequate lighting, heating, and ventilation. Depending on their assignment, they may spend a lot of time interacting with other people, including police officers, suspects, and the general public. Police aides assigned to parking or traffic control work outdoors and spend a lot of time walking or standing.

Police aides generally work standard five-day, 40-hour weeks. They may have to work weekends and some holidays. They may be assigned to rotating shifts. In some cases they may be required to wear special uniforms.

Employment

Police aides are government employees who work in law enforcement agencies at the local, county, and state levels. In 1992, there were about 259,000 general office clerks employed in state and local government. This number represents just 4 percent of all occupations in the industry.

Training, Other Qualifications, and Advancement

Police aides are usually hired on a probationary basis and receive on-the-job training. In some cases, training may include classroom instruction.

On-the-job training for police aides covers subjects such as orientation, rules and regulations, government agencies, and communication skills. Police aides are trained in using communications equipment and departmental forms. They may learn traffic codes and traffic direction techniques and receive instruction in the use of firearms.

Police aide positions are sometimes filled by high school graduates who are planning to pursue careers as police officers. They are usually between the ages of 17 and 21 and are enrolled in police science programs at two- or four-year colleges. All applicants for police aide positions generally have to pass a civil service examination as well as an oral interview. They may also have to pass a qualifying medical examination and submit to a background check.

Police aides are detail-oriented individuals with an interest in organized, clearly defined activities. They must be patient and methodical. Written and oral communication skills are important. Police aides often intereact with the general public and must have a neat appearance and courteous manner.

Advancement depends to a great extent on the nature of the employing agency. Depending on how a department is structured, police aides may be able to advance to senior or supervisory positions. Police aides sometimes continue their education and training and become police officers.

Job Outlook

The Bureau of Labor Statistics does not publish separate employment projections for police aides. However, employment of general office clerks by state and local government agencies is projected to increase by nearly 20 percent between 1992 and 2005.

Employment prospects for police aides are expected to be favorable. Police departments recognize the advantages of hiring civilians to fill police aide positions. The most openings for police aides are likely to occur in large police departments located in urban and suburban areas.

Earnings

Limited salary data is available for police aides. Earnings vary by region and the size of the police department, with larger departments generally paying higher salaries. According to *American Salaries and Wages Survey*, the average annual salary for police aides in South Dakota was around $12,000 in 1991-92. General office clerks employed by the federal government earned an annual average salary of approximately $22,800 in 1993. Most police departments provide police aides with a benefits package covering medical insurance, paid vacation, and sick leave.

Related Occupations

Other occupations concerned with records processing and information transmittal include dispatchers, reservation clerks, general office clerks, court clerks, municipal clerks, and alarm operators.

Sources of Additional Information

Contact state and local government agencies for information about employment opportunities. For more information about police careers, contact:

- National Police Officers Association of America, PO Box 22129, Louisville, KY 40252-0129. Phone: (800)467-6762.

- National Police and Fire Fighters Association, 3801 Biscayne Blvd., Miami, FL 33137. Phone: (305)573-0700.

POLICE DISPATCHERS

At a Glance

- **D.O.T.:** 379.362-010 and 379.362-018

- **Preferred Education:** High school diploma or equivalent

- **Average Salary:** $18,000 to $24,000

- **Did You Know?** In some communities or municipalities, all 911 emergencies go to the police department and dispatchers may coordinate the action of police, fire, ambulance, and rescue units.

Nature of the Work

Life-threatening emergencies occur every few seconds and people depend on police dispatchers to send the needed assistance as quickly as possible.

Police dispatchers receive telephone calls from citizens concerning crimes and other emergencies, along with nonemergency calls. These dispatchers perform a very important role because they are often the first to be contacted by people needing police or emergency assistance.

Dispatchers calmly question a caller to identify the type, seriousness, and location of a problem, and then determine the best type of action to resolve it. For instance, they determine whether a crime is in progress or has already been committed, and whether or not it is a life-threatening situation. Each call may require different action.

False reports and crank calls are screened to prevent police delays to serious emergencies. Police dispatchers must also decide which calls are not within police jurisdiction and direct the caller to the appropriate agency. For instance, a person concerned about garbage not being collected is not considered a matter that requires police assistance.

During an actual or perceived police emergency, police dispatchers record information from the caller that includes the name, address, and telephone number of caller; type of emergency; geographic location of emergency; and any other pertinent facts, such as a description of individuals or vehicles, which could be helpful to police. This information is forwarded to a police radio dispatcher, who broadcasts the order and any instructions to available patrol units in the vicinity of the problem. In smaller police forces, the police dispatcher may broadcast directly to patrol units.

In some communities or municipalities, all 911 emergencies go to the police department and dispatchers may coordinate the action of police, fire, ambulance, and rescue units. When it is appropriate, dispatchers stay in close contact with the dispatched units and the caller. If it is necessary, dispatchers may give first aid instructions while the caller is waiting for the ambulance or other emergency unit. In many situations, dispatchers serve as a link between the caller and the emergency unit, which is continuously updated on the victim's condition.

Dispatchers verify assignment location of police units through radio contact. They assist these police officers by providing descriptions of suspects or stolen vehicles. Police dispatchers may receive and transmit messages between their own agency and others. Police dispatchers may also monitor silent or automatic alarm systems that indicate a possible burglary, and dispatch police units directly to the scene.

To perform their jobs, police dispatchers sit at desks or cubicles wearing telephone headsets and type relevant information into computer terminals. Police dispatchers have a thorough knowledge of their police department so that they can efficiently handle emergency situations.

Working Conditions

Police dispatchers typically work 40 hours per week, including rotating shifts (day and night), weekends, and holidays. Their offices may or may not be modern. Dispatchers in larger metropolitan areas often work in small cubicles in an office shared with several other dispatchers. Agencies usually require uniforms or professional attire.

Police dispatchers are often under a lot of stress. At times, they must handle many phone calls and calls by people who are undergoing life-threatening or high-anxiety situations. It is the dispatcher's responsibility to quickly assess a situation

and make sure police and other necessary help gets to the caller as soon as possible. Sometimes police dispatchers must calmly and clearly direct a distressed caller on how to handle a situation until help arrives. The final outcome of a call may be very disappointing if a person does not survive the emergency situation; however, positive outcomes and the knowledge that dispatchers provide help can be very satisfying.

Employment

According to the U.S. Bureau of Labor Statistics, there were 75,000 police, fire, and ambulance dispatchers employed in the United States in 1992. Police dispatchers are employed by police agencies at local, county, and state levels.

Training, Other Qualifications, and Advancement

Police dispatchers should have a high school diploma or equivalent. Applicants must have a qualifying civil service examination score (which may include a written and typing test) and pass an oral interview. They must also successfully complete a physical exam. Employers want dispatchers who are able to speak clearly, pay close attention to detail and remain alert at all times. Police dispatchers must have patience and perform their duties efficiently, methodically, tactfully, and courteously, regardless of the anxiousness of the caller or the number of incoming calls. They must be able to think quickly, clearly, and calmly in emergency situations. Police dispatchers must want to have contact with the public and have the ability to sit in their work stations for a long period of time.

Beginning police dispatchers receive classroom and on-the-job training. They learn communications skills, human relations skills, use of communications equipment, police code language, geographic arrangement of areas within jurisdiction, departmental rules and regulations, functions of the police agency, and functions of other governmental agencies. There is a six-month to one-year probationary period.

Advancement opportunities may be available to those who continue their education. Police dispatchers may become senior dispatchers or supervisors.

There are unions that police dispatchers may wish to join.

Job Outlook

According to the U.S. Bureau of Labor statistics, jobs openings for police dispatchers will increase by 16.3 percent by the year 2005, as fast as average for all occupations. The job outlook for police dispatchers is considered good. The growing population and increasing crime rates bring need for more emergency services and police personnel and support personnel, which includes police dispatchers.

Earnings

Earnings for police dispatchers varies according to geographic location, employer, and experience. Larger metropolitan municipalities typically pay more than smaller ones. The pay range for police dispatchers is usually $10,000 to $35,000 a year. Police dispatchers also receive benefits such as paid vacations and holidays, sick leave, health and life insurance, and retirement plans.

Related Occupations

Other occupations in public safety include police officers, fire fighters, paramedics, and ambulance drivers. Other dispatcher occupations include truck dispatchers, bus dispatchers, train dispatchers, taxicab dispatchers, tow truck dispatchers, and gas and water service dispatchers.

Sources of Additional Information

For more information on a career as a police dispatcher, contact:

- Associated Public Safety Communications Officers, 2040 S. Ridgewood Ave., South Daytona, FL 32119. Phone: (904)322-2500.

REAL ESTATE ASSISTANTS

At a Glance

- **D.O.T.:** 219.362-046

- **Preferred Education:** High school diploma

- **Average Salary:** $7.22 to $8.24 per hour

- **Did You Know?** Job openings for real estate assistants are projected to increase 44.1 percent by the year 2005, faster than average for all occupations.

Nature of the Work

Purchasing a home is one of the most important and expensive financial transactions that a person can make. Anyone who has purchased a home or investment property is aware of the myriad of paperwork and details involved in buying or selling real estate. On the other side of the real estate paperwork fence are real estate assistants, who are responsible for handling a multitude of real estate administrative tasks.

Real estate assistants perform a number of duties, chiefly concerning maintaining records connected with the rental, sale, and management of real estate. They calculate the amount of principal, interest owed, taxes due, and penalty payment on mortgage loans. They hold collateral in escrow to ensure contracts are fulfilled in transferring real estate and property titles. They check due notices on taxes and the renewal dates of insurance and mortgage loans to take follow-up action. They type contracts and other legal documents involved in the sale and purchase of property. They send out rent notices to tenants. They write checks in payment of bills due, keeps record of disbursements, and examine canceled returned checks for endorsement. They maintain and balance

bank accounts for sales transactions and operating expenses. They secure estimates from contractors for building repairs. They maintain a log of sales and commissions received by real estate agents.

Real estate assistants type real estate sales and rentals listings for distribution to local trade publications, local newspaper classified sections, and for use as reference data by other office departments. Similarly, they submit photographs and descriptions of property to be advertised in newspapers and trade magazines for publication. They may also be responsible for other direct marketing mailings to prospective clients. In contrast, they compile prospect lists from leads in newspapers and trade periodicals to locate prospective real estate purchasers.

Similar to other administrative assistants, real estate assistants, they open, sort, and distribute office mail; answer telephone calls; take messages for salespersons; greet clients; use office equipment, including personal computers, fax machines, and copy machines; and perform other typical clerical duties.

Working Conditions

Real estate assistants usually work about 40 hours per week, five days a week. Real estate offices are sometimes open on evenings and weekends, and assistants may have to work during this time.

Real estate assistants work in clean, comfortable offices. They spend most of their time sitting at a desk. They may work alone or with other real estate assistants, depending on the size of the real estate firm. There are usually no great physical demands, but as with other types of administrative assistants, they run the risk of computer eyestrain and carpal tunnel syndrome and must handle hectic schedules and deadline pressures.

Employment

According to the U.S. Bureau of Labor Statistics, there were 24,000 real estate assistants employed in 1992. Real estate assistants are employed by real estate firms. The highest concentration of jobs are in urban areas and areas with growing populations. Many real estate assistants are employed part-time.

Training, Other Qualifications, and Advancement

Employers require that real estate assistants have a high school diploma and proficient typing skills. Employers also prefer that real estate assistants be versed in computer skills, such as word processing, spreadsheets, and database management. Real estate assistants must also have good oral and written communication skills, as well as reliable arithmetic skills. Accuracy and neatness are requirements. Knowledge of real estate terminology and legal terms is helpful.

Typing, word-processing, and other business skills can be learned in high school and at a business school or vocational school. Although a lot of real estate knowledge is gained on the job, laws prohibit real estate assistants from performing real estate activities that require a license.

To become a real estate sales agent or a real estate closer additional training and formal licensing is required.

Job Outlook

According to the Bureau of Labor Statistics, job openings for real estate assistants will increase 44.1 percent by the year 2005, faster than average for all occupations. Job openings may be somewhat tempered by increased computer automation that streamlines some of the clerical tasks associated with real estate sales, property management, and record keeping.

Earnings

Earnings for real estate assistants varies by experience, employer, and geographic location. According to American Salaries & Wages Survey, in the early 1990s, real estate assistants in southern and central regions averaged $7.22 to $8.24 per hour. Newly hired assistants may earn slightly above the minimum wage, and more experienced workers can earn more than $13 per hour. Full-time real estate assistants may receive benefits such as paid vacations and holidays, health and life insurance, and retirement plans.

Related Occupations

Other occupations similar to real estate assistants include underwriting clerks, budget clerks, securities clerk, mortgage clerks, mortgage loan closers, vault cashier, deposit clerks, credit analysts, and escrow officers.

Sources of Additional Information

- National Association of Realtors, 430 N. Michigan Ave., Chicago, IL 60611. Phone: (312)329-8200.

SURVEY WORKERS

At a Glance

- **D.O.T.:** 205.367-054

- **Preferred Education:** High school diploma

- **Average Salary:** $4.25 to $10 per hour

- **Did You Know?** Survey workers are employed by government agencies, market research firms, independent polling firms, and other businesses that survey public opinion.

Nature of the Work

Facts, figures, and statistics on people, businesses, opinions, tastes, and habits are very important to businesses, organizations, and government agencies. This information provides a snapshot of the world we live in and can form the basis of many critical decisions. This type of data is collected by survey workers.

Survey workers interview the public to compile statistical information for polling firms, market research companies, and government agencies. They seek information on consumer buying habits, opinion on public issues, and population facts and figures.

Survey workers work as part of a team under the supervision of a team leader or supervisor. Survey workers contact people by telephone or in person, at their homes or places of business, or approach them randomly on the street. They perform the survey following set procedures. They collect data either orally or by questionnaire, depending on the method of contact. Survey workers may request personal information such as name, address, age, marital status, number of people in household, number of children, occupation, income, hobbies, and sometimes race, religion, or political affiliation. Sometimes they want to know about spending habits, product usage, and future product or service needs. Other questions may be about beliefs or opinions on issues. Responses may be detailed or a simple yes or no.

Once the data is collected, survey workers enter the data into a computer to tabulate final results. Survey workers may arrange information in a specified order or grouping, such as by name, gender, location, occupation, or affiliation. They record, classify, and review the data from answers collected. They may prepare reports or charts to show survey results. They keep records of the surveys and analyze data from old records. The organizations that request this information may make it available for public use or use it for business or other decisions.

Working Conditions

Survey workers typically work 40 hours per week, five days a week. They often work during the evening when people are usually home from work. They perform much of their work at a desk inside an office. In-person surveying requires travel such as visiting people's homes or surveying customers at a business establishment or on the street.

Employment

According to the U.S. Bureau of Labor Statistics, there were 71,000 interviewing clerks (not including personnel and social welfare clerks) employed in 1992. Some reports estimate that about 22,000 were survey workers.

Survey workers are employed by government agencies, market research firms, independent polling firms, and other businesses that survey public opinion.

Survey workers employed by the U.S. Bureau of the Census work on a permanent, part-time basis; on some projects they work 40 hours per week for one or two weeks a month.

Many survey workers employed by other businesses also work part-time or on a temporary basis. In 1992, 2.8 percent of survey workers were self-employed, contracted by polling firms and agencies.

Training, Other Qualifications, and Advancement

Employers require that survey workers have at least a high school diploma or equivalent. Federal agencies require that prospective employees pass a civil service examination. Survey workers receive on-the-job training. If travel is required, survey workers must have a valid driver's license and reliable transportation.

Survey workers must enjoying dealing with the public. They must be able to speak clearly and have good vision and hearing (either naturally or with correction). They must also be able to perform organized, routine tasks.

Survey workers who demonstrate leadership ability and technical skills may advance to become a team leader or supervisor. Furthering education is helpful in other advancement opportunities.

Job Outlook

According to the U.S. Bureau of Labor Statistics, job opportunities for information clerks will increase 34.4 percent by the year 2005, higher than average for all occupations. Because survey work involves contact with people, it is not significantly affected by changes in technology, improving its expected rate of job growth. Some openings will come from business and organization expansion, while most will come from the need to replace experienced workers who leave the occupation.

Earnings

According to *American Salaries and Wages Survey*, in 1992, survey workers in the state of New York earned an average wage of $254 per week. Wages in other states ranged anywhere from minimum wage to $10 per hour in 1992. Survey workers' salaries may vary depending on personal experience, size of employer, and geographic location.

Benefits for full-time survey workers vary by employer. Some employers may offer paid vacations and holidays, sick leave, health insurance and retirement plans. Other employers, especially government agencies, may offer educational assistance.

Related Occupations

Other occupations that involve collecting information, interviewing, and assisting people in completing application forms include census enumerators, hospital admitting clerks, customer service representatives, civil service clerks, mortgage loan interviewers, claims clerks, bonding agents, credit clerks, and employment clerks.

Sources of Additional Information

For more information on a career as a survey worker, contact:

- American Marketing Association, 250 S. Wacker Dr., Chicago, IL 60609.

- Society for Marketing Professional Services, 99 Canal Center Plz., Ste. 250. Alexandria, VA 22314.

- United States Office of Personnel Management, Federal Job Information Center, 1900 E St. NW, Rm. 1416, Washington, DC 20415.

TAX PREPARERS

At a Glance

- **D.O.T.:** 219.362-070

- **Preferred Education:** High school diploma or equivalent

- **Average Salary:** $450 per week

- **Did You Know?** The Internal Revenue Service estimates that every year 45 to 60 million Americans pay for professional tax return preparation.

Nature of the Work

Taxes are an inescapable part of life. With the amount of paperwork and math involved as well as continuously changing tax laws, filing tax returns can be a very complicated process. It is not surprising that many people turn to tax preparers for help in filing returns.

Tax preparers prepare federal, state, and local income tax returns for individuals and small business. Tax returns may be filed both annually or quarterly. Tax preparers review each clients' financial records, such as wage and income statements, interest and dividend statements, documentation of expenditures and allowances (retirement contributions, charitable contributions, medical expenses, expense receipts, mileage logs), property tax records, alimony payments, and past tax return forms. Tax preparers also obtain additional information directly from their clients regarding taxable income and deductible expenses and allowances. Once all the necessary information is gathered, tax preparers are able to determine which forms are needed to prepare an individual return.

Using the collected information and following tax form instructions and tax tables, tax preparers calculate the amount of taxes their clients owe and complete the appropriate entries on the tax forms. Tax preparers use calculators and computers to calculate figures for tax form entries. They may also consult tax law handbooks or bulletins to determine the proper procedure for preparing complex returns. Because it is essential that tax returns be without errors, tax preparers will often have their calculations verified by another tax preparer, or if self-employed, double-check their own figures.

After a tax return is completed, tax preparers notify the client of any refund or the amount owed to the government. As required by law, on every tax return prepared, tax preparers must sign, and provide their Social Security number and/or federal employment identification number and their firm's name and address. Tax preparers determine the preparation fee according to the complexity of the return and amount of time required in preparation. Tax preparers provide their client with a copy of the return and keep a copy for their files.

Working Conditions

Tax preparation is largely a seasonal occupation; part-time tax preparers work only during tax season, which is late January through April 15th. Naturally, this time of year is also the busiest period for full-time tax preparers, who prepare quarterly income tax returns and provide other tax and accounting services during the year. Whether a part-time or full-time tax preparer, as the April 15th tax filing deadline approaches, work hours become longer and more hectic. Near tax deadlines, tax service firms may be open 12 hours a day, seven days a week. To stay competitive, self-employed tax preparers also work late evenings and during weekends.

Tax preparers work in an office atmosphere or, if self-employed, may work out of their home.

Employment

Tax preparers may be self-employed or work for tax service firms. Tax preparers who are licensed to represent taxpayers before the Internal Revenue Service are known as *enrolled agents*.

Tax preparers work in all geographic locations. The exact number of employed tax preparers is unknown due to the seasonal nature of the work. The National Association of Enrolled Agents reports having more than 30,000 active members.

Training, Other Qualifications, and Advancement

Employers prefer that tax preparers have a high school diploma or equivalent. Some states may require licensing or registration. State laws may also demand that tax preparers be at least 18 years of age.

Employers request that tax preparers successfully complete an in-depth training course, ranging from 60 to 80 hours, on tax preparation, tax regulations, and the Internal Revenue Code. Because tax laws change every year, tax preparers may be required to take updated courses annually.

In California, for instance, a tax preparer must register with the state every year and meet one of the following sets of requirements: have completed 60 hours of approved instruction within the past 18 months; have been a paid preparer for federal and state personal income tax returns for others for at least an average of 15 hours per week during two tax seasons within the last four years; or have been a paid preparer for federal and state personal income tax returns for others for at least an average of eight hours per week during four tax seasons within the last six years. In Oregon, a tax preparer must be licensed with the state and renew the license every year, and successfully complete a board-approved, 80-hour course on basic tax law. The preparer must pay a fee for both the examination and the license.

Tax preparers who represent taxpayers before the Internal Revenue Service must meet specific requirements. To become an enrolled agent, a tax preparer must pass the IRS Special Enrollment Examination (SEE) or have a minimum of 5 years' continuous employment with the IRS in a position that regularly applied and interpreted provisions of the Internal Revenue Code and regulations relating to income, employment, estate, gift, or excise taxes. Those who pass the test must then submit an enrollment agent application to the IRS. Applications are then investigated by the IRS, and it may take four to six months before candidates are notified of acceptance or rejection. Accepted applicants are issued an enrollment card and certificate and are required to complete 72 hours of continuing professional education every three years.

Tax preparers may advance to become enrolled agents. Advancement to a professional occupation, such as an accountant, requires at least a bachelor's degree and board certification.

Job Outlook

The Internal Revenue Service (IRS) estimates that every year 45 to 60 million Americans pay for professional tax return preparation. Complicated and continually revised tax laws will ensure the need for qualified tax preparers.

Computer technology, however, may reduce some job opportunities as routine processes are streamlined. Also, current requirements for tax preparers are expected to become standardized in the coming years, according to the National Association of Tax Practitioners. This may deter some preparers who may have little training.

Earnings

Earnings for tax preparers vary according to the tax preparer's experience, whether working full-time or part-time, the employer, and the complexity of the tax return. According to *American Salaries and Wages Survey*, in 1991 tax preparers in New York earned an average of $449 per week and tax preparers in Kansas earned $15.45 to $17.76 per hour. Tax preparers may charge a flat fee per tax return. This usually ranges from $50 to $500 per tax return, largely depending on the complexity of the tax return.

Full-time, year-round tax preparers earn more and charge higher fees. Those who work for firms or the IRS usually receive benefits that include paid vacations and holidays, health and life insurance, and a retirement plan. Seasonal or part-time workers are sometimes paid minimum wage plus commission. Self-employed and part-time tax preparers are responsible for their own benefits.

Related Occupations

Other occupations similar to tax preparers include accounting clerks, credit card clerks, mortgage loan computation clerks, brokerage clerks, collection clerks, dividend clerks, policy-change clerks, margin clerks, and underwriting clerks.

Sources of Additional Information

For more information on a career as a tax preparer,

contact:

- National Association of Tax Practitioners, 720 Association Dr., Appleton, WI 54914. Phone: (414)749-1040.

- National Association of Enrolled Agents, 200 Orchard Ridge Rd., No. 302, Gaithersburg, MD 20878. Phone: (301)212-9608.

- National Association of Tax Consultors, 454 N. 13th St., San Jose, CA 95112. Phone: (408)298-1458.

- American Institute of Certified Public Accountants, 1211 Avenue of the Americas, New York, NY 10036.

UTILITIES CUSTOMER SERVICES REPRESENTATIVES

At a Glance

- **D.O.T.:** 239.362-014

- **Preferred Education:** High school diploma or equivalent

- **Average Salary:** $200 to $800 per week

- **Did You Know?** The largest percentage of employment growth in public utilities is expected to be in water supply and sanitary services industry.

Nature of the Work

In today's modern times, it is almost unimaginable to live without electricity, running water, gas heat, telephone service, or even cable television. Yet, these utilities are not given to us automatically, freely, and without the occasional complication. When someone needs assistance with his or her utility services, they must first contact a utilities customer services representative.

Utility customer service representatives talk to customers in person or by telephone. They interview applicants for electric, gas, water, telephone, or cable service. They receive orders for service installation, start up, discontinuance, or changes in service.

Utility customer service representatives fill out contract forms and calculate the charges for services. They may also collect deposits or fees and prepare or update records that reflect changes of address or new or additional services.

Utility customer service reps listen to customer complaints concerning service or billing. They adjust billing errors or try to explain to the customer why they were charged for a certain item. With service problems, a customer service representative may try to determine if the problem is minor and offer a solution to the customer; if it is a more extensive problem or an emergency, the customer service rep will directly contact the service department or connect the customer with the service department.

Utility customer service representatives, especially telephone and cable service reps, often explain the operation of a specific service or equipment to customers.

A utility customer service representative may contact customers to determine when they will pay overdue bills. Some customer service representatives solicit customers by telephone to use their company's services and explain the benefits of its services.

Working Conditions

Utilities customer services representatives work in clean, well lighted, well ventilated offices. They work at desks, often in a large room with other customer service reps, have their own computer terminal to access customer records, and may wear headsets to speak with customers by telephone.

Utilities customer services representatives work 40-hour weeks. Some work evening or night shifts and Saturdays. Overtime is not usual, but may occasionally be required.

Utilities customer service reps spend a great deal of time sitting at their desks, and are subjected to the noise of other reps talking to customers. They must sometimes try to calmly resolve problems with angry or upset customers.

Employment

According to the U.S. Bureau of Labor Statistics, there were 127,000 utilities customer service representatives employed in the United States in 1992. The communications (telephone and cable) segment of the public utilities industry employed the most workers, consisting of nearly 65 percent of all public utilities workers. Electric services employed 12.7 percent, government agencies over 10.5 percent, gas production and distribution 5.4 percent, and water and sanitary services, 1.3 percent. There were no self-employed workers.

Training, Other Qualifications, and Advancement

Employers expect applicants to have a high school diploma or equivalent, or an Associate's Degree, although education beyond the high school level is not usually a requirement to become a utilities customer services representative.

Employers provide on-the-job training. Some customer service reps begin as trainees or are on probation for a specified period of time, and advance to full-time positions after demonstrating the necessary skills to work as a customer services representative.

Those who demonstrate the ability for more responsible work may eventually advance to become supervisors or managers.

Most utilities customer services representatives are required to join a union, such as the Utility Workers of America, Communications Workers of America, or International Brotherhood of Electrical Workers.

Job Outlook

According to the Bureau of Labor Statistics, job opportunities for utilities customer services representatives are expected to grow 19.1 percent, as fast as average for all occupations, by the year 2005.

The largest percentage of employment growth in public utilities is expected to be in the water supply and sanitary services industry, followed by the combination utility services industry, and the electric services industry. There is expected to be a decrease in employment opportunities within the gas production and distribution industry.

The increasing population, advanced technologies and the demand for better services will account for some new openings, however, most will come from attrition as workers retire, transfer to new jobs, etc.

Earnings

In 1993, utilities customer services representatives had earnings ranging anywhere from $200 to $800 per week. Earnings for customer service reps working for electric and gas companies were reportedly slightly higher than those working for telephone and water companies. Full-time customer service representatives receive benefits that include paid vacations and holidays, sick leave, health and life insurance, and retirement plans.

Related Occupations

Other occupations in public utilities include installation-maintenance technicians, central office technician, service dispatchers, electrical engineers, mechanical engineers, nuclear engineers, scientists, computer systems analysts, and plant operators.

Sources of Additional Information

- American Gas Association, 1515 Wilson Blvd., Arlington, VA 22209.

- American Public Power Association, 106 W. 11th St., Ste. 1800, Kansas City, MO 64105.

- American Water Works Association, 6666 W. Quincy, Denver, CO 80235.

- Communications Workers of America, 1925 K St. NW, Washington, DC 20006.

- Edison Electric Institute, 701 Pennsylvania Ave. NW, Washington, DC 20004-2696.

- International Brotherhood of Electrical Workers, 1125 15th St. NW, Washington, DC 20005.

- Utility Workers of America, 815 16th St. NW, Ste. 605, Washington, DC 20006.

Service Occupations

Protective Service Occupations

ANIMAL CONTROL OFFICERS

At a Glance

- **D.O.T.:** 379.263-010

- **Preferred Education:** High school diploma

- **Average Salary:** $12,678-$25,564

- **Did You Know?** Animal control officers pick up stray animals and transport them to a shelter for treatment or care. They also remove animals from traps or other inhumane conditions.

Nature of Work

Just as police officers protect the safety of humans, animal control officers protect animals from cruelty and neglect. In many cities, animal control specialists are responsible for enforcing animal control ordinances.

Animal control officers inspect pet shops, kennels, and other businesses to make sure animals are receiving proper care. They also investigate people who may be abusing their pets. Animal control officers often interview witnesses to determine if laws are being violated. If a person is breaking the law by mistreating an animal, the animal control officer warns the violator or reports the violator to the police. The police may then arrest the violator.

Animal control officers generally patrol the streets in a truck or van equipped with a cage. They pick up stray animals and transport them to a shelter for treatment or care. They also remove animals from traps or other inhumane conditions. Some specialize in rescuing trapped or injured animals. Animal control officers enforce local laws involving rabies and other inoculations. They are required to write reports on all their activities.

Animal control officers may work with other government departments, such as the police and health departments, and wildlife and conservation agencies.

Working Conditions

Animal control officers usually work regular hours. They spend most of their time patrolling streets in their vehicles. The rest of their time is often spent in animal shelters and police stations where they write reports. Some animal control officers may be required to work evenings or weekends. They may be on call to pick up stray animals during their off hours. Animal control officers risk being bitten, scratched, or attacked by animals.

Employment

Animal control officers work for animal shelters, humane societies, wildlife agencies, and local governmental agencies.

Training, Advancement, and Other Qualifications

Animal control officers are usually required to have a high school diploma or its equivalent. While most animal control officers receive on-the-job training, experience with and knowledge of animals is helpful. Some colleges and universities offer courses in animal control. Other beneficial courses include criminology, animal science, and veterinary technology. Certification may be required in some states.

High school students interested in a career as an animal control officer should take courses in English, biology, computers, typing, and physical education. They can gain practical experience by working at a veterinary clinic, kennel, or humane society. They can also learn by caring for their own pets.

Animal control officers should like animals. They should have common sense, patience, and good judgement. They also need the ability to work alone or as part of a team.

Job Outlook

Employment opportunities for animal control officers will increase about as fast as the average through they year 2005. This is because the number of dogs and cats has increased significantly over the last 10 years and is expected to continue to increase.

Earnings

According to the *American Salaries and Wages Survey*, the average earnings of animal control officers in the South was $12,678-$25,564 per year in 1993.

Related Occupations

Animal control officers provide a protective service. Similar occupations include wildlife control agent, public safety officer, fish and game warden, regional wildlife agent, canine service instructor-trainer.

Sources of Additional Information

• National Animal Control Association, 806 S. New York, Liberal, KS 67901 Phone: (800)828-6474.

• Humane Society of the United States, 2100 L St. NW, Washington, DC 20037 Phone: (202)452-1100.

BAIL BOND AGENTS

At a Glance

■ **D.O.T.:** 186.267-010

■ **Preferred Education:** High school diploma

■ **Average Salary:** $25,000 per year

■ **Did You Know?** Bail bond agents are empowered to make arrests in any jurisdiction. A century-old Supreme Court decision also allows them to enter private homes without a warrant if they believe a bail jumper is inside.

Nature of the Work

There were more than 30,000 arrests made of skips in 1993, according to the National Association of Bail Enforcement Agents. Skips are people who have been arrested, posted bond, and fail to shown up in court when scheduled. Bail bond agents have the authority to arrest skips without a warrant, and can take them across state lines (except in Illinois, Kentucky, and Oregon) without extradition papers.

The work of bail bond agents combines the duties of an insurance agent with those of law enforcement. A bail bond is a form of insurance because it insures that the person who has been arrested will show up in court as scheduled. States that license bail bond agents usually do so through the same departments of insurance that also license insurance agents and brokers.

People who have been arrested usually contact bail bond agents to post their bond so they do not have to remain in jail. Bail bond agents generally screen their clients, reducing the probability of potential skips. They do not have to post bond for everyone who requests it. Individuals arrested for drug dealing, for example, are generally considered bad risks by bail bond agents. Individuals who live in the same city where they have been arrested are more reliable than individuals who live elsewhere.

When people who have been arrested contact bail bond agents to post bond, the agents charge 10 percent of the total amount as their fee. If the full amount of the bond is $60,000, then the bail bond agent receives a $6,000 fee or commission. Many bonds are arranged through third parties who know the arrested person. Once the bond has been paid, the arrested person is freed from jail. If the person does not show up for the scheduled court date, the bail bond agent has 90 days to find and return the bail jumper. Otherwise, the bail bond agent must pay the full amount of the bond to the court.

Bail bond agents spend a relatively small amount of their time actually posting bond. Most of their time is spent tracing skips, even though only a small percentage of people jump bail. Agents who specialize in locating bail jumpers are known as bail enforcement agents, or bounty hunters. They collect fees from government agencies and bail bond agents for locating and returning bail jumpers.

Bail bond agents utilize many different investigative techniques to locate bail jumpers. They may search computerized databases to check for credit records, debt proceedings, land ownership, and even death certificates. They question individuals who know or are related to the bail jumper, and are often willing to pay these individuals for information.

Once a bail jumper has been located, bail bond agents determine the best method of arresting them. They are empowered to make arrests in any jurisdiction, not just the state in which they do business. A century-old Supreme Court decision allows them to enter homes without a warrant if they believe a bail jumper is inside.

Sometimes a show of force is necessary. Bail bond agents often have a permit to carry a weapon and may call on local law enforcement officials to help them make arrests. Locally, most bail bond agents have good working relationships with the sheriff's and police departments.

In other cases bail jumpers can sometimes be tricked into returning to where they can be easily apprehended. Bail bond agents may send out letters granting phoney amnesties or offering prizes to entice bail jumpers. Whatever they do to locate and apprehend bail jumpers, bail bond agents are always exposed to danger when they make an arrest.

Working Conditions

Bail bond agents often unconventional hours since someone must be on call 24 hours a day. Bail bond agents spend time frequently speaking and listening to other individuals, giving and receiving information in person or over the telephone.

When they have to arrest bail jumpers, bail bond agents are often exposed to physical danger. There is also some stress involved when they have to deal with criminals. While most bail jumpers are arrested locally, bail bond agents occasionally have to travel to locate skips.

Employment

There were approximately 11,000 bail bond agents employed throughout the country in 1994. There are no bail bond agents in Illinois, Kentucky, and Oregon, the only states that have laws prohibiting bail bond agents. Bail bond agents are either self-employed and own their own bail bonding firm, or they work for other bail bond agents.

Training, Other Qualifications, and Advancement

Bail bond agents usually have a background in insurance, law enforcement, or private investigations. They have one to two years of specific vocational training that can be learned on the job. The National Institute of Bail Enforcement offers training programs to help bail bond agents learn techniques for skip tracing and arresting bail jumpers.

Bail bond agents must be knowledgeable about the legal aspects of bonding. Some states that license bail bond agents require them to also have an insurance license. While not all states license bail bond agents, those that do usually require them to have a clean record and to meet other requirements. State licensing usually takes place through state insurance departments.

Bail bond agents may need to be able to use a firearm and be licensed to carry a weapon. They must be familiar with investigative techniques in order to locate bail jumpers, and trained to handle sometimes dangerous arrest situations.

Bail bond agents must have good communication skills when dealing with criminals, family members, fugitives, and law enforcement officials. They must be able to develop good working relationships with other members of the law enforcement community as well.

Bail bond agents can advance in their careers by gaining experience and becoming more adept at skip tracing. Some agents go on to open their own bail bond firms.

Job Outlook

The Bureau of Labor Statistics (BLS) does not publish separate employment statistics for bail bond agents. The amount of business as well as the demand for bail bond agents decreases when individual states adopt lenient release programs for people who have been arrested. However, the trend seems to be for states to be moving away from such release programs, creating more of a demand for bail bond agents.

Earnings

Earnings data for bail bond agents is scarce. A typical starting salary for an employee of a bail bond firm is $25,000. Experienced agents can earn more. Experienced agents that specialize in locating skips can earn $50,000 or more per year.

Related Occupations

Related government law enforcement occupations include police officers and detectives, sheriffs and deputy sheriffs, Federal Bureau of Investigation (FBI) special agents, and other federal special agents. Guards, bailiffs, correction officers, fire marshals, fish and game wardens, and U.S. marshals also work in law enforcement. Other related occupations include private detectives and insurance agents.

Sources of Additional Information

- National Association of Bail Enforcement Agents, National Institute of Bail Enforcement, PO Box 1170, Tombstone, AZ 85638. Phone: (520)457-9360.

BAILIFFS

At a Glance

- **D.O.T:** 377.667-010

- **Preferred Education:** Written and physical exam

- **Average Salary:** When not attending court sessions, bailiffs may perform a variety of clerical, personal, and administrative tasks for judges.

- **Did You Know?** When not attending court sessions, bailiffs may perform a variety of clerical, personal, and administrative tasks for judges.

Nature of the Work

Each year, millions of cases are tried in the American judicial system. The courts rely on bailiffs to keep order during these trials.

Bailiffs maintain security in state and local courtrooms and protect the judge, jury, and other participants during hearings and trials. Working under the supervision of the judge, bailiffs provide general services in the operation of a court. They escort jury members and prisoners in and out of the courtroom, deliver case files, and call witnesses and defendants to the stand.

Bailiffs start the day by inspecting the courtroom for cleanliness, checking equipment, and searching for security violations. They call court into session by announcing the entrance of the judge. While court is in session, bailiffs maintain order and respond to any potentially dangerous situations that may arise. They make sure jurors, witnesses, attorneys, news reporters, and spectators are seated in specific areas. Bailiffs eject persons who disrupt the court's proceedings.

Bailiffs are also responsible for the security of the jury during deliberations. They escort jurors in and out of the courtroom and accompany the jury to all meals. When a jury is held overnight, bailiffs arrange for food, lodging, and transportation. They also prevent jurors from having outside contact with the public during a trial, which may cause a mistrial.

When not attending court sessions, bailiffs may perform a variety of clerical, personal, and administrative tasks for judges. These include running errands, writing reports, screening visitors, answering the telephone, and making appointments.

Working Conditions

Bailiffs generally are found in courthouses. Here they inspect the courtrooms for cleanliness, orderliness, and proper heat, light, and ventilation. They also escort prisoners and jury members in and out of the courtroom.

Employment

Bailiffs work for state and local courts all across the United States. The U.S. Bureau of Labor Statistics classifies bailiff as a miscellaneous law enforcement occupation. Workers in this classification held 38,000 jobs in 1992.

Training, Advancement, and Other Qualifications

Graduation from high school or its equivalent is usually required to become a bailiff. Most states also require applicants to pass a written and physical exam. Since bailiffs work with all types of people on a daily basis, they need good communication skills. This means they must be able to understand and follow written instructions and express themselves clearly and concisely. Tact and courtesy are especially helpful. In addition, it is important for bailiffs to have knowledge of office practices, court procedures, and legal terminology and forms. Some courts require bailiffs to be skilled in the use of firearms. Bailiffs employed by larger courts may advance to supervisory positions.

Job Outlook

According to the Bureau of Labor Statistics, employment for bailiffs is expected to increase as fast as the court system expands. Courts are expanding to keep pace with the rising number of offenders and the need to speed up the handling of cases. The bureau expects the number of miscellaneous law enforcement officers, which includes bailiffs, to grow 14.4 percent between the years 1992 and 2005.

Earnings

According to the *American Salaries and Wages Survey*, the average wage offered to bailiffs in South Dakota was $5.30 per hour in 1992.

Related Occupations

Other occupations that involve enforcing law and order, maintaining order in court, and serving summonses include identification and communication officers, deputy sheriff, court deputy, deputy United States Marshall, and grand jury deputy sheriff.

Sources of Additional Information

For information on recruitment, training and salary information for court personnel, contact the personnel office of the state court administrator's office. Local offices of state employment services may have additional information.

BODYGUARDS

At a Glance

- **D.O.T.:** 372.667-014

- **Preferred Education:** Background in the military or law enforment

- **Average Salary:** $28,496 per year.

- **Did You Know?** Clients of bodyguards include well-known actors and actresses, musicians, political figures, and professional athletes.

Nature of the Work

Celebrities, musicians, government officials, and professional athletes are some of the people who hire bodyguards for protection. Bodyguards may be responsible for overall security measures, including protecting a private residence, or they may protect their clients only in public.

Bodyguards may drive vehicles for their clients. In public places, they may plan the safest route into and out of buildings and escort their clients to protect them from bodily injury.

Bodyguards carry guns and generally have other skills such as a knowledge of martial arts. They monitor crowds and watch for unusual circumstances. If a potential danger arises, they respond quickly to keep the situation under control and keep their clients safe.

Working Conditions

Being a bodyguard is dangerous work. Bodyguards must be in good physical condition and must be prepared to defend their client at all times. Bodyguards need good vision to scan crowds of people for unusual situations. Hours for bodyguards vary depending on the type of assignment. Bodyguards for entertainers may work many evening and weekend shifts when many performances are scheduled.

Employment

Bodyguards work independently or for private security companies. Clients include well-known actors and actresses, musicians, political figures, professional athletes, and others who find themselves in high-profile situations or who feel threatened for personal reasons. Bodyguards may be hired for only one evening, or they may have a long-term assignment.

Training, Advancement, and Other Qualifications

There are no formal education requirements for bodyguards. However, many bodyguards have military or law enforcement backgrounds. Specialized training courses in bodyguard techniques are also available.

Training may include martial arts, surveillance tactics, use of firearms, escort techniques involving one person or a team, driving skills, recognizing explosive devices, and basic emergency medical skills.

Bodyguards must be observant and capable of reacting quickly to unexpected situations. They must have the ability to anticipate threats and respond with good judgment. Bodyguards who carry firearms must have a state license.

Job Outlook

According to the International Bodyguard Association, there is an annual 25 percent increase in political violence worldwide. Other factors affecting the employment outlook for bodyguards include an increase in celebrity stalking by obsessive fans and kidnapping for ransom.

Employment of guards as a whole is expected to increase much faster than the average for all occupations, mainly due to a high employee turnover and large number of people employed in security services.

Earnings

According to *American Salaries and Wages Survey*, the average wage paid to bodyguards in New York was $548 per week, or $28,496 per year in 1991. Wages can be significantly higher depending on experience and client.

Related Occupations

Related occupations include armored car guards, special agents, security inspectors, correction officers, and jailers.

Sources of Additional Information

- International Bodyguard Association, 458 W. Kenwood, Brighton, TN 38011 Phone: (901)837-1915.

- American Society for Industrial Security, 1655 N. Ft. Myer Dr., Ste. 1200, Arlington, VA 22209 Phone: (703)522-5800.

BORDER PATROL OFFICERS

At a Glance

- **D.O.T.:** 375.363-010

- **Preferred Education:** Training course

- **Average Salary:** $22,500 to $24,500

- **Did You Know?** In recent years, illegal immigration has become a concern in a number of border states, resulting in pressure on the federal government to take action.

Nature of the Work

More than 8,000 miles of land and seacoast make up the international boundaries of the continental United States. Border patrol agents are responsible for monitoring the border and preventing people from entering the country illegally.

These highly-trained officers work for the Immigration and Naturalization Service, which is an agency of the U.S. Department of Justice. To detect and prevent illegal entries into the country, they patrol the border on foot, in jeeps and cars, in motor boats, and in airplanes.

Border patrol agents often rely on high-technology equipment to do their jobs. These include electronic sensing devices, night vision scopes, and electronic communications systems. For example, agents conceal electronic sensors at strategic points along the border. When these devices are activated, border patrol agents are sent to the scene to investigate.

Sometimes, border patrol agents use binoculars to scan the border for illegal aliens. Another method is the jeep-plane team. These teams use aircraft to survey large areas, such as agricultural sites, and detect possible illegal aliens. Once the lawbreakers are discovered, border patrol agents in jeeps are dispatched to the site for further investigation.

Border patrol agents frequently stop cars and trucks along the border to check the citizenship of the occupants. They also inspect and search trains, buses, trucks, aircraft, and boats to find illegal aliens. Agents look for illegal workers on farms and ranches near the border. During these searches, many of which are along the border between Mexico and the U.S., agents may find it useful to speak and understand Spanish.

When illegal aliens are discovered, border patrol agents are authorized to arrest them, using physical force or firearms if necessary. Agents sometimes find evidence of smuggling activities and may report this evidence to customs agents. Border patrol agents arrange for the prosecution or deportation of illegal aliens. They also make detailed reports of their activities and may be called upon to testify in court.

Working Conditions

Border patrol agents work rotating shifts that often involve working at night. They usually work more than 40 hours per week. Agents work under stressful and dangerous conditions. There is often the risk of physical injury during the performance of their duties.

Employment

There were more than 4,400 border patrol agents employed by the Immigration and Naturalization Service in 1995. Newly hired agents are assigned to duty stations along the southwest border of the United States. Many of these stations are located in small, isolated communities in California, Arizona, New Mexico, and Texas. <Subhead 1>Training, Advancement, and Other Qualifications

Border patrol agents are trained during a 16-week training program at the Federal Law Enforcement Training Center in Glynco, Georgia. At this program, they undergo physical training and learn the basics of the job. Courses include regulations and procedures, criminal law, border patrol methods and operations, tracking and surveillance, and firearm use and safety. They must also study Spanish.

Applicants for the border patrol training program must pass an entrance examination. A high school diploma or its equivalent is required to take the exam. High school students can prepare for a career as a border patrol agent by taking courses in English, Spanish, history, and communications.

Border patrol agents can advance by gaining experience and additional training. After three years of continuous service, agents receive a permanent career appointment. They may be promoted to immigration inspectors, deportation officers, or special agents. Advancement is based on the needs of the agency as well as on merit.

Job Outlook

In recent years, illegal immigration has become a concern in a number of border states, resulting in pressure on the federal government to take action. As reported in *Newsweek* in December of 1994, the federal government increased INS appropriations by $225 million, much of which was designated for 1,000 new agents and additional equipment along the southwestern border of the U.S.

According to the Bureau of Labor Statistics, however, overall job opportunities for police officers, detectives and special agents are expected to increase more slowly than the average for all occupations through the year 2005. For federal agencies in particular, the number of qualified applicants generally exceeds the number of open positions.

Earnings

Entry-level border patrol agents employed by the Immigration and Naturalization Service are paid by the GS rating system. In 1995, entry-level border patrol agents (GS-5) in Texas earned a salary of $22,500. Entry-level agents in California earned $24,500. After six months, agents can be promoted to GS-7 level. GS-7 agents in Texas earned $25,000 per year. GS-7 agents in California earned $28,000. Agents also receive other benefits given to federal employees.

Related Occupations

Border patrol officers help protect the public and maintain law and order. Similar occupations include traffic officer, commanding officer, highway patrol pilot, special agent, chief detective, narcotics investigator, and police inspector.

Sources of Additional Information

For additional information on a career in border patroling contact:

• Immigration and Naturalization Service, 425 I St. NW, Washington, DC 20536. Phone: (202)514-2643.

• United States Government Federal Information Center. Check phone number in local directory.

FINGERPRINT TECHNICIANS

At a Glance

■ **D.O.T.:** 375.387-010

■ **Preferred Education:** Specific Vocational Preparation

■ **Average Salary:** $14,000 to $20,000 per year.

■ **Did You Know?** The FBI is the largest single employer of fingerprint technicians.

Nature of the Work

When people touch things with their hands and fingers, they usually leave a partial or complete set of fingerprints. An individual's fingerprints are unique and cannot be altered or imitated. On the basis of these characteristics, fingerprints have become the most reliable form of personal identification in the 20th century.

Fingerprint impressions serve a number of useful purposes in law enforcement. They disclose whether an individual has a prior criminal record or is currently being sought by other law enforcement agencies. For security and employment background checks, fingerprints can be used to check and verify a person's history. They are also used to identify missing persons, unidentified bodies, and amnesia victims.

Fingerprint technicians are forensics experts who provide fingerprint evidence from crime scenes and suspected crime scenes to police detectives and special agents to help them with investigations. Police detectives and special agents rely on fingerprint technicians to identify crime victims, suspects, and other individuals at a crime scene by matching newly obtained fingerprints with those on file. In the course of an investigation, fingerprint technicians do not interpret findings; they leave that up to the detectives and others on the law enforcement team.

Fingerprint technicians routinely record the fingerprints of individuals who have been arrested. This process involves cleaning the subject's fingertips, inking the fingertips, and taking impressions of each fingerprint. Care must be taken to take a good impression. The subject then signs the fingerprint card, and the fingerprint technician notes the subject's weight, height, eye and hair color, and any distinguishing physical features.

The information contained on fingerprint cards is entered into the law enforcement agency's main recordkeeping system. It may also be sent to state or federal law enforcement agencies routinely to add to their databases. Most fingerprint information is now routinely computerized to facilitate retrieval and sharing among different law enforcement agencies. Fingerprint data from arrest records is compiled by law enforcement agencies into databases for future access and retrieval.

When fingerprint technicians obtain fingerprints from

crime scenes and suspected crime scenes, they may use chemical powders and dust to retrieve latent prints that are invisible to the naked eye. Prints may be lifted by using flexible tape. The tape is then taken back to the laboratory for further analysis.

New fingerprints taken from crime scenes, unidentified bodies, and other sources are compared to those already on file. It is at this point in a criminal investigation that access to as many fingerprint records as possible is most helpful. Computerized identification systems make it easier for law enforcement agencies to access fingerprint data that may be scattered among several agencies and their databases.

Fingerprint technicians analyze and classify new fingerprints according to an established system. There are three main types of fingerprints, known as the arch, the loop, and the whirl. Within each main category there are several subgroups. Fingerprint technicians use a number and letter classification system to establish a fingerprint's precise subgroup. A final classification formula is then assigned before the prints are filed.

In order to find a match, fingerprint technicians may have to make hundreds or thousands of comparisons with fingerprints already on file. In larger agencies, computerized identification systems perform many of the steps involved in matching fingerprints. Fingerprint technicians may call on the resources of the Federal Bureau of Investigation (FBI), which routinely assists other law enforcement agencies with fingerprint identification on the basis of the extensive files they hold.

Working Conditions

Fingerprint technicians spend most of their time working under moderate noise levels in clean, well-lighted and ventilated offices and laboratories where they analyze, classify, and compare fingerprint evidence. They also travel occasionally to crime scenes and other locations to obtain fingerprint evidence.

While the work of fingerprint technicians is not physically demanding, they may experience eyestrain from the visual requirements of the job. As part of a criminal identification unit that operates around the clock, fingerprint technicians typically work rotating shifts including evenings and weekends.

Employment

The FBI is the largest single employer of fingerprint technicians. They also work for state and local law enforcement agencies located throughout the United States. Fingerprint technicians are a small occupational group within forensics.

Training, Other Qualifications, and Advancement

A high school diploma or equivalent is the basic prerequisite for entry into the field of fingerprint identification. Fingerprint technicians generally have one to two years of specialized training. Some law enforcement agencies require two years of college in police science or a combination of education and practical experience. Individuals seeking employment with the FBI as fingerprint technicians must pass a written examination. Once hired, they work as clerks until vacancies for fingerprint technicians occur and then receive on-the-job training for about 90 days. Most law enforcement agencies require applicants to be U.S. citizens. They must also pass a background check and a physical examination.

The work of fingerprint technicians requires accuracy and careful attention to detail. It is sometimes painstaking and requires a good memory and a great deal of patience. Fingerprint technicians must have an interest in scientific investigation and be comfortable working with scientific procedures and equipment. They must have good reasoning skills to apply scientific principles and solve practical problems. They must be able to interpret instructions that are written or diagrammed. Good interpersonal skills are helpful when working as part of a forensics team or criminal identification unit.

Fingerprint technicians advance by working for different law enforcement agencies or applying for positions with the FBI. They may learn additional identification and forensics skills and advance from an assistant's position to one where they work independently and eventually become a project leader or head of an investigative or identification unit.

Job Outlook

The Bureau of Labor Statistics does not provide an employment forecast for fingerprint technicians or forensics experts. This is a relatively small occupational group whose numbers may increase slightly because of factors such as rising crime rates, population increases, and greater emphasis on scientific procedures in criminal investigations.

Earnings

The FBI pays approximately $14,000 a year to entry-level employees in its Identification Division. Salaries at state and local law enforcement agencies for fingerprint technicians range from $12,000 for new hires to $20,000 with a couple of years of experience. Most agencies provide a benefits package that includes paid vacation and sick leave, holiday and overtime pay, medical insurance, and retirement benefits.

Related Occupations

Related occupations in forensics include identification technicians and evidence technicians. There are related occupations in laboratory technology, including laboratory assistants, graphologists, testers, mine samplers, weather observers, document examiners, pharmacist assistants, and photo-optics technicians.

Sources of Additional Information

• American Academy of Forensic Sciences, 410 N. 21st St., Ste. 203, PO Box 669, Colorado Springs, CO 80901-0669. Phone: (719)636-1100.

• Forensic Sciences Foundation, 410 N. 21st St., Ste. 203, PO Box 669, Colorado Springs, CO 80901-0669. Phone: (719)636-1100.

• International Association for Identification, PO Box 2423, Alameda, CA 94501. Phone: (510)865-2174.

FIRE INSPECTORS

At a Glance

■ **D.O.T.:** 373.267-010 and 373.367-010

■ **Preferred Education:** Specialized training

■ **Average Salary:** $27,000

■ **Did You Know?** In addition to checking buildings for fire risks, fire inspectors may also perform the duties of a fire fighter or fire captain.

Nature of the Work

Equally as important as fighting fires is the prevention of fires. To prevent fires, fire inspectors check buildings for fire hazards and enforce regulations pertaining to fire safety.

Most buildings are subject to a regular fire inspection, but schools, hospitals, nursing homes, restaurants, hotels, theaters and other public places are particularly important. Fire inspectors prevent fires by inspecting buildings' interiors and exteriors for potential fire hazards and safety violations. Buildings are inspected for hazardous and flammable substances and chemicals. Buildings are also inspected for faulty, worn, or exposed electrical wiring. Storage areas are examined for trash, debris, and other materials that could easily ignite. Fire inspectors make certain there are clearly-defined building exits and unobstructed doorways and stairways. They test smoke and fire alarms and other fire-control devices for proper operation. They examine building machinery and equipment, such as furnaces or fuel storage tanks, to make sure it conforms to fire and safety codes.

Fire inspectors discuss the completed inspection with the building owner or manager, inform them of any unsafe conditions that must be corrected, such as defective electrical wiring or obstructed escape areas. Recommendations are also made regarding safe methods for storing flammables or other hazardous materials.

If a building passes the fire inspection, the fire inspector issues a permit that declares the building's safe operating conditions. If a building does not pass inspection according to local ordinances and state laws, a violations report is prepared, and the owner or manager must see that corrections are made immediately. If any fire hazards have not been corrected before the next inspection, the fire inspector will issue a summons and enforce code.

Fire inspectors also inspect fire stations. Within the station, fire inspectors inspect fire equipment such as hoses and pipes to make sure that everything is working properly.

Fire inspectors keep files of inspection records. They may be responsible for collecting permit and license fees. A fire inspector may also perform the duties of a fire fighter or fire captain.

Working Conditions

Fire inspectors usually work 40-hour, five-day weeks. Evening and weekend work is sometimes necessary. Fire inspectors usually work alone, but sometimes as a member of a team. They work indoors and outdoors, depending on the premises under inspection and the type of inspection. The types of buildings inspected vary in size and condition. A fire inspector's office is usually within the main fire department.

Employment

According to the U.S. Bureau of Labor Statistics, 14,000 fire inspectors were employed in 1992. Most fire inspectors are employed by municipal or county fire departments. Others are employed by federal and state agencies, airports, and private companies, such as insurance agencies. Large urban areas may have several fire inspectors, while smaller communities only one.

Training, Other Qualifications, and Advancement

Qualifications vary by employer, but a high school diploma is typically required. Some employers may require a college education. Age (at least 21 years old) and physical requirements are usually enforced. A medical examination and a physical performance test determining strength and agility may be necessary. Fire inspectors must also successfully complete a written examination. Some employers require applicants to undergo a personal background investigation.

Beginning fire inspectors are given several weeks of intensive classroom and practical training on fire prevention and safety at the department's training center. Training may be ongoing as new techniques or new fire hazards are discovered.

Fire inspectors must have excellent oral communication skills and be able to communicate clearly with people.

Job Outlook

According to the U.S. Bureau of Labor Statistics, job openings for fire inspectors are expected to grow only two percent through the year 2005. Fire inspectors make up the smallest segment of the fire fighting industry. Turnover is generally low and layoffs are rare. Most growth will occur in smaller communities with growing populations. Other openings will result from retirements. Fire fighting occupations, which offer a relatively high income, attract many people.

Earnings

Earnings for fire inspectors vary by experience, employer, and geographic location of employer. A reported median annual salary for fire inspectors was $27,000 in 1993.

Fire inspectors receive benefits such as paid vacations,

sick leave, health and life insurance, and a retirement pension.

Related Occupations

Other occupations in fire prevention and control include fire-protection engineers, fire fighters, fire marshals, fire chiefs, and arson investigators. Related occupations in health and safety regulations includes public health service officers, safety inspectors, industrial hygienists, water-pollution control inspectors, radiation-protection specialists, agricultural commodities inspectors, and pesticide-control inspectors.

Sources of Additional Information

For more information on a career as a fire inspector, contact:

* International Association of Fire Fighters, 1750 New York Ave. NW, Washington, DC 20006-5395. Phone: (202)737-8484.

* National Fire Protection Association, 1 Batterymarch Park, PO Box 9101, Quincy, MA 02269-9101. Phone: (617)770-3000.

* International Association of Fire Chiefs, 4025 Fair Ridge Rd., Fairfax, VA 22033-2868 Phone: (703)273-0911.

FIRE LOOKOUTS AND SPOTTERS

At a Glance

* **D.O.T.:** 452.367-010

* **Preferred Education:** On the job training

* **Average Salary:** $7 per hour

* **Did You Know?** There are approximately 200 to 300 paid fire lookouts in the U.S. Forest Service. They work primarily in national parks and forests in the western United States.

Nature of the Work

Fire lookouts play a key role in the U.S. Forest Service's fire protection program. They are usually the first ones to spot a lightning strike in a forested area. After determining the precise location of the fire, they radio its location to headquarters or a base camp, which then dispatches a firefighting team.

The sooner a lightning strike fire is spotted and pinpointed, the quicker firefighting teams can respond to suppress the fire. Quick action on the part of fire lookouts is crucial to successful fire control. While the Forest Service estimates that 95 percent of all such fires are contained and suppressed, the 5 percent that are "escaped" fires cause about

95 percent of the resource damage and suppression costs in forested areas.

Stationed in remote lookout towers overlooking vast tracts of forested land, fire lookouts perform other duties in addition to watching for lightning strikes. They record, process, and report daily data related to weather conditions, including temperature, relative humidity, wind direction and velocity, and type of cloud formations. They transmit messages regarding weather forecasts, fire hazard conditions, emergencies, accidents, and other information to base camps, mobile units, and law enforcement and governmental agencies.

Fire lookouts use a device known as a fire locator to pinpoint the coordinates of a lightning strike. The fire locator is similar to a range finder. By looking through the fire locator at a lightning strike, fire lookouts can pinpoint the fire's location and relay that information to a base camp or headquarters office. When a dry thunderstorm is in the area, many small fires can be started in a matter of minutes.

During a fire it is the fire lookout's responsibility to keep the base camp, mobile units, and other government and law enforcement agencies informed of weather conditions. Fire lookouts may serve to relay messages between firefighting units and their control centers. They use radios or telephones to keep all parties informed of wind changes and fire conditions.

Fire lookouts have to maintain their lookout station and keep it in working order. When visitors stop by, they may have to make presentations explaining federal and state fire laws, timber company policies, fire hazard conditions, and fire prevention methods.

Working Conditions

Fire lookouts typically work in remote areas of the northwest United States and southern Canada. They may live in the nearest town and drive to their lookout tower. In many cases they live at the lookout tower, receiving food and supplies via helicopter. They may spend long periods of time--days and even weeks--alone.

To relieve their isolation, fire lookouts are usually given blocks of time off. They may work five days a week and have weekends off. Other schedules have them working ten days in a row, with the next ten days off. Their work is seasonal, typically starting in the spring and ending in the fall.

Fire lookouts may spend long periods of time without having to report a fire. Then, a dry thunderstorm may pass over, causing several lightning strikes all at once. Then fire lookouts become extremely busy, trying to report the fires as quickly as possible so that firefighting teams can be dispatched. When there are fires, fire lookouts may have to work around the clock.

Employment

There are approximately 200 to 300 paid fire lookouts in the U.S. Forest Service. They work primarily in national parks and forests in the western United States. In addition, volunteers work at some lookout stations that are located mainly in the eastern United States.

Most fire lookouts are either women, retired persons, or

college students. Employment is seasonal. Some fire lookouts who are full-time employees of the Forest Service are given other assignments during the off-season. In some cases married couples are hired to be lookouts.

Training, Other Qualifications, and Advancement

Fire lookouts generally learn their responsibilities on the job. The Forest Service requires that applicants have some knowledge of forestry procedures and the ability to operate equipment in the lookout tower. These basic skills can be learned through previous experience as a volunteer or lookout relief person. Some familiarity with fire and weather behavior is considered helpful.

Fire lookouts must have good vision, especially to see at a distance and to see all areas within their field of vision. Good health and physical condition are also needed.

Most importantly, fire lookouts must be self-reliant and able to spend long periods of time alone. They are usually people who enjoy being outdoors. They must be self-starters who are able to work on their own and fulfill their responsibilities without close supervision.

Fire lookouts have to interpret basic mathematical information. They should know how to compute ratios and percentages and be able to interpret graphs. They must be able to apply common sense understanding to carry out written, oral, or diagrammed instructions. They should also be able to write reports and read instruction manuals.

Fire lookouts can use their experience to advance to other positions involving fire protection and forestry.

Job Outlook

Some consider the use of fire lookouts to be the old way of spotting lightning strikes and forest fires that will be replaced by automated weather stations and satellite cameras. While the Forest Service does rely to some extent on aerial observers and electronic lightning-detection systems, lookout towers remain a cheap and efficient way to provide early detection of lightning strikes. Fire lookouts can spot a fire quicker than an automated system that identifies the location of lightning strikes without indicating which strikes have become fires.

The Forest Service is in the process of closing some fire lookout towers, while at the same time new ones are being opened. Most employment opportunities for fire lookouts are in the western United States, where timber is a high-value resource. Most of the new lookout stations are being opened in the western states. In the East many stations are staffed by volunteers.

Earnings

Fire lookouts employed by the Forest Service earn about $7 hour, based on the GS rating system. If they are seasonal employees, they do not receive any benefits. Volunteer lookouts generally receive a modest daily stipend to cover expenses.

Related Occupations

Fire rangers are involved with fire prevention and spend a lot of time patrolling forested areas for fires. Other occupations concerned with the protection of property and people include parking enforcement officers, airline security representatives, bodyguards, security guards, and detectives.

Related forestry and logging occupations include forest firefighters, tree planters, log markers, chain saw operators, rafters, and log sorters.

Fire lookouts transmit and receive information. Other occupations with similar duties include dispatchers, telegraphers, switchboard operators, and alarm operators.

Sources of Additional Information

- Forest Service, U.S. Dept. of Agriculture, PO Box 96090, Washington, DC 20090-6090.

- Society of American Foresters, 5400 Grosvenor Ln., Bethesda, MD 20814. Phone: (301)897-8720.

- Fire Lookout Information Center, PO Box 624, Eureka, CA 95502. Phone: (707)444-7015.

FISH AND GAME WARDENS

At a Glance

- **D.O.T.:** 379.167-010

- **Preferred Education:** 2 to 4 years postsecondary education

- **Average Salary:** $18,340 to $22,717 (federal government)

- **Did You Know?** Most government agencies require that applicants for fish and game warden positions be at least 21 years old and pass a written examination.

Nature of the Work

Fish and game wardens, also known as conservation officers, prevent fish and game law violations. They also investigate reports of crop and property damage by wildlife, and compile biological data.

Fish and game wardens are typically assigned an area to patrol. They may travel through their assigned area on foot or by car, horse, boat, or airplane. They are often equipped with firearms, cameras, binoculars, maps, charts, diagrams, first aid kits, and camping gear.

When observing fishers and hunters, fish and game wardens make sure that all fishing and hunting methods and equipment are lawful, and they issue warnings or citations to violators. At times, fish and game wardens must serve warrants, seize unlawfully-used equipment, arrange for the disposition of illegally obtained fish and game, and arrest uncooperative violators. In the event of an arrest, fish and game wardens must prepare reports and present evidence in court.

Fish and game wardens also help fishers and hunters by investigating and reporting hunting and fishing accidents. They assist in search and rescue missions and help promote hunter safety programs.

In addition to monitoring fishing and hunting activities, fish and game wardens study and report information on the number and condition of fish and wildlife as well as the condition of their habitat. They determine the availability of wildlife food and cover. In overpopulated areas, fish and game wardens recommend modification to obtain balance and implement authorized methods of relocating animals. They also investigate claims of property and crop damage caused by wildlife.

Fish and game wardens investigate violations and enforce laws to reduce water pollution, protect wetlands, and eliminate littering. They patrol and protect parks and forests. They sometimes enlist the aid of others to implement lake and stream rehabilitation and game habitat improvement.

In some cases, fish and game wardens address schools, civic groups, and sports organizations to disseminate conservation information and promote conservation public relations. They teach people the importance of conservation and safety practices and develop and oversee programs on hunting and recreational vehicle safety.

Working Conditions

Fish and game wardens usually work alone in an assigned area, under the direction of a regional supervisor. The greatest amount of their time is spent outdoors in all types of weather conditions, including rain, snow, storms, very hot and very cold temperatures, and high humidity. Most indoor work is spent preparing reports.

Fish and game wardens typically work 40 hours per week and often work weekends and holidays, when hunting and fishing activities are heaviest. A fish and game warden's workday may start very early and end late. The busiest times are during summer and hunting seasons in the fall and winter.

Fish and game wardens are at possible risk of injury from wildlife or, even more likely, from individuals resisting arrest. They also do a great deal of standing, walking, stooping, crouching, crawling, kneeling, and lifting and carrying.

Employment

According to the U.S. Bureau of Labor Statistics, fish and game wardens were a part of the 38,000 people employed in law enforcement occupations that did not include fire fighting, police and detectives. Fish and game wardens are employed by federal, state, and local government agencies. Most work in rural areas or areas with a great abundance of wildlife.

Training, Other Qualifications, and Advancement

Employers want fish and game wardens to have at least a high school diploma, although some desire a two-year degree. Increasingly, due to competition, many fish and game wardens have bachelor's degrees.

There is usually an age requirement (at least 21 years of age) for fish and game wardens. Most government agencies require that applicants pass a written examination. Fish and game wardens must have a clean criminal record and be free of even minor infractions, including certain traffic law violations. Fish and game wardens must be in good physical condition, pass a physical examination, and have a valid driver's license. Fish and game wardens usually must complete police training.

Fish and game wardens must be able to hear well and have good vision (with or without corrective lenses). They must be capable of dealing with all kinds of people. They must also demonstrate the ability to react quickly in unexpected or dangerous situations.

Job Outlook

Job opportunities for fish and game wardens are expected to increase 14.4 percent by the year 2005. Protecting the environment continues to be an important issue and boosts the need for fish and game wardens. Governmental conservation agencies, however, are often subject to budget cutbacks, which during economic downturns has a negative effect on new job opportunities for fish and game wardens. Most job openings for fish and game wardens will be the result of retirements.

Earnings

According to *American Salaries and Wages Survey*, in 1992 fish and game wardens in Hawaii were offered an average starting wage of $9.32 per hour, while those in South Dakota were offered $6.40 per hour.

Other sources report that in 1994 fish and game wardens employed by the federal government had annual starting salaries between $18,340 and $22,717. More experienced officers earned $33,623 to $43,712 annually. Supervisors could earn more than $70,000 per year.

Conservation officers typically receive benefits that include paid vacations and holidays, sick leave, tuition reimbursement, health and life insurance, and retirement plans.

Related Occupations

Other occupations similar to fish and game wardens include wildlife agents, animal cruelty investigation supervisors, animal treatment investigators, wildlife control agents, and public-safety officers.

Sources of Additional Information

For more information contact:

• National Association of Conservation Districts, 509 Capitol Ct. NE, Washington, DC 20002 Phone: (202)547-6223.

- National Parks and Conservation Association, 1776 Massachusetts Ave., Ste. 200, Washington, DC 20036 Phone: (202)223-6722.

- National Wildlife Federation, 1400 16th St. NW, Washington, DC 20036-2266.

- U.S. Department of the Interior, Fish and Wildlife Service, 1849 C St. NW, Washington, DC 20240 Phone: (202)208-5634.

FOREST FIRE FIGHTERS AND SMOKEJUMPERS

At a Glance

- **D.O.T.:** 452.134-010, 452.364-014 and 452.687-014

- **Preferred Education:** Two years of firefighting experience and training course

- **Average Salary:** $10 base pay plus overtime

- **Did You Know?** Smokejumpers are typically hired by the Forest Service for 180 days or less.

Nature of the Work

Every summer, it seems, spectacular forest fires focus national attention on the brave men and women whose job is to fight the fires. Some of these fire fighters are known as smokejumpers. Smokejumpers parachute from small airplanes into remote areas to fight forest fires. Those who hang or drop from helicopters are known as helitacks.

Smokejumpers typically work in teams under the direction of a team leader or supervisor. They are taken in small planes that circle over forest fires. They use hand signals to communicate with the pilot to help position the plane in relation to the fire. Then they parachute onto a "jump spot" in order to contain fires and keep them from changing direction.

Smokejumpers use advanced parachutes that give them the ability to maneuver in the air, even slowing almost to a stop in mid-air if necessary. They jump wearing about 60-70 pounds of jump-related equipment, which includes main and reserve chutes, helmet, harness, let-down rope, pack-out bag, padded jumpsuit, and a small day-pack.

The tools and equipment used by smokejumpers are dropped separately, as are food, water, and camping gear. Once on the ground, smokejumpers may join with ground crews of firefighters to clear fire lines around the fire. The purpose of digging fire lines is to remove fuel from the fire's path. Fire lines are typically 18-inch-wide areas that are cleared around a fire by removing brush, cutting trees, and digging trenches. Digging a fire line can be very difficult if the terrain is rough. Smokejumpers use tools such as chain saws and pulaskis (a combination ax and hoe named for its inventor) to make fire

lines.

Experienced ground forest firefighters are sometimes called "hotshots." They carry saws, axes, and hoes into the brush and use them to remove fuel from fires. They are driven as close to the fire as possible, or when necessary are transported to fires by helicopter. They are directed by crew chiefs or squad leaders to accomplish specific tasks. They wear protective gear, including heavy leather work boots, fire-resistant shirts and trousers, heavy leather gloves, a hard hat and hood, plastic goggles, and a nylon harness to carry such items as a canteen, first-aid kit, fire tent, radio, and pack. They may be required to carry 20 to 40 pounds of gear over rough terrain.

Smokejumpers and forest firefighters may use hand- or engine-driven water or chemical pumps to extinguish flames and embers to suppress a fire. They may light controlled backfires to bring a blaze under control. They make sure a fire is completely out by marking off squares and sifting the dirt with their bare hands to see if it is hot. Warm ground is sprayed and then stirred up. Team or crew chiefs are usually responsible for making sure a fire is completely dead.

Once the fire has been put out, smokejumpers and forest firefighters have to carry out most of their gear. They may have to carry 100-pound packs for miles over steep terrain.

When not involved with fighting fires, smokejumpers maintain a rigorous physical conditioning program. Forest firefighters who work on the ground may patrol certain areas looking for fires. They may relieve fire spotters and lookouts.

Working Conditions

The work of smokejumpers and forest firefighters can be risky and hazardous. Since smokejumping was first introduced in 1940, 19 smokejumpers have died in fires or parachuting accidents through the end of 1994. Three of these deaths occurred in 1994 when smokejumpers were among 14 firefighters killed by a raging forest fire in western Colorado. Particularly hazardous are strong winds that can turn a fire unexpectedly into the path of firefighters. Smokejumpers often have to parachute into dangerous terrain and risk injury when landing. Other hazards include falling down cliffs and being hit by falling rocks or trees. Even getting to the fire by land or air can be hazardous.

When fighting fires smokejumpers and forest firefighters are subject to hot, smoky, and dusty conditions. Their eyes may sting from smoke, and they may develop coughs from inhaling smoke-filled air. They are subject to extremes of weather and other atmospheric conditions, particularly hot and wet conditions.

The work requires a great deal of physical strength. Smokejumpers and forest firefighters must be able to carry packs weighing 100 pounds for several miles, sometimes over rough terrain. They may be required to climb to high altitudes. They may be called upon to fight two different fires with little time for rest between action.

Work hours can be long and vary widely. Twelve- to 18-hour days are not uncommon. Smokejumpers and forest firefighters typically work both day and night shifts. They are often away from their families for days, weeks, or even months at a time.

Smokejumpers and forest firefighters enjoy the action, challenge, and teamwork required to effectively fight forest fires. They also enjoy traveling to remote locations. In between fighting fires they may experience boredom as they wait for their next assignment.

Employment

There were fewer than 30,000 forest firefighters employed in 1992, with about 400 men and women employed as smokejumpers. The major federal agencies that employ smokejumpers and forest firefighters are the U.S. Forest Service, U.S. Park Service, and Bureau of Land Management. State departments of forestry also employ them, especially in states with large tracts of forests.

While most employment opportunities are in the western states, many opportunities also exist along the east coast where forests are maturing. The largest base for Forest Service smokejumpers is located in Missoula, Montana.

Employment may be seasonal or year-round. Smokejumpers are typically hired by the Forest Service for 180 days or less. There are relatively few women smokejumpers, but a higher percentage are employed as forest firefighters. Most smokejumpers and forest firefighters are in their twenties.

Training, Other Qualifications, and Advancement

The U.S. Forest Service requires at least two years of firefighting experience to become a smokejumper. Parachuting experience can be helpful, but training will be provided. Applicants must also meet minimum physical requirements regarding height, weight, and vision. Once hired, smokejumper trainees undergo a six-week training program that includes crawling through corrugated drainage pipes, climbing 60-foot utility poles, and other exercises similar to the U.S. Army's boot camp. Parachute and firefighting training are also part of the program. In approximately three weeks trainees learn how to parachute by using simulators and making practice jumps. Smokejumpers also learn how to sew their own uniforms, packs, and harnesses and to repair their own parachutes.

Beginning ground forest firefighters do not need any particular training or experience. Once hired they receive basic firefighting training. They must also pass a physical test. Once they become a crew member, they are qualified to use shovels or other hand tools. They may also learn how to drive large trucks and operate chain saws. With one or more years of experience fighting forest fires, individuals may join established crews known as "hotshots" that fight fires all over the United States. Previous firefighting and safety training, including first-aid training, may be required for seasonal firefighters.

Smokejumpers and forest firefighters must be in top physical condition. They are people who enjoy working outdoors. They must be aggressive and enthusiastic. Having common sense and good judgment, being able to think and react quickly, and reliability are also very important.

Beginning forest firefighters can become members of

hotshot teams after one year of experience. With two years of experience they can apply to become smokejumpers. Individuals with extensive firefighting or smokejumping experience are often hired by government agencies to fill other permanent positions in forestry and fire protection.

Job Outlook

While the Bureau of Labor Statistics does not keep separate statistics for smokejumpers and forest firefighters, employment of all types of firefighters is projected to increase by 16 to 17 percent between 1992 and 2005, a rate somewhat lower than the average for all occupations.

There are approximately 40 openings per year in the Forest Service for smokejumpers. In general, the field is highly competitive, with many more applicants than available positions at the federal and state level. Demand for forest firefighters and smokejumpers increases when dry weather conditions result in more fires.

Earnings

Seasonal smokejumpers employed by the U.S. Forest Service earn a base pay of about $10 per hour (GS-5 level, GS-6 for returning smokejumpers). They are typically hired for 180 days or less. With overtime, they can earn $200 a day or $1,200 a week. When Yellowstone National Park burned in 1988, smokejumpers earned about $40,000 for the season.

Forest firefighters employed by a federal agency are also paid by the GS rating system, starting out at GS-3 and earning a base pay of about $14,100 per year for an eight-hour day. In addition, firefighters earn a lot of overtime at time-and-a-half. One hundred hours of overtime in a two-week period is not uncommon. They can also earn other bonus pay for night and hazardous duty.

According to *American Salaries and Wages Survey*, forest firefighters in Colorado earned between $5.70 and $9 per hour in 1990-91. Smokejumpers in South Dakota earned an average of $4.75 per hour in 1991-92.

Related Occupations

Related occupations that can be involved with fighting forest fires include support personnel such as pilots, medics, lookouts, fire camp workers, weather researchers, fire behavior specialists, and transportation workers. Fire rangers and fire lookouts spend time locating forest fires. Fire protection engineers and firefighters employed by cities or counties are also involved with fire protection.

Other occupations that involve responding to emergencies include emergency medical technicians and law enforcement officers.

Sources of Additional Information

For more information on careers as smokejumpers and forest firefighters, contact:

- Forest Service, U.S. Dept. of Agriculture, PO Box 96090, Washington, DC 20090-6090.

- Society of American Foresters, 5400 Grosvenor Ln., Bethesda, MD 20814. Phone: (301)897-8720.

- National Interagency Fire Center, 3905 Vista Ave., Boise, ID 83705. Phone: (208)389-2575.

For information on other firefighting careers, contact:

- International Association of Fire Chiefs, 4025 Fair Ridge Dr., Fairfax, VA 22033-2868. Phone: (703)273-0911.

- International Association of Fire Fighters, 1750 New York Ave. NW, Washington, DC 20006-5395. Phone: (202)737-8484.

LIFEGUARDS

At a Glance

- **D.O.T.:** 379.364-014 and 379.667-014

- **Preferred Education:** High school diploma recommended

- **Average Salary:** $4.25 to $17.50 per hour

- **Did You Know?** The American Red Cross administers a lifeguard training program that emphasizes surveillance, lifeguard professionalism, and the prevention of aquatic emergencies.

Nature of the Work

Lifeguards are trained to monitor activities at beaches and pools, provide assistance to swimmers, and prevent accidents. Lifeguards work almost anywhere public swimming is allowed. Depending on where they work, lifeguards may be designated *pool lifeguards* or *surf lifeguards*.

Lifeguards usually sit in towers or elevated chairs to best monitor beach or pool users' activities and detect distressed swimmers, disorderly conduct, and safety violations. Lifeguards are equipped with a whistle or megaphone to call orders to swimmers. Lifeguards on beaches use binoculars. Sometimes lifeguards patrol beach areas on foot or by motor vehicle.

When lifeguards spot a swimmer in trouble, they react quickly to begin rescue efforts. Using trained rescue techniques, a lifeguard may be able to pull the swimmer to shore or pool-side using a rescue tube, pole, or other rescue device. A lifeguard may have to swim out to the swimmer and tow the person to safety, also using trained rescue techniques and equipment. Once safely out of the water, if the swimmer is unconscious or has stopped breathing, a lifeguard must perform mouth-to-mouth resuscitation or cardiopulmonary resuscitation (CPR) until the person is revived or until a emergency medical unit arrives. If the swimmer has received only minor injuries, such as cuts or bruises, the lifeguard will apply first aid. Lifeguards must record in detail all emergency incidents.

Lifeguards prevent accidents by watching for situations that could lead to accidents. They do not allow swimmers to travel too far from shore or into unsafe areas. They make sure young children are not left unattended by an adult.

Lifeguards maintain order by monitoring disorderly conduct and enforcing rules pertaining to alcoholic beverages, or the use of dangerous objects. At times, lifeguards must ask disorderly people to leave the beach or pool area.

Lifeguards keep track of boats and surfers to make sure that they do not enter swimming zones. Lifeguards in ocean beach areas track approaching high tide and sometimes watch for sharks and other dangerous marine life.

Lifeguards also perform non-protective services. They may give directions, reunite lost children with parents, pick up discarded articles, and turn lost articles into lost-and-found. Lifeguards who work at facilities with swimming pools may also keep the pool clean.

When not on duty, many lifeguards give swimming lessons or operate booths that rent recreation equipment.

Working Conditions

Lifeguards typically work 40 hours per week. A lifeguard's schedule usually includes evening and weekend hours, the time when most people are able to use recreational facilities. Overtime is sometimes necessary.

Lifeguards who work outdoors are exposed to various weather conditions. The weather is often sunny and the temperatures hot, but it can also be cloudy, chilly, and rainy. Outdoor lifeguards must wear protective sunscreen lotion, sunglasses, and hats to prevent sunburn and other sun-related damage.

Lifeguards must remain alert at all times and know how to determine if a swimmer is in trouble. In an emergency, a lifeguard must be able to get a person of any size safely out of the water; sometimes a victim may be panicking or unconscious. Although there is a lot of satisfaction in saving lives, sometimes lifeguards must also deal with the reality that the drowning victim they tried to save did not survive.

Lifeguards may be required to perform daily physical exercise to remain fit.

Employment

According to the U.S. Bureau of Labor Statistics, in 1992, 26,000 persons held protective service occupations within the amusement and recreation industry. This figure includes lifeguard positions. The United States Lifesaving Association reports having 6,000 members.

Lifeguards are employed at indoor and outdoor swimming facilities, including lake, river, and ocean beaches, water parks, state and national parks, health clubs, the YMCA and YWCA, municipal recreation centers, hotels, resorts, and other public and private establishments.

Lifeguarding is largely a seasonal occupation. In many

climates, lifeguards who work outdoors are employed only during summer months, often between Memorial Day and Labor Day. Many employers hire high school and college students (at least 16 years of age) who are available to work as lifeguards during their summer vacations.

Training, Other Qualifications, and Advancement

The specific requirements to be a lifeguard vary according to local standards, but there are many universal prerequisites to becoming a lifeguard. Usually a lifeguard must be at least 16 years of age, or older in some states. Lifeguards must be strong swimmers, and have successfully completed a training course in lifeguarding, first aid, and cardiopulmonary resuscitation (CPR). The American Red Cross administers a lifeguard training program that emphasizes surveillance, lifeguard professionalism, and the prevention of aquatic emergencies. In the program, the use of a rescue tube or other appropriate equipment is mandatory, and there is an emphasis on surveillance and victim recognition.

Many states require that lifeguards be licensed. A lifeguard may be licensed to work in surf areas (water with waves), non-surf areas (calm waters), or swimming pools only. Some employers require that lifeguards have at least 20/30 uncorrected vision in each eye. Full-time lifeguards must have a high school diploma.

State employment requires a physical examination. Lifeguards must also complete a practical examination, and a proficiency test in surf conditions or non-conditions if working at a beach.

Lifeguards with experience, demonstrated lifeguarding skills, and leadership abilities may advance to become lifeguard captains, training officers, facility managers or pursue other aquatics careers.

Job Outlook

According to the Bureau of Labor Statistics, job openings for workers such as lifeguards will increase 37 percent by the year 2005. With physical fitness awareness spurring an increase in the use of recreational and workout facilities, the need for qualified lifeguards should remain steady.

Earnings

Beginning lifeguards usually start their pay slightly above minimum wage, which is $4.25 per hour in 1995. According to *American Salaries and Wages Survey*, in 1991-1992 lifeguards earned an average of $4.50 to $6.26 per hour. Some reports show that lifeguards on average earn $7.50 to $12.50 per hour, and as high as $17.50 per hour for highly experienced and medically-trained lifeguards. Earnings increase with experience. Private lifeguards tend to earn more than those who are employed by public facilities. Those who work in coastal urban areas also tend to earn more.

Related Occupations

Related protective service occupations include park rangers, bouncers, ski patrollers, gambling monitor, bailiffs, and patrol officers.

Sources of Additional Information

For more information on becoming a lifeguard, contact a local chapter of the American Red Cross or the YMCA, or write to:

- United States Lifesaving Association, PO Box 366, Huntington Beach, CA 92648. Phone: (714)536-5283.

PRIVATE DETECTIVES AND INVESTIGATORS

At a Glance

- **D.O.T.:** 376.267-018 and 376.367-014
- **Preferred Education:** Specialized training
- **Average Salary:** $36,700
- **Did You Know?** Among the types of businesses that employ private detectives and investigators are retail stores, shopping malls, hotels, resort and recreational facilities, law firms, financial institutions, and insurance companies.

Nature of the Work

Staking out private homes, finding missing persons, compiling confidential information, and preventing thefts are some of the varied duties of private detectives and investigators. In addition to conducting investigations, they may provide security services by protecting property in business establishments, accompanying the transfer of valuable property, or acting as bodyguards.

There are many different types of private detectives and investigators. Some may specialize in a particular type of investigation, while others are known as general investigators. General investigators are given a range of assignments from their employer, usually a small investigative firm. They may be required to conduct background investigations, physical surveillance, or computer searches. They may obtain information for use in civil or criminal trials by interviewing witnesses, compiling evidence, and conducting stakeouts. They may spend time verifying facts through telephone calls, interviews, and visiting specific locations.

Store detectives and detectives who work for large companies, shopping malls, and similar facilities specialize in preventing theft and the destruction of company property. They may conduct investigations, monitor company property, question suspects, apprehend thieves and others engaged in criminal activity, file complaints, and testify in court. They usually have to write case reports for their employers. Other areas of interest to corporate investigators include employee fraud and substance abuse.

Legal investigators specialize in matters dealing with the

courts and lawyers. They may assist attorneys in preparing a defense by locating witnesses, interviewing police officers, and gathering and reviewing evidence. They may take photographs and testify in court. In cases involving injured parties and insurance claims, investigators interview prospective witnesses, collect information, and search for additional evidence.

Some investigators specialize in financial investigations. These involve compiling confidential financial profiles of parties involved in financial transactions. Financial investigators may provide investment bankers and attorneys with financial information concerning proposed corporate mergers and acquisitions. By searching commercial databases, reporting services, and public records, investigators are able to compile financial profiles with the help of contacts in the banking industry.

Working Conditions

Private detectives and investigators usually work irregular hours and are not subject to a fixed routine. Some work is conducted in an office setting, including computer searching and making telephone calls, while much of their work is done outside of the office. They may have to work undercover and disguise their identity. When conducting surveillance, they may have to stand or sit for long periods of time. They usually work alone or in pairs.

When conducting interviews and working away from the office, private detectives and investigators may be exposed to a variety of settings. Their work can be confrontational and even dangerous at time. They frequently deal with all types of people.

Employment

Private detectives and investigators are either self-employed, work for an investigative agency or private security company, or are employed by a business. Among the types of businesses that employ private detectives and investigators are retail stores, shopping malls, hotels, resort and recreational facilities, law firms, financial institutions, insurance companies, and other large companies. A high percentage of private detectives and investigators are employed on a part-time basis.

According to the Bureau of Labor Statistics, there were 59,000 private detectives and investigators employed in 1992. Approximately 17 percent were self-employed, and an estimated 40 percent worked for investigative or security firms. Fully one-third of all private detectives and investigators worked for department stores.

Training, Other Qualifications, and Advancement

There are no specific educational requirements for private detectives and investigators, although many employers prefer at least a high school graduate. Detectives involved in property protection and theft detection receive about one to three months of on-the-job training. Investigators may receive up to one year of specific vocational preparation.

Many private detectives and investigators are former police officers or detectives who have worked for federal, state, or local government agencies. Individuals may obtain specialized training through private investigation schools that offer classroom instruction or provide correspondence courses. Some companies may require staff investigators and detectives to have a college degree. Appropriate subjects include law enforcement, police science, criminal justice, or a business-related field.

Many states require private detectives and investigators to be licensed or registered. Licensing requirements vary considerably from state to state, and in some states they only apply to self-employed private detectives and investigators, or those working for detective agencies. Staff investigators and detectives working for a law firm, store, or other business generally do not have to be licensed. Typical licensing requirements involve passing an examination, posting a bond, and in some cases having a minimum amount of relevant experience or education.

Private detectives and investigators have a genuine interest in protecting people and property. Investigators should enjoy the mental challenge of conducting an investigation. An inquisitive mind, good observation skills, and a strong memory are needed to succeed. Private detectives and investigators should also be honest, ingenious, persistent, and assertive.

They must have highly developed reasoning abilities and language skills. They often have to deal with numerous variables in different types of situations. They must be able to read complex documents and write reports and summaries. Good oral communication skills are needed to obtain information through interviews.

Private detectives and investigators advance by conducting successful investigations and preventing theft and destruction of property. Those who are successful and gain experience receive better assignments. They may also benefit from the high turnover rate among private detectives and investigators. In some firms there are supervisory and management positions available. Some private detectives and investigators advance by opening their own private investigative or security firm.

Job Outlook

The Bureau of Labor Statistics projects that employment of private detectives and investigators will increase by 70 percent between 1992 and 2005, much faster than the average for all occupations. Several factors support a growing demand for private investigative services. These include the growth of computer technology, which has made large amounts of data easily accessible and led to an increase in white-collar crime. Growth in population, economic activity, and domestic and global competition will be accompanied by increases in crime, litigation, and the need for confidential information.

Earnings

Earnings of private detectives and investigators depend on whether they are self-employed, work for a detective agency, or are employed by a store or corporation. Geographic location and area of specialization also affect earnings. Store detectives tend to earn less than private investigators working for an agency, with corporate investigators being the highest paid on average.

According to the *Occupational Outlook Quarterly*, store detectives averaged about $16,100 a year in 1993, while private investigators earned an average of $36,700 a year. Starting salaries for general investigators ranged from $15,000 to $18,000. Experienced private investigators earned between $20,000 and $125,000 annually. Those in charge of their own agency earned between $40,000 and $300,000.

Corporate investigators earned starting salaries in the $40,000 range, reaching $50,000 after a few years of experience. Investigators and detectives in supervisory positions at corporations earned $70,000 and more per year.

Most private detectives and investigators do not receive benefits unless they are employed by a large corporation. Corporate investigators generally receive a standard benefits package that includes health insurance, pension plan, profit-sharing plan, and paid vacations.

Related Occupations

Related investigative occupations include sheriffs, police officers, fire marshals, public detectives and investigators, fire wardens, and special agents. Other occupations that involve the protection of people and property include security guards, parking enforcement officials, and gate guards.

Sources of Additional Information

- International Security and Detective Alliance, PO Box 6303, Corpus Christi, TX 78466-6303. Phone: (512)888-6164.

- Council of International Investigators, PO Box 266, Palmer, MA 01069-0266. Phone: (413)283-7003.

- National Association of Investigative Specialists, PO Box 33244, Austin, TX 78764. Phone: (512)719-3595.

- World Association of Detectives, PO Box 1049, Severna Park, MD 21146. Phone: (410)544-0119 or 800-962-0516.

SKI PATROLLERS

At a Glance

- **D.O.T.:** 379.664-010

- **Preferred Education:** Skiing experience and specialized training

- **Average Salary:** $6.00 per hour

- **Did You Know?** The National Ski Patrol System includes 2,000 registered professional ski patrollers and about 25,000 volunteers.

Nature of the Work

Few people can combine their favorite recreational activity with their occupation. Ski patrollers, however, are part of that rare group. Ski patrolling can be a great way to help others while perfecting personal skills. But working as a ski patroller is very demanding work.

Ski patrollers are primarily concerned with the safety of other skiers. Their main duties include providing emergency care for injured or ill skiers, performing avalanche control work, and putting up boundary ropes and signs. They spend their working hours skiing down ski trails and slopes. Patrollers are the first skiers on the slopes in the morning. They look for hazardous conditions and make sure the signs and ropes along the course are in place.

When accidents occur on the slopes, ski patrollers rescue the injured skiers. They administer first aid on the scene and often use toboggans to move injured skiers to an ambulance. Ski patrollers wear radios so they can contact medical personal when there are serious injuries.

Ski patrollers are responsible for enforcing the rules of ski etiquette. They often hand out warnings to violators. Defusing avalanches is another part of a ski patroller's job. Ski patrollers work with demolition crews to trigger avalanches before skiers arrive on the slopes. They also help evacuate ski lifts in case of an emergency. Ski patrollers go down the lifts on the cables and lower the stranded skiers to the ground by rope.

After the lifts close at the end of the day, ski patrollers make one last run down the course to make sure all skiers are off the slopes. This is called a "sweep." They also inspect the ski lifts and tow ropes, and report any wear or damage to the management. Ski patrollers may give instruction to beginning skiers.

Working Conditions

The work of ski patrollers is physically demanding and requires a great deal of skill and stamina. Ski patrollers spend most of their time outdoors, often working more than 40 hours per week during peak skiing season. Their work can be stressful and dangerous, especially when assisting injured skiers and skiing in extreme weather conditions.

Employment

The National Ski Patrol System includes 2,000 registered professional ski patrollers. Many of these professional ski patrollers work at large ski areas, especially in the western United States. Smaller ski areas in Virginia, West Virginia, Maryland and southern Pennsylvania employ professional ski patrollers on weekdays when volunteers are not available. The National Ski Patrol System has 25,000 volunteers who also patrol the slopes. Other ski resort states include Vermont, Maine, New Hampshire, and Michigan.

Ski patrolling is a seasonal occupation. The ski season runs from mid-November to the third week in April. Patrollers, therefore, generally work other jobs during the summer.

Training, Advancement, and Other Qualifications

Ski patrollers must be experienced and confident skiers and be able to demonstrate their skills. They must then pass an intensive, 60- to 80-hour course called Winter Emergency Care (WEC), which is similar to emergency medical technician training but emphasizes cold weather-related injuries. Candidates must also pass a course in cardiopulmonary resuscitation (CPR). They may receive additional training in toboggan handling, avalanche control, search and rescue tactics, lift evacuation, and ski mountaineering.

Ski patrollers should be able to work well in a team, which may become necessary during rescue efforts. They should also have an interest in helping others and a willingness to educate fellow skiers about safety on the slopes. Ski patrollers must be able to handle stress and make decisions quickly in an emergency situation.

Ski patrollers can advance by perfecting their skills and becoming certified or senior patrollers. They may choose to work at larger ski resorts or be promoted to ski patrol directors. This job has the additional responsibilities of recruiting, training, and supervising ski patrollers.

Job Outlook

Because ski patrollers are highly regarded among fellow skiers, competition exists for ski patrol positions even among volunteers. However, due to the demanding nature of the job, few patrollers make it a lifelong career. Therefore, new positions open every year due to attrition and employee turnover.

Earnings

Ski patrollers do not receive high wages. For example, workers at ski resorts in Colorado often earned a starting wage of $6 per hour in 1994. Experienced ski patrollers and supervisors receive better pay. Ski patrollers often earn more money through their summer jobs. Some ski resorts offer benefits such as health insurance. Other benefits include the opportunity to live in scenic locations, the camaraderie of fellow workers, and free ski passes.

Related Occupations

Other occupations involving safety responsibilities include lifeguards, park rangers, border guards, golf-course rangers, and bouncers. Additional occupations at ski resorts include ski lift operators, maintenance vehicle operators, snow makers, and ski instructors.

Sources of Additional Information

- National Ski Patrol System, Ski Patrol Bldg., Ste. 100, 133 S. Van Gorden St., Lakewood, CO 80228. Phone: (303)988-1111.

- Ski Industries America, 8377-B Greensboro Dr., Mc Lean, VA 22102. Phone: (703)556-9020.

Food and Beverage Preparation and Service Occupations

BAKER, PASTRY COOK, PASTRY CHEF

At a Glance

- **D.O.T.:** 313.381-010, 313.381-026, 313.131-022

- **Preferred Education:** High school diploma

- **Average Salary:** $6 to $7 per hour

- **Did You Know?** In addition to learning how to prepare food and use kitchen equipment, culinary students are also trained in menu planning, cost control, food storage, and the safe handling of food.

Nature of Work

Restaurants, hotels, retail bakeries, and institutional kitchens all employ bakers and pastry cooks to prepare a wide assortment of baked goods such as breads, rolls, pastries, pies, and cakes.

Bread bakers prepare bread, rolls, muffins, and biscuits, generally doing most of the work by hand. Following recipes, bread bakers measure and mix ingredients to form dough or batter. Then, they cut the dough with a knife or divider, and mold the dough into loaves or rolls. After placing the dough on cooking pans, bakers often spread or sprinkle on toppings such as jelly, cinnamon, and poppy seeds. Bakers let the dough rise in a proof box. Once it has risen, the dough is placed in an oven to bake. Baked goods are removed from the oven and placed on a cooling rack before they are served to customers.

Pastry cooks have a job similar to bread bakers, only they bake desserts such as cakes, cookies, pies, and puddings. They also do most of their work by hand. They measure and mix ingredients to create dough or batter. Pastry cooks then shape the dough by hand, or with a rolling pin or cookie cutters. Like bread, the dough is placed in an oven and allowed to bake. Pastry cooks also prepare the ingredients used for pastry fillings, puddings, and custards. They make icings used for decorating cakes, cookies, and other pastries. Some pastry cooks specialize in preparing one type of pastry or desert.

Pastry chefs supervise pastry cooks. They plan production for the pastry department based on a menu or special requirements. They also supply pastry cooks with recipes and offer baking suggestions and tips. Pastry chefs may help in preparing deserts. Other responsibilities include ordering supplies and equipment, and maintaining production records.

Working Conditions

Bakers and pastry cooks work in kitchens. They generally work 40 hours per week. Work hours may include early morning, late evening, weekend, and some holidays. They must be able to work in close quarters during busy periods. The work can be physically demanding. Bakers and pastry cooks stand for hours at a time, and must frequently lift heavy pots and kettles. Job hazards include slips and falls, cuts, and burns. Some bakers and pastry cooks belong to a union. Nearly one-third of all bakers and restaurant and institutional cooks work part time.

Employment

According to the U.S. Bureau of Labor Statistics, bread and pastry bakers held 146,000 jobs in 1992. Most chefs, cooks, and other kitchen workers work in restaurants or similar establishment. Others work for institutional kitchens, grocery stores, hotels, private clubs, catering establishments, banquet halls, and many other food service establishments.

Training, Advancement, and Other Qualifications

Although it is not required, a high school diploma is recommended for those considering a career as a baker or pastry cook. Some bakers and pastry cooks receive their training through trade schools, vocational centers, professional associations, and colleges. These programs can range from a few months to 2 years or more. Bakers and pastry cooks also can be trained in apprenticeship programs offered by professional culinary institutes, industry associations, and trade unions. Some large hotels and restaurants operate their own training programs.

Students generally learn their skills through actual practice. They spend most of their time learning to prepare food and use kitchen equipment. Other topics include menu planning, cost control, and food storage. Students also learn sanitation and health rules for handling food.

Bakers and pastry chefs should be able to work as part of

a team. They need a keen sense of taste and smell. Personal cleanliness is also important. Most states require health certificates for kitchen workers.

There are excellent advancement opportunities for chefs and cooks. By learning new skills and moving from one job to another, many acquire higher paying positions. Advancement depends on culinary skills, the ability to supervise other workers, and the ability to work efficiently and control costs. Some cooks and chefs go into business for themselves as caterers or restaurant owners. Others may become instructors at culinary schools or other academic institutions.

Job Outlook

According to the U.S. Department of Labor, job openings for chefs, cooks, and other kitchen workers are expected to be excellent through the year 2005. Employment opportunities will increase with the growth of the economy. Other factors contributing to employment growth will be population growth, rising family and personal incomes, more leisure time, and more women joining the work force. The popularity of baked breads and pastries should ensure rapid growth in the employment of bakers. The U.S. Bureau of Labor Statistics estimates that 69,000 new jobs for bread and pastry bakers will be created between 1992 and 2005.

Earnings

According to a survey conducted by the National Restaurant Association, bread and pastry bakers had median hourly earnings of $6.25 in 1992; most earned between $6.00 and $7.00 per hour. In Minnesota, for example, the median hourly wage paid to bread and pastry bakers in 1992 was $6.90. Top bakers in Minnesota earned $11.75 or more per hour in 1992.

Related Occupations

Workers who perform tasks similar to those of bakers and pastry cooks include chefs, cooks, specialty cooks, pie makers, short-order cooks, pizza bakers, and barbecue cooks.

Sources of Additional Information

For additional information contact:

- American Bakers Association, 1350 Eye St. NW, Ste. 1290, Washington, DC 20005-3005 Phone: (202)789-0300

- American Institute of Baking, 1213 Bakers Way, Manhattan, KS 66502 Phone: (913)537-4750

- American Culinary Federation, 10 San Bartola Rd., P.O. Box 3466, St. Augustine, FL 32085-3466 Phone: (904)825-4468

- American Hotel & Motel Association, 1201 New York Ave. NW, Ste. 600, Washington, DC 2005 Phone: (202)289-3100

- Educational Foundation of the National Restaurant Association, 250 S. Wacker Dr., No. 1400, Chicago, IL 60606 Phone: (312)715-1010

BARTENDERS

At a Glance

- **D.O.T.:** 312.474-010

- **Preferred Education:** High school diploma

- **Average Salary:** $250 per week

- **Did You Know?** Bartenders may be responsible for determining when a customer has had too much to drink, and may refuse to serve an inebriated customer any more.

Nature of the Work

Many adults like to relax and socialize with an alcoholic drink, and unless they do this at their home or a friends, their drinks will be prepared by a bartender. Bartenders take orders for alcoholic drinks from customers at bars, prepare and serve the drinks, and collect payment. Bartenders also fill drink orders that waiters and waitresses take from customers in restaurants, hotel lounges, and other places that serve alcoholic beverages. Bartenders may prepare nonalcoholic beverages, too. Whatever the beverage request, bartenders serve customers quickly and accurately, even during the busiest periods.

Bartenders serve draught or bottled beer, wine, liquors, and other alcoholic beverages. Following standard recipes, they also mix ingredients, such as liquor, soda, ice, fruit or vegetable juices, sugar, salt, and bitters to prepare cocktails and other drinks. Some establishments, especially larger ones, use automatic equipment to mix drinks at the simple push of a button. Nevertheless, bartenders know how to prepare drinks that are not handled by automatic equipment and are able to mix drinks when the automatic machine isn't working. Some people prefer their cocktails made a particular way and bartenders will mix drinks to suit a customer s taste. For many drinks, especially cocktails, bartenders may slice and pit fruit to garnish the drinks. Bartenders collect money for drinks served, operate the cash register, and clean up counters and tables after customers leave.

While maintaining their work efficiency, bartenders often socialize with customers. They listen to customers and make them feel welcome. Bartenders may be responsible for determining when a customer has had too much to drink, and may refuse to serve an inebriated customer any additional alcohol. A bartender may also see that an inebriated customer does not drive and call a cab for the customer if the person is alone. By law, bartenders are required not to serve alcohol to persons under 21 year of age. Bartenders who serve alcoholic drinks directly to customers are responsible for determining that customers are of legal drinking age. To determine this, bartenders will ask customers to show a valid drivers license.

Bartenders arrange bottles and glasses in an attractive display and often wash glassware at the bar. They may prepare appetizers, such as pickles, cheese, and cold meats, or set out snacks such as pretzels. Bartenders may also be responsible for ordering and maintaining the inventory of liquor, mixes, and other bar supplies.

Working Conditions

Bartenders may work part-time or full-time. Their work day usually starts in the afternoon and a shift may last 10 to 12 hours. Bartenders busiest hours are late evenings, nights and weekends. Many work holidays. Bartenders often work on a daily, weekly, or monthly rotating shift.

Bartenders work indoors in a relatively safe work environment, although they are exposed to smoke from customer cigarettes. Bartenders spend most of their time standing. During busy times, bartenders schedules can be hectic and stressful.

Employment

According to the U.S. Department of Labor, there were 382,000 bartenders employed in 1992. Bartenders work in bars, restaurants, hotels and other lodging establishments, casinos, resorts, cruise ships, and country clubs. Bartenders are employed throughout the country, but jobs are concentrated in large cities and tourist areas.

Training, Other Qualifications, and Advancement

Bartenders must be at least 21 years of age, the legal drinking age in the United States, but many employers prefer to hire individuals who are at least 25 years old. Employers prefer that bartenders have a high school diploma. Prior to employment, bartenders must be familiar with state and local laws and regulations concerning the sale of alcoholic beverages.

Some bartenders learn their skills through bartending school or a vocational or technical school that offers courses in bartending. These schools often assist graduates with finding jobs. Other bartenders learn on the job by starting as a bartender s helper or as a waiter or waitress.

Bartenders should be friendly and enjoy working with different types of people. They must be well organized and be able to remember how to prepare drinks and customer orders. Bartenders should be good in arithmetic and be able to calculate a customer bill without relying on a cash register.

Job Outlook

According to the U.S. Department of Labor, job opportunities for bartenders are expected to be very good. Jobs in eating and drinking establishments are expected to increase 33 percent through the year 2005. Job turnover is relatively high and most openings will result from the need to replace bartenders who left for another opportunity. Increased leisure time and growing populations will also contribute to job growth.

Earnings

Bartenders obtain their earnings from a combination of hourly wages and customer tips. Those employed in public bars may receive more than half of their earnings from tips.

Earnings for bartenders vary by employer, geographic location, and experience. Tips can vary by the customer, but efficient bartenders usually get higher tips. According to the National Restaurant Association, bartenders earned a median hourly wage of $5.36. According to the U.S. Department of Labor, in 1992 full-time bartenders had median earnings of about $250 per week, including tips. According to *American Salaries & Wages Survey*, in 1994, average hourly wages for bartenders varied from $4.25 to $9.43. Bartenders in Los Angles, CA, however, averaged $35,000 per year.

Related Occupations

Other occupations similar to bartenders include waiters, waitresses, flight attendants, hosts, hostesses, counter attendants, and fast-food workers.

Sources of Additional Information

For more information on a career as a bartender, contact:

- The Educational Foundation of the National Restaurant Association, 250 S. Wacker Dr., Ste. 1400, Chicago, IL 60606.

BREWMASTERS

At A Glance

- **D.O.T.:** 183.167-010

- **Preferred Education:** 4 to 10 years of experience.

- **Average Salary:** $25,000 and above

- **Did You Know?** Many brewmasters have knowledge in a relevant science such as microbiology, biology, or chemistry.

Nature of the Work

There are nearly 500 commercial breweries located in the United States. Fewer than 20 of them account for 99 percent of U.S. beer production. The other 480 or so are part of what is known as the craft brewing industry, which includes regional specialty breweries, microbreweries, and brewpubs.

All of these breweries employ brewmasters to oversee beer production and ensure the quality of the beer that is produced. The brewing process begins when malted barley or other grains are mashed in large kettles to convert malt starches into sugar. Mashing creates a sweet barley juice called wort that is brought to a boil. Hops are added according to a recipe to add bitterness and flavor. Fruit and spices may also be added. Brewmasters are responsible for creating and executing recipes calling for specific amounts of hops and other ingredients.

The brew mixture is allowed to boil for a few hours after the hops have been added, then it is transferred to a whirlpool tank for clarification. The hops solids and wort protein are separated from the brew, which is allowed to cool. After cooling it is transferred to a fermentation tank where yeast is added. Brewmasters are careful to use only clean yeast that does not have any bacteria. They may supervise laboratory personnel to ensure that no bacteria are present. The yeast and brew are sealed in an airtight tank and allowed to ferment.

Brewmasters may oversee the production of several different brews at a time. The fermentation process is typically a two-week cycle, followed by cold maturation that may take from ten days to three months. After yeast solids are removed for use in other batches of brew, the beer is filtered and put in kegs or bottles.

In the largest commercial breweries, brewmasters may be responsible for production scheduling, staffing, equipment, quality control, and inventory control. They monitor beer standards by testing and inspecting the raw materials that go into brewing beer as well as the finished product and the equipment that is used. They may develop new products and experiment with formulas and brewing techniques.

Brewmasters in small and medium-sized breweries have similar duties but supervise fewer employees. In the smallest craft breweries, they are likely to be directly involved in beer production. In medium-sized craft breweries brewmasters may be in charge of all plant operations. They may direct and supervise brewery workers who perform the tasks associated with brewing beer. They are familiar with all of the equipment in the plant and are able to assist workers when there is a breakdown or questions arise. In addition to overseeing the brewing process, brewmasters may also oversee the bottling and shipping operations of craft breweries.

Working Conditions

Brewmasters divide their time between working in the plant and in their office. Their work is not physically demanding, but it can be stressful. Brewmasters spend a lot of time interacting with other employees. In some cases they may act as liaisons between brewery workers and higher level executives. They often have to deal with people under pressure from production schedules and deadlines.

Brewmasters often have to work more than 40 hours per week. They may be required to work in shifts if the brewery is on a 24-hour production cycle. They may be called on at any time to handle emergencies that may arise at the brewery.

Employees of craft breweries are generally not unionized. Brewmasters may belong to professional organizations such as the Association of Brewers or the Master Brewers Association of the Americas.

Employment

Brewmasters are employed at large commercial breweries and at smaller craft breweries such as regional specialty breweries, microbreweries, and brewpubs. There were nearly 500 commercial breweries in the United States by the end of 1994, according to the Beer Institute. Fewer than 20 are major breweries. The rest are part of the craft brewing industry, which is spread throughout the United States.

Training, Other Qualifications, and Advancement

While there are no specific educational or experience requirements for brewmasters, they may spend anywhere from four to ten years perfecting their knowledge of the brewing process. Many breweries look for college graduates with a background in a relevant science such as microbiology, biology, or chemistry. Others may hire people with experience working in breweries.

There are two major schools that have programs in brewing technology. One is the Siebel Institute of Technology located in Chicago, Illinois. It offers a 10-week program that leads to a diploma in brewing technology. Students are typically experienced brewers with strong backgrounds in math and science. Among the courses offered are sensory evaluation of beer, quality control, and brewing microbiology. The other program is offered by the University of California at Davis, which is the only university to offer a brewing studies course leading to an academic degree. The American Brewers Guild offers a two-week apprenticeship program in microbrewing.

Brewmasters are industrial production managers who are good at speaking and writing effectively. They are able to deal tactfully with workers as well as executives. It is helpful to be detail oriented and to have exacting standards. Well developed mathematics and reasoning skills are also required.

Brewmasters can advance by working for larger breweries. Brewmasters in the craft brewing industry can advance by developing a reputation for quality brewing. They may be given additional responsibilities as their brewery expands its operations. They may also become involved in industry associations and activities to improve their professional standing. Some brewmasters may decide to start their own breweries.

Job Outlook

According to the Beer Institute, the craft brewing industry is the fastest growing segment of the commercial brewing industry. Fewer positions are expected to be available at large commercial breweries as they flatten their management structures. Within smaller operations, candidates with training and experience will have the best prospects.

Earnings

According to the *Occupational Outlook Quarterly*, the average annual salary for brewmasters can range from $25,000 in brewpubs to more than $250,000 in a major commercial brewery. Brewmasters generally receive a standard benefits package that includes health and medical insurance, paid vacations, and pension plans. In smaller operations they may be offered a percentage of sales as part of their compensation package.

Related Occupations

Other managerial occupations in manufacturing and processing include general supervisors, production managers, and branch managers in any industry, food processing plant managers, wine makers, quality control managers, customer services managers, railroad car construction superintendents, logging superintendents, and concrete mixing plant superintendents.

Sources of Additional Information

- Association of Brewers, PO Box 1679, Boulder, CO 80306-1679. Phone: (303)447-0816.

- Beer Institute, 1225 Eye St. NW, Ste. 825, Washington, DC 20005. Phone: (202)737-BEER.

- Brewers Association of America, PO Box 876, Belmar, NJ 07719-0876. Phone: (908)280-9153.

- Master Brewers Association of the Americas, 2421 N. Mayfair Rd., No. 310, Waukatusa, WI 53226-1403 Phone: (608)231-3446.

- Siebel Institute of Technology, 4055 W. Peterson Ave., Chicago, IL 60646. Phone: (312)463-3400.

CATERERS

At a Glance

- **D.O.T.:** 187.167-106

- **Preferred Education:** On-the-job training

- **Average Salary:** Varies

- **Did You Know?** Work experience in restaurants and hotels, especially as a cook, can be helpful in obtaining employment as a caterer or starting a catering business.

Nature of the Work

Wedding receptions, awards banquets, luncheon meetings, and dinner parties are some of the special events that require the services of caterers. Their job is to prepare and present food for large groups of people. Catering businesses range from single-person operations to million-dollar companies that prepare regular meals for schools or businesses or cater meals for hundreds of special events per year.

When catering special events, caterers meet with their clients to discuss the details of the event, including a budget. Together the client and caterer discuss such matters as food choice and whether the meal will be served or presented in a buffet. They may decide upon specific decorative items such as flower arrangements or table settings. During the planning stages, caterers and clients are in frequent contact by telephone or in person to finalize the necessary details.

Once a price and menu have been decided upon, caterers determine what food and supplies will be needed for the event.

They may obtain food from grocery stores or wholesale food suppliers. They may provide the table settings, including dishes, glasses, silverware, and table linens, all of which may be rented if the caterer does not own them. They make arrangements to obtain flowers and other decorations for the event. If the event is to be held outdoors, they may rent or buy a tent or canopy.

Caterers may prepare the food in their own homes or kitchens or at the site of the event. Whenever possible the food is prepared ahead of time. If the event is a large banquet or reception held in a hotel or a rented hall with kitchen facilities, they usually prepare the food there. In the case of formal dinner parties held at a client's home, a caterer might prepare some of the food in the client's kitchen. Caterers typically visit the site several times in advance of a special event to plan precisely how the food will be prepared and served.

Depending on the size of the event, caterers usually have to supervise other workers including kitchen assistants and servers. They typically hire assistants or have staff members help prepare and serve the food. They may hire other assistants to transport the food, decorations, and other supplies to the event.

In addition to food preparation, caterers have business responsibilities. To attract new clients, caterers must market their services in a variety of ways. They may advertise locally in newspapers and magazines or obtain leads from other businesses such as florists, bakers, and rental companies. They may also be able to leave menus, samples of their food, or business cards in gourmet shops, specialty stores, and selected restaurants where their clientele is likely to shop and eat. Contacting organizations that are likely to hold special events is another way of obtaining leads.

In addition to marketing their services, single-person operations, known as home caterers, and owners of small catering companies may have financial responsibilities such as monitoring budgets and ordering supplies. In larger companies, these functions may be given to separate departments.

Working Conditions

The work of caterers can be physically demanding. They frequently have to lift up to 10 pounds and are often on their feet for long periods of time. Most of the special events they cater take place in the evening or on weekends. Holidays are the busiest time for caterers. Their hours can be long as well as irregular.

Like others involved in service industries, caterers work under pressure to please their customers and clients. Caterers generally work under pressure to make sure food is prepared in a timely fashion.

Caterers work in a variety of locations. They may do some of their work in their own kitchens, but they also frequently work in other facilities as dictated by each event. Caterers who work outdoors may be exposed occasionally to extremes of weather. Their work involves frequent reaching and handling, and they spend a lot of time talking and listening to others.

Employment

Catering is a good occupation for people who like to be self-employed. They can be home caterers, mobile caterers, or owners of small catering companies. Mobile caterers use trucks or vans to sell prepared food at busy outdoor locations. Some caterers provide food through vending machines. For those who prefer working for an established firm, there are many large catering companies that prepare and serve meals on a regular basis in institutional settings such as schools or businesses. Even meals that are served on airplanes are usually prepared by professional caterers.

Training, Other Qualifications, and Advancement

Caterers usually have two to four years of specific vocational preparation that can be learned on the job. Most catering companies provide training. Work experience in restaurants and hotels, especially as a cook or in the kitchen, can be helpful in obtaining employment as a caterer or starting one's own catering business.

Although college is not required, caterers can study food service and preparation in culinary schools and community colleges. These programs prepare students for careers in food service through a combination of classroom and kitchen training. Similar classes and programs are also offered at two- and four-year colleges. Many universities offer degree programs in home economics and restaurant management. Courses in small business management can be helpful in starting a catering business.

Regulation and licensing of caterers varies from state to state and city to city. Depending on their location, caterers may have to obtain state or local food service licenses. Catering companies usually need a business license as well, and some places may require employees to be licensed or registered. Additional licenses are needed if alcoholic beverages are served.

Caterers combine their creativity in preparing and serving food with the management skills necessary to provide a business service. In addition to being good cooks, they must have good communication skills. They must be polite and efficient and able to speak persuasively to clients, suppliers, and employees. A neat, clean appearance is also important.

Caterers must be well organized and able to make decisions on the spot. They must be able to plan and manage complex events. They have to be able to handle emergencies and unexpected situations. They should know how to run a business and be familiar with basic concepts of marketing, accounting, and mathematics.

Independent caterers can develop their business by expanding their client base and increasing the size of their operation. They may branch out into the gourmet food store business or open a restaurant. Within large catering firms there are opportunities for employees to advance to management-level positions.

Job Outlook

While the Bureau of Labor Statistics does not make projections specifically for caterers, employment of food service and lodging managers is expected to increase by 43.5 percent between 1992 and 2005, much faster than the average for all occupations.

Other factors indicate a strong demand for the services of caterers. Employment opportunities in large catering firms will grow as a result of the continued demand for food services by institutions such as hospitals and colleges as well as by business and industry. A growing number of special business events for employees and clients will require more caterers. Greater affluence combined with longer working hours suggest that more independent caterers will be needed to meet the demand for special event catering ranging from wedding receptions to formal dinner parties.

Competition among caterers is expected to remain keen, especially as more highly qualified individuals open their own catering businesses. In addition many restaurants are adding catering services. In general the demand for catering of special events tends to reflect the overall economy and has similar ups and downs.

Earnings

Earnings of caterers vary widely and depend on such factors as size of the catering firm and whether caterers are self-employed or employees. According to *American Salaries and Wages Survey*, starting salaries for food service managers, including caterers, ranged from about $8,500 to $19,000 annually in 1991-92. With some experience they earned between $10,000 and $23,500. High-end salaries for food service managers were over $40,000 annually.

Related Occupations

Related food and beverage preparation occupations include chefs, cooks, bakers, and kitchen workers. Occupations involving food and beverage service include waiters and waitresses, bartenders, hosts and hostesses, dining room attendants, counter attendants, and fast-food workers. Related business management occupations include food and beverage directors, dietary managers, flight kitchen managers, food services directors, and managers of other types of businesses.

Sources of Additional Information

For additional information contact:

- International Food Service Executives Association, 1100 S. State Rd. 7, Ste. 103, Margate, FL 33068. Phone: (305)977-0767.

- Mobile Industrial Caterers Association, 1240 N. Jefferson St., Ste. G, Anaheim, CA 92807 Phone: (714)632-6800.

- National Association for the Specialty Food Trade, 8 W. 40th St., New York, NY 10018. Phone: (212)921-1690.

- National Association of Catering Executives, 60 Revere Dr., Ste. 500, Northbrook, IL. 60062 Phone: (708)480-9080.

Health Service Occupations

AMBULANCE DRIVERS AND ATTENDANTS

At a Glance

- **D.O.T.:** 913.683-010 and 355.374-010

- **Preferred Education:** On-the-job training

- **Average Salary:** $5 to $10 per hour

- **Did You Know?** Ambulance drivers and attendants can advance by attaining the education necessary to become emergency medical technicians.

Nature of the Work

Ambulance drivers and attendants transport sick, injured or convalescent people to hospitals or nursing homes. Along with emergency medical technicians (EMTs), they are often the first people to arrive at the scene of an accident or other emergency.

Ambulance drivers use their driving skills and knowledge to reach an emergency quickly and safely. Once at the scene of an emergency, they place patients on stretchers and carry them into the ambulance. They may have to administer first aid if necessary or restrain violent patients. They may be required to report facts related to the emergency to law enforcement officials or hospital personnel.

Ambulance attendants generally assist ambulance drivers on calls by helping to lift patients onto stretchers, administering oxygen, and providing other first aid such as bandaging and splinting.

Working Conditions

Like emergency medical technicians, ambulance drivers and attendants are on call to assist in emergencies, which may happen at any time of the day or night. Their work takes them to a variety of locations, and they frequently perform their duties outdoors in various weather conditions. Their work is physically demanding and requires that they be able to lift and carry patients on stretchers, with the help of others. In addition, working in emergency situations is stressful.

Employment

According to the Bureau of Labor Statistics, there were 15,000 ambulance drivers and attendants employed in 1992, not including emergency medical technicians. A high percentage of these people worked part-time. There are also many volunteers working in this capacity. Emergency medical services are provided by hospitals, police and fire departments, and private ambulance companies.

Training, Other Qualifications, and Advancement

Unlike emergency medical technicians, who must meet formal training requirements, ambulance drivers and attendants generally learn their skills on the job. Ambulance drivers are usually at least 18 years old, have a valid driver's license and a good driving record. They may also be required to be certified by the American Red Cross in first aid and CPR.

People interested in becoming ambulance drivers or attendants should have an interest in caring for other people. They must be able to follow oral and written instructions and respond quickly to directions. They must also be in good physical condition.

Ambulance drivers and attendants can advance by attaining the education necessary to become emergency medical technicians. (Consult the *Occupational Outlook Handbook* for more information on emergency medical technicians.)

Job Outlook

The number of jobs for ambulance drivers and attendants is expected to increase to 18,000 by 2005, which is about as fast as the average for all occupations. Employment of emergency medical technicians, however, is expected to increase faster than average in response to a growing population and large number of older Americans. According to the Bureau of Labor Statistics, job openings will result primarily from the need to replace workers who leave the occupation. High employee turnover is largely due to the stressful working conditions.

Earnings

According to *American Salaries and Wages Survey*,

ambulance drivers and attendants earned wages ranging from $5 to $10 per hour, or $10,400 to $20,800 annually, in 1993-94. The average starting salary for people with EMT-Ambulance or Basic training was $20,092 in 1993, according to the *Journal of Emergency Medical Services*. Earnings for ambulance drivers and attendants vary depending on their employer, geographic location, and experience. Those employed by emergency medical services that are part of police and fire departments typically earn more than those employed by hospitals and private ambulance services. In rural locations, positions for ambulance drivers and attendants may be filled by volunteers.

Related Occupations

Related occupations concerned with patient care include first-aid attendants, physical therapy aides, birth attendants, emergency medical technicians, dental assistants, nurse assistants, and certified medical technicians. Other occupations that involve driving include bus drivers, car rental deliverers, taxi drivers, tow truck operators, funeral car chauffeurs, and health-equipment servicers. Firefighters and police officers are additional occupations that involve responding in emergency situations.

Sources of Additional Information

For information on training and requirements for EMTs, as well as ambulance drivers and attendants, write to the Emergency Medical Services Director in the appropriate state. For information on EMTs, contact:

- National Association of Emergency Medical Technicians, 102 W. Leake St., Clinton, MS 39056. Phone: (601)924-7744.

For information on the emergency medical services industry, contact:

- American Ambulance Association, 3800 Auburn Blvd., Ste. B, Sacramento, CA 95821. Phone: (916)483-3827.

GERIATRIC AIDES

At a Glance

- **D.O.T.:** 355.674-014
- **Preferred Education:** On-the-job training
- **Average Salary:** $10,400 to $13,200
- **Did You Know?** Geriatric aides are often the principal caregivers to nursing home residents.

Nature of the Work

Geriatric aides are health care workers who provide direct patient care to elderly people in nursing homes and similar facilities. They work under the supervision of licensed nurses or other members of the medical staff. Also called nursing home assistants or geriatric nurse assistants, they have duties similar to those of nurse aides and assistants who work with the general population.

Geriatric aides are often the principal caregivers to nursing home residents. They have more contact with patients than the rest of the staff. They often develop special relationships with their patients, who may remain nursing home residents for months and even years.

Geriatric aides respond when their patients need assistance, which may be at any time of the day or night. They serve food and feed patients who need assistance. They change bed linens, empty bed pans if necessary, and turn and reposition patients who must remain in bed most of the time. They may also bathe, dress, and undress their patients.

When patients need to leave their room, geriatric aides may transport them using wheelchairs. They may help patients walk. They may dress patients for examinations and treatments, remaining with them during examinations to hold instruments and adjust lights. Aides may be directed to take and record patients' temperatures, blood pressure, pulse, and respiration rates as well as food and fluid intake. They observe patients' mental, physical, and emotional condition and report any changes to the nursing or medical staff.

Working Conditions

Geriatric aides work under relatively quiet conditions in clean, well-lighted health care facilities such as nursing homes, residential care facilities, and other places with elderly patients. Their work requires moderate physical strength, with frequent lifting of weights up to 25 pounds and occasionally as much as 50 pounds. Geriatric aides frequently have to help people out of bed or assist them in walking and are subject to back strain when performing these duties.

Geriatric aides often have to perform unpleasant duties, such as emptying bedpans, changing soiled linen, and dealing with disoriented or irritable patients. Geriatric aides and others involved in direct patient care in nursing and personal care facilities have a higher rate of occupational injury than comparable workers in hospitals or the private sector. In addition to back strain, they must guard against exposure to radiation and caustic chemicals and infectious diseases such as AIDS and hepatitis.

It is normal for geriatric aides to work evenings, nights, weekends, and holidays. According to the Bureau of Labor Statistics, nonsupervisory workers in nursing and personal care facilities, including geriatric aides, worked an average of 32.2 hours per week in 1993. Many are on part-time schedules.

Employment

According to the Bureau of Labor Statistics, there were approximately 1,308,000 nursing aides employed in 1992. Approximately half of them, or 659,000, were geriatric aides working in nursing homes. In addition to working in private nursing homes, geriatric aides also are employed in nursing homes operated by the U.S. Department of Veterans Affairs. Other employers of geriatric aides include retirement communities, senior centers, hospitals, and residential care facilities.

Training, Other Qualifications, and Advancement

Not all employers require geriatric aides to have a high school diploma or previous experience. Geriatric aides can acquire the necessary training at their place of employment in three to six months. Those who work in certified nursing facilities may be required to complete 75 hours of mandatory training and pass a competency evaluation program within the first four months of employment. After completing the program, aides are placed on their state's registry of nursing aides. To maintain their standing they must complete at least 12 hours of in-service education every year.

Some states require geriatric aides or nursing home assistants to become certified. Requirements typically include completing an approved training program and passing a competency examination. Geriatric aides generally receive training similar to that given to nursing aides, with an emphasis on care of the elderly. Individuals who wish to obtain training prior to employment may do so in high school, vocational school, and community college. Relevant courses include body mechanics, nutrition, anatomy and physiology, infection control, communication skills, and hygiene skills.

Geriatric aides are individuals with a genuine interest in helping others with their physical and health concerns. They must use common sense and their special skills to attend to the needs of their patients. They must be able to follow oral and written instructions. They must be flexible enough to adapt to changes in job duties and emergency situations. Other qualities that are important for geriatric aides include being healthy, tactful, patient, understanding, emotionally stable, and dependable.

Geriatric aides may have difficulty advancing without additional education. Their position is an entry-level one that often provides individuals with their first work experience. Larger facilities provide the best opportunities for promotion and advancement. Additional experience and education are usually required to advance within the health care field.

Job Outlook

According to the Bureau of Labor Statistics, employment of nursing aides including geriatric aides is projected to increase much faster than the average for all occupations. The 1,308,000 nursing aides employed in 1992 are expected to increase to 1,903,000 by 2005, an increase of more than 45 percent.

Several factors support the growth in employment of nursing aides and geriatric aides. The segment of the United States population age 85 and older is the fastest growing age group. Advances in medical technology serve to prolong life and increase the need for extended care. Nursing and personal care facilities will increase in number, providing new employment opportunities for geriatric aides. In addition, many opportunities will occur as a result of the need to replace workers who leave this occupation.

Earnings

Median annual earnings for geriatric aides working in chain nursing homes was $11,600 in 1992-93, according to a survey conducted by the American Health Care Association. Half of them earned between $10,400 and $13,200 a year. Some nursing homes provide benefits, including paid vacations and sick leave, medical insurance, and pension plans.

The Bureau of Labor Statistics reports that nonsupervisory workers in nursing and personal care facilities, including geriatric aides, earned an average of $262 per week in 1993, based on average hourly earnings of $8.15 and working an average of 32.2 hours per week, or approximately $13,600 annually.

Related Occupations

Related occupations involving patient care include nursing aides, psychiatric aides, home health aides, childcare attendants, occupational therapy aides and assistants, and physical therapy aides and assistants. Social service occupations that provide an opportunity to work with older people include home-delivered meal workers, information and referral clerks, janitors and cleaners, outreach coordinators, senior center van drivers, and volunteer coordinators.

Sources of Additional Information

- American Health Care Association, 1201 L St. NW, Washington, DC 20005. Phone: (202)842-4444.

- American Nursing Assistant's Association, PO Box 2734, Fort Riley, KS 66442-0734.

HEARING AID SPECIALISTS

At a Glance

- **D.O.T.:** 276.354-010

- **Preferred Education:** 1 to 2 years of training

- **Average Salary:** Varies

- **Did You Know?** According to the International Hearing Society, there were approximately 26 million hearing impaired people in 1994, and only six million of them had hearing aids.

Nature of the Work

Technological advances in quality and design have revitalized the hearing aid industry. Hearing aids can now be matched to the wearer's skin tone or inserted out of sight in the wearer's ear canal. They can even be programmed for different listening environments.

Hearing aid specialists are trained individuals who fit and dispense hearing aids, much the same way that opticians fit and dispense eyeglasses. Their services are available in retail outlets as well as in specialized hearing loss clinics and hearing aid stores.

Hearing aid specialists are not the same as audiologists, who test for hearing loss, make diagnoses, and recommend courses of treatment. Audiologists who also fit and dispense hearing aids are known as dispensing audiologists. Hearing aid specialists, on the other hand, may test for hearing loss and provide hearing aid devices to correct the problem. However, they are generally required by law to recommend that their patients undergo a medical examination by a physician, audiologist, or other ear specialist. They may not sell a hearing aid device to someone who has not been examined by a physician, audiologist, or other ear specialist without a waiver signed by the customer.

Hearing aid specialists use specialized testing equipment to test the hearing levels of their customers, following standardized evaluation procedures. They interpret and evaluate the hearing test results. They confer with their customers to select an appropriate hearing aid. Customers may be hearing impaired individuals who have come on their own, or they may have been referred by physicians or other ear specialists.

Hearing aid specialists take measurements to fit hearing aids for each customer, adapting and modifying them as necessary. They may make impressions of a client's ear for use in fitting. They may send the fitting data to a hearing aid manufacturer who will supply the hearing aid device. Once the hearing aid device has been received from the manufacturer, hearing aid specialists may adjust and modify it as needed.

Other duties performed by hearing aid specialists may include repairing hearing aid devices. If their clients are confined to their homes, hearing aid specialists may visit them at home to conduct hearing tests.

Working Conditions

Hearing aid specialists generally work in clean, well-lighted stores. Their work is not physically demanding and is carried on under relatively quiet conditions. They may spend a lot of time on their feet, and they frequently interact with their customers. They usually work standard 40-hour work weeks.

Employment

According to the International Hearing Society, there were approximately 12,000 hearing aid specialists and dispensing audiologists employed in 1994. Many hearing aid specialists are sole proprietors and own their own businesses. Others have purchased franchises, such as Beltone or Miracle Ear. Hearing aid specialists may also work for other hearing aid dealers and dispensers.

Training, Other Qualifications, and Advancement

Hearing aid specialists generally have one to two years of training. They may learn by apprenticing with an experienced hearing aid specialist, or they may take correspondence courses that are available from the International Hearing Society and other organizations.

Most states require that hearing aid specialists be licensed or registered. While requirements vary from state to state, typical licensing requirements include passing a licensing examination to demonstrate competence to fit and dispense hearing aids.

Hearing aid specialists are individuals with a knack for salesmanship. They must have good communication skills to interact with their customers. They need well developed reasoning abilities to rationally solve practical problems in situations where there is only limited standardization.

Hearing aid specialists can advance by becoming more competent and opening their own business. With additional education, they may decide to become audiologists.

Job Outlook

According to the International Hearing Society, there were approximately 26 million hearing impaired people in 1994, and only six million of them had hearing aids. Older Americans represent the fastest growing population segment and are the most likely to suffer hearing loss. In addition, many middle-aged "baby boomers" are experiencing early hearing loss due to overexposure to loud music and other noisy conditions in their youth.

Recent technological advances in hearing aids should also result in a growing demand for the services of hearing aid specialists. More people are likely to accept hearing aids, once they discover how easily they can be fitted and worn. The success of hearing aid franchises and the subsequent growth in hearing aid advertising should also stimulate demand among people who are hearing impaired.

Earnings

There is limited data regarding the earnings of hearing aid specialists. Earnings depend a great deal on the employment setting. Hearing aid specialists may be paid a salary or work strictly on commission, or they may be paid a combination of salary and commission. According to *American Salaries and Wages Survey*, hearing aid specialists in the West earned an average of $6 per hour in 1993. Specialists who own their own businesses can earn considerably higher salaries.

Related Occupations

There are many related occupations in retail sales. Other occupations using similar skills include manufacturers' and wholesale trade sales workers, service sales representatives, counter and rental clerks, real estate sales agents, wholesale and retail buyers, and insurance sales workers.

Sources of Additional Information

- Academy of Dispensing Audiologists, 3008 Millwood Ave., Columbia, SC 29205. Phone: (803)252-5646.

- Hearing Industries Association, 515 King St., Ste. 320, Alexandria, VA 22314. Phone: (703)684-5744.

- International Hearing Society, 20361 Middlebelt Rd., Livonia, MI 48152. Phone: (810)478-2610.

OCCUPATIONAL THERAPY ASSISTANTS AND AIDES

At a Glance

- **D.O.T.:** 076.364-010 and 355.377.010

- **Preferred Education:** Certificate or associate degree

- **Average Salary:** $20,954

- **Did You Know?** Persons interested in becoming occupational therapy assistants can receive the necessary education through a two-year associate degree program or a one-year certificate program.

Nature of the Work

Most people never consider the many skills they need to live independent, productive lives. Once learned, simple tasks such as eating, dressing, and washing become second nature. But people who have suffered emotional or physical traumas often need to relearn these basic skills. Occupational therapy assistants and aides help treat these patients.

Occupational therapy assistants and aides work under the direction of occupational therapists. While occupational therapy assistants help administer treatment programs and work directly with patients, occupational therapy aides perform support services, such as maintaining supplies and equipment.

Occupational therapy assistants help occupational therapists evaluate patients and help determine the extent of their abilities and limitations. These patients may have physical or emotional disabilities. Others may be mentally impaired. Occupational therapy assistants help occupational therapists design specific programs for each individual patient based on the patient's needs. For example, one patient may need to relearn job skills after suffering a serious injury. Another patient may have trouble coping with the demands of daily life after suffering an emotional crisis.

Occupational therapy assistants use a variety of educational and recreational programs to help patients. They often involve physical and social activities. They also teach patients through creative activities such as arts and crafts. Sometimes, occupational therapy assistants teach these skills to patients in groups. Other times, they teach patients in individual sessions.

Occupational therapy assistants teach patients and their families how to use therapy equipment such as splints and braces. They also participate in evaluating patients and report information to their supervisors. Occupational therapy assistants may be responsible for maintaining patient records and preparing reports. They also may help prepare work materials, maintain equipment, and order supplies.

Occupational therapy aids support occupational therapists by transporting patients, assembling equipment, and preparing and maintaining work areas. They do not provide direct care to patients, but may help occupational therapists and assistants demonstrate therapy activities.

Working Conditions

The working conditions of occupational therapy assistants and aides vary depending upon their patients' needs. They generally work indoors in specially-designed therapy rooms, but may work outside during certain recreational activities. While physical demands are generally light, occupational therapy assistants and aides may be required to help move patients from wheelchairs or beds. A high percentage of occupational therapy assistants and aides work part time.

Employment

According to the Bureau of Labor Statistics, there were 12,000 occupational therapy assistants and aides employed in 1992. Many are employed by hospitals, while others work for nursing homes, clinics, rehabilitation facilities, long-term care facilities, extended care facilities, sheltered workshops, schools, camps, and community agencies.

Training, Other Qualifications, and Advancement

People interested in becoming occupational therapy assistants can receive the necessary education through a two-year associate degree program or a one-year certificate program. These programs are offered by colleges and universities, medical schools, and technical and vocational schools. A high school diploma or equivalent is required for admission into an occupational therapy assistant program. Courses include occupational therapy principles and practice skills, the occupational therapy process, treatment planning, and management services. Students also receive supervised field work experience.

Following the completion of all educational requirements, individuals take a national certification exam administered by the American Occupational Therapy Association. Many states also regulate the practice of occupational therapy and require occupational therapy assistants to obtain a state-approved license. Occupational therapy assistants can become occupational therapists by gaining four years of experience and passing a certification exam or by completing the additional two years of a bachelor's degree program.

Job Outlook

Job opportunities for occupational therapy assistants and aides will grow much faster than average through the year 2005. The Bureau of Labor Statistics estimates the need for 21,000 occupational therapy assistants and aides by 2005, up from 12,000 in 1992.

Earnings

According to a recent survey by the American Occupational Therapy Association, the average salary for occupational therapy assistants is $20,954. According to *American Salaries and Wages Survey,* the average wage offered to occupational therapy assistants and aides in the Midwest ranged from $6 to $14 per hour in 1992.

Related Occupations

Occupational therapy assistants treat and rehabilitate persons with mental or physical disabilities or disorders. Similar occupations include music, dance, art, exercise, and recreation therapists. Occupations similar to occupational therapy aide include physical therapy aide, ambulance attendant, certified medication technician, psychiatric aide, and mental-retardation aide.

Sources of Additional Information

* American Occupational Therapy Association, 4720 Montgomery Ln., PO Box 31220, Bethesda, MD 20824-1220. Phone: (310)652-2682.

* American Occupational Therapy Certification Board, 4 Research Pl., Ste. 160, Rockville, MD 20850-3226. Phone: (310)990-7979.

OPHTHALMIC MEDICAL ASSISTANTS

At a Glance

- **D.O.T.:** 078.361-038

- **Preferred Education:** Certificate program or associate degree

- **Average Salary:** $15,000 to $18,000

- **Did You Know?** As of 1994, there were 15,000 certified ophthalmic medical assistants, technicians, and technologists employed in the United States.

Nature of the Work

Ophthalmic medical assistants, including technicians and technologists, are medical support personnel. They work under the direction of an ophthalmologist, a doctor of medicine or osteopathy (M.D. or D.O.) who specializes in eye and vision care. They provide assistance by collecting data, helping with the management of patients, and administering tests or supervising treatment ordered by the ophthalmologist.

Ophthalmic medical assistants use precision instruments to administer diagnostic tests covering such areas as visual acuity, color vision, and lensometry. They measure and record a patient's vision and test the functioning of eyes and eye

muscles. As they become more experienced and skilled, ophthalmic medical assistants are able to perform more advanced tests. They may even take over part of the ophthalmologist's workload. However, they are not independent practitioners, and they do not generate medical or surgical diagnoses or prescriptions for patients.

Ophthalmic medical assistants may be designated as ophthalmic surgical assistants and provide pre-operative preparation of the patient. They are responsible for identifying, selecting, and maintaining ophthalmic surgical instruments. They may sterilize and set up instruments for ophthalmic surgical procedures and assist the ophthalmic surgeon in an office or hospital operating room.

Other duties of ophthalmic medical assistants include taking patient histories and providing other basic patient services. They may show patients how to use eye dressings, protective shields, and safety glasses. They may assist in the fitting of contact lenses and show the patient how to insert, remove, and care for them.

Ophthalmic medical assistants may administer topical medications, including eye drops, ointments, and irrigating solutions, under the direction of an ophthalmologist. Such medications may be used to anesthetize, dilate, or medicate the patient's eyes.

Working Conditions

Like other medical assistants, ophthalmic medical assistants work in a clean, well-lighted environment typical of a medical office. They generally work a 40-hour week, including some evenings and weekends. They work closely with their supervising ophthalmologist, who is ultimately responsible for their performance. They frequently interact with others and handle varied tasks throughout the day.

Employment

Ophthalmic medical assistants work for ophthalmologists in private practice or in a hospital setting. As of 1994, there were 15,000 certified ophthalmic medical assistants, technicians, and technologists employed in the United States. In addition, there are approximately 10,000 to 15,000 noncertified individuals employed as ophthalmic medical assistants, according to estimates of the American Academy of Ophthalmology.

Training, Other Qualifications, and Advancement

Some ophthalmic medical assistants may obtain employment with a practicing ophthalmologist and receive their training on the job. Other assistants complete a one-year certificate program, while ophthalmic technicians complete a two-year associate degree program. Ophthalmic technologists have the most education and generally obtain a four-year degree.

A high school diploma or equivalent is usually required to enter a formal training program or gain employment with a practicing ophthalmologist who will provide on-the-job training. A background in math and science is helpful. Formal training programs and self-study programs are subject to accreditation by the Commission on Accreditation of Allied Health Education Programs (CAAHEP) or approval by the Joint Review Committee for Ophthalmic Medical Personnel (JRCOMP). Such programs may be taken at a variety of colleges, universities, and specialized institutes throughout the United States and Canada. Canadian programs are accredited by the Canadian Medical Association.

While a high school diploma or equivalent may be sufficient to gain entry into a basic program, more advanced programs may require some college level coursework in anatomy, physiology, chemistry, psychology, and math. Physics, microbiology, and law and ethics are other advanced subjects that candidates may need to study.

The Joint Commission on Allied Health Personnel in Ophthalmology (JCAHPO) offers three levels of certification for ophthalmic medical assistants: assistant, technician, and technologist. Candidates for certification must have a high school diploma or equivalent, must have completed an approved program for ophthalmic medical assistants within the past three years, and must have at least one year of full-time work experience under the supervision of an ophthalmologist.

Certification candidates may substitute completion of an approved home-study course for the educational requirement. In addition, candidates must possess nationally recognized certification in cardiopulmonary resuscitation (CPR). Assistant-level certification may then be attained by passing a written certification examination covering six major areas: patient history taking, basic skills and lensometry, patient services, basic tonometry, instrument maintenance, and general medical knowledge including CPR, anatomy, physiology, systemic diseases, ocular diseases, ocular emergencies, and microbial control. Higher levels of certification require knowledge of ocular pharmacology, microbiology, and advanced general medical knowledge.

Certified ophthalmic medical assistants are required to complete a certain amount of continuing education every three years for recertification. There are a variety of continuing education opportunities, including taking courses, self-study, teaching, and authorship of scientific publications, oral presentations, or posters.

Ophthalmic medical assistants are genuinely interested in helping others with their physical problems, especially as they relate to the eyes and vision. A pleasant and courteous manner is needed, and they should be able to put patients at ease. They must have good language and communication skills. They should have reasoning skills sufficient to interpret a variety of instructions and deal with concrete variables in situations where only limited standardization exists.

Ophthalmic medical assistants may advance to greater levels of responsibility through experience and study. They may progress in their careers by obtaining professional certification at higher levels.

Job Outlook

Medical assistants, including ophthalmic medical assistants, are in one of the fastest growing occupations, according to the Bureau of Labor Statistics. Employment is projected to increase by nearly 74 percent between 1992 and 2005.

Earnings

The average starting salary for graduates of accredited medical assistant programs was about $15,059 per year in 1992, according to the Committee on Allied Health Education and Accreditation. According to the American Association of Medical Assistants, the average annual salary for medical assistants in 1991 was $18,334. Medical assistants with under two years of experience generally earned less, while those with several years of experience earned higher wages.

Related Occupations

Medical assistants who work for physicians, podiatrists, and chiropractors perform similar duties in different specialties. Other medical support occupations include medical secretaries, hospital admitting clerks, pharmacy helpers, medical record clerks, dental assistants, occupational therapy aides, and physical therapy aides. Other vision-related occupations include optician's assistant, dispensing optician, optometrist, and ophthalmologist.

Sources of Additional Information

- Joint Commission on Allied Health Personnel in Ophthalmology, 2025 Woodlane Dr., St. Paul, MN 55125-2995. Phone: (612)731-2944, (800)284-3937. Fax: (612)731-0410.

- American Association of Medical Assistants, 20 N. Wacker Dr., Ste. 1575, Chicago, IL 60606-2903. Phone: (312)899-1500, (800)228-2262.

PHARMACY ASSISTANTS AND TECHNICIANS

At a Glance

- **D.O.T.:** 074.381-010 and 074.382-010

- **Preferred Education:** 6 months to 2 years

- **Average Salary:** $13,000 to $18,000

- **Did You Know?** There is a trend toward increased educational requirements for pharmacy technicians as their roles expand to provide greater support to licensed pharmacists.

Nature of the Work

Working in the pharmacy departments of hospitals, nursing homes, and other healthcare institutions, pharmacy technicians perform many of the routine and technical tasks associated with drug preparation and distribution, recordkeeping, and supplies. They are also known as pharmacy technologists or pharmacy assistants.

Pharmacy technicians work under the direct supervision of licensed pharmacists. Their work is subject to quality-control checks to ensure accuracy. By delegating more routine and technical tasks to pharmacy technicians, pharmacists are able to devote more of their time to clinical and management duties rather than to preparing and dispensing medication.

One of the major duties of pharmacy technicians is to perform tasks associated with the dispensing and distribution of drugs. They may prepare daily patient medication profiles and fill medication carts with unit doses of each patient's prescribed medication. They may have to repackage and relabel drug products into unit doses. They work with pharmacists to ensure that medication is delivered promptly and on time. In healthcare facilities, they participate in daily deliveries and bring unit-dose carts and other drug supplies to patient-care units. In some cases technicians may also perform quality-assurance functions related to unit-dose carts.

Pharmacy technicians also prepare medications that will be administered intravenously (IV). They prepare specified injectable medications, including prefilled syringes, chemotherapy compounds, and large-volume sterile solutions. They are responsible for labeling IV medications and recording the schedule of IV medications. They may assist in patient preparation for surgery. Other duties may include answering the IV room telephone, screening questions, and preparing IV room products for delivery.

In hospital pharmacies, pharmacy technicians prepare and dispense outpatient prescriptions. They may also assist pharmacists in filling prescriptions by preparing labels, maintaining appropriate records, transcribing patient profiles, and handling the cash or credit transactions.

Pharmacy technicians also perform many of the administrative tasks associated with pharmacy departments. These may include front counter scheduling, which involves processing, scheduling, and pulling doses for new orders. In departments with computerized records, pharmacy technicians enter data to keep each patient's records up-to-date.

Another area of responsibility that is often handled by pharmacy technicians is inventory control and purchasing. They order, price, and stock drugs. They check and replace all out-of-date medication. They check in narcotics and controlled substances and reconcile usage with inventory levels. They charge requisitioned medications and handle inpatient charging.

Other routine and secretarial duties that may be handled by pharmacy technicians include answering the telephone, directing and screening calls, entering daily charges, entering drug and patient information into the computer, monitoring the office printer, and answering requests at the pharmacy window.

Pharmacy technicians may specialize in one area of responsibility, such as drug dispensing and distribution, or they may handle a combination of responsibilities. Since they may be required to fill in for other pharmacy technicians, they

generally must be trained in all aspects of pharmacy technology. The trend is for pharmacy technicians to take on additional duties as licensed pharmacists spend more time providing clinical services to patients.

Working Conditions

Pharmacy technicians generally work in healthcare institutions that are clean and well-lighted. They work under quiet to moderately noisy conditions. They work closely with pharmacists and other pharmacy technicians and frequently interact with other individuals. Some manual dexterity is required for the frequent reaching, handling, and fingering involved in their daily work. They must be able to read labels and other small type at close range and have normal color vision.

Employment

According to the Bureau of Labor Statistics, there were 54,000 pharmacy assistants employed in 1992. A high percentage are employed on a part-time basis. Major employers include hospitals, nursing homes, home health agencies, and other healthcare institutions with pharmacy departments. They may work in community pharmacies and are also employed by pharmaceutical companies.

Training, Other Qualifications, and Advancement

There is a trend toward increased educational requirements for pharmacy technicians as their roles expand to provide greater support to licensed pharmacists. The emphasis has changed from on-the-job training to formal training programs. These programs range from six months to two years and lead to a certificate, diploma, or associate degree in pharmacy technology. They are offered by community colleges, secondary and postsecondary vocational and technical schools, and military schools. Some programs are accredited by the American Society of Hospital Pharmacists.

Pharmacy technician training programs combine classroom instruction with practical experience in community pharmacies and healthcare institutions. Depending on the length of the program, students are instructed in different aspects of pharmacy technology, including laws and ethics, medical terminology, calculations and dosages, and pharmacology. Some programs include additional coursework in anatomy, physiology, therapeutic agents, chemistry, microbiology, and related sciences.

While only a handful of states require pharmacy technicians to be licensed, some states have established voluntary certification programs for pharmacy technicians. Individuals may obtain Pharmacy Technician Certification by passing a competency examination and fulfilling other requirements. Throughout their careers pharmacy technicians are expected to continue their education by attending seminars and other professional programs and reading professional journals.

Among the skills and abilities required of pharmacy technicians are a knowledge and ability to use scientific and technical language and symbols. They must have good hand-eye coordination and manual dexterity to use delicate equipment. Accuracy and careful attention to detail are essential for determining and measuring precise differences in shape, color, quantity, and texture. Pharmacy technicians must also be able to follow technical and sometimes complex instructions.

Some pharmacy departments may have established different levels of competency, providing pharmacy technicians with a definite career ladder. Pharmacy technicians may also be able to advance by transferring to larger institutions. With additional education they may become licensed pharmacists.

Job Outlook

The Bureau of Labor Statistics projects that employment of pharmacy assistants will increase much faster than the average for all occupations. The 54,000 pharmacy assistants employed in 1992 are expected to increase to 76,000 by 2005, an increase of nearly 42 percent. A number of factors will support the increasing employment of pharmacy technicians, including an aging population, an increase in the size and number of healthcare institutions, and the trend for pharmacists to spend more time fulfilling clinical and management responsibilities.

Earnings

According to *American Salaries and Wages Survey*, pharmacy technicians and assistants working in healthcare institutions earned an average starting salary of approximately $13,000 in 1993-94. Their average salary with some experience was about $18,000 per year. Higher-end salaries approached $30,000 per year.

Related Occupations

Other occupations in patient care include ambulance attendants, birth attendants, chiropractor assistants, emergency medical technicians, medical assistants, nurse aides, practical nurses, orderlies, and surgical technicians. Related occupations in laboratory technology include laboratory testers, laboratory assistants, laboratory technicians, and scientific helpers. There are also many shipping, receiving, and stock checking occupations in various industries.

Sources of Additional Information

For additional information contact:

- American Foundation for Pharmaceutical Education, 618 Somerset St., PO Box 7126, N. Plainfield, NJ 07060. Phone: (908)561-8077.

- American Pharmaceutical Association, 2215 Constitution Ave. NW, Washington, DC 20037. Phone: (202)628-4410 or (800)237-APHA.

- American Society of Hospital Pharmacists, 7272 Wisconsin Ave., Bethesda, MD 20814. Phone: (301)657-3000.

PHYSICAL THERAPY ASSISTANTS AND AIDES

At a Glance

- **D.O.T.:** 076.224-010 and 355.354-010

- **Preferred Education:** Associate degree for assistants; 3 to 6 months of training for aides

- **Average Salary:** $24,000 to $28,000 for assistants; $10,000 to $20,000 for aides.

- **Did You Know?** Most states require that physical therapy assistants (not aides) be licensed or registered.

Nature of the Work

People who are born with physical handicaps as well as those suffering from disabilities due to accidents, illnesses, and sports injuries are some of the people who seek the help of physical therapists and their assistants and aides. Physical therapy assistants and aides work under the supervision and direction of licensed physical therapists, providing support in many ways.

Physical therapy assistants play a greater role in patient treatment than aides, who are restricted by law. Physical therapy assistants instruct patients in treatments that may include simple body movements, weight lifting, riding a stationary bike, or exercising on a treadmill to improve physical condition and muscle strength. They may assist patients with therapeutic exercises, give massages, and administer heat, light, sound, water, and electrical modality treatments to relieve pain.

Physical therapy assistants also administer traction to relieve neck and back pain. Following instructions from a physical therapist, they may fit patients with orthopedic braces, prostheses, and other support devices such as crutches, wheelchairs, walkers, and canes. They may record information about patients' body measurements and assess their flexibility and range of motion prior to fitting them with such devices and during treatment.

Physical therapy assistants monitor patients and their progress during therapy. They provide written or oral reports to the physical therapist. Much of their time is spent communicating with others, including therapists, patients, and patients' families. They attend meetings with other members of the health care team to plan, modify, and coordinate treatment programs.

Physical therapy aides, who have less training than assistants, generally perform duties related to treatment sessions. They may be responsible for keeping the treatment area clean and organized and ready for the next patient. They may help patients prepare for their therapy sessions by helping them get dressed and undressed and escorting them to the treatment area. They may help patients put on and remove support devices such as braces, splints, and slings, before and after treatment.

During therapy sessions, aides help patients with their exercises and provide encouragement. They watch how patients are performing their exercises and make sure the exercises are being done correctly. If patients are having difficulty with treatment, aides will notify a physical therapist or assistant. Aides may administer routine treatments such as hydrotherapy, hot and cold packs, and paraffin baths.

Aides may also perform clerical and record-keeping duties such as keeping track of supplies and equipment, ordering replacements, and maintaining patient records. They may also answer telephones and fill out forms.

Working Conditions

Physical therapy assistants and aides must be in reasonably good physical condition. Their work requires frequent stooping, kneeling, and crouching. They must be strong enough to provide patients with physical support. They frequently have to lift or move the equivalent of 10 to 25 pounds, and occasionally 20 to 50 pounds.

Physical therapy assistants and aides usually work with other healthcare professionals in clean, well-lighted settings. Those who work in private clinics may have to work some evenings and weekends.

Employment

Approximately 30 percent of all physical therapy treatment takes place in hospitals. More than half of all physical therapy assistants and aides work in hospitals or private physical therapy offices. In addition, physical therapy assistants and aides may be employed by community health centers, nursing homes, sports teams and facilities, corporate and industrial health centers, research institutions, home health agencies, schools, pediatric centers, and colleges and universities.

According to the Bureau of Labor Statistics, there were 61,000 physical therapy assistants and aides employed in 1992. An estimated 80 percent of them worked on a full-time, salaried basis.

Training, Other Qualifications, and Advancement

Physical therapy assistants may complete a two-year associate degree program, many of which are offered at community and junior colleges. Such programs usually consist of one year of general education and one year of technical courses on physical therapy procedures, including hands-on clinical experience. Academic courses of study include algebra, anatomy and physiology, biology, chemistry, and psychology.

Assistants can advance to become physical therapists by completing the necessary education, usually a bachelor's degree. Some employers have outlined steps for career advancement as assistants gain experience and expertise.

Physical therapy aides generally need less training than assistants. Aides are typically high school graduates, who learn the basics of their work in three to six months. They receive clinical training on the job. With additional study, physical therapy aides can qualify as physical therapy assistants.

Physical therapy assistants and aides share a genuine interest in helping people overcome their physical problems. They need good communication skills and the ability to work with people. In addition, they must be physically strong enough to help patients with their treatment.

Most states require that physical therapy assistants (not aides) be licensed or registered. Licensing requirements vary from state to state, but typical requirements include completing an approved course of study and passing an examination. Physical therapy assistants may also need to be certified for cardiopulmonary resuscitation (CPR).

Job Outlook

According to the Bureau of Labor Statistics, employment of physical therapy assistants and aides is projected to increase by 93 percent between 1992 and 2005, much faster than the average for all occupations. Overall the occupation of medical assistants, including physical therapy assistants, is projected to increase by 70.5 percent between 1992 and 2005.

Increased demand for physical therapy services will be supported by an aging population and the increasing popularity of physical and outdoor activities. In addition, since physical therapy allows some patients to shorten their hospital stay by undergoing treatment on an outpatient basis, it is becoming more frequently prescribed as a means of controlling health care costs.

Earnings

Physical therapy aides generally earn less than physical therapy assistants. According to *American Salaries and Wages Survey*, starting salaries for aides range from $10,000 to $13,000. More experienced aides can earn as much as $20,000 annually.

The Bureau of Labor Statistics reported that starting salaries of physical therapy assistants averaged between $24,000 and $28,000 in 1992. Earnings of assistants employed in hospitals tended to be lower than those in private practice. Experienced assistants in private practice earned between $30,000 and $35,000.

Related Occupations

Other healthcare occupations that involve working under the supervision of licensed professionals include dental assistants, medical assistants, occupational therapy assistants, optometric assistants, recreational therapy assistants, and pharmacy assistants.

Physical therapy aides are involved in patient care. Related patient care occupations include orderlies, practical nurses, birth attendants, ambulance attendants, psychiatric aides, nurse assistants, respiratory therapy aides, and emergency medical technicians.

Sources of Additional Information

For additional information contact:

• American Physical Therapy Association, 1111 N. Fairfax

St., Alexandria, VA 22314. Phone: (703)684-2782.

• U.S. Physical Therapy Association, 1803 Avon Ln., Arlington Heights, IL 60004.

• National Rehabilitation Association, 633 S. Washington St., Alexandria, VA 22314. Phone: (703)836-0850.

PODIATRIC ASSISTANTS

At a Glance

■ **D.O.T.:** 079.374-018

■ **Preferred Education:** 1 to 2 years of postsecondary education

■ **Average Salary:** $15,000 to $18,000

■ **Did You Know?** The American Podiatric Medical Association reports that the outlook for podiatry in general is affected in part by the increasing number of men and women involved in some sort or exercise, resulting in an increase in foot and ankle injuries.

Nature of the Work

Podiatric assistants aid licensed podiatrists in attending to their patients and handling office tasks. Podiatrists specialize in foot and ankle care, dealing with such ailments as ankle and foot injuries, arch problems, heel spurs, calluses, and infections. The specific duties of podiatric assistants depend upon the podiatrist's type of practice, volume of patients and number of assistants employed. In general, podiatric assistants are responsible for chairside assisting, surgical assisting, and business office procedures.

Chairside assisting involves responding to patient needs and preparing them for treatment. Podiatric assistants also take and record patient histories. Surgical assisting involves preparing and sterilizing instruments and equipment, giving post-operative instructions to patients, and applying surgical dressings. Podiatric assistants also expose and develop x-rays, and assist in biomechanical evaluations and plaster casting.

When they are not dealing directly with patients in the office, podiatric assistants handle clerical procedures. They answer telephones, schedule appointments, maintain inventory supplies, process insurance and billing paperwork, and receive payments.

Working Conditions

Like other types of medical assistants, podiatric assistants work in clean, well-lighted clinical settings. Full-time medical assistants generally work 40 hours per week. There are also a significant number of part-time workers. Medical assistants spend much of their time interacting with others. They may be required to handle several tasks at once.

Employment

According to the Bureau of Labor Statistics, approximately 21,720 medical assistants, or 12 percent, worked for health practitioners such as podiatrists, chiropractors, and optometrists in 1992. During this same time, 14,700 podiatrists were employed. The number of podiatric assistants employed in individual offices depends primarily on the volume of patients.

Podiatric assistants work for podiatric physicians primarily in private practices, but also in hospitals, group practices, and public health departments. According to the Bureau of Labor Statistics, there is a concentration of podiatrists in or near the seven states with colleges of podiatric medicine. These states include California, Florida, Illinois, Iowa, New York, Pennsylvania, and Ohio. Areas such as the South and Southwest as well as non-metropolitan areas have few podiatrists.

Training, Other Qualifications, and Advancement

Podiatric assistants, like other medical assistants, should have a high school diploma. Appropriate high school courses include biology, health, mathematics, and office procedures. In some cases, podiatric assistants may be trained on the job. However, formal training in medical assisting is often preferred by employers. Formal training involves attending a one-year certificate program or a two-year degree program at a postsecondary vocational school, vocational-technical school or community college. (Consult the *Occupational Outlook Handbook* for more information on training requirements for medical assistants.)

Podiatric medical assistants can attain the designation Podiatric Medical Assistant Certified (PMAC), which is awarded by the American Society of Podiatric Medical Assistants. To be eligible, candidates must be members of the Society for at least one year and pass a certification examination.

Like other medical assistants, podiatric assistants must have a pleasant manner and be able to put patients at ease. They must be able to explain physicians' instructions and respect the confidential nature of medical information. They may advance to become office managers or medical records clerks. They may also attain additional education and pursue occupations in nursing or medical technology.

Job Outlook

According to the Bureau of Labor Statistics, employment of all types of medical assistants is expected to grow much faster than average for all occupations through the year 2005. The American Podiatric Medical Association reports that the outlook for podiatry in general is affected in part by the increasing number of men and women involved in some sort or exercise, resulting in an increase in foot and ankle injuries. Another factor affecting the demand for podiatrists and their assistants is the increasing percentage of older Americans, who commonly experience foot problems. Prospects will be best for medical assistants with formal training.

Earnings

The average starting salary for graduates of accredited medical assistant programs was about $15,059 per year in 1992, according to the Committee on Allied Health Education and Accreditation. According to the American Association of Medical Assistants, the average annual salary for medical assistants in 1991 was $18,334. Medical assistants with under two years of experience generally earned less, while those with several years of experience earned higher wages.

Related Occupations

Other types of medical assistants work for physicians, chiropractors, and optometrists. Other medical support occupations include medical record clerks, pharmacy helpers, medical secretaries, and hospital admitting clerks. Related occupations concerned with patient care include occupational therapy aides, ambulance attendants, physical therapy aides, nurse assistants, and surgical technicians.

Sources of Additional Information

- American Society of Podiatric Medical Assistants, 2124 S. Austin Blvd., Cicero, IL 60650.

- American Podiatric Medical Association, 2124 S. Austin Blvd., Cicero, IL 60650. Phone: (708)863-6303.

For information on medical assistants, contact:

- American Association of Medical Assistants, 20 N. Wacker Dr., Ste. 1575, Chicago, IL 60606-2903. Phone: (312)899-1500, (800)228-2262.

Building and Grounds Service Occupations

ARBORISTS

At a Glance

- **D.O.T.:** 408.181-010

- **Preferred Education:** 1 to 2 years on-the-job training

- **Average Salary:** $12,500 to $25,000

- **Did You Know?** The average life span of an urban tree is only 60 years; the same tree in a rural forest may live several times that long.

Nature of the Work

Arborists are tree care professionals who help trees survive in our harsh urban and suburban environments. Their skills are needed more than ever as we have come to recognize the environmental, economic, and social benefits of trees. Properly placed and cared for, trees provide shade, deflect harsh winds, screen unsightly views, add beauty to the environment, and help purify the air we breathe.

Arborists perform many tasks relating to tree care including pruning, fertilizing, pest management, tree planting, tree removal, and bracing. Arborists who do this type of work may be known as *tree surgeons, tree trimmers, tree pruners,* or *tree planters.* Their job titles include crew member, climber, and crew leader. They may have to hire, train, and direct the activities of a small crew of workers. Arborists who provide cost and value estimates and diagnose tree problems may be known as *consulting arborists.*

Arborists spend much of their time pruning shade and ornamental trees. Pruning is often required to shape a tree or remove dead or diseased limbs. Pruning may also be necessary when trees interfere with power or telephone lines. Depending on the size of the tree, arborists may have to climb the tree, using a climber's belt or saddle and a climber's rope. They may use hand and power saws, pole pruners, and hand shears. In some cases, the necessary height is reached using a bucket truck or aerial lift. Logs may have to be maneuvered using cranes and winches. Bush chippers are used to dispose of unwanted branches.

Fertilization is an important part of tree care handled by arborists. They may use an earth auger to drill holes into the ground and fill the holes with a dry tree food mixture. Another method of fertilizing trees involves using a power sprayer to inject a liquid chemical fertilizer into the ground. Fertilizers may also be injected directly into a tree and be distributed through the tree's circulatory system. Fertilizing serves to increase a tree's strength and its resistance to damaging insects and diseases.

Arborists employ different pest management techniques and strategies in their work. Pest management is preventive as well as corrective and is used to control plant diseases as well as insects. Many tree species have their own particular insect problems. Arborists must be able to diagnose the problem accurately and take appropriate action.

Before applying pesticides to control plant diseases and insects, arborists use other preventive measures. These may include monitoring the insect population, using resistant varieties of plants, and releasing natural insect predators or parasites. When pesticides are needed, arborists apply them using one or more types of hydraulic sprayers. Special permits are usually needed to apply pesticides that are controlled by state and federal regulations.

Arborists may also plant trees, following a plan of their own or one developed by a landscape architect or designer. They select appropriate species of trees based on their knowledge of environmental conditions. They transplant the trees following established procedures that ensure the trees will survive.

Other tree care duties performed by arborists include repairing damaged trees using cables and braces. Arborists may also need to remove trees that are diseased, dead, or otherwise undesirable.

Working Conditions

The work of arborists is physically demanding, not in the sense of lifting heavy weights, but in terms of climbing trees and using a variety of hand and power tools. Arborists are frequently climbing, balancing, stooping, kneeling, and crouching, often at some distance above the ground.

Most of their work is carried on outdoors, so arborists are exposed to all types of weather conditions. The work of arborists is sometimes hazardous. They may have to operate hand-held power tools high above the ground. They may be subject to windy weather conditions. Injuries such as cuts, sprains, and bruises are common.

Arborists typically work in urban and suburban environments. Their busiest time of the year is during the late spring in May and June, when they work longer hours. Storm and emergency work may also require them to work extra hours. In some parts of the country, they may be laid off or work at other jobs during the winter months.

Employment

Commercial tree service firms offer arborists the most stable employment. Some arborists open their own tree service businesses and become self-employed. Other employers include public utility companies, state and local government agencies, nurseries and garden centers, equipment and chemical manufacturers, cooperative extension services, colleges and universities, arboreta and tree research centers, and landscape architectural planning and development firms.

Arborists are employed throughout the United States. The most employment opportunities tend to be with tree service firms that service affluent suburbs.

Training, Other Qualifications, and Advancement

Arborists generally have one to two years of training that can be learned on the job. Tree service firms usually provide on-the-job training to entry-level employees. These on-the-job training programs may include home study, audiovisual materials, and safety training.

Arborists are usually high school graduates. In addition, they may take college-level courses as part of a two- or four-year certificate or degree program. Urban forestry programs are offered by many forestry departments at colleges and universities. Basic courses include oral and written communication, dendrology, soil science, economics, botany, and several forestry courses. Advanced courses may include entomology, park and recreation operations, tree physiology, personnel management, small business management, pathology, urban forestry, and arboriculture. Many courses include lab work and practical experience in addition to classroom instruction. Graduates of urban forestry programs are qualified to start their own commercial tree service businesses.

The International Society of Arboriculture offers two levels of voluntary certification for arborists: Certified Arborist (CA) and Certified Arborist Technician (CAT). Certification requirements include passing written and practical tests. Arborists may continue their education through courses sponsored by industry associations and agencies, federal and state funded training programs, and technical schools.

Arborists are people who like physical activity and working outdoors. They must be in good physical condition. Working high above the ground requires a good sense of balance. Some manual dexterity is needed to operate equipment and power tools.

Arborists possess common sense and good judgment to observe safety precautions and respect the property of clients and employers. They need good communication skills and the ability to develop positive relationships with clients and fellow workers.

Advancement generally depends on such factors as skill, knowledge, experience, efficiency, and ability to get along with others. Entry-level arborists can advance with experience to positions such as tree climber and crew leader. Experienced arborists may be promoted to management positions. Arborists who own their own tree service firms can expand their business, hire more workers, and upgrade their equipment.

Higher level positions, such as park superintendent, municipal arborist, and utility arborist, generally require two to four years of college. Arborists with appropriate educational backgrounds may take forestry positions with federal and state government agencies.

Job Outlook

While the Bureau of Labor Statistics does not publish separate employment projections for arborists, the related occupations of gardeners and groundskeepers are expected to increase faster than the average for all occupations through 2005. People leaving these occupations are also expected to create a large number of job openings.

Among the factors supporting an increased demand for arborists are the development and building of new homes and offices that require landscaping and tree care services. As more people come to regard ornamental trees and shrubs as valuable resources, homeowners will utilize the services of tree care specialists. Homeowners will continue to use arborists in ever-increasing numbers to enhance the beauty and value of their property.

As suburban developments increase and populations expand, these communities will create a strong demand for arborists and tree service companies. However, competition among commercial tree service companies will intensify. Newly established companies will likely find it difficult to attract new customers.

Earnings

Earnings for arborists vary with their skill levels and the responsibilities of their positions. According to the National Arborist Association, yearly earnings based on working 2,000 hours per year for ground personnel range from $12,500 to $18,000.

Tree climbers can earn from $10,000 to $25,000, and foremen from $11,000 to $35,000. Employees of tree service firms often receive some benefits, including medical insurance and paid vacation time.

Related Occupations

Other occupations involving managerial work with plants and specialty cropping include special effects gardeners, bonsai culturists, greens superintendents, specialty growers, landscape gardeners, nursery managers, and landscape contractors. Many farming occupations also involve working outdoors with plants.

Sources of Additional Information

- American Society of Consulting Arborists, 5130 W. 101st Cir., Westminster, CO 80030. Phone: (303)466-2722.

- International Society of Arboriculture, PO Box GG, Savoy, IL 61874-9902. Phone: (217)355-9411.

- National Arborist Association, The Meeting Place Mall, Rte. 101, PO Box 1094, Amherst, NH 03031-1094. Phone: (603)673-3311 or (800)733-2622.

BUILDING MAINTENANCE WORKERS

At a Glance

- **D.O.T.:** 899.381-010

- **Preferred Education:** Training and experience

- **Average Salary:** $17,000 to $19,000

- **Did You Know?** In larger establishments, building maintenance workers may specialize in tasks such as plumbing, painting, electrical wiring, carpentry, floor covering, and landscaping.

Nature of the Work

Apartment complexes, offices, hotels, and other commercial and industrial buildings that we live and work in require regular maintenance and upkeep. Walls need repainting. Floors need new carpet. Light fixtures must be replaced. These are some of the tasks performed by building maintenance workers.

Building maintenance workers do routine preventive maintenance in and around buildings. They monitor and inspect the physical condition of buildings. When necessary, they may make drywall and plaster repairs, fix roofs, and build partitions. They may replace windows, lay floor tile, fix plumbing, and repair appliances such as air conditioners and refrigerators. Building maintenance workers employ a wide range of tools, equipment, and materials in their work. They may use carpentry tools, lumber, paint, brushes, cleaning supplies, scaffolds, and ladders. Their duties may change frequently, from painting a room to repairing a heating system.

For more complex repair jobs, building maintenance workers may consult repair manuals, blueprints, building codes, parts catalogs, and other reference books. They may have to inspect and diagnose problems. They may use specialized equipment and electronic test devices. They may obtain supplies and repair parts from a storeroom or distributor and fix or replace broken or worn parts on different types of equipment and machinery in buildings. Repair work usually calls for the use of common hand and power tools, including hammers, wrenches, drills, saws, and screwdrivers.

In larger establishments, building maintenance workers may specialize in tasks such as plumbing, painting, electrical wiring, carpentry, floor covering, and landscaping. In smaller establishments, building maintenance workers may perform most of the repair and maintenance work themselves.

Working Conditions

Building maintenance workers may work standard 40-hour weeks, or they may work various shifts to provide maintenance on evenings, weekends, and holidays. Depending on where they are employed, such as apartment complexes, building maintenance workers may live on site, receiving free or low-cost housing. Many building maintenance workers belong to unions such as the Service Employees International Union, the Association of Federal, State, County, and Municipal Employees (AFSCME), or the United Auto Workers (UAW).

Some of the jobs performed by building maintenance workers can be physically demanding. They may frequently have to lift or move objects weighing 25 pounds and occasionally as much as 50 pounds. They may have to stand for long periods of time or work in awkward and cramped positions.

Building maintenance workers repair and maintain buildings and equipment on the inside as well as outside. They may be frequently exposed to extremes of weather. Hazards of the job include minor cuts, bruises, burns, and electrical shocks. They may have to work from ladders and scaffolding. Most risks of injury, however, can be minimized by following standard safety precautions.

Employment

There were about 1,145,000 building maintenance workers employed in 1992. Manufacturing, real estate, wholesale and retail trade, and educational services including colleges and universities accounted for more than half of all employment of building maintenance workers. Other industries employing building maintenance workers include government, construction, business services, health care including hospitals and nursing homes, and transportation and public utilities.

Training, Other Qualifications, and Advancement

Building maintenance workers do not have to be high school graduates, but they generally have one to four years of training. They may gain experience and training by starting out as building maintenance helpers. Helpers are usually given less complicated jobs to perform and gradually gain enough experience and skills to become building maintenance workers.

Building maintenance workers may also obtain training and skills in high school courses and by taking postsecondary programs in trade and vocational schools. Appropriate high school and postsecondary subjects include general math, blueprint reading, shop mechanics, wood shop, appliance repair, electricity and electronics, machine shop, small engine repair, and heating, air conditioning, and refrigeration. Building maintenance programs may cover subjects such as fundamentals of building trades, building maintenance, equipment repair, plumbing repair, electrical repair, air conditioning systems, boiler maintenance, grounds maintenance, swimming pool maintenance, and the use of hand and power tools.

Building maintenance workers generally have a mechanical aptitude and enjoy applying mechanical principles to practical situations. They must have well developed reasoning skills to solve complicated problems when things need to be fixed or repaired. They must be able to read and apply instructions found in technical manuals and reference works. Newer buildings are using computerized control systems, so building maintenance workers will find that they need to become familiar with computers.

With additional training and experience, building maintenance workers may become journey workers such as electricians, plumbers, and heating, air conditioning, and refrigeration mechanics. They may also advance to become maintenance mechanics in factories, hospitals, and schools, maintenance supervisors, building maintenance instructors, and building rehabilitation contractors.

Job Outlook

The Bureau of Labor Statistics projects that employment of building maintenance workers will increase faster than the average for all occupations between 1992 and 2005. New employment opportunities will result from the building of new office buildings, hospitals, apartment buildings, shopping centers, and other commercial and industrial structures. Additional opportunities will arise from the need to replace workers who leave this large occupational category to find work in other occupations.

Earnings

Earnings of building maintenance workers vary according to industry, employer, union affiliation, experience, and geographic location. The U.S. Department of Labor reported that the median earnings of building maintenance workers in metropolitan areas were approximately $18,740 in 1992. In service businesses, the median was slightly less at $17,500 annually, while building maintenance workers in manufacturing had median annual earnings of approximately $19,800.

According to *American Salaries and Wages Survey*, building maintenance workers can earn salaries ranging from $8,800 to $30,000 depending on geographic location. Building maintenance workers employed by the State of Michigan earned between $22,000 and $34,000 in 1994.

Building maintenance workers generally receive a standard benefits package from their employer that includes paid vacations and holidays, medical insurance, and pension plans.

Related Occupations

Other mechanical crafts occupations include roofers, glaziers, dispensing opticians, motorcycle and bicycle frame repairers, pipe installers, carper layers, and high riggers. Other related occupations include plumbers, industrial machinery mechanics, electricians, and HVAC (heating, ventilation, and

cooling) mechanics.

Sources of Additional Information

- Building Service Contractors Association International, 10201 Lee Hwy., Ste. 225, Fairfax, VA 22030. Phone: (703)359-7090.

- Cleaning Management Institute, 13 Century Hill Dr., Latham, NY 12110-2197. Phone: (518)783-1281.

- Service Employees International Union, 1313 L St. NW, Washington, DC 20005. Phone: (202)898-3200.

GOLF COURSE SUPERINTENDENTS AND GREENSKEEPERS

At a Glance

- **D.O.T.:** 406.137-010, -014 and 406.683.010

- **Preferred Education:** On-the-job training for greenskeepers; associate or bachelor's degree for golf course superintendents

- **Average Salary:** $11,000 to $19,000 for greenskeepers

- **Did You Know?** Superintendents direct the overall turf management programs at golf courses, using the principles of agronomy, entomology, and other sciences.

Nature of the Work

In many ways golf courses set the standard in landscape and design, with their manicured fairways and greens. Their grounds and greens must be well-kept to attract golfers. Maintaining a golf course in top condition is often the key to its continued success.

Golf courses rely on a staff of greenskeepers, usually working under the direction of golf course superintendents, to keep their greens, fairways, hazards, and other features in top condition. The staff may include entry-level greenskeepers who operate tractors with attachments to till, cultivate, and grade new turf areas. They apply prescribed amounts of fertilizer, insecticide, and fungicide to the courses. They also operate tractors to mow fairways and roughs at specified heights, taking care not to injure trees, plants, and shrubs on the course. They use hand and power mowers to cut greens and tee areas.

Entry-level greenskeepers are supervised by experienced greenskeepers. Supervisory greenskeepers may consult with golf course superintendents to plan and review work projects. They establish work priorities and assign workers to specific tasks. They may mix and prepare fertilizers, pesticides, insecticides, and fungicides. They may also supervise the repair and maintenance of equipment, including tractors, hand mowers, and power mowers.

The entire greenskeeping staff, which may range from 10 to 20 or more people, works under the overall direction of a golf course superintendent, also known as a greens superintendent. Superintendents direct the overall turf management programs at golf courses, using the principles of agronomy, entomology, and other sciences. Superintendents balance environmental concerns with the need to provide a golf course that is challenging as well as enjoyable.

Among the specific duties of golf course superintendents are planning work programs, planning new areas or changes in a course, directing workers to accomplish those changes, reviewing test results of soil and turf samples, touring grounds to ascertain work progress, and inspecting turf to determine the height and frequency of mowing. Some superintendents specialize as construction superintendents, working with developers, golf course architects, and builders on new course construction.

Golf course superintendents also have administrative duties that include budgeting, purchasing, cost control, inventory control, and payroll. They may keep records of the weather, course conditions, and management practices. Superintendents are also responsible for keeping records to comply with applicable governmental regulations.

Working Conditions

Greenskeepers and superintendents enjoy an attractive, outdoor work setting. Greenskeepers are exposed to weather conditions; many positions are seasonal. They may be exposed to hazards associated with pesticides, fertilizers, and other chemicals. They also work with potentially dangerous equipment, including power mowers, tractors, chain saws, and electric clippers. Such equipment is often loud and may emit fumes.

Employment

According to the Bureau of Labor Statistics, there were approximately 43,200 gardeners and groundskeepers who cared for athletic fields and golf courses in 1992. The Golf Course Superintendents Association of America reported a membership of 14,000 in 1995.

Golf course superintendents and greenskeepers are employed at different types of golf courses. Employers include private clubs, daily fee courses open to the public, municipal courses operated as part of a city or county's recreation program, and resort facilities. Course sizes may range from nine-hole, par-three courses to multi-course layouts.

Training, Other Qualifications, and Advancement

Greenskeepers may have different levels of training and vocational preparation, depending on their responsibilities and duties. While most greenskeepers are high school graduates, some jobs may be performed by high school students or individuals who have not graduated. Entry-level greenskeepers can learn the basics of their job in one to three months. Individuals who apply pesticides generally have to meet state certification requirements.

Advancement to supervisory positions and to golf course superintendent requires additional training. Supervisory greenskeepers generally have one to two years of specific vocational preparation. They may take courses in plant science and landscape management, including turfgrass management. Courses in business and general science are also recommended.

Golf course superintendents have more formal training than greenskeepers. According to the Golf Course Superintendents Association of America, approximately two-thirds of all golf course superintendents have completed a two- or four-year degree program. The trend is for new superintendents to have earned a bachelor's degree in turfgrass management. Individuals with some college who are considering a career change to turfgrass management typically take a two-year program leading to an associate degree.

Turfgrass management programs combine academic study with practical experience working on golf courses. Courses include plant science, general science, special problems in plant management, landscape management, and business. Other electives that may be taken include genetics, physics, meteorology, range management, water control and utilization, and soil conservation and land use, among others. Continuing education is needed to keep up with new developments in the field.

Greenskeepers are individuals who enjoy working outdoors with plants. Entry-level workers must be responsible and self-motivated, since they often work with little supervision. Advancement requires technical ability as well as leadership skills. Supervisors and superintendents must have good communication skills.

Greenskeepers can advance to supervisory positions by gaining experience and receiving additional training. With additional education, they may become golf course superintendents.

Job Outlook

According to the Bureau of Labor Statistics, employment of gardeners and groundskeepers is expected to grow somewhat faster than the average for all occupations. In the agricultural services industry, employment of gardeners and groundskeepers (except farm) is projected to increase by nearly 58 percent between 1992 and 2005.

In the amusement and recreation services industry, employment of gardeners and groundskeepers (except farm) is projected to increase by 27 percent between 1992 and 2005.

The demand for greenskeepers and golf course superintendents will be supported by the explosive growth of golfing as a leisure pursuit. Golf's growth is especially strong in the United States, Europe, Australia, Japan, and throughout Southeast Asia. New golf courses will create additional employment opportunities. Many entry-level positions will arise as the result of people leaving the occupation.

Earnings

Earnings for greenskeepers and golf course

superintendents depend on such factors as geographic location, type of golf course, level of duties, and amount of education and experience. According to the Bureau of Labor Statistics, median weekly earnings for gardeners and groundskeepers were between $210 and $365 in 1992, or between $11,000 and $19,000 annually. The Golf Course Superintendents Association of America reports that salaries of golf course superintendents are comparable to those of other business executives.

Related Occupations

Other occupations that involve elemental nursery and groundskeeping work include flower pickers, orchid transplanters, yard workers, agricultural landscape laborers, tree surgeon helpers, horticultural workers, landscape specialists, lawn service workers, and garden workers. Related occupations involving managerial work with plants include nursery managers, landscape contractors, landscape gardeners, and tree surgeons.

Other outdoor occupations include gardeners, construction workers, landscape architects, nursery workers, farmers, and forest conservation workers.

Sources of Additional Information

- Golf Course Superintendents Association of America, 1421 Research Park Dr., Lawrence, KS 66049-3859. Phone: (913)832-4444.

- Professional Grounds Management Society, 120 Cockeysville Rd., Ste. 104, Hunt Valley, MD 21031. Phone: (410)584-9754.

LAWN SERVICE WORKERS

At a Glance

- **D.O.T.:** 408.684-010 and 408.684-014

- **Preferred Education:** On-the-job training

- **Average Salary:** $11,000 to $19,000

- **Did You Know?** Many lawn service jobs are seasonal, with jobs available only during the spring and summer.

Nature of the Work

Many people take great pride in the appearance of the landscape surrounding their homes and businesses. For this reason, a growing number of homeowners and businesses are relying on professional lawn service workers to care for their lawns, shrubs, trees, and gardens.

Lawn service workers specialize in maintaining lawns and shrubs for a fee. They perform a full-range of duties, including mowing, edging, trimming, and fertilizing. Those working for chemical lawn service companies, generally known as hand sprayers, inspect lawns for problems and apply fertilizers, weed killers, and other chemicals.

Lawn service workers mow lawns with power mowers. They edge along the curb and walkways with edgers. They also trim grass along the sides of buildings, lawn furniture, or light poles. After they finish mowing, edging, and trimming, lawn service workers remove clippings from sidewalks with brooms or power blowers. To cultivate lawns, lawn service workers use power aerators to pierce holes in the soil. Then, using a spreader, they distribute fertilizers, pesticides, and fungicides on the lawn.

Instead of a spreader, hand sprayers use a hose to spray herbicides, pesticides, and fungicides on trees, shrubs, and lawns. The hose is connected to a chemical tank mounted on a truck. Hand sprayers pull the hose from the truck, turn the knob, and point the nozzle at weeds, trees, or shrubs. They may also use portable spray equipment. In addition, hand sprayers may remove infested bushes and destroy diseased trees.

Working Conditions

Many lawn service jobs are seasonal with jobs available only during the spring and summer. Lawn service workers work outdoors in all kinds of weather. They must exercise safety precautions when working with pesticides, fertilizers, and other chemicals. Power lawn mowers and other equipment can also be dangerous.

Like many in the agricultural services industry, lawn service workers may work 6 or 7 days a week during the busy season. The work is very physical. Standing, stooping, lifting, and operating heavy machinery are routine tasks. Many workers spend much of their time pushing power lawn mowers.

Employment

According to the U.S. Department of Labor, lawn and garden service companies employed approximately 353,000 workers in 1992. These companies work for residential homeowners and commercial clients, such as office buildings, shopping malls, multi-unit residential buildings, and hotels and motels. Many lawn services workers are self-employed.

Training, Other Qualifications, and Advancement

Lawn service requires little or no prior training or experience. The basics tasks associated with the job usually can be learned in less than a week. Most newly hired workers are trained on the job under the supervision of an experienced employee or supervisor. Employers look for workers who are responsible and self-motivated, are in good physical condition, and like to work outdoors.

Lawn service workers can advance to supervisory positions or start their own lawn service companies.

Job Outlook

According to the Bureau of Labor Statistics, wage and

salary jobs in agricultural services, which includes lawn care, are expected to increase 41 percent from 1992 through the year 2005. A growing number of homeowners will use lawn maintenance and landscaping services to enhance the appearance of their property and conserve leisure time. In addition, the increasing number of commercial buildings and similar facilities will add to the demand for these services.

Earnings

According to the Bureau of Labor Statistics, median weekly earnings for gardeners and groundskeepers, which includes lawn service workers, were about $275 per hour in 1992. The middle 50 percent earned between $210 and $365. The lowest 10 percent earned less than $175. The top 10 percent earned more than $475 per week.

Related Occupations

Others whose jobs are related to lawn service workers include tree surgeons, tree trimmers and pruners, greenskeepers, plant care workers, landscape gardeners, nursery workers, and forest conservation workers.

Sources of Additional Information

* Professional Lawn Care Association of America, 1000 Johnson Ferry Rd., N.E., Ste. C-135, Marietta, GA 30068-2112. Phone: (404)977-5222.

PEST CONTROLLERS AND ASSISTANTS

At a Glance

■ **D.O.T.:** 383.361-010, .364-010, .684-010, .687-010, 389.134-010 and .684-010

■ **Preferred Education:** On-the-job training

■ **Average Salary:** $6 to $10 per hour

■ **Did You Know?** The entire field of pest control is heavily regulated. Nearly every state requires that pest controllers be licensed, registered, and/or certified.

Nature of the Work

Owners of residential and commercial buildings use pest controllers to rid their structures of rodents, insects, termites, and other pests. Also known as exterminators and fumigators, pest controllers and their assistants use chemicals and mechanical traps to control the spread of unwanted pests in buildings. They also advise their customers on proper methods to keep pests from returning.

Pest controllers may operate under service contracts to periodically apply chemicals and set traps at commercial and residential buildings such as hotels, condominiums, and food stores. During the day, they may travel established routes to these locations as well as respond to individual service requests.

Once on site, they apply chemicals in floor and wall cracks, under sinks, and in other places that attract pests. They may set mechanical traps containing poisonous bait in places where they will not contaminate food or endanger children or pets. When necessary, they conduct inspections of premises to determine the extent of the pest problem and the most effective solutions.

Termite control is a specialized area of pest control that calls for more extensive and complicated measures. Termite specialists may have to treat termites that live in underground colonies by placing a chemical barrier around the affected structure. In some cases, they must make structural changes in buildings. Foundations may have to be raised or infested wood replaced. Termite specialists may have to drill holes in basement floors to pump chemicals into the soil under the structure. If extensive alterations are required, a building contractor or carpenter may be called in to provide assistance.

Pest controllers may also be involved with fumigation, where poisonous gases are released into sealed areas that may encompass parts of a structure or an entire building. When fumigation is required, pest controllers first conduct an inspection of the premises to determine the best way to seal off the infested area. They take measurements and determine the volume of fumigant required. They seal off the infested area by taping vents, pulling a tent or tarpaulin over the building, and fastening the edges to make the building airtight.

When the fumigation is to take place, pest controllers post warning signs and lock the doors to the building. They release the compressed fumigant through a hose into the building. During fumigation they check the edges of the tent or tarpaulin and vents to detect any leaks. They advise clients when it is safe to return to the building after the tent or tarpaulin has been removed.

Pest controllers and their assistants keep records of every application. They must read directions on chemical containers and make decisions concerning the type and amount of chemicals to use in each case. They may have to mix the chemicals and load machines prior to application.

Working Conditions

Pest controllers are frequently exposed to fumes, odors, dusts, and other atmospheric conditions during the course of their work. They often handle toxic chemicals, although such chemicals are applied in quantities that are not harmful to humans or household pets. Their work involves frequent balancing, stooping, and kneeling as well as manual dexterity.

The physical demands of the job range from light to heavy, depending on the task to be performed. Routinely applying chemicals and setting traps is light work. Termite exterminators and their assistants who treat infested wood in structures normally lift or move objects weighing from 10 to 25 pounds, and occasionally as much as 50 pounds. Fumigators have the most physically demanding work, having to frequently lift or move objects weighing 50 pounds or more.

Employment

According to the Bureau of Labor Statistics, there were 49,000 pest controllers and assistants employed in 1992. A very high percentage of them work part-time. Pest controllers may be self-employed and run their own structural pest control service, or they may work for other pest controllers.

Most pest controllers are employed in urban areas where there are older buildings. Termite technicians tend to work in suburban areas where there is a concentration of wooden frame buildings. There is a greater need for pest controllers in states with warm climates that are conducive to insects and pests.

Training, Other Qualifications, and Advancement

Pest controllers generally have six months to one year of specific vocational preparation that usually consists of on-the-job training. Entry-level positions are available without experience to individuals with a good background and high school education. Some knowledge of biology, entomology, and chemistry is helpful prior to employment.

The entire field of pest control is heavily regulated. All states require that pest control businesses be licensed, and nearly every state requires that pest controllers be licensed, registered, and/or certified. Under the Federal Insecticide, Fungicide, and Rodenticide Act (FIFRA), every state will eventually have to establish certification requirements for pest controllers. While existing requirements vary from state to state, they typically involve passing practical and written examinations designed to measure an individual's competency. Candidates for certification usually have to complete a period of training under the guidance of a certified operator. Pest controllers keep up with new technical information by reading trade journals, taking training courses, and earning continuing education credits.

Individuals who are pest controllers must be in good health and physical condition and be able to lift fairly heavy weights. Manual dexterity and some mechanical ability are important. Technicians must be able to drive a vehicle. In some cases pest controllers are bonded and must have a clean legal record.

Pest controllers and their assistants can advance in their occupation in several ways. They may study and obtain certification in a variety of pest control specialties. Assistants may advance to become fully certified operators. Employees of pest control businesses may become supervisors and direct other applicators. Some may choose to become self-employed and run their own pest control business. Most pest control businesses have sales and customer service positions that represent an advancement for pest controllers and their assistants.

Job Outlook

The BLS has projected little change in the employment of pest controllers and their assistants between 1992 and 2005. Many job openings in this field are created by replacement needs resulting from individuals leaving the field. Overall, the pest control industry is growing at a healthy pace, and the demand for pest controllers and their assistants is not expected to decline.

Earnings

According to *American Salaries and Wages Survey*, pest controllers and their assistants can expect to earn an entry-level wage ranging from minimum wage to about $6 per hour. Wages for experienced pest controllers range from $6 per hour to $10 per hour. Full-time pest controllers may earn as much as $23,000 annually. Self-employed pest controllers who run their own businesses have the opportunity to increase their earnings considerably.

Related Occupations

Pest controllers who work with buildings may consider other pest control specialties, including lawn sprayers, agricultural pesticide applicators, forest pesticide applicators, water pesticide applicators, and highway pesticide applicators. Other cleaning and building service occupations include institutional cleaning supervisors, home restorers, sextons who take care of church buildings, and janitors and cleaners.

Sources of Additional Information

- National Pest Control Association, 8100 Oak St., Dunn Loring, VA 22027. Phone: (703)573-8330.

Animal Caretakers, Except Farm

ANIMAL TRAINERS

At a Glance

- **D.O.T.:** 159.224-010

- **Preferred Education:** High school diploma; some college course work recommended

- **Average Salary:** Dog trainer/$20,000 per year; racehorse trainer/$35-$50 per day; show horse trainer/$30,000-$35,000 per year; performance animal trainer/$21.55 per hour

- **Did You Know?** According to the Bureau of Labor Statistics, the best opportunities for animal trainers is being in dog obedience training.

Nature of the Work

If you know something about animals and enjoy working with them, including all kinds of pets and their owners, then a career as an animal trainer may be for you. Animal trainers usually specialize in one type of animal, although trainers who work with animals that appear in movies have to be able to train all types of animals. The most common specialty among animal trainers is dog obedience trainers. Horse trainers and the subspecialty of racehorse trainers form another large category of animal trainers. Other trainers specialize in lions, elephants, and other wild animals. Even birds and cats can be professionally trained.

Regardless of what kind of animals they are working with, trainers use their technical skills to teach an animal to perform certain feats, tasks, or movements upon command. Using their knowledge of an animal's habits and learning abilities, animal trainers conduct training programs to achieve the desired behavior. They evaluate each animal's temperament, ability, and aptitude. Training methods typically involve repeating certain instructions or movements, then rewarding the animal when it performs as desired. Animal trainers may teach animals to obey specific commands, compete in shows or exhibitions, or perform tricks to entertain an audience.

Dog obedience trainers are concerned with developing a manageable pet who responds to its owner's commands and directions. They work closely with both the pet and its owner. They may work with dogs one-on-one or conduct obedience classes with several pet owners. Dogs that are shown and exhibited may receive several levels of advanced obedience training designed to enhance their performance.

Training dogs to assist blind, visually impaired, and/or deaf people is a specialized type of dog obedience training. A typical training program begins with obedience training, in which the dogs are taught commands such as come, sit, stay, and heel. During this phase the trainer learns the general characteristics of the dog and studies its habits and temperament. Once these assist dogs complete obedience training they receive basic training in tasks related to assisting people, including observing curbs, pedestrians, parking meters, and low awnings. Advanced training consists of training the dogs to deal with more complex and confusing situations, such as heavy traffic, crowded areas, revolving doors, elevators, and noisy construction areas.

Leader dog trainers must also train the individuals who will be using these dogs. At the Leader Dogs for the Blind School in Rochester, Michigan, students spend 25 days living in the facility's dormitory. During this period, students and dogs learn together. With the help of their trainer they learn to negotiate heavy traffic and find stores and corners. Students must learn to feed, exercise, and groom their leader dogs, and most importantly, they need to establish a relationship with their dogs.

Another specialized area of dog training is training working dogs for law enforcement and other governmental agencies. Dogs may be trained to act as guard dogs or to perform tasks such as detecting specific scents at border crossings or airport terminals or finding injured people trapped in buildings following an earthquake or other type of disaster. Guard dogs are usually given obedience training at an early age, then are trained to learn specific tasks.

Horse trainers work with horses and their riders to accomplish different objectives. They may train horses to be ridden or put in harness. Training horses for casual riding involves getting them accustom to human contact, and getting them to accept a harness, bridle, saddle, and other riding gear. Riding horses learn commands that are either spoken or signalled by the rider using reins or legs. Instead of training horses for riding, horse trainers may train draft horses to pull wagons or other loads.

Specialized areas of horse training include training show horses, horses for equestrian competitions, and racehorses. These specialized horse trainers usually give each horse a special training program tailored to the animal's peculiarities. Racehorse trainers spend time exercising and clocking their horses, coaching jockeys, and advising owners on new horse purchases.

Animal trainers of all kinds typically have other duties in addition to training animals. They often have to exercise, groom, and feed the animals they are training. In some cases they may have to clean up after the animals and perform duties associated with animal caretakers.

Other trainers specialize in lions, elephants, and other wild animals. Some specialize in training marine mammals such as whales, seals, dolphins, otters, porpoises, and sea lions. These wild animal trainers may work in zoos and amusement or theme parks that have the animals on display. Other wild animal trainers train animals that appear in movies or perform in circuses. Movie-animal trainers rehearse the animals for each scene, walking them through their routines. The trainers remain on the set at all times, protecting the cast and crew from any mishaps and keeping the animals calm.

Working Conditions

Most animal trainers have some exposure to weather extremes and other atmospheric conditions. Dog trainers may be exposed to scratches and bites. The work of wild animal trainers and handlers is somewhat more dangerous.

They work with people as much as with animals in many cases, including pet owners, horse riders and owners, and assist dog companions.

Working conditions, including hours, vary considerably for animal trainers depending on the type of animal being trained. Some work is seasonal in nature.

Employment

Animal trainers may be employed in a variety of areas depending on their specialty. Dog trainers may run their own dog training facilities or academies as well as kennels. They may be employed at such facilities or work for schools that train assist dogs, and may even also work for government agencies, including the U.S. Customs Service, the military, or state and local law enforcement agencies. Dog obedience trainers account for the greatest number of employed animal trainers.

Horse trainers may be employed by owners of show horses or racehorses. They may work for large stables or horse farms. Trainers of animals used for entertainment may work for circuses, amusement and theme parks, carnivals, zoos, and motion picture studios. Animal ranches in California that supply animals for motion pictures also employ animal trainers.

Training, Other Qualifications, and Advancement

There are no strict standards for animal trainers. Some employers may require previous experience or some formal education in related subjects. The Humane Society of the United States recommends that anyone pursuing a career involving contact with animals have a good general background in courses such as biology, natural history, ecology, zoology, animal learning, and other animal behavior topics. General humanities courses can also be valuable for people concerned about animals.

Animal trainers generally have one to two years of specific vocational preparation that is usually learned on the job. They often start their careers as animal caretakers, learning all they can about the different animals they may eventually train. Apprenticeships with experienced trainers are sometimes available, and can last up to five years. Another way of gaining experience is to be a seasonal volunteer at a zoo or theme park working as an animal handling or caretaker.

Dog trainers employed by leader dog or assist dog schools usually have to meet higher standards. Typical qualifications include high school graduation and three years of previous experience training guide dogs. Leader dog trainers must be familiar with the psychological aspects of blindness, as well as its causes. Having knowledge in dog psychology is also helpful.

Other specialties have different requirements. Racehorse trainers, for example, need a state license. While licensing requirements vary from state to state, racehorse trainers must generally be at least 18 years of age and be able to demonstrate their qualifications through prior experience or by passing an examination. Move-animal trainers are often required to have some knowledge of motion picture production techniques and cinematography in addition to knowing about animals.

Animal trainers are people who genuinely like animals and enjoy working with them. They must know the habits and needs of specific types of animals. Patience is an important quality for animal trainers to possess as well as excellent communication skills.

Animal trainers can advance from apprentices to fully qualified trainers. They may supervise and direct assistant trainers. Some trainers go into business for themselves, opening a training facility or working as an independent contractor.

Job Outlook

The Bureau of Labor Statistics (BLS) does not publish separate employment statistics or projections for animal trainers. The demand for animal trainers does not appear to be great, and there is a great deal of competition among qualified individuals for available positions. Training facilities often have small staffs and tend to promote from within.

The best opportunities for animal trainers are for dog obedience trainers and trainers of assist dogs and guard dogs. A modest demand for horse trainers is also expected to accompany the growth of the horse population in the United States. Demand for trainers of animals for entertainment purposes is expected to remain limited.

Earnings

Earnings of animal trainers vary greatly depending on the type of animal being trained and place of employment.

Based on limited information, dog trainers can expect to earn anywhere from $20,000 and up.

Related Occupations

Other occupations that involve animal training include horse exercisers, animal ride managers, canine service instructors and trainers, and farm horse trainers. Related animal service occupations include dog groomers and bathers, stable attendants, animal caretakers, aquarists, and farriers.

Sources of Additional Information

- National Congress of Animal Trainers and Breeders, 23675 W. Chardon Rd., Grayslake, IL 60030. Phone: (708)546-0717. Fax: (708)546-3454.

- Leader Dogs for the Blind, 1039 S. Rochester Rd., Rochester, MI 48307-3115. Phone: (810)651-9011.

- National Association of Dog Obedience Instructors, P.O. Box 432, Landing, NJ 07850-0432.

- Society of North American Dog Trainers, c/o ASPCA-CAS, 424 E. 92nd St., New York, NY 10128. Phone: (212)243-7862.

- Humane Society of the United States, Higher Education Section, 2100 L St. NW, Washington, DC 20037. Phone: (202)452-1100. Fax: (202)778-6132.

- American Horse Council, 1700 K St. NW, Ste. 300, Washington, DC 20006. Phone: (202)296-4031.

DOG GROOMERS

At a Glance

- **D.O.T.:** 418.674-010 and 418.677-010

- **Preferred Education:** Apprenticeship training or grooming school

- **Average Salary:** $18,000 to $20,000

- **Did You Know?** A high percentage of dog groomers are self-employed or work part-time.

Nature of the Work

Dog groomers are one of many different animal caretakers who help pet owners care for their pets. Grooming not only improves appearance, it also helps pets stay healthy.

During a typical grooming session, groomers begin by thoroughly brushing and trimming the dog's coat to remove all matted hair. This prepares the dog's coat for initial clipping and shaping. Most groomers also trim toe nails and clean dogs' ears. Groomers then bathe the dog using a special shampoo. When necessary, groomers also use special bathing solutions to kill ticks and fleas. Groomers then dry the dog using either a towel or hair dryer. A final combing and clipping finishes the grooming session.

Some dog groomers may be known as *pet groomers*, who trim and groom dogs according to owner preference, regardless of the breed. An important part of the job for these groomers' involves communicating effectively with pet owners. They must listen carefully to pet owners in order to provide their dogs with the desired grooming. In some cases, they must tell pet owners that their preferred grooming style is not feasible or may even be unhealthy.

Other groomers may be known as *master groomers*, who attempt to achieve the breed standard appearance. These dog groomers must be familiar with all breeds of dog and be able to give each breed an appropriate grooming. Some breeds require more care than others. Poodles require a lot of grooming and are usually a substantial part of a groomer's business.

Groomers also check dogs for signs of illness and infection. They may advise pet owners to take their pet to a veterinarian. They examine the dog's muscle tone and bone structure as well as its eyes, ears, coat, and skin to detect abnormalities. However, groomers are not licensed to prescribe any form of treatment for pet illnesses and infections.

Dog groomers who own their own shops may also sell pet-related products and grooming supplies, which requires a general knowledge of pet care and nutrition.

Working Conditions

Dog grooming is physically demanding. Groomers frequently have to lift animals weighing from 20 to 50 pounds--and sometimes more--into tubs and onto grooming tables. They risk back strain as well as being bitten or scratched. They are sometimes exposed to diseases and must use caution when working with the toxic chemicals in flea dips and shampoos. Like other animal caretakers, they generally work under noisy conditions. A love of dogs, however, often outweighs many negative elements of the job.

Employment

There were an estimated 30,000 dog groomers employed in 1992, accounting for nearly one-third of the total 103,000 animal caretakers. A high percentage of dog groomers are self-employed or work part-time. Self-employed dog groomers may work out of their homes, their own grooming shop, or have a mobile facility. Other dog groomers work for veterinary hospitals, pet stores, boarding kennels, grooming shops, and grooming schools. Many of these dog groomers work for a percentage of income generated from grooming, such as 50 or 60 percent. Some employers provide groomers with all the necessary supplies.

Training, Other Qualifications, and Advancement

There are several ways dog groomers learn their trade. Many groomers are involved in breeding and showing dogs and gain experience grooming their own pets. Others learn on-the-job by working as an apprentice to an experienced groomer for three to six months. With the help of books as teaching guides, they can then practice on their own pets and those of friends until they gain experience. Finally, dog groomers can attend a trade school that specializes in grooming. There are numerous accredited dog grooming programs and more than 50 grooming schools accredited by the National Dog Groomers Association of America (NDGAA). Classes in grooming are usually small and emphasize learning through practical experience.

The NDGAA also offers professional registration or certification to dog groomers who meet established standards. Throughout their careers, dog groomers continue their learning and training by keeping up with developments in the field. They read trade journals and other publications on grooming and animal care. They may attend conventions and seminars, take classes, and enter competitions to improve their skills.

Dog groomers genuinely care for dogs and are interested in activities involving animals. They must learn the needs and habits of different breeds. They have to be patient and gentle with animals that may be nervous or uncooperative. They need good communication skills to talk to, sympathize with, and receive instructions from pet owners.

Dog groomers can advance in their careers by managing a grooming shop or service and eventually opening their own shop. Some groomers become certified instructors and teach at grooming schools. They may also become kennel operators, breeders, or trainers.

Job Outlook

While the Bureau of Labor Statistics does not make projections specifically for dog groomers, employment of animal caretakers as a whole is projected to increase by nearly 40 percent between 1992 and 2005. This is faster than the average for all occupations.

Several factors point to a strong demand for the services of dog groomers. These include a growing population and expanding economy along with an increasing number of dogs and cats as pets. As pet ownership increases, there will be a growing demand for dog groomers. Many openings will also occur for dog groomers as a result of people leaving the field.

Earnings

Earnings for dog groomers depend on type of employment and average number of hours worked per week. Some full-time groomers average $18,000 to $20,000 per year, while experienced groomers can make considerably more. Self-employed groomers and those owning their own services or shops generally make more than those who work for pet shops and other employers. Groomers familiar with the specific requirements of various breeds tend to make more than those who do general grooming.

Related Occupations

Other pet care occupations include kennel attendants, dog trainers, handlers, animal breeders, pet store caretakers, and pet shop owners.

Other animal caretaker occupations include animal attendants, stable workers, zookeepers, veterinary technicians, veterinary assistants, laboratory animal technologists, laboratory animal technicians, and assistant laboratory animal technicians.

Other occupations that involve working with animals include agricultural and biological scientists, veterinarians, retail sales workers in pet stores, gamekeepers, game-farm helpers, poultry breeders, ranchers, and artificial-breeding technicians.

Sources of Additional Information

For more information about dog groomers and accredited grooming schools, contact:

- National Dog Groomers Association of America, PO Box 101, Clark, PA 16113. Phone: (412)962-2711.

FARRIERS

At a Glance

- **D.O.T.:** 418.381-010

- **Preferred Education:** 1-2 years of specific vocational preparation

- **Average Salary:** Self-employed farriers can earn between $37,500 and $62,500.

- **Did You Know?** Farriers can shoe from six to ten horses a day.

Nature of the Work

Farriers are blacksmiths who specialize in shoeing horses. They use a wide variety of hand and power tools to fit, shape, and nail aluminum or steel shoes to horses' hooves. In some cases they may forge special fitting shoes from steel bars. A relatively small proportion of farriers work out of a traditional blacksmith shop. Most farriers have a van, truck, or trailer that is outfitted as a mobile shop to take them where horses are located.

The job of horseshoeing usually begins with the removal of worn or defective shoes from the horse's hooves, using nail snippers and pincers. Most horses need to be trimmed or reshod every six to eight weeks. Farriers use knives and snippers to trim and shape an animal's hoof as needed. In making new shoes for horses, farriers typically start with machine-made, or "keg," shoes that come in a variety of sizes, styles, weights, and materials. In some cases they hand forge and fabricate horseshoes from metal bar stock, especially if they are doing corrective or therapeutic shoeing.

The process of hand forging a special horseshoe, or in

some cases a special tool, involves heating the metal to the desired temperature in a coal, oil, or gas fitted furnace. Farriers determine the temperature of the metal by using a pyrometer or watching the color of the fire. When the proper temperature is reached, they remove the metal from the fire with a pair of tongs and place it on an anvil. A hammer or rasp is used to shape the metal into a shoe or tool on the anvil.

Farriers use a variety of tools to shape the horseshoe to its proper size and contour to fit the horse's hoof. They use measuring devices such as calipers, dividers, and scales to take measurements of the hooves. During the shaping process they may use a variety of tools, including the hardy, pritchel, flatter, swedge block, and forepunch. The metal shoe may be held in a bench vise while it is being shaped.

After the shoe has been shaped to the foot of the animal, it is hardened by tempering it in air, oil, or water. Horseshoe borium may be applied by using an acetylene torch to harden the wearing surface of the shoe. Farriers then finish the surface of the shoe using hand files and rasps or a power grinder.

Farriers can shoe from six to 10 horses a day, depending on such factors as how cooperative the animals are and how far they must travel between animals. The quality of work being done and the stamina of the farrier also determine how many horses can be shod in a day.

Working Conditions

Farriers may face a variety of adverse conditions as they work on horses outdoors or in stables. They often encounter flying insects, odors, dust, and temperature extremes. Working in close quarters with horses, farriers are exposed to such hazards as biting, scratching, and kicking from the animals.

Due to the nature of the work, injuries are not uncommon, including cuts, bruises, burns, and mashed fingers. Some protection is afforded by wearing a leather apron, goggles, and steel-toed shoes. Much of the work of farriers is performed in a stooping or crouching position. In addition to holding tools and working with both hands together, farriers often have to bend, twist, reach, grip, lift, carry, and handle the animals they are working on.

Farriers receive instructions from and interact with horse owners. They may work under the direction of a Doctor of Veterinary Medicine (DVM). Their work often involves putting up with distractions from other animals, people, and automobiles in their work area.

Employment

Most farriers are self-employed. It is usually difficult to establish a new practice. Once established, farriers can decide how much or how little work they will do, and they can usually choose where they work. Some farriers are on retainer from specific farms or stables. Others specialize in working with racehorses and follow the racing circuit from track to track.

Training, Other Qualifications, and Advancement

Farriers generally have from one to two years of specific vocational preparation before they are fully qualified. They may be self-taught or serve an apprenticeship with an experienced farrier. They may learn their trade at one of approximately 50 farrier schools located in the United States and Canada. Courses of instruction range from three days to four months. Individuals can prepare for working as farriers by learning how to use hand tools and working with animals. Courses in anatomy and other biological and physical sciences are also helpful.

In addition to learning the physical skills involved in forging and shaping horseshoes, farriers should acquire as much knowledge as possible about the theory of horseshoeing. Relevant areas of study include anatomy, physiology, and animal psychology. A thorough knowledge of horses' anatomy and physiology will help in diagnosing imbalances and understanding the probable results of any shoeing or trimming. They should be able to read and understand radiographs and know enough medical terminology to communicate with a DVM. Since most farriers are self-employed, basic courses in business management and public relations are also recommended.

The American Farrier's Association (AFA) offers two levels of professional certification of farriers. Candidates must demonstrate their abilities and pass a written certification examination. In addition, the AFA recently began offering a special endorsement in therapeutic horseshoeing. Individuals must pass a three-part examination consisting of a written exam, two oral presentations, and a practical test involving specimen shoes.

The work of farriers requires that they have average physical strength and be in good physical condition. Stamina and agility are needed, along with good hand-eye coordination, manual dexterity, and a sense of balance and angles.

Farriers enjoy working around animals. They must be able to handle horses and work with horse owners and Doctors of Veterinary Medicine. Common "horse sense" is often needed to handle situations that arise.

Job Outlook

The Bureau of Labor Statistics includes farriers with the broad category of animal caretakers, except farm. Employment projections for this occupational group are much better than the average for all occupations, with employment projected to increase by nearly 40 percent between 1992 and 2005. The demand for farriers in particular is expected to remain strong, since the equine population has increased each year. There are an estimated 10 million horses in the United States, and most animals have to be trimmed or shod every six to eight weeks throughout the year.

Earnings

Farriers earn different rates depending on the services they perform. Their overall earnings depend on the services they are willing to do and the amount of time they are willing to work. Rates range from $5 for trimming an unshod animal to $18 to $26 for a normal shoeing. If the horseshoes are handmade, $35 to $75 is usually charged. Therapeutic or corrective work is billed at higher rates based on the nature of the work. Self-employed farriers who average six to 10 horses a day, five days a week, 50 weeks a year, can expect to earn between $37,500 and $62,500. Offsetting those earnings are expenses involved in traveling, overhead spent on tools and equipment, and other costs of doing business.

Related Occupations

Related occupations involving horses include stable workers, trainers, veterinary technicians, and a variety of other positions at racetracks, ranches, stables, and farms. Other occupations involving blacksmithing and metalworking include boilermakers, jewelers, machinists, metalworking machine operators, tool and die makers, and welders and cutters.

Sources of Additional Information

- American Farrier's Association, 4059 Iron Works Pike, Lexington, KY 40511. Phone: (606)233-7411. Fax: (606)231-7862.

VETERINARY TECHNICIANS

At a Glance

- **D.O.T.:** 079.361-014

- **Preferred Education:** Associate degree

- **Average Salary:** $15,000 to $25,000

- **Did You Know?** The American Veterinary Medical Association (AVMA) has accredited more than 60 two-year associate degree programs in veterinary technology.

Nature of the Work

Preparing animals for surgery, administering medication, and conducting laboratory tests are some of the varied responsibilities of veterinary technicians. Veterinary technicians serve as professional assistants to veterinarians, biomedical researchers, and other scientists.

In veterinary practices, technicians assist in diagnostic, medical, and surgical procedures. They check animals for parasites, give vaccines, and dress wounds. For surgeries, veterinary technicians sterilize instruments, set up equipment, and administer anesthesia. Veterinary technicians may also collect specimens and perform laboratory procedures. They may position animals for x-rays, calculate radiation exposure, and develop the film. They may be responsible for medical supplies inventory and control.

An important part of the job for veterinary technicians involves obtaining information from clients regarding animal history and condition. They also communicate with clients and educate them regarding animal care. Veterinary technicians

may specialize in the care of either small or large animals.

In other facilities, such as biological research laboratories, drug companies, or zoos, veterinary technicians may be responsible for animal care and feeding, laboratory procedures, equipment maintenance, and record-keeping.

Working Conditions

Veterinary clinics are often noisy, and veterinary technicians may be at risk of animal bites and scratches as well as diseases. The work requires moderate strength to be able to lift and maneuver animals weighing from 20 to 50 pounds or more. At animal clinics, veterinary technicians frequently interact with animal owners as well as other staff members during the course of their work day. They may also supervise and interact with veterinary assistants and animal attendants.

Employment

Most veterinary technicians are employed by practicing veterinarians in veterinary clinics. Other facilities that employ veterinary technicians include biological research laboratories, drug or feed manufacturing companies, animal production facilities, zoos, and food processing and packing plants. Public health organizations, research and academic institutions, and universities also employ individuals trained in veterinary technology.

Training, Other Qualifications, and Advancement

Most states require that veterinary technicians be licensed or registered with the state. While requirements vary from state to state, licensing requirements typically include graduation from a nationally accredited or state approved program in veterinary technology, or equivalent experience working for a practicing veterinarian. Other licensing requirements usually include passing a national or state examination and paying a license fee.

The American Veterinary Medical Association (AVMA) has accredited more than 60 two-year associate degree programs and five bachelor's degree programs in veterinary technology. The core curriculum of these programs includes the fundamentals of chemistry, applied mathematics, communication skills, humanities or liberal arts, and biological science. High school courses in these subjects provide applicants with a good background for the study of veterinary technology.

In addition, AVMA accredited programs include a number of required areas specifically related to veterinary technology. Among the topics studied are ethics and jurisprudence, anatomy and physiology, anesthetic nursing, biochemistry, medical terminology, office management, animal nutrition and feeding, animal care and management, animal husbandry, diseases and nursing of animals, surgical nursing, and several others. Students are given practical experience with animals in addition to scientific and theoretical instruction. Most courses are taught by experienced veterinarians or veterinary technicians.

Personal qualifications of veterinary technicians include a natural affinity with animals and a desire to help them. Veterinary technicians must also have well developed reasoning skills to apply scientific findings and principles to practical problems in medicine. Good communication and interpersonal skills are very important to work as part of an animal health care team and communicate with animal owners. Veterinary technicians must be able to work under supervision and follow directions.

Veterinary technicians generally advance to higher salary levels through good performance on the job. They may also decide to continue their education to become veterinarians.

Job Outlook

The overall outlook for animal caretakers, except farm, calls for a 40 percent increase in employment between 1992 and 2005, which is faster than the average for all occupations. Within the field of animal care, prospects are best for individuals trained as veterinary technicians. According to the Bureau of Labor Statistics, many employers report a shortage of properly trained veterinary technicians.

Also affecting the need for veterinary technicians is the growing senior citizen population, many of whom have pets for companions. Some studies indicate that pet owners visit veterinarians twice as often as they did 10 years ago for animal vaccinations and physicals.

Earnings

Earnings for veterinary technicians depend on experience, size of employer, and geographic location. The average salary for veterinary technicians working in private practices ranges from $15,000 to $25,000 per year. Those working for companies involved in scientific research can earn an average salary ranging from $27,000 to $40,000.

Related Occupations

Related occupations that involve animal care and handling include laboratory animal technicians, zookeepers, animal attendants, kennel and stable operators and helpers, agricultural and biological scientists, veterinarians, gamekeepers, poultry breeders, ranchers, and artificial breeding technicians. Other fields that include related occupations are animal protection and control, pet services, animal trainers, wildlife management, and conservation and environmental protection.

Sources of Additional Information

For additional informaiton contact:

- American Veterinary Medical Association, 1931 N. Meacham Rd., Ste. 100, Schaumburg, IL 60173-4360. Phone: (708)925-8070 or (800)248-2862.

- Humane Society of the United States, 2100 L St. NW, Washington, DC 20037. Phone: (202)452-1100.

ZOOKEEPERS

At a Glance

- **D.O.T.:** 412.674-010 and -014

- **Preferred Education:** B.S. in animal behavior, animal science, conservation biology, marine biology, wildlife management, or zoology

- **Average Salary:** $9,000 to $30,000

- **Did You Know?** All major zoological parks require entry-level zookeepers to have a four-year college degree.

Nature of the Work

Wild and exotic animals are sometimes held in captivity for conservation, research, public education, and recreation. A healthy, well-adjusted group of animals is the responsibility of a specialized team of animal care specialists that includes curators, veterinarians, and zookeepers, among others. Zookeepers are charged with providing the daily care of captive animals. In addition, they often serve as frontline public relations representatives by answering questions from the zoo's visitors.

Zookeepers' basic duties include feeding the animals and keeping their enclosures clean. They may prepare food for animals by chopping or grinding meat, mixing prepared feeds, or unbaling forage grasses. Following the directions of a veterinarian, they may add vitamins or medication to the food. They keep the animals' water containers filled and place and remove food from cages as directed.

Zookeepers keep their animals' enclosures clean by using a rake, water hose, and disinfectant. In addition they may help design, build, and repair animal enclosures. They are sometimes responsible for plants and vegetation in and around the exhibits. They monitor the temperature and humidity of the enclosures and adjust controls as needed. When animals are transferred from one location to another, zookeepers make sure it is done properly.

Zookeepers are required to observe the animals under their charge closely. They must learn the habits and behaviors of each animal and group of animals in order to be able to detect subtle changes in their physical or psychological condition. They watch animals for illnesses and injuries and notify the head zookeeper or veterinarian when they occur. They may assist veterinarians in treating illnesses and injuries. They keep records regarding the animals' behavior, feeding, and health.

Zookeepers may also be involved in research projects, conservation efforts, and reproductive husbandry. They work closely with zoo managers and provide them with data based on their observations.

Zookeepers often answer questions from visitors. They must be knowledgeable about the animals, their natural habitats and habits, and zoos in general. As representatives of the zoo, they help increase public awareness of the role of zoos in wildlife conservation and other areas.

Zookeepers may become highly specialized. Those who work in children's zoos often care for newborn and young animals in a zoo nursery. They also care for the mothers of newborn animals. They may conduct physical examinations of young animals and keep records of their growth. Other areas of specialization include caring for specific species, such as exotic birds, reptiles, or elephants.

Working Conditions

Zookeepers may be subject to animal bites and scratches as well as diseases. As a result, direct contact with animals is kept to a minimum. The work requires moderate strength, with frequent lifting or moving of 10 to 25 pounds. Zookeepers frequently have to stoop, kneel, crouch, and reach during the course of their work. Zookeepers regularly interact with other zoo employees, zoo managers, and the general public. The zoo atmosphere is often noisy.

Zookeepers often work outdoors and are frequently exposed to unpleasant weather conditions. Work schedules usually include weekends and holidays, as animals must be fed and cared for daily. A 40-hour work week is standard, although some zookeepers may work 50 hours a week.

Employment

Zookeepers work in large zoological parks and smaller zoos. These parks and zoos are usually located near large and medium-size cities and other populated areas. The number of employers is limited, and zookeepers may find some difficulty in entering the field. A list of potential employers is available from the American Zoo and Aquarium Association.

Training, Other Qualifications, and Advancement

All major zoological parks require applicants for entry-level zookeepers to have a four-year college degree. Appropriate fields of study include animal science, zoology, marine biology, conservation biology, wildlife management, and animal behavior. Some colleges, notably Santa Fe Community College in Gainesville, Florida, and Moorpark College in California, offer specific programs oriented toward working in zoos. Curatorial internships are available at some zoos.

Many zoos require previous experience handling animals, which may be obtained at smaller zoos, animal hospitals, or by working as a volunteer. Newly hired zookeepers receive on-the-job training, in which the basic responsibilities are taught during the first three to six months. Additional on-the-job training may last for years.

Zookeepers must have a genuine interest in taking care of animals, usually in an outdoor setting. They must learn the habits and physical needs of specific types of animals. They must be keen observers in order to detect changes in animal behavior that may signal physical or psychological distress. Zookeepers' concern for animal welfare is expressed in terms of dedication, commitment, and patience on the job.

Zookeepers can advance while still maintaining hands-on responsibility for the care and handling of captive animals. Especially in larger institutions, they may advance from keepers to senior keepers who take care of a specific species or class of animals. Head keepers supervise a section or department of a zoo and provide training and scheduling for keepers. Curatorial and management positions higher than head keeper usually require an advanced degree.

Job Outlook

The overall outlook for animal caretakers, except farm, calls for a 40 percent increase in employment between 1992 and 2005. Within the field of animal care, prospects for zookeepers are less favorable. Competition for available positions, slow growth in zoo capacity, and low turnover among zookeepers are cited as reasons for the low number of positions available.

Earnings

A zookeeper's salary may range from minimum wage to more than $30,000 a year, according to the American Zoo and Aquarium Association. Education, skills, and length of employment are the major factors determining salary level in this field.

Related Occupations

Related occupations that involve animal care and handling include laboratory animal technicians, veterinary technicians, animal attendants, kennel and stable operators and helpers, agricultural and biological scientists, veterinarians, gamekeepers, poultry breeders, ranchers, and artificial breeding technicians. Fields that contain other related occupations are animal protection and control, pet services, animal trainers, wildlife management, and conservation and environmental protection.

Sources of Additional Information

For additional information contact:

• American Association of Zoo Keepers, Topeka Zoological Park, 635 SW Gage Blvd., Topeka, KS 66606. Phone: (913)272-5821.

• American Zoo and Aquarium Association (American Association of Zoological Parks and Aquariums), Office of Membership Services, Ogleby Park, Wheeling, WV 26003-1698. Phone: (304)242-2160.

Personal Service Occupations

CHILD DAY CARE WORKER

At a Glance

- **D.O.T.:** 359.677-010

- **Preferred Education:** High school diploma

- **Average Salary:** $260 per week

- **Did you know?** One third of all full-time day care providers work more than 40 hours per week.

Nature of Work

With the increasing number of women in the work force, more and more American children under the age of six are being raised by day care workers. Child day care workers supervise and care for young children while their parents are at work or otherwise away from home. Child day care workers may be employed by day care centers or be self-employed and caring for children in their own homes.

Whatever the setting, child day care workers generally have the same responsibilities. They plan and supervise activities, offer basic care, help keep the children healthy, and encourage their physical, emotional, intellectual, and social development.

Child day care workers feed, diaper, comfort, and play with infants. They help older preschoolers explore their interests, develop their talents and independence, build self-esteem, and learn how to behave with others. When children misbehave, day care workers may be required to discipline them.

Child day care workers balance each day's activities with individual and group play and quiet and active time. A typical day may begin with breakfast, followed by indoor play activities such as arts and crafts, a juice break, and outdoor play. In the afternoon, child day care workers may serve lunch, read stories, and take children to the playground or on field trips. Naps are also included in the daily schedule.

Although child day care workers are not officially considered teachers, they often combine basic care with teaching duties. Young children mainly learn through play.

For example, storytelling and acting games help children develop language skills. Counting and balancing blocks introduces children to basic concepts and helps develop motor skills.

Child care workers who are employed by day care centers generally work under a supervisor or director. They typically follow a structured program and have few administrative responsibilities. Self-employed child care workers, on the other hand, have the additional responsibility of running a business. This includes purchasing food and supplies and keeping detailed business records.

Working Conditions

Day care centers may be located in private homes, schools, religious institutions, private buildings, community centers, or office buildings. Regardless of the setting, areas in which children are cared for should be clean and comfortable. The working hours can be long. Many centers are open 12 or more hours a day. One third of all full-time day care providers work more than 40 hours per week. There are also many opportunities for part-time work. Self-employed day care workers who work in their own homes can care for their own children and run errands while they work.

Day care workers spend much of their time walking, standing, bending, stooping, and lifting. The work environment can be loud and active. Day care workers must be constantly alert and able to anticipate and prevent accidents. Dealing with disruptive children can make the job physically and emotionally demanding.

Employment

Child care workers held approximately 684,000 jobs in 1992. Approximately one in five were self-employed; most were assumed to be family care providers, while others were self-employed managers of child care centers. Child care operations vary greatly in size. Self-employed workers typically care for a few children in their homes. Large corporate centers, meanwhile, often employ large staffs. Most centers are small, however. Two-thirds have nine or fewer employees. Jobs in child-care can be found across the country.

Training, Advancement, and Other Qualifications

Typically, there are no training requirements or

125

qualifications for child day care workers who work out of their homes. Some states have, however, established minimum education requirements for day care center employees. Directors may be required to have a college degree. Teachers must have a high school diploma and, in many cases, a combination of college education and experience. Many states require a Child Development Associate (CDA) credential, which is offered by the Council for Early Childhood Professional Recognition. Other day care workers usually need a high school diploma but it is not always a requirement.

Many states also require other types of training for staff members, including health and first aid, fire safety, and child abuse detection and prevention. Most states also mandate criminal record checks for all child-care staff.

Child day care workers should be mature, patient, and understanding. They also need plenty of energy and physical stamina. Those who are self-employed must have good business skills.

As they gain experience, child day care workers can move into supervisory or administrative positions in large day care operations. These jobs often require formal education, such as a bachelor's degree. Some workers open their own day care businesses.

Job Outlook

The U.S. Department of Labor expects wage and salary jobs in the child care services industry to grow 42 percent between 1990 and 2005, which is much faster than the average for all industries. An unusually large number of job openings will result each year from the need to replace experienced workers who leave the industry. This high turnover rate reflects the low wages and relatively meager benefits received by child care workers. But, rapid growth and high turnover should create excellent employment opportunities.

Although the number of children age 5 and under is expected to decline, the proportion of youngsters in day care and preschool is expected to increase.

Earnings

Earnings for child day care workers depend on the employer and the educational background of the worker. Although child care is among the lowest paid occupations in the country, more education sometimes means higher earnings.

According to 1992 figures from the U.S. Department of Labor, median weekly earnings of full-time, salaried child-care workers were $260. Early childhood teacher assistants earned $220 per week. The top 10 percent of child-care workers earned at least $460; assistants, at least $420. The bottom 10 percent of child-care workers earned less than $140; teacher assistants, less than $150.

Earnings of self-employed child-care workers vary depending on the hours worked, number and ages of the children cared for, and the location.

Benefits for child-care workers also vary. Many receive free or discounted child care from their employers. Some employers offer full benefits, including health insurance and paid vacation, while others offer no benefits at all.

Related Occupations

Child-care workers need patience, creativity, and an ability to nurture, motivate, and teach children. Others who work with children and need these skills include teacher aides, children's tutors, kindergarten and elementary school teachers, nannies, child psychologists, and preschool teachers.

Sources of Additional Information

- Council for Early Childhood Professional Recognition, 1341 G St. NW, Ste. 400, Washington, DC 20005 Phone: (202)265-9090

- Child Care Action Campaign, 330 7th Ave., 17th Fl., New York, NY 10001 Phone: (212)239-0138

- National Association for Family Day Care, 1331-A Pennsylvania Ave., NW. Ste. 348, Washington, DC 20004 Phone: (602)838-3446

- Child Welfare League of America, 440 1st St. NW, Ste. 310, Washington, DC 20001 Phone: (202)638-2952

MAKEUP ARTISTS

At a Glance

- **D.O.T.:** 333.271-010

- **Preferred Education:** Training and experience

- **Average Salary:** Varies.

- **Did You Know?** The most employment opportunities for theatrical makeup artists are in major metropolitan areas and cities with an active cultural life, including New York, Los Angeles, Washington, D.C., Chicago, and Atlanta.

Nature of the Work

Achieving the right look in real life has never been easy. It's even more difficult to make actors and actresses, news anchors, talk show hosts, and fashion models look natural in the harsh light of artificial settings. Thanks to the work of makeup artists, television and stage performers can look their best at all times.

Makeup artists improve, enhance, or alter the appearance of performers or other individuals. To accomplish this, makeup artists generally have a full range of cosmetic products available for their use, including face powder, blush, lipstick, and eye shadow. When makeup artists require a shade, color, or texture that is not available commercially, they may mix their own makeup using greases, oils, coloring, and other materials. Some top makeup artists have even developed their own commercial lines of cosmetics. Other makeup artists serve as consultants to makeup and cosmetics manufacturers, advising them on what products to introduce.

Makeup artists in television, film, and theater work closely with other production personnel, including directors, production designers, costume designers, costumers, and production hairstylists. In smaller productions, makeup artists may also serve as hairstylists. Makeup artists on television shows and film productions review production schedules to determine if there are any special makeup needs for the day's shooting.

Makeup artists are sometimes required to create a look or appearance for a character in a television show, film, or stage play. They may research the character first by reading the script and consulting with directors, writers, and actors. In some cases makeup artists will try to achieve a completely natural look to make a character look like a real person. In other cases they may try to achieve a more elaborate look that goes beyond realism.

When doing makeup for news and talk shows, commercials, and many kinds of realistic television shows, films, and plays, makeup artists try to achieve a natural look. Since the harsh lighting used in many productions tends to wash out certain aspects of a person's appearance and accentuate others, makeup artists apply makeup in such as way as to minimize the effects of lighting and create a natural appearance. Makeup artists can also make people appear older, younger, heavier, or thinner.

Makeup artists may apply makeup to exposed parts of a performer's body in addition to the face. For example, if a scene involves a telephone call, makeup artists may apply makeup to the character's hand. When characters have been in an accident, makeup artists can make their bodies look bruised or injured. Makeup artists can add blood, scars, and wounds to characters' faces, arms, and other body areas to make it appear they have been in a fight.

Working Conditions

Makeup artists are at work on the set before, during, and after a film or show is shot or a play performed. Consequently they often work long hours. They may start working at midnight to prepare makeup for morning talk and news show hosts and their guests. In theatrical productions, they usually arrive at the theater a few hours before the performance. They must remain in the theater during the performance to reapply makeup, make changes, and do touch-ups for the actors.

Makeup artists are under a certain amount of pressure to achieve a certain look for a performer and may have a limited time in which to work. Like others in the film and theatre industry, they may have to travel to various locations and work under different conditions.

Employment

Makeup artists work for motion picture studios and production companies, television stations and production companies, and video production companies. Makeup artists may work on staff or as freelancers for various productions, including sitcoms, dramas, soap operas, motion pictures and films, commercials, and corporate broadcasts. Makeup artists are typically hired for specific productions, so they may not work regularly. When one production is completed, they must find work elsewhere. Many makeup artists in New York, Los Angeles, and elsewhere belong to the International Alliance of Theatrical Stage Employees and Moving Picture Machine Operators of the U.S. and Canada (IATSE). Local chapters of the IATSE usually keep a list of makeup artists and other stage and film production workers who are available for work.

Theatrical makeup artists may work for Broadway plays, Off- and Off-Off-Broadway plays, cabaret and dinner theater productions, regional and stock theater productions, and ballets and operas. The most employment opportunities for theatrical makeup artists are in major metropolitan areas and cities with an active cultural life, including New York, Los Angeles, Washington, D.C., Chicago, and Atlanta.

Some makeup artists work regularly in cosmetology salons as cosmetologists, facialists, or hairstylists in between productions. Some makeup artists are self-employed and work on a freelance basis. Others may own their own beauty salon.

Training, Other Qualifications, and Advancement

Makeup artists can learn their skills in many different ways. They can obtain first-hand experience through internships or apprenticeships, learning from experienced practitioners. Apprenticeship and internship programs are available from some television stations and film production companies. Where no apprenticeships or internships are available, makeup artists can work as assistants to experienced makeup artists and learn from them.

Makeup artists may also obtain formal training in college by majoring in subjects such as television, film, or theater arts and production. They may attend makeup schools that specialize in television, film, and theatrical makeup. Additional training may be had in courses, workshops, and seminars offered by colleges, universities, and television or film studios. Makeup artists may attend cosmetology schools to learn the techniques of professional manicurists, facialists, estheticians, hairstylists, and cosmetologists.

Some states may require makeup artists to be licensed as cosmetologists, hairstylists, or facialists. While licensing requirements vary from state to state, they generally include taking a course of study at an approved cosmetology school and passing a practical and written licensing examination.

Makeup artists are generally people who are artistically inclined and like to express themselves visually. They should have a good sense of color, form, and shape and be able to select the appropriate tools, materials, and techniques to achieve a desired result. They need manual dexterity to mix, handle, and apply cosmetics. They must have good vision to work closeup and have good color vision.

Makeup artists have different opportunities for advancement. With experience they may advance to work on larger productions. Theatrical makeup artists at the top of their field work on Broadway productions. Television makeup artists strive to work on regularly scheduled programs such as sitcoms, soap operas, and news and talk shows. Other possibilities for advancement include becoming a makeup consultant for a cosmetics manufacturer or developing one's own line of cosmetic products.

Job Outlook

According to the Bureau of Labor Statistics, overall employment of cosmetologists, including makeup artists, is projected to increase faster than the average for all occupations between 1992 and 2005. Within the motion picture industry, employment of artists and commercial artists, including makeup artists, is projected to increase by approximately 50 percent between 1992 and 2005.

Earnings

Earnings for makeup artists depend on such factors as employment situation, geographic location, ability to work regularly, type and size of productions worked on, and individual experience, qualifications, and responsibilities. Entry-level makeup artists can expect to earn approximately $12,800 or more to start.

Members of the IATSE and other unions may have their base-level earnings set for them. Makeup artists working on Broadway productions must belong to the IATSE, which has established a minimum weekly earnings level of approximately $700 for them. Experienced makeup artists earn considerably more than the IATSE minimum. In film and television, salaries for makeup artists range from $500 per week to more than $2,500. Top names in the field can earn as much as $2,500 per day.

Related Occupations

Related occupations include cosmetologists, barbers, hairstylists, facialists, estheticians, and manicurists. Other occupations in the cosmetology industry include barber and cosmetology instructors, beauty supply distributors, makeup consultants, and wig specialists. Other preproduction occupations in film and television include art directors, illustrators, scenic designers, model makers, set decorators, and costume designers.

Sources of Additional Information

- American Association of Cosmetology Schools, 901 N. Washington St., Ste. 206, Alexandria, VA 22314-1535 Phone: (703)845-1333.

- Association of Cosmetologists and Hairdressers, 1811 Monroe, Dearborn, MI 48124. Phone: (313)563-0360.

- International Alliance of Theatrical Stage Employees and Moving Picture Machine Operators of the U.S. and Canada (IATSE), 1515 Broadway, Ste. 601, New York, NY 10036. Phone: (212)730-1770.

- National Accrediting Commission of Cosmetology Arts and Sciences, 901 N. Stuart St., No. 900, Arlington, VA 22203. Phone: (703)527-7600.

- National Cosmetology Association, 3510 Olive St., St. Louis, MO 63103. Phone: (314)534-7980.

MANICURISTS AND NAIL TECHNICIANS

At a Glance

- **D.O.T.:** 331.674-010

- **Preferred Education:** Training and classroom study

- **Average Salary:** $14,500 to $29,100

- **Did You Know?** In most states, manicurists must have a license, which requires passing a written and practical test.

Nature of the Work

More than $3 billion is spent each year on the services of professional nail technicians, also known as manicurists. Such services include manicures, pedicures, and artificial nails. In addition to giving basic manicures and pedicures (care of the feet), nail technicians shape and color nails using a variety of techniques. Increasingly, nail technicians use their artistic ability to create original nail designs.

When a customer visits a nail technician, the technician provides a consultation by examining the nails, making sure they are healthy, and determining what color and shape the client prefers. Nail technicians take into consideration the shape of the client's hands, length of fingers, and type of work the client does, which may have an affect on their hands and nails. In some cases, nail technicians may have to refer a client to a physician if the client has a nail or skin disorder.

After the consultation, technicians may remove nail polish with liquid polish remover and cotton swabs. They also use orangewood sticks to loosen cuticles around the base of the nail and a steel pusher to push back excess cuticle growth. They shape the nails with emery boards or nail files. During the process, they use antibacterial soap, creams and oils to soften cuticles, and nail strengthener. After the nails are prepared, nail technicians apply colored polish.

Most nail technicians are skilled in additional services such as nail tips, nail wraps, and acrylic nails. Nail tips are artificial nails made of plastic, nylon, or acetate. Nail wraps are pieces of cloth or paper bonded to the front of the nail to repair or strengthen natural nails. Acrylic nails, or sculptured nails, are made by combining a liquid acrylic product with a powdered acrylic product and shaping them into natural looking nails.

Beyond these services, nail technicians may use airbrushing or stencils to create designs, and make decorations with tiny gems, foils, tapes, and other materials. Clients may only wish to have one nail decorated, which may take two or three minutes, or they may want complex designs on all ten.

Working Conditions

Nail technicians work in clean, well-lighted salons. They work with their customers at manicure tables that contain their equipment and materials. Many of the chemicals used by nail technicians can be hazardous when they are improperly used or stored, and nail technicians may have to wear gloves or dust masks during certain procedures to avoid contact or overexposure to these chemicals. In addition, nail technicians are at some risk of infection if they perform services on customers who are not healthy. To minimize risk, technicians must follow strict state guidelines regarding various nail services, the use of certain chemicals, and sanitation procedures.

Employment

According to the Bureau of Labor Statistics, there were 35,000 manicurists employed in 1992. Manicurists may work in full-service salons that provide several cosmetology services such as hair styling and makeovers, or they may work in salons devoted solely to manicures. These salons may be located in department stores, hotels, and in some cases private homes. Many nail technicians are self-employed.

Training, Other Qualifications, and Advancement

Approximately 4,000 cosmetology and beauty schools in the United States offer programs for manicurists. These programs can take from 100 class hours to 2,100 class hours to complete. They include classes, lectures, and demonstrations. Students also learn from practical experience.

During their classes, students learn about the structure and composition of nails. They study the different types of equipment and supplies needed for their jobs. In courses covering proper sanitation, students learn how to care for their tools and how to use chemicals safely. Some schools offer apprenticeship programs. Most offer services to the public so students can work with actual customers.

In most states, manicurists must have a license. To receive a license, students must pass a written and practical test. Many states also have age and educational requirements for licensure. For more information on licenses, students should check with their state board of cosmetology.

Nail technicians should have a basic knowledge of the structure of the human body and its functions. Appropriate areas of study include anatomy and physiology. Nail technicians must have artistic ability and good communication skills to interact with their clients. After receiving their license, nail technicians should be prepared to continue their education to keep up with changing technologies and state requirements. As they develop knowledge and skills, nail technologists may choose to teach nail technology in cosmetology schools, demonstrate manufacturers' products at stores and conventions, open their own salon, or become the personal nail technician for a fashion model or actor.

Job Outlook

According to the Bureau of Labor Statistics, job openings for manicurists will increase 54 percent by the year 2005. This is faster than the average for all occupations and reflects the growing popularity of nail services. Combined sales of more than $3 billion are reported for the manicuring, pedicuring and artificial nail industry. In some areas, this represents a 25 percent increase over previous years.

Earnings

Depending on the size of their clientele and the services they offer, nail technicians can earn between $14,500 and $29,100 per year. Manicurists who provide specialty services can earn much more than those who do only basic manicures. In 1992, for example, manicurists charged between $7 and $15 for a basic manicure, while charging as much as $85 for a full set of sculpted, acrylic nails. Some clients pay as much as $125 an hour for services. Many manicurists also receive tips from their customers. Self-employed manicurists must pay their own expenses, social security, and state and federal taxes.

Related Occupations

Related personal service occupations include barbers, hair stylists, make-up artists, electrologists, masseurs and masseuses, and weight reduction specialists.

Sources of Additional Information

- National Cosmetology Association, 3510 Olive St., St. Louis, MO 63103. Phone: (314)534-7980 or 800-527-1683.

NANNIES

At a Glance

- **D.O.T.:** 301.677-010
- **Preferred Education:** High school graduate
- **Average Salary:** $4.25 to $18 per hour
- **Did You Know?** As of 1994, demand for child care far outstripped the supply of trained nannies.

Nature of the Work

Nannies, also known as child monitors, provide working parents with an alternative to child day care centers by caring for their children in the children's own home. Nannies may commute from their own home or they may be hired to live with the families that employ them.

Nannies care for infants as well as children, who may be as old as 10 or 12 years. If there are infants in their care, nannies are responsible for feeding them. They prepare formula and sterilize bottles and other equipment. They supervise the infant's bathing and care for them when they are sick, giving them medicine according a doctor's instructions. They rock and cuddle the infants and change their diapers.

With young children, nannies help them dress. They do their laundry and keep their clothes clean and neat. They may also straighten up the children's rooms, but they usually don't have heavy cleaning responsibilities. Nannies may shop with young children and help them pick out their clothes. They usually cook and prepare meals for the children. When the children become sick, nannies take care of them and give them their medicine. Children like to play, and every day nannies have to plan playtime activities for them. Nannies may play games with the children and read or sing with them.

Nannies may also assist with the education of pre-schoolers and young children in school. Some nannies are trained to tutor children in certain subjects. They may make sure that children do their homework or provide them with educational materials to read and play with.

While nannies spend a lot of time in the home taking care of the children, they also have duties that take them outside of the house. They may be required to go on vacation with the family, for example. Nannies may have to transport children to and from school, to doctor's appointments, and to other activities. They may take walks with the children or accompany them to a playground.

During the day when the children's parents are not at home, nannies usually have the authority to discipline children. Parents and nannies discuss the parents' philosophy of raising their children, and nannies are expected to act in accordance with the parents' rules, values, and expectations.

Working Conditions

Nannies may be day-workers who live in their own homes and travel to work. Some nannies live in the home of their employer, generally with their own room and bath. Families that hire nannies usually live in urban apartments or suburban homes. While most of the work is done in their employer's home, nannies also spend time out of the home with the children. They may travel occasionally if their employer expects them to go on vacation with the family.

Hours of employment vary with each family. Nannies typically work more than 40 hours a week and sometimes as much as 50 to 60 hours during a five-day week. Nannies who live in their employer's home generally work longer hours than those who live in their own home. The long hours may make it difficult for nannies to establish their own social life, although nannies are usually given weekends and holidays off.

Employment

Traditionally, nannies were employed by upper class families who lived in large homes and estates. With the dramatic growth of dual-income families in recent years, families in which both parents work have become the major employers of nannies. Nannies are also employed by single-parent families.

According to the Bureau of Labor Statistics, there were 350,000 child care workers, including nannies, employed in private homes in 1992.

Training, Other Qualifications, and Advancement

Nannies are usually high school graduates who have had experience caring for children. In some cases, they learn the specific responsibilities of their position on the job. In other cases, families look for specially trained nannies. Graduates of nanny schools receive an intensive three- to four-month training program. Subjects of study include infant care and stimulation, family relations, creative play activities, nutrition, child psychology, special needs children, first aid, and similar topics. Applicants to nanny schools usually have to be at least high school graduates, have a driver's license, and be in good health.

Other educational programs that can prepare one for being a nanny are given at community and four-year colleges. Relevant areas of study include child growth and development, nutrition, infant care, creative play, health, safety, and first aid.

Nannies are people who are genuinely interested in helping others. They enjoy caring for other people, especially children. They should be honest, discreet, dependable, courteous, and neat. Some physical stamina is needed to take care of children for long hours at a time.

Opportunities for advancement as a nanny are limited. Nannies can earn higher wages by working for affluent families or families with more children. However, their experience in child care may lead to jobs in day care centers, preschools, or other positions involving children.

Job Outlook

Although the Bureau of Labor Statistics projects that employment of child care workers in private households will decrease by about 35 percent between 1992 and 2005, employment opportunities for nannies in particular are expected to be excellent. The reason is that many people leave this occupation, so that an estimated 151,000 openings for child care workers in private households will occur each year.

Other factors point to an increasing demand for the services of nannies. In particular the trend toward more families with two working parents and the growth of single-parent families means that there will be more demand for nannies and other types of child care. As of 1994, demand far outstripped the supply of trained nannies. As more women join the workforce, they will need help running their households and raising their children.

Earnings

Earnings depend on several factors, including geographic location, type of household, and number of hours worked. According to *American Salaries and Wages Survey*, nannies earn between minimum wage ($4.25) or less and $18 per hour. Higher-end wages are earned by trained nannies and those who work in affluent areas. Live-in nannies are given room and board and may receive other benefits such as use of a car.

Related Occupations

Related occupations include private household workers such as general houseworkers, child care workers, governesses, housekeepers, butlers, cooks, caretakers, child day care center workers, preschool workers, and home health aides.

Sources of Additional Information

For more information about nannies and nanny schools, contact:

- American Council of Nanny Schools, Delta College, University Center, MI 48710. Phone: (517)686-9417.

- International Nanny Association, PO Box 26522, Austin, TX 78755-0522. Phone: (512)454-6462.

- National Academy of Nannies, Inc., 1681 S. Dayton St., Denver, CO 80231. Phone: (303)333-NANI or (800)222-NANI.

Travel and Leisure Occupations

AMUSEMENT AND RECREATION ATTENDANTS

At a Glance

- **D.O.T.:** 340, 341, 342

- **Preferred Education:** No minimum educational requirement

- **Average Salary:** Begins at $4.25 per hour

- **Did You Know?** Job opportunities for amusement and recreation attendants are expected to increase faster than the average for all occupations through the year 2005.

Nature of the Work

Whether its plummeting down a roller coaster, pumping tokens into a video game, skiing down a snowy slope, or scoring a hole-in-one, most people enjoy engaging in leisure activities at amusement and recreation facilities. Amusement and recreation attendants play a very important role in ensuring that people have the most fun possible while visiting recreation facilities.

There are a wide variety of amusement and recreation attendant occupations—from arcade attendants and golf course caddies, to ride attendants and ski-tow operators—but all attendants are employed to help customers safely enjoy leisure activities. The following is a description of some of the many amusement and recreation occupations available.

Caddies carry golf bags, push or pull golf bag carts, and drive golf cars around golf courses. They hand requested clubs to the golfer, locate driven golf balls, hold marker out of cup while the golfer putts, and advise the golfer, as requested, on the selection of proper golf clubs.

Ride operators run or inform patrons how to operate riding mechanisms (rides) at amusement parks or carnivals. They instruct patrons how to fasten their seat belt or safety bar; control the start, stop, and speed of roller coasters, Ferris wheels, merry-go-round, swings, and other rides or equipment; speak to patrons by microphone regarding safety procedures or what patron will experience on the ride; drive vehicles, such as trains or boats, which patrons ride; space rides to avoid collisions; and decide whether mechanical or weather conditions make the ride unsafe for use.

Ski-tow operators tend gasoline, diesel, or electric lifts that transport skiers up a slope or mountainside; control levers that start, stop, and regulate the speed of lifts, such as a chair lift, T-bar, J-bar, or rope tow; collect fee or tickets from passengers; and assist passengers onto and from lift. Ski-tow operators may also maintain and make minor repairs to equipment.

Game attendants operate concession booth games at amusement parks, carnivals, and fairs. They persuade customers to play the game, describe the objection of the game, collect the fee, supply patrons with game equipment (i.e. balls or toss rings), and distribute prizes to customers who win the game.

Bowling alley desk clerks assign bowling alleys to patrons, collect fees, rent bowling shoes to patrons, reserve alleys for individuals or bowling leagues, issue score sheets, inspect alleys to ensure bowling equipment is available, observe bowlers to determine misuse of alleys or equipment and record receipts and number of games played.

Recreation facility attendants schedule use of recreation facilities, such as softball diamonds, tennis courts, golf courses, according to the public park or private club's regulations. They collect fees from patrons; rent or sell sports equipment; coordinate facilities to prevent players from interfering with one another; inform patrons of facility rules, dress codes, proper equipment use, and conduct rules; eject or enforce rules on unruly or unauthorized persons; inspect facilities or equipment for damage or misuse; and report damage of facilities or equipment. Recreation facility attendants may also give first aid to injured patrons.

Arcade attendants assist patrons with facility game machines, such as video games, pinball machines, and photo booths, by explaining operation of games, exchanging paper currency for coins or tokens, and attending to customer complaints about machine malfunction. They make minor repairs to game machines, return lost money to patrons, place out-of-order signs on defective machines, and notify maintenance of machines in need of repair. They also ask disruptive patrons to leave facility.

Working Conditions

Working conditions for amusement and recreation attendants depends upon the job. The hours usually range between 20 and 40 hours per week, depending upon whether the job is part-time or full-time. Most amusement and recreation attendants work on weekends, during the evening, and at night—the time when most people have time for leisure activities. They may also work during the day depending on where they are employed.

The work can be indoors or outdoors. Those who work indoors (i.e. bowling allies, skating rinks, indoor sports facilities) may work in pleasant, modern, air conditioned buildings, or older, poorly maintained facilities. Those who work outdoors (i.e. golf courses, parks, ski lodges) may work in warm summer months or cold winter months. Those working outdoors in the summer may have to work in the rain, but most facilities temporarily shut-down during poor weather conditions. Game attendants work in small booths. Carnival workers may live in small, uncomfortable, mobile living quarters.

Employment

According to the U.S. Bureau of Labor Statistics, in 1992 there were 207,000 amusement and recreation attendants employed in the United States.

Most amusement and recreation attendants are employed part-time. Employment is seasonal due to the fact that many amusement and recreation activities are enjoyed outdoors. Many attendants work only during the summer months—the time when outdoor amusement and recreation facilities, such as amusement parks and golf courses, are open. On the other hand, attendants who work for ski facilities and winter recreation facilities are employed in winter months.

Employers very often hire students who are able to work during their summer vacations or part-time after school.

Training, Other Qualifications, and Advancement

There are no specific educational requirements for amusement and recreation attendants. Most receive on-the-job training from an experienced employee or manager. Larger amusement and recreation facilities may have formal training sessions for new employees.

There is little opportunity for advancement for amusement and recreation attendants. Those with a lot of experience may become managers or supervisors.

Job Outlook

Job opportunities for amusement and recreation attendants are expected to grow 46 percent, faster than the average for all occupations, through the year 2005. Since job turnover is very high in this industry, many jobs should be available to first-time job seekers, people with limited skills, and displaced workers.

Earnings

Most beginning amusement and recreation attendants

earned $4.25 per hour in 1994, which is the minimum wage. More experienced workers earn a little more. Amusement and recreation attendants are generally paid an hourly wage, and employed part-time or temporarily (during peak seasons). Full-time amusement and recreation attendants may receive benefits such as paid vacations, sick leave, and retirement plans.

Related Occupations

There are numerous other careers in amusement and recreation, including caddie supervisors, skate-shop attendants, golf range attendants, ride supervisors, weight guessers, barkers, fun-house operators, and wharf attendants.

Sources of Additional Information

For more information on a career as an amusement and recreation attendant, contact:

- American Association for Leisure and Recreation, 1900 Association Dr., Reston, VA 22091 Phone: (703)476-3472.

- National Recreation and Parks Association, 2775 S. Quincy St., Ste. 300, Arlington, VA 22206 Phone: (708)820-4940 or 800-626-6772.

- Outdoor Amusement Business Association, 4600 W. 77th St., Minneapolis, MN 55435 Phone: (612)831-4643.

BAGGAGE PORTERS AND BELLHOPS

At a Glance

- **D.O.T.:** 324.137-010, 324.137-014, 324.477-010 and 324.677-010

- **Preferred Education:** High school diploma

- **Average Salary:** $3.25 to $6 hourly

- **Did You Know?** Travel and tourism is predicted to be the number one industry by the year 2000.

Nature of the Work

Whether they are working in a busy hotel in midtown Manhattan or a quiet resort on the island of Maui, baggage porters and bellhops play a vital role in the multi-billion-dollar lodging industry. By handling luggage and providing special services, baggage porters and bellhops make sure guests have an enjoyable stay.

Bellhops carry luggage, escort incoming guests to their rooms, and introduce guests to hotel services and facilities. They make sure the hotel room is in order by checking lights and room temperature. Bellhops show guests how to use the room's television, radio, air-conditioner tand door locks. They also let guests know about local special events and entertainment attractions.

Bellhops often run errands for guests. They deliver messages and room service orders. They also pick up articles of clothing for laundry and valet service. Bellhops call taxis for guests and sometimes drive guests around the premises in a car or van. When guests are ready to leave, bellhops carry luggage back to the front desk.

Bellhops keep detailed records of their service calls. In large hotels and resorts, bellhops are managed by a *bell captain*. Bell captains train new bellhops, inspect the bellhops' work, and set work schedules. Bell captains sometimes provide special services for guests, such as securing tickets to the theater, concerts or sporting events. They make reservations at popular restaurants. Bell captains also handle customer complaints when something goes wrong.

Baggage porters handle luggage for hotel and resort guests. They move trunks, luggage, and other packages to and from the hotel's storage room. Baggage porters mail or ship packages for guests. They provide guests with travel information, such as transportation rates, routes and schedules.

Some baggage porters help the hotel prepare for special events. They help the hotel salespeople by setting up rooms for meetings, conventions and parties. This can include moving furniture, podiums and equipment.

Baggage porters often report to head baggage porters. *Head baggage porters* have duties similar to bell captains. They supervise baggage porters by giving directions, setting work schedules, and passing out assignments. They hire and train new baggage porters. Bell captains keep time records and handle customer complaints about lost or mishandled baggage.

Working Conditions

Baggage porters and bellhops have physically demanding jobs. They carry luggage between the front desk and guestrooms. Each piece of luggage can weigh up to 50 pounds. Occasionally, baggage porters and bellhops may lift trunks weighing up to 100 pounds. The hotel industry has many incidences of occupational injury and illness. Work hazards include sprained muscles and wrenched backs from heavy lifting.

Baggage porters and bellhops spend long hours standing and walking. They usually work 8-hour shifts. Like most hotel employees, baggage porters and bellhops work evenings, weekends and holidays. While bellhops are generally required to wear uniforms, baggage porters often wear their own clothes. Both types of employees must be well-groomed while they are on the job.

Employment

According to the U.S. Bureau of Labor Statistics, there were 34,000 baggage porters and bellhops employed in the United States in 1992. Like most jobs in the hotel industry, employment is concentrated in highly populated cities and resort areas. Most jobs in the hotel industry are in establishments with more than 100 employees, mostly part-time. These larger establishments employ over 60 percent of all workers in the hotel industry. Many of the industry's workers are younger than age 30.

Training, Other Qualifications, and Advancement

There are no specific educational requirements for baggage porters and bellhops. Most receive on-the-job training from an experienced employee or the manager. Some large hotel and resort chains have formal training sessions for new employees.

Baggage porters and bellhops must have a certain amount of physical strength. They must enjoy assisting people. They need patience and the ability to understand and follow instructions.

Job Outlook

Job opportunities for baggage porters and bellhops are expected to grow 45.9 percent, faster than average for all occupations, through the year 2005. Since job turnover is high in the hotel industry, many jobs should be available for people with limited skills, first-time job seekers and displaced workers.

Earnings

According to the Colorado Career Information Center, most baggage porters and bellhops earn an hourly wage, generally between $3.25 and $6 per hour. However, wages may vary depending on geographic location and employer. Baggage porters and bellhops in the Northeast earned from $4 to $6.50 per hours, according to *American Salaries and Wages Survey*. Those in the Southeast earned from $2.50 to $6.56 per hour, and those in the wester United States earned from $5.07 to $7.52 per house.

Baggage porters and bellhops rely heavily on tips for most of their incomes. Those who are pleasant and courteous receive larger tips and can substantially increase their annual incomes.

Related Occupations

Other occupations similar to baggage porters and bellhops include room service clerks, checkroom attendants, porters, and baggage checkers.

Sources of Additional Information

For more information contact:

- American Hotel and Motel Association, 1201 New York Ave. NW, Washington, DC 20005. Phone: (202) 289-3100.

- Council on Hotel, Restaurant, and Institutional Education, 1200 17th St. NW, Washington, DC 20036-3097. Phone: (202) 331-5990.

- Hotel Employees and Restaurant Employees International Union, 1219 28th St. NW, Washington, DC 20007. Phone: (202) 393-4373 or 800-HERE-WAY.

- Service Employees International Union, 1313 L St. NW, Washington, DC 20005. Phone: (202) 898-3200.

GAMBLING DEALERS

At a Glance

- **D.O.T.:** 343.464-010

- **Preferred Education:** Specialized training

- **Average Salary:** $14,000 to $32,000 per year

- **Did You Know?** Gambling dealers receive a salary, but most of their income comes from tips.

Nature of the Work

Craps, blackjack, roulette, poker and baccarat are the types of games run by gambling dealers or *croupiers*, in hundreds of casinos throughout the United States and Canada. While specific duties vary depending on the type of game, the work of gambling dealers is similar regardless of which game they are running.

Dealers monitor bets and make sure that they are placed correctly before each game begins. In some games, dealers announce winning numbers or hands. They make payoffs on winning bets, calculating the correct odds. They collect all of the losing bets.

Gambling dealers represent the house in the games they run. In card game such as poker, blackjack, and baccarat they shuffle cards and pay off winning hands. In poker they generally do not play the game but simply pay off the winner of each hand and collect the house percentage from the pot. In baccarat there may be three dealers running the game, two to handle money and one to shuffle the cards and call out the winner. In blackjack gambling dealers deal themselves a hand which represents the house, with all other players playing against the dealer.

Gambling dealers also run roulette and craps (dice) tables. Roulette dealers spin the roulette wheel and announce when all bets must be placed. They then drop a steel ball over the wheel and announce the winning number. They pay off winning bets according to posted odds and collect all losing bets. Dice or craps dealers do not play the game but simply pay off winning players and collect from losers. They handle all of the bets placed at the craps table.

Working Conditions

Gambling dealers are constantly interacting with people. They occasionally have to deal with players who are compulsive gamblers, drunk, or otherwise unpleasant. They are closely supervised and must conduct their games according to strict rules and procedures. Their work can sometimes be stressful. They must work at a rapid pace while maintaining a friendly attitude toward all players. Casinos may become crowded and noisy at times.

Many casinos are open twenty-four hours a day. Gambling dealers typically work nine or ten hour shifts, with breaks after each hour. They usually have to work different shifts

during the course of a year and often have to work on weekends. Many dealers prefer night and weekend shifts, when they receive better tips. Dealers may sit or stand depending on the games they are running, and their work is generally not physically demanding.

Employment

Gambling is a growing industry. There are nearly 700 casinos with slot machines and/or table gaming in the United States and Canada, many of them run by Indian tribes. Some casinos are land-based, others are located on the docks of rivers or on river boats. Gambling is also conducted aboard ocean-going cruise ships.

Most of the employment opportunities for gambling dealers are in Las Vegas and Reno, Nevada, and in Atlantic City, New Jersey, where there are concentrations of casino gaming. Many of the other casinos in the United States and Canada are located in small towns or cities. New opportunities will arise as more states and municipalities legalize different types of casino gaming.

Both men and women commonly become gambling dealers. Dealers are often relatively young, and there is a high turnover among workers in this occupation.

Training, Other Qualifications, and Advancement

Gambling dealers generally have six months to one year of training, including a combination of formal schooling and on-the-job experience. In some states dealers must attend a dealer school. It takes four to eight weeks of schooling to learn each game. The International Dealers School of Las Vegas, Nevada, offers a 36-week course for casino croupiers that covers all of the basic games in addition to six to eight week courses on individual games including roulette, craps, blackjack, poker, and baccarat/pai gow poker.

Most states that have legalized casino gaming require that all casino employees be licensed by the state gaming commission. Licensing requirements vary from state to state, but virtually every state that licenses casino employees requires that they do not have any felony convictions. Most states require that casino employees be at least 18 years old or 21 years old for some positions. Some states require all casino employees to be over 21. Nevada and New Jersey, among other states, require that gambling dealers have graduated from a state-approved school for dealers. Based on a survey of selected private institutions, nearly 600 people graduated from schools for gambling dealers in 1991-92 in the United States.

Gambling dealers must have good mathematical skills and be able to think quickly. Gambling dealers must have sufficient manual dexterity to conduct their games efficiently and reliably. They must be able to handle money and be familiar with their state's gambling regulations.

Gambling dealers can advance in their careers by performing well and being promoted to higher stakes tables. They may improve their position by becoming adept at all of the major casino games. Within many casinos there is an established hierarchy that offers the opportunity for job advancement, from dealer to floor supervisor, pit boss, shift supervisor, and ultimately casino manager. Individuals interested in casino management should have some college or a degree in hotel administration.

Job Outlook

While the Bureau of Labor Statistics (BLS) does not publish separate employment projections for casino and gaming employees, the occupational category of amusement and recreation attendants is projected to increase by 52 percent between 1992 and 2005, much faster than the average for all occupations. Casinos and other gambling establishments are a rapidly growing segment of the amusement and recreation services industry.

The number of casinos has grown steadily since the passage in 1988 of the Indian Gaming Regulatory Act, which permitted legalized gambling on property owned by Indian tribes under certain circumstances. The established gaming centers of Las Vegas, Reno, and Atlantic City have also shown an increase in the size and number of casinos offering employment for gambling dealers. Other states have legalized gambling on their waterways, resulting in many new floating casinos and river boats that offer gambling.

Earnings

Gambling dealers receive a salary, but most of their income generally comes from tips, or tokes as they are called in the casino industry. They typically receive a base salary that ranges from minimum wage to six or eight dollars an hour. The International Dealers School reports that dealers can expect to earn between $14,000 and $25,000 during their first year of employment. With tips they can earn between $24,000 and $32,000 per year, according to the Casino School of Atlantic City. Salaries in Nevada and Atlantic City tend to be higher than in other parts of the country.

Related Occupations

Other occupations in the gaming industry include change persons, slot attendants, keno runners, keno writers, bingo paymasters, slot cashiers, cage cashiers, cardroom attendants and supervisors, floor bosses, pit supervisors, and shift supervisors.

The amusement and recreation industry includes many occupations such as waiters and waitresses, food counter and fountain workers, coaches, athletic trainers, fitness instructors, musicians, actors, and recreation workers.

Occupations in sales services include arcade attendants, parking lot attendants, automatic car wash attendants, retail sales clerks, and a variety of other amusement and recreation service attendants.

Sources of Additional Information

- International Dealers School, 503 E. Fremont, Las Vegas, NV 89101. Phone: (702)385-7665.

- Nevada Casino Dealers Association, Phone: (702)699-5656.

- Casino Schools, Inc., 1535 Bacharach Blvd., Atlantic City, NJ 08401 Phone: (609)345-5423.

- New Jersey Casino Association, 1325 Boardwalk, Atlantic City, NJ 08401 Phone: (609)347-0800.

MUSEUM ATTENDANTS

At a Glance

- **D.O.T.:** 109.367-010

- **Preferred Education:** High school diploma

- **Average Salary:** $12,000 to $25,000 per year

- **Did You Know?** Museum attendants have an occupation that technology can't automate.

Nature of the Work

Every day, students, tourists, and people of all ages visit museums. Museums are great warehouses of knowledge, so much in fact that visitors often need guides to assist them with the learning. Museums hold valuable, irreplaceable objects that must be carefully protected. Museums are also public institutions that must be monitored for the safety, comfort, and enjoyment of visitors. For these reasons, museums hire museum attendants to conduct the general operation of the museum and provide visitors with information about its exhibits, facilities, and regulations.

Museum attendants are the museum's principal representatives. They open and close the museum at its designated hours, greet visitors, and invite visitors to sign the guest register. They also collect any admission fees, and distribute museum layout maps and other materials concerning the museum s collections. Museum attendants also give out promotional materials, such as brochures or fliers on upcoming exhibits or presentations.

Museum attendants answer a lot of questions concerning museum facilities, exhibits, and regulations, serving as the main source of information for most museum visitors. Throughout the day, visitors ask attendants about museum facilities, especially directions to rest rooms and the museum restaurant, but also the location of a particular exhibit. Museum attendants also arrange tours for schools or other groups.

Most attendants can tell stories behind the exhibits as well as facts. In an art museum, for example, a visitor may want to know more about a particular artist or sculptor whose artwork is on display. In a science museum, an attendant may demonstrate an experiment and answer "how, what, and why" questions about scientific displays. In a historical museum, visitors may want to know more about a particular time period. Museum attendants in historical museums may wear clothing indicative of particular era and demonstrate a period craft, such as weaving or spinning on a loom, and prepare and serve food in a historically authentic way.

Museum visitors are of all ages and educational and cultural backgrounds, thus requiring attendants to be able to talk to scholarly researchers as well as children. No matter who they are speaking with, museum attendants answer questions pleasantly and professionally.

Besides serving visitors, museum attendants protect the museum collection by guarding the exhibits against harm. They discreetly observe visitors, cautioning anyone who is not following museum regulations. Most museum regulations prohibit visitors to touch exhibits. At times museum attendants must tell children not to run through the halls, or reunite a lost child with a parent or teacher. If an exhibit is very popular and draws a large crowd, the museum attendant keeps everyone orderly. Museum attendants also watch for suspicious people, those who may harm the exhibits as well as those who could pose a threat to visitors. In case of an emergency such as a fire, museum attendants evacuate visitors from the building. To perform guarding duties in large institutions, museum attendants may make regular rounds of the building, using hand radios to communicate with other attendants.

Protecting the museums collection may also mean checking thermostats and climate controls to ensure that temperature and humidity levels are accurate. A delicate painting or fragile historical item can be easily destroyed by humid conditions. Attendants also periodically examine exhibit facilities and collection objects. They notify the appropriate museum personnel, typically a curator, when there is damage or a repair is needed.

The duties of a museum attendant varies with needs of the museum. Large museums have several attendants, each assigned a particular responsibility. In very small museums, the attendant may also be the director.

A museum may be dedicated to the visual arts, displaying the paintings and sculptors of great artists; or to history, exhibiting antique automobiles, furniture, and aircrafts that served in wars; or to natural science, displaying gigantic dinosaur skeletons, prehistoric fossils, and ancient pottery. On the other hand, museums can be very specialized, featuring one particular historical figure, ethnic group, family, town, sport, hobby, type of music, or collection—there are even museums exclusively displaying chamber pots, old fans, bottles, and nuts.

Working Conditions

Museum attendants typically work 20 to 40 hours per week. Some work full-time, others part-time. Museum attendants spend long hours standing and walking through the museum. They must always be attentive and courteous to visitors. At times, they must be strict with unruly museum visitors.

Employment

Museum attendants are employed by museums of all types. Museums are located throughout the country, but the best employment opportunities are found at large museums in big metropolitan areas.

Training, Other Qualifications, and Advancement

Although there is no special formal training required, most employers prefer museum attendants to have at least a high school diploma. College education is very helpful. Employers also desire museum attendants to have a genuine interest and considerable knowledge of museum displays.

Museum attendants must like working with the public. They must be able to communicate clearly and be able to discuss museum exhibits with visitors. They should have a pleasant manner, but be able to be strict when dealing with visitors who are behaving inappropriately. Attendants must also be very attentive to making certain museum exhibits are not damaged or harmed.

Job Outlook

Museum attendants have an occupation that technology can't automate. This fact suggests the employment outlook for museum attendants is good. Economic downturns, however, can have a negative affect on job openings. During these times, many museums are affected by budget cuts, forcing directors to put a freeze on hiring and cut staff hours.

Earnings

Museum attendants' earnings varies by employer, geographic location, and experience. Sources claim that in early 1990s, annual salaries ranged from $12,000 to $25,000. Large museums in big metropolitan areas pay more than small museums in areas with low populations. For example, *American Salaries & Wages Survey* reports that the average wage for a museum attendant working in South Dakota was $4.80 per hour in 1994.

Related Occupations

Related occupations in museum, library, and archival sciences include tour guides, library assistants, security guards, information scientists, museum research associates, library shelving supervisors, research assistants, encyclopedia research workers, museum armor technicians, paper and prints restorers, craft demonstrators.

Sources of Additional Information

For more information on a career as a museum attendant, contact:

- American Association of Museums, 1225 I St. NW, Washington, DC 20005.

- American Institute for Conservation of Historic and Artistic Works, 1400 16th St. NW, Washington, DC 20036.

- National Trust for Historic Preservation, Office of Personnel Administration, 1785 Massachusetts Ave. NW, Washington, DC 20036.

Tour Guides

At a Glance

- **D.O.T.:** 353.167-010, 353.363-010, 353.367-010 and 353.367-014

- **Preferred Education:** On-the-job training

- **Average Salary:** Varies.

- **Did You Know?** For some tour guides, tips make up two-thirds of their earnings.

Nature of the Work

Whether they are leading a group of sightseers on an African safari, escorting a group of students through a museum, or directing an out-of-town visitor to local points of interest, tour guides perform a wide range of important services.

Some tour guides, who are also called *travel guides*, lead groups of tourists on special package tours. These tours can include trips to far off locations. Tour guides arrange for transportation and handle all other arrangements, such as making hotel and restaurant reservations and planning recreational activities. They prepare and follow a planned itinerary and escort the group through the entire trip.

During the trip, tour guides describe points of interest. They make sure their guests have all the appropriate travel certificates, such as visas, passports, and health certificates. They also convert their guests' dollars into foreign currency, when necessary.

There are also tour guides who lead groups on one-day sightseeing trips. These *sightseeing guides* travel with their guests on buses or vans and speak to the group about points of interest along the tour. These points of interest can include historic sites, buildings, museums, and art galleries. Sightseeing guides sometimes escort their tour groups through these buildings or sites, often lecturing on the history or significance of the location.

Another tour guide occupation is the *establishment guide*. These tour guides also escort groups through important sites or buildings. Unlike sightseeing guides, however, these tour guides specialize in one location. For example, an establishment guide at an art gallery may give detailed lectures on the history and importance of each piece of art in the gallery. They also answer questions from the group.

Visitor guides escort out-of-town guests around a city. These guests often include convention delegates, business people, and representatives of foreign governments. Visitor guides help their guests find buildings and other points of interest. They also escort visitors to designated locations. Some visitor guides drive their guests in cars or vans. They often carry their equipment and luggage. Guides working with visitors from other countries may be required to speak foreign languages.

Working Conditions

Working as a tour guide can be very demanding work. Travel guides must be on call 24 hours-a-day while conducting a tour. They can work seven days-a-week for up to 15 to 25 straight weeks, then have several weeks off. The day-to-day demands of the job, especially making sure all the guests are happy, can be stressful. Also, because of the long trips away from home, maintaining relationships can be difficult.

Other tour guides may work more traditional hours. Their work may be performed indoors or outdoors, depending on the type of tour. Tour guides spend a great deal of time walking, standing, and talking.

Employment

According to the *Occupational Outlook Quarterly*, there are over 160,000 guides and ushers in the United States. Travel guides usually work for travel agents or exotic vacation companies. Many are self-employed and work on a contract basis. It is generally not a full-time position.

Training, Advancement, and Other Qualifications

Most tour guides learn their skills on the job, often by working with more experienced guides. Some travel agencies and tour companies prepare their guides through formal training programs. Degrees in tourism are available through some colleges. Although a college degree is not required to become a tour guide, it can be helpful, especially if a guide plans to lead tours in foreign countries. These guides should be fluent in foreign languages. Courses in art, history, and communications are also beneficial.

Tour guides must be able to get along with all types of individuals. They should be well organized and patient. They must be able to deal with crises or unexpected events. It is also important that they enjoy learning about a certain subject and sharing that information with others.

Job Outlook

Spending on travel is expected to increase significantly through the year 2005. More people are expected to travel on vacation, and do so more often. Since the travel industry is sensitive to economic conditions, job opportunities may fluctuate.

Earnings

The salaries of tour guides are typically low. However, talented tour guides can supplement their incomes with tips from satisfied clients. For some tour guides, tips make up two-thirds of their earnings. Tour guides also receive commissions from agents. The major benefit of becoming a tour guide, however, is the ability to travel free or at low cost. Some guides receive free meals and accommodations while conducting tours.

Related Occupations

Other occupations concerned with escorting individuals

on trips or tours include hunting and fishing guides, alpine guides, and dude wranglers. Other occupations in the travel industry include travel agents, flight attendants, and airline reservation agents.

Sources of Additional Information

- National Tour Association, 546 E. Main St., P.O. Box 3071, Lexington, KY 40596. Phone: (606)226-4444.

- Professional Guides Association of America, 2416 S. Eads St., Arlington, VA 22202. Phone: (703)892-5757.

- Travel Industry Association of America, 1100 New York Ave. NW, Ste. 450, Washington, DC 20005 Phone: (202)408-8422)

- American Sightseeing International, 490 Post St., Ste. 1701-A, San Francisco, CA 94102. Phone: (415)986-2082.

USHERS AND TICKET TAKERS

At a Glance

- **D.O.T.:** 344.677-014; 344.677-010

- **Preferred Education:** On the job training

- **Average Salary:** Varies.

- **Did You Know?** Ushers, lobby attendants, and ticket takers can often hear or view events while they are working, which is a unique benefit of this occupation.

Nature of the Work

Movie theaters, sports stadiums, concert halls, music festivals, and other public events all employ ticket takers and ushers to collect tickets, help patrons find their seats, and maintain order.

Ticket takers collect tickets and passes from customers as they enter entertainment events. They check the tickets or passes for authenticity and make sure only those with valid tickets enter the event. They also may refuse to admit customers for other reasons such as intoxication or improper attire. Once the show or event has begun, ticket takers usually count and record the number of tickets collected.

Ushers have many of the same responsibilities as ticket takers but their main job is to help customers find their seats. Depending on the type of performance or event, ushers may walk patrons directly to their seats or indicate where the seats are located. They also help patrons find exits, concession stands, telephones, restrooms, and other facilities. In addition, ushers often hand out programs and help customers find lost items or companions. After the performance, ushers direct people to the most convenient exit. Another part of their job is helping coworkers change advertising displays and signs.

Ushers are required to enforce rules and regulations. At large events, ushers may be responsible for maintaining order. For example, ushers help calm unruly fans at sporting events and rock concerts. When seating problems arise, ushers must solve the problem quickly and quietly. If a fire, emergency, or accident occurs, ushers direct people to emergency exits.

Working Conditions

Ticket takers and ushers work both indoors and outdoors, depending on the type of event. Those who work outdoors must be prepared to do so in all types of weather. Ticket takers and ushers often work weekends, evenings, and holidays. Part-time work is usually available. Ushers and ticket takers spend most of their time standing and walking. Many wear uniforms that are provided by their employers. Some ushers belong to labor unions.

Employment

Ushers, lobby attendants, and ticket takers held approximately 56,000 jobs in 1992. They work for movie theaters, sports stadiums, circuses, concert halls, and music festivals throughout the country. Some ushers work for companies that specialize in providing ushers for public gatherings and events. These ushers may work a different type of event every day. The number of ticket takers and ushers employed in a theater, stadium, or arena depends on the size of the facility.

Many jobs in the amusement and recreation services industry are part time or seasonal positions, as in the case of outdoor entertainment and sports events.

Training, Advancement, and Other Qualifications

There are no formal educational requirements for these occupations, but a high school diploma or its equivalent is preferred by many employers. Most employers train their own ushers and ticket takers on-the-job. The training period is usually less than one hour long.

In most instances, the job of an usher or ticket taker is an entry-level position. Ushers and ticket takers can advance to jobs in more prestigious facilities. Ushers may seek the position of head usher. Some ushers in theaters take the job as an opportunity to meet others in the business and move on to particular areas of interest, such as acting.

Ushers and ticket takers should be articulate, pleasant, and friendly people. An ability to deal tactfully with others is necessary. Since a good portion of their working time is spent either standing or walking, these workers need good physical stamina. Ushers and ticket takers also must have the ability to remain calm in a crisis.

Job Outlook

Employment opportunities for ushers, lobby attendants, and ticket takers are expected to increase faster than the average for all occupations through the year 2005. The U.S. Bureau of Labor Statistics projects the number of jobs in this field will grow from 56,000 in 1992 to 72,000 in 2005, an increase of nearly 30 percent. Two reasons for this growth will be higher individual incomes and more leisure time. Americans with more disposable income and the time to use it will provide a larger market for establishments providing amusement and recreational facilities and services.

Earnings

Depending on their responsibilities, salaries for ushers, lobby attendants, and ticket takers can range from minimum wage to $10 per hour or more. In Minnesota, for example, low-end wages for ushers, lobby attendants, and ticket takers were $4.25 per hour in 1992; others earned more than $6.50 per hour. Ushers who belong to unions have their minimum salaries set by the union. Ushers, lobby attendants, and ticket takers can often hear or view events while they are working, which is a unique benefit of this occupation.

Related Occupations

Other occupations concerned with taking tickets, distributing programs, and escorting patrons to seats include ride attendant, children's attendant, escort, passenger service representative, ski-tow operator, head usher, and conductor.

Sources of Additional Information

For additional information on ushers and ticket takers, contact:

- International Association of Auditorium Managers, 4425 W. Airport Freeway, Irving, TX 75062. Phone: (214)255-8020.

- National Association of Theater Owners, 4605 Lankershim Blvd., North Hollywood, CA 91602 Phone: (818)506-1778.

- International Alliance of Theatrical Stage Employees and Moving Picture Machine Operators, 1515 Broadway, New York, NY 10036. Phone: (212)730-1770.

- Service Employees International Union, 1313 L St. NW, Washington, DC 20005. Phone: (202)898-3200.

Agriculture, Forestry, and Related Occupations

APIARISTS

At a Glance

- **D.O.T.:** 413.161-010

- **Preferred Education:** Knowledge of entomology, biology, and agriculture

- **Average Salary:** $35 per bee colony for pollination services.

- **Did You Know?** Some beekeepers run as many as 50,000 hives.

Nature of Work

Apiarists, or beekeepers, are an important part of the agricultural community. Not only do their honey bees produce honey, they also pollinate a variety of crops.

Apiarists keep bees in wooden beehives, which they often build themselves with hand tools. The basic elements of a wooden beehive include the bottom board, which forms the floor of the hive; brood chambers (where the bees live, the queen lays her eggs, the young are raised), and wax combs, where the honey is stored; honey supers, to store excess honey; a queen excluder that keeps the queen from laying eggs in the honey; and top and bottom covers to protect the bees.

To make honey, bees fly from plant to plant looking for nectar. The foraging bees return to the hive and regurgitate nectar into the mouths of "house" bees. These bees add enzymes to the mixture and store the mixture in the cells of the comb. The center of every hive is the queen bee. A queen can lay as many as 2,000 eggs a day. The eggs quickly turn to larvae. They are cared for by infertile female bees, often called worker bees. Worker bees make up more than 98 percent of the hive's population. They also clean and defend the hive. The few male bees in the hive, called drones, live only to mate with the queen and die shortly afterwards.

Apiarists are responsible for maintaining the hives and ensuring the health of the bee colonies. To inspect the hives,

they puff smoke from a smoker into the hive entrance. The smoke calms the bees while the apiarist checks their condition. Apiarists must make sure each colony has a healthy queen and enough honey to feed the colony. The excess honey is harvested.

Apiarists harvest honey by removing the frames of honeycombs from the hive. They cut off the wax cap seals and use an extractor to remove the honey. They drain the honey into a storage tank. To remove impurities, apiarists pour the honey through strainers. The honey is then bottled and sold. The wax can also be sold.

During their search for nectar, honey bees carry pollen from plant to plant. This pollination is beneficial to many types of crops, including blueberries, pears, watermelons, and apples. Farmers often allow apiarists to set up hives on their land in exchange for the pollination service of the bees. Other farmers rent bee colonies from apiarists. Some apiarists travel across the country, transporting their hives on trailers and renting them out to farmers.

Apiarists keep accurate records of their bees and hives. The records include information on the size of the colonies, the ages of the queens, and the number of filled honeycombs.

Working Conditions

Obviously, the main hazards of beekeeping are bee stings. Most apiarists wear a protective veil, gloves, and coveralls when working near a hive. Also, apiarists avoid working with bees early in the morning, late in the afternoon, and evenings when bees are most defensive. Apiarists may become immune to bee venom over time, but people allergic or sensitive to stings should avoid this occupation.

Employment

According to the U.S. Department of Labor, there are an estimated 190,000 apiarists in the United States. Most are hobbyists who do not raise bees for profit. About 20 percent of all beekeepers make half their annual earnings or more from keeping bees. Only 4 percent, or about 7,600 apiarists, depend solely on beekeeping for income. There are some very large beekeepers that run as many as 50,000 hives.

Apiarists operate bee colonies in all 50 states. Most are located in Florida and California. Some apiarists in cold weather states move their bee colonies to southern or west coast states during the winter, where they can pollinate citrus crops or maintain honey production.

Training, Other Qualifications, and Advancement

There are no qualification requirements for becoming an apiarist. Some junior colleges offer apiculture courses. Apiarists should have some knowledge of entomology, biology, agriculture, woodworking, and business management.

Job Outlook

Cutbacks in government price supports for honey could negatively impact small beekeeping operations. American beekeepers also face strong competition from countries such as China, Mexico, and Argentina.

Earnings

Starting a commercial beekeeping business is expensive. Since new colonies do not produce much surplus honey the first year, it can take 3 to 5 years to become profitable. This is why many beekeepers are hobbyists who do not raise bees for profit. In 1993, beekeepers received 52 cents for one pound of honey. Farmers paid apiarists about $35 per bee colony for pollination services.

Related Occupations

Other occupations concerned with breeding, raising, and caring for wild animals and birds include animal keeper, animal nursery worker, game farm helper, and game bird farmer.

Sources of Additional Information

- American Beekeeping Federation, Inc., P.O. Box 1038, Jesup, GA 31545 Phone: (912)427-8447.

- Bee Culture Magazine, The A.I. Root Co., publishers, 623 W. Liberty St., Medina, OH 44256 Phone: (216)725-6677.

DIVERS

At a Glance

- **D.O.T.:** 899.261-010, 899.664-010, and 379.384-010

- **Preferred Education:** Specialized training

- **Average Salary:** $20,000 to $45,000

- **Did You Know?** Most divers work for firms that provide offshore drilling services for oil companies.

Nature of Work

From taking photographs to searching for lost valuables to laying pipelines, professional divers perform a variety of tasks underwater. Their assistants, called diver helpers or diver tenders, stay above the water's surface and help divers perform their jobs safely.

Divers generally use one of three types of diving equipment. Scuba (Self-Contained Underwater Breathing Apparatus) equipment allows divers to carry a supply of air in a tank strapped to their backs. This equipment is used for dives down to 100 feet below the surface. Deeper dives require the use of a diving suit and an air hose which supplies air from the surface. Divers using an air hose can work at a depth of 200 feet. When diving to great depths, in extremely cold water, or in swift currents, submersible vehicles are used to lower divers to the ocean floor. Submersible vehicles serve as a base between expeditions and supply air to the divers.

Using diving equipment is only part of a diver's job. When they are under water, divers perform many different tasks. Some divers are construction workers who build docks, bridges, and oil drilling platforms. They work on underwater pipelines, cables, and sewers. These divers use handtools, and cut and weld steel with arc welding equipment.

Salvage divers search for lost, missing, or sunken objects such as boats, automobiles, or valuables. They fasten lines or chains around heavy objects so they can be raised to the surface. Some divers may rig explosives to demolish underwater obstacles or remove undeeded equipment. Some divers repair boats and ships. They replace missing or leaking rivets with bolts, caulk leaks, and inspect propellers. They may remove barnacles and other marine growth from vessels. Underwater photographers take photos of sunken ships, underwater structures, and marine life.

Diver assistants inspect the diving equipment and help divers get into their suits. They help divers into the water and hand them equipment. Diver assistants remain on the surface and maintain communication with submerged divers by a lifeline or telephone. They make sure that there are no clogs in the airhose and that the air pressure remains in a safe range. Diver assistants watch for dangerous weather conditions. They also make sure the diver does not remain underwater too long.

Working Conditions

Diving is dangerous and physically demanding work. There is always the risk of drowning. Other risks include health problems from cold temperatures and changes in pressure in deep waters. Working hours vary with the assignments. Their working hours often include preparing for the dive. Deep sea dives can take longer than shallower dives. Also, it can take much longer to complete a task underwater than it does on land. Divers often travel from job to job. Those working on off-shore drilling rigs or on research ships may live on them for weeks at a time.

Employment

Compared to most occupations, there are relatively few divers. Most work for diving firms that provide offshore drilling services for oil companies. Much of this work takes place in the Gulf of Mexico, supporting oilfield operations off the coasts of Texas, Louisiana, Mississippi, and Alabama. Other divers work for construction companies that build bridges, dams, and tunnels. Some divers work for waterfront businesses such as boatyards and shipping companies. Telephone companies, government agencies, police departments, insurance companies, and security agencies also employ the services of divers.

Training, Advancement, and Other Qualifications

Although there are no specific educational credentials required to become a diver, extensive training is essential. Some commercial divers receive their training in the military. There are also many colleges and private schools that offer programs in diver training. Along with diving, students may study boating, marine biology, electronics, underwater operations, and physical oceanography. Divers specializing in a specific line of work may need additional training. For example, underwater construction workers need to learn skills such as carpentry and welding. Underwater photographers need photography training.

Divers must be physically fit. They should be able to work alone and as part of a team. They also need self-confidence and courage. Divers with experience may start their own businesses. The best divers are proficient in a number of skills. Those who earn advanced degrees have good advancement potential.

Job Outlook

Despite the growing use of robot submarines and other underwater vehicles, there will always be a need for divers. Remote controlled devices are safer because they are controlled from the surface, but many tasks still require direct observation as well as the coordination and adaptability of a human being.

Earnings

According the published sources, salaries for divers typically range between $20,000 and $45,000 per year, depending on skills, experience, and working conditions. Divers with highly specialized skills or those who work under extremely dangerous conditions may earn up to $100,000 per year.

Related Occupations

Related occupations involving diving include diver assistants and salvage divers. Workers in other occupations that require some of the same skills include construction workers, welders, riveters, service mechanics, boat riggers, pipe installers, and salvage supervisors.

Sources of Additional Information

- Association of Commercial Diving Educators, c/o Marine Technology Program, Santa Barbara City College, 721 Cliff Dr., Santa Barbara, CA 93109-2394 Phone: (805)965-0581

- Association of Diving Contractors, 2611 FM 1960W, Ste. F204, Houston, TX 77068 Phone: (713)893-8388

- National Association of Underwater Instructors, P.O. Box 14650, Montclair, CA 91763 Phone: (714)621-5801

FISHING AND HUNTING GUIDES

At a Glance

- **D.O.T.:** 353.161-010

- **Preferred Education:** Skill and knowledge of a particular region

- **Average Salary:** Varies.

- **Did You Know?** Hunters are required to have professional guides in certain wilderness areas in the western United States as well as Canada.

Nature of the Work

When people hunt or fish in unfamiliar territory, they often choose to employ the services of a professional guide. Hunting and fishing guides work in different environments, but both have similar objectives. By combining their sporting skills with a knowledge of a particular geographic region, hunting and fishing guides lead their clients to where they are most likely to find fish and game.

Fishing guides are expert fishers who may know a lot about a particular species of fish or of a particular region. They often scout the rivers and lakes in that region to determine the best locations and time of day for fishing. Depending on the type of fishing expedition, guides may provide clients with equipment such as rods, reels, and line. They obtain the necessary bait prior to the trip or assist in tying flies.

Fishing guides also keep their clients informed of applicable laws and regulations regarding the size, number, and species of fish that they are allowed to take. They may provide their clients with fishing tips or give lessons on how to fish for different species or use different types of rods and tackle.

If fishing guides use a boat rather than fishing from land, their duties include keeping the boat clean and running smoothly. Some guides also serve as charter boat captains, taking fishing parties out for full- or half-day expeditions on oceans or lakes.

Hunting guides also generally specialize in a certain region or species of animal. They may guide wild turkey hunters around the outskirts of farms and forests, or they may take hunting parties into wilderness country in search of elk and other big game. Using their hunting expertise and knowledge of the region, hunting guides discuss hunting strategy with their clients and lead them to likely areas. Guides are usually the first to spot game; they then set up a stalk so their clients can get a fair shot.

Guides and their clients often hike or ride horses or mules

to their destination. Wilderness guides usually work for outfitters, who arrange for meals and camping facilities on the trip. Outfitters may also arrange to have cooks and other support personnel. However, in some situations, hunting guides have numerous responsibilities on the trip that range from cutting wood for fires to taking care of horses.

Once an animal has been shot, hunting guides dress and transport the meat and trophy from field to camp. At the end of the hunt they may also arrange to have the meat taken to a locker for butchering and have the trophy taken to a taxidermist.

Working Conditions

The work of fishing and hunting guides is active and often physically demanding. Fishing guides may row boats for their clients, while hunting guides may hike for long distances or ride horses to reach wilderness campsites. Some wilderness campsites are also reached by airplane or helicopter, and campsite conditions vary from walled tents with showers to small tents with few amenities.

A large part of a guide's responsibilities involve interacting with their clients, who may range from novices to experts. Guides must be able to determine the level of challenge their clients are seeking and decide the best locations and how much assistance to provide.

Hunting and fishing guides spend a lot of time scouting territory and often work long hours preparing for and guiding trips. Some guided trips last for several days, while others last for a single day or less.

Hunting and fishing guides can be under a certain amount of pressure for their clients to be successful. Guides may be hindered, however, by factors beyond their control such as poor weather conditions or clients with unrealistic expectations.

Employment

Hunting and fishing guides typically work on a seasonal basis, and many work part-time. Some guides work on weekends only, while doing other jobs during the week.

Guides may work for outfitters or they may be self-employed. Most professional hunting guides work in the western part of the United States, including Alaska. Others work where hunting and fishing are common, especially in sparsely populated areas with forests, lakes and rivers.

Training, Other Qualifications, and Advancement

Hunting and fishing guides are skilled hunters and fishers who have a familiarity with a certain geographic region. Experience is the primary requirement. Guides gain the necessary experience by hunting and fishing on their own, then working with experienced guides.

Some states require hunting and fishing guides to be licensed and bonded. While requirements vary from state to state, guides typically must have some experience hunting or fishing in the areas in which they will be serving as guides. Some states require that guides also pass a licensing examination. Fishing guides who also serve as charter boat captains must obtain a license from the U.S. Coast Guard.

Hunting and fishing guides are people who enjoy nature and working outdoors. They must be in good physical condition and have good vision. They must be able to talk easily with other people, give clear instructions, and be tactful. Good judgment and reasoning are needed to be able to handle emergencies and unexpected situations. A knowledge of first aid is helpful.

Guides can advance in their occupation by gaining more experience and building their own reputation and clientele. Some guides go into business as outfitters. Fishing guides with their own boats can use their boats to generate additional income by providing other types of guided tour services.

Job Outlook

Employment prospects for hunting and fishing guides are limited and vary from region to region. Those with skill and a thorough knowledge of a particular region will have the best opportunities. Certain wilderness areas in the western United States as well as Canada require people to hunt with professional guides, which will support employment to some degree. Another factor affecting the long-term outlook is the increasing number of people attracted to outdoor activity.

Earnings

Annual earnings for fishing and hunting guides are difficult to calculate, since much of the work is seasonal, and many guides work part-time. Other guides offer their services as part of a larger outfitting business.

In general, however, hunting guides can expect to begin earning $40 or $50 per day, including room and board. Experienced guides may earn or charge $100 to $200 per day. Fishing guides employed by outfitters typically start at approximately $125 per day. Self-employed guides must deduct their overhead costs for fuel, bait, tackle, etc., from the fees they charge to determine their actual earnings.

Related Occupations

Related outdoor occupations include fishers, hunters, trappers, captains of fishing vessels, harbor pilots, game wardens, forest rangers, zookeepers, and wildlife management specialists.

Other occupations that involve escorting people for recreation and amusement include guides who escort people on tours, trips, and cruises, and cruise ship directors.

Other related occupations include ushers, interpreters and translators, ticket agents, and porters and bellhops.

Sources of Additional Information

- America Outdoors, PO Box 1348, Knoxville, TN 37901. Phone: (615)524-4814.

- Deer Unlimited of America, PO Box 1129, Abbeville, SC 29620. Phone: (803)391-2300.

- International Game Fish Association, 1301 E. Atlantic

Blvd., Pompano Beach, FL 33060-6744. Phone: (305)941-3474.

- National Hunters Association, PO Box 820, Knightdale, NC 27545. Phone: (919)365-7157.
- North American Outfitters, Inc., PO Box 505, Boise, ID 83701. Phone: (208)342-1438.
- Sport Fishing Institute, 1010 Massachusetts Ave. NW, Ste. 320, Washington, DC 20001. Phone: (202)898-0770.

Contact the following state associations for information about guides in specific states:

- Alaska Professional Hunters Association, PO Box 91932, Anchorage, AK 99509.
- Colorado Outfitters Association, PO Box 440021, Aurora, CO 80044. Phone: (303)368-4731.
- Idaho Outfitters and Guides Association, PO Box 95, Boise, ID 83701. Phone: (208)342-1919.
- Montana Outfitters and Guides Association, PO Box 1248, Helena, MT 59624. Phone: (406)449-3578.
- New Mexico Council of Outfitters and Guides, 160 Washington SE, #75, Albuquerque, NM 87108. Phone: (505)743-2504.
- Oregon Guides and Packers Association, PO Box 10841, Eugene, OR 97440. Phone: (503)683-9552.
- Washington Outfitters and Guides Association, 22845 N.E. 8th, Ste. 331, Redmond, WA 98053. Phone: (206)392-6107.
- Wyoming Outfitters and Guides Association, PO Box 2284, Cody, WY 82414. Phone: (307)527-7453.

Forestry Technicians

At a Glance

- **D.O.T.:** 452.364-010
- **Preferred Education:** Associate degree
- **Average Salary:** $15,000 to $20,000
- **Did You Know?** Of all the forested land in the United States, 58 percent is owned by private individuals, 14 percent by corporations, and 28 percent by federal, state, or local governments.

Nature of the Work

Forestry technicians assist foresters in managing and caring for the nations forested areas. Forest technicians patrol the land to monitor forest conditions. They inspect trees for harmful insects or disease, spray pesticides, and assist in fire prevention and control. They also plant trees and measure trees to be harvested. Their activities vary to a large extent depending upon the time of year.

Forestry technicians often compile data about the size, content, and condition of specific forest tracts. Their fieldwork involves walking through forested lands in designated patterns to gather information about topography, tree species and population, disease and insect damage, fire conditions, and timber harvesting. They may mark specific trees for harvesting, based on species, condition, and tree size.

During their fieldwork, forestry technicians often use hand-held instruments to help them collect data. They may use a Haga altimeter to measure tree height, and carry portable computers to record their findings. They may collect rain samples from rain collectors placed in forests and examine rain gauges to determine amounts of rainfall.

Forestry technicians may also assist in surveying property lines, timber sale boundaries, and road and recreation sites. They hold stadia rods, clear survey lines, measure distances, and record survey data. Some forestry technicians supervise road building crews.

Forestry technicians often lead, train, or instruct other workers. They may train conservation workers in seasonal activities such as planting tree seedlings, collecting seed cones, suppressing fires, maintaining recreational areas and facilities, and clearing fire breaks and access roads. Visitors to forest areas and parks may be instructed by forestry technicians in regulations that apply to camping, vehicle use, and fire safety.

Forestry technicians who work for tree seedling nurseries may supervise all activities related to collecting seeds, managing the nursery beds, and lifting the seedlings.

Working Conditions

Forestry technicians spend most of their time outdoors. They may have to live in the park or forest where they work. Some isolated wilderness areas can be reached only by airplane or helicopter.

Like other conservation workers, forestry technicians must be in good physical condition to meet the demands of their job. They often have to walk long distances over rugged terrain in all weather conditions.

Forestry technicians typically work as part of a team. Depending on where they work, they may interact with other people on a regular basis, including forest workers, other forestry technicians, professional foresters, and the general public.

Employment

Of all the forested land in the United States, 58 percent is owned by private individuals, 14 percent by corporations, and 28 percent by federal, state, or local governments. Employment of professional foresters and forestry technicians in these sectors breaks down to about one-third by the federal government, one-third by state and local governments, and one-third by the private sector.

The largest federal employer of forestry technicians is the U.S. Forest Service, an agency in the Department of Agriculture. As of 1991, the Forest Service employed nearly 7,500 forestry technicians and nearly 5,300 professional foresters. Other federal agencies that employ forestry technicians are the Soil Conservation Service, Bureau of Land Management, National Park Service, and Army Corps of Engineers. State forestry agencies and state Cooperative Extension Services also employ forestry technicians. With the rise of urban forestry, county and municipal governments may be the fastest-growing public employers of forestry personnel.

In the private sector, employers include companies that manage forests for lumber and related products as well as companies that utilize forest products and suppliers of forest equipment and machinery. Tree farms and tree seedling nurseries also employ forestry technicians, as do forest management and consulting services.

Although opportunities for forestry technicians exist in every state, employment opportunities are concentrated in the western and southeastern areas of the United States where many national and private forests and parks are located. Depending on geographic location, the work of forestry technicians may be seasonal, with increased employment opportunities available during the summer months.

In addition, some private companies involved in forestry have international operations. Some overseas positions are available with the Forest Service, and the Peace Corps has been engaged internationally in reforestation projects that require forestry technicians.

Training, Other Qualifications, and Advancement

Forestry technicians generally have a two-year associate degree in forestry. These two-year forestry technician programs are offered at junior and community colleges and universities. The Society of American Foresters (SAF) has recognized 21 technician programs in the United States and three in Canada as of 1994. Some forestry technicians may have a four-year bachelors degree in forestry, although such an educational background would qualify them for positions as professional foresters.

Training programs for forestry technicians emphasize the practical aspects of forestry. Courses provide opportunities for hands-on experience along with technical instruction. Specialization opportunities exist in such areas as forest management, urban forestry, nursery production, forest pest control, and park operations. Taking high school classes in science, math, and communications will provide a good foundation for studying forestry.

Some degree of continuing education is necessary to keep up with new developments in the field. Forestry technicians can take advantage of a variety of professional conferences, seminars, publications, and home study materials available in print, audio, and video formats.

Individuals who become forestry technicians are genuinely interested in the outdoors and nature. They must be in good physical condition and be able to work outdoors every day. Good interpersonal skills are needed to work effectively as part of a team.

Forestry technicians are promoted on the basis of their experience and performance. Within the U.S. Forest Service, forestry technicians may advance from grade three to grade 12. Forestry technicians who have earned a bachelor's degree in forestry may advance to become professional foresters.

Job Outlook

The overall employment outlook for forest and conservation workers, including forestry technicians, is expected to increase about as fast as the average for all occupations. The Bureau of Labor Statistics projects a 22.4 increase in the employment of forest and conservation workers between 1992 and 2005.

Factors supporting an increased demand for forestry personnel include growing public interest in and concern over such issues as land use, soil preservation, parks administration, and conservation. Despite these trends, competition exists for jobs as forestry technicians, due to the large number of young people interested in working outdoors.

Earnings

Median earnings for forestry technicians were about $15,000 in 1992, according to the Bureau of Labor Statistics. Half of all those employed as forestry technicians earned between $10,000 and $20,000. In 1993, those who worked for the federal government earned $26,000 on average. Forestry technicians are generally employed by government agencies or private companies that provide a standard benefits package.

Related Occupations

Related occupations concerned with trees and their environment include arborists, gardeners, groundskeepers, horticulturists, landscapers, nurserymen, nursery workers, range aides, and soil conservation technicians. Forestry technicians may also consider the wide range of logging occupations available.

Sources of Additional Information

For additional information on a career as a forestry technician, contact:

- Society of American Foresters, 5400 Grosvenor Ln., Bethesda, MD 20814. Phone: (301)897-3690.

- U.S. Forest Service, Department of Agriculture, 14th St. and Independence Ave. SW, Washington, DC 20013.

NURSERY WORKERS

At a Glance

- **D.O.T.:** 405.684-014 and 405-687-014

- **Preferred Education:** High school diploma

- **Average Salary:** $11,000

- **Did You Know?** Horticultural training is provided in high schools, vocational schools, junior and community colleges, universities, nurseries, and public gardens.

Nature of the Work

Nursery workers plant, cultivate, and harvest flowers, trees, shrubs, and vegetables in nurseries, greenhouses, arboreta, and outdoors. Duties range from hauling topsoil to monitoring plant growth. Generally, nursery workers in large facilities specialize in one area, while those in smaller facilities perform a variety of duties. They usually work under the supervision of trained horticulturalists or professional nurserymen.

Whether they work indoors or outdoors, nursery workers may haul and spread topsoil, fertilizer, peat moss, and similar materials. They may dig, rake, and screen soil and fill plant beds to prepare them for planting. They plant, spray, weed, and water plants, shrubs, and trees. They may sow seeds and plant sod as well as cutting, rolling, and stacking sod.

Other duties include planting shrubs and other plants in containers and preparing flowers, plants, shrubs, and trees to fill orders. They dig up shrubs and trees, wrapping the roots with burlap. They may make boxes for packing horticultural products out of cardboard or other materials.

More experienced nursery workers work under less supervision, following instructions from a manager or grower. They monitor the condition of plants by checking leaf texture, bloom development, and soil condition to determine nutrient and moisture requirements. The look for germ and pest infestations, applying herbicides, fungicides, or pesticides as needed.

Experienced nursery workers working in greenhouses, nurseries, and garden centers regulate the humidity, ventilation, and carbon dioxide levels by reading and interpreting sensors and other measuring instruments. They may graft seedlings and pollinate, prune, transplant, and pinch plants to make sure they grow into saleable products. They also harvest, pack, and store plants.

Nursery workers also repair and maintain nursery equipment and structures, including hydroponic and environmental control systems. They may keep records concerning chemicals, soils, environmental conditions, plant progress, and other matters related to the growth and development of plants.

Working Conditions

Nursery work is physically demanding. Nursery workers frequently have to lift or move material weight from 25 to 50 pounds, and occasionally 50 to 100 pounds. Their work involves frequent stooping, kneeling, and reaching as well as handling plants and other objects. Nursey work occasionally requires climbing and a good sense of balance.

Working in environmentally controlled structures, such as greenhouses, exposes nursery workers to wet or humid conditions. Working outdoors they are often exposed to weather extremes. Occasionally nursery workers are exposed to unpleasant atmospheric conditions such as fumes, noxious odors, and poor ventilation.

Employment

According to the Bureau of Labor Statistics there were 72,000 nursery workers employed in 1992. They are employed in the horticultural industry at such facilities as wholesale and retail nurseries, public parks and gardens, greenhouses, and arboreta. Large institutions with extensive grounds, such as colleges and universities, and industrial and commercial facilities also employ nursery workers. Other employers include state and federal agricultural extension services, landscape contractors, and landscape management services. A high percentage of nursery workers are employed on a part-time basis.

Training, Other Qualifications, and Advancement

Entry-level nursery workers don't need much in the way of training or experience. Tasks can be explained on the spot, and within a month they usually have learned the basics of the job. After one to three months they generally are able to work under less supervision. Students can start gaining experience as early as high school by taking on a part-time job or participating in an internship or co-op program.

Nursery workers must be in excellent physical shape to be able to lift and move heavy objects. They should enjoy working with plants and handling and manipulating things. Those working under close supervision should be able to apply common sense to carry out simple instructions. Experienced nursery workers are able to carry out more detailed instructions and deal with problems involving a few concrete variables.

With additional education and training, nursery workers can advance to become supervisors or managers. They may enter state certification programs for nurserymen based on study, experience, and passing an exam. Certification covers such areas as plant identification, pruning, fertilizing, turf management, watering and soils, crew efficiency, plant pests and diseases, and solving landscape problems through proper design.

After they obtain a two-year associate degree nursery workers can advance to sales positions as well as more hands-on positions involving landscape maintenance. A four-year bachelor of science degree is generally required to be a professional horticulturalist or to advance to an administrative position.

Job Outlook

According to the Bureau of Labor Statistics, employment

of nursery workers will increase much faster than the average for all occupations. The 72,000 nursery workers employed in 1992 is projected to increase to 116,000 by 2005, a growth of 62 percent.

Earnings

Earnings of nursery workers are related to geographic location and experience. Those who works in states with longer growing seasons, such as California or Florida, tend to earn more. According to *American Salaries and Wages Survey*, nursery and greenhouse workers in the Northwest started at approximately $9,500 annually in 1991. The average wage was about $11,000, and the top wage slightly more than $20,000 annually.

Related Occupations

Related occupations include farm workers, groundskeepers, gardeners, yard workers, landscape specialists, tree-surgeon helpers, flower pickers, and other nursery and groundskeeping positions.

Sources of Additional Information

- American Association of Botanical Gardens and Arboreta, 786 Church Rd., Wayne, PA 19087. Phone: (215)688-1120.

- American Association of Nurserymen, 1250 I St. NW, Ste. 500, Washington, DC 20005. Phone: (202)789-2900.

- Professional Plant Growers Association, PO Box 27517, Lansing, MI 48909. Phone: (517)694-7700 or 800-647-7742.

- Wholesale Nursery Growers of America, 1250 I St. NW, Ste. 500, Washington, DC 20005. Phone: (202)789-2900.

PARK TECHNICIANS

At a Glance

- **D.O.T.:** 249.367-082

- **Preferred Education:** No specific requirements

- **Average Salary:** $18,000 to $25,000 per year.

- **Did You Know?** Park technicians assign camping sites, collect camping fees, replenish firewood, and enforce park rules.

Nature of the Work

Millions of visits are recorded every year to national and state parks throughout the United States. As the number of visitors continues to climb dramatically each year, the task of preserving and protecting our national and state parks becomes a more difficult one. It is the responsibility of park technicians, or park aides as they are also known, to inform visitors of the park's rules that are designed to protect and conserve the park's fragile environment.

The first person a park visitor makes contact with is likely to be a park technician. Park technicians meet and greet park visitors when they first arrive at the park. They may provide visitors with maps and other printed materials, give them directions, collect entrance fees, and explain some of the rules.

If the visitors are there for camping, park technicians may assign them camping sites and collect their camping fees. Other park technicians monitor campsites, replenish firewood, and enforce the rules. When injuries occur, park technicians provide first aid and assist those who are more seriously injured.

Park technicians may also perform many other duties in national and state parks. They may serve as interpreters who provide oral presentations to groups of visitors about different aspects of the park or historic site. They may operate sound and light equipment to assist presentations by park rangers. They may guide groups of visitors on tours of certain areas of the park. Sometimes the tours last for two days and require an overnight stay.

Park technicians may also work on maintenance crews, helping groundskeepers maintain the camping and recreational areas. They may assist with landscaping and other outdoor maintenance. They may be called on to assist in firefighting activities. They may work on building restorations, excavations of archaeological sites, and other conservation projects.

Park technicians may also serve as administrative assistants at nationals parks and at the national and regional offices of the National Park Service. They may provide administrative support in departments such as personnel, budgeting, supply procurement, and property management.

In the private sector park technicians may work in different settings as assistants to head groundskeepers, gardeners, landscapers, and similar supervisors. These settings include resorts, golf courses, and private park and recreational facilities.

Working Conditions

Most park technicians work during the summer season and are subject to extreme weather conditions. Their work is conducted out of doors for the most part. They spend a lot of time interacting with other people. Seasonal workers are often assigned to different parks each summer, so they have to be willing to move around.

Work schedules vary depending on job assignments. Park technicians may work four ten-hour days, or they may have to work weekends. They are usually given meals and lodging while they are employed at the park.

Employment

At the federal level park technicians are employed by the National Park Service of the Department of Interior at national parks and other sites located throughout the United States.

While there are some full-time year-round positions available, most park technicians are employed on a seasonal basis during the summer months. There are also some winter seasonal positions. Altogether, the National Park Service fills more than 100,000 seasonal park positions every year.

Many of these positions are filled by high school and college students. Others are filled by teachers and other professionals desiring to work in a national park for the summer. Individuals who have completed one summer of work for the National Park Service are given priority for next year's openings.

Park technicians are also employed by state governments, typically by their natural resources or fish and game departments. In the private sector park technicians may find employment with resorts, public and private golf courses, and large companies or industrial centers with groundskeeping staffs.

Training, Other Qualifications, and Advancement

Park technicians generally receive on-the-job training and instruction that can be completed in three months or less. While there are no specific educational requirements, applicants with an interest in the environmental sciences have an advantage over other applicants. Individuals whose summer employment at a park fits in with their career goals may be given preference over others.

In addition to having an interest in the outdoors, park technicians must be good communicators. They must be able to speak well and communicate with different kinds of people. They may be required to give presentations in front of groups of visitors. Park technicians must be tactful, polite, and well groomed in order to perform well. High school and college teachers may be given preference for positions that require them to speak comfortably before groups of visitors.

In some cases park technicians start out as volunteers before they are hired as seasonal employees. They may work at different parks each summer. They can advance to full-time permanent positions with the National Park Service.

Job Outlook

While the Bureau of Labor Statistics (BLS) does not make employment projections for park technicians, the demand for this occupation is expected to remain strong. As the number of visitors to national and state parks continues to increase, there will be a need for more park technicians. At the same time, competition for these positions will remain fierce, since there are many people who are interested in this type of work.

Earnings

Seasonal park technicians hired by the National Park Service usually start at a GS-3 or GS-4 salary level. In 1992 the annual GS-3 salary range went from $14,082 to $18,303, the GS-4 range from $15,808 to $20,551. Many technicians report earning close to minimum wage during the summer. However, they are given meals and lodging while they are employed at the park.

Related Occupations

Related occupations that involve working outdoors include foresters, forestry technicians, park naturalists, park rangers, and recreation workers. Other occupations that involve spoken communications to register individuals include government registrars, hotel clerks, recreation facility attendants, animal shelter clerks, election clerks, and public health registrars.

Sources of Additional Information

For addtional information on a career as a park technician, contact:

- National Park Service, Dept. of the Interior, PO Box 37127, Washington, DC 20013-7127. Phone: (202)208-4649. Fax: (202)208-7520.

- National Parks and Conservation Association, 1776 Massachusetts Ave. NW, Ste. 200, Washington, DC 20036. Phone: (202)223-6722 Fax: (202)659-0650.

- National Recreation and Park Association, 2775 S. Quincy St., Ste. 300, Arlington, VA 22206. Phone: (703)820-4940. Fax: (703)671-6772.

- National Society for Park Resources, 2775 S. Quincy St., Ste. 300, Arlington, VA 22206. Phone: (703)820-4940. Fax: (703)671-6772.

Mechanics, Installers, and Repairers

ALARM SERVICE TECHNICIANS

At a Glance

- **D.O.T.:** 822.361-018, 822.361-022

- **Preferred Education:** Specialized training

- **Average Salary:** $5 to $10 per hour

- **Did You Know?** In some states, alarm service technicians must have their fingerprints on record with their local authorities.

Nature of the Work

Burglaries, fires, and medical emergencies are unfortunate facts of life. For peace of mind, people often choose to protect their families, personal property, and businesses against these hazards with protective alarm systems. Although simple to use, these potentially life-saving alarm systems consist of complex equipment that require the expertise of professional alarm service technicians to install, inspect, repair, and replace them.

When a customer requests to have a protective alarm system installed, the technician may meet at the customer's home or business to determine what function the alarm will serve, such as a burglary or fire warning; the type of alarm, such as a warning siren, or a silent signal that is monitored by a protective services station; means of alarm activation, such as a motion detector, contact switch, or control panel; and the physical areas the alarm system will cover, such as first-floor doors and windows. Once these factors are determined, the technician begins to design and install a system that works best for the customer.

Alarm service technicians have many duties: they read blueprints for building design and electrical layout; install new alarm systems; inspect existing systems to ensure proper function; investigate potential alarm system problems; perform tests on equipment; and repair or replace defective alarm system parts.

Alarm service technicians work with a wide variety of equipment and parts, including wires, conduits, motion sensors, contact switches, horns, video cameras, and lights. The job requires that they also use a variety of tools, including electric drills and other power tools, voltmeters, ohmmeters, test probes, wire cutters and strippers, soldering irons, and hand-held vacuums. Sometimes technicians must read service and installation manuals to assure proper installation of an alarm system.

Alarm service technicians receive their installation, inspection, or repair jobs from their employer. The employer provides information prior to the job on the type of work to be done and the location of the job site. Depending upon the amount of work an individual job site requires, technicians often visit several job sites each day. Technicians must keep detailed records on the type of service they perform at each job site. Alarm service technicians typically must speak directly with the customer in order to access the job site and ensure that the requested service is performed.

Working Conditions

Alarm service technicians work mostly indoors in residential, office, commercial, and industrial buildings. The job requires frequent standing, stooping, kneeling, crouching, climbing, and handling of parts, equipment, and tools. Technicians occasionally need to carry equipment that weighs between 25 and 50 pounds.

Alarm service technicians typically work 40-hour weeks, which sometimes includes Saturdays. Evenings and Sundays are occasionally necessary.

The job requires alarm service technicians to drive to their work sites—usually located within the employer's area or region. Alarm service technicians must wear employer-provided uniforms and may have to purchase their own tools.

Employment

According to the Michigan Occupation Information System 1995, approximately 20,000 alarm service technicians were employed in the United States in 1992.

Most alarm service technicians are employed or contracted by alarm service companies that provide security alarm systems to private residences and businesses.

Training, Other Qualifications, and Advancement

A high school diploma or GED certificate is highly recommended, although not always a requirement to become an alarm service technician. Many employers, however, do insist that prospective alarm service technicians have classroom training or vocational education classes specific to the field. Alarm service technicians find most of their experience is gained from on-the-job training or through apprenticeship. An aptitude in algebra, mechanics, and science is helpful. Technicians must be able to read alarm system manuals.

Alarm service technicians must have a valid driver's license, mostly for transportation to job sites. Some states require that employees of protective services companies have their fingerprints and other identification on police record. Accordingly, employees of protective services companies must have no criminal record. Some states require that alarm service technicians be at least 21 years old.

Advancement is achieved through experience. Those with enough experience may become estimators, supervisors, or superintendents, or eventually head their own company.

Job Outlook

Due to increasing societal awareness of the need for protective alarm systems, the demand for alarm system technicians is predicted to grow. A segment of the electrical technicians field, overall jobs are expected to rise 19.3 percent through the year 2005, according to the U.S. Bureau of Labor Statistics.

Earnings

Most alarm service technicians are paid an hourly wage, which may vary according to geographic location, employer, and experience. According to *American Salaries & Wages Survey*, protective alarm service technicians in heavily populated New York state earned an average wage of $383 per week; those working in less populated states like Hawaii and South Dakota earned an average between $5 and $7 per hour.

Full-time technicians receive benefits such as paid vacations and holidays, sick leave, health and life insurance, and retirement plans.

Related Occupations

Other occupations similar to alarm service technicians include electricians and data communications technicians.

Sources of Additional Information

For more information on a career as an alarm service technician, contact:

- National Burglar and Fire Alarm Association, 7101 Wisconsin Ave., No. 1390, Bethesda, MD 20814.

- Independent Electrical Contractors, Inc., 507 Wythe St., Alexandria, VA 22314 Phone: (703)549-7351.

AUTOMOTIVE EMISSIONS TECHNICIANS

At a Glance

- **D.O.T.:** 620.281-014

- **Preferred Education:** 2 to 4 years advanced training

- **Average Salary:** $20,000 to $30,000

- **Did You Know?** Opportunities for auto emissions technicians will be best for those who have graduated from accredited training programs.

Nature of the Work

Automotive emissions technicians are automotive service technicians who specialize in testing and repairing a vehicle's emissions control system. In addition to using conventional tools, emissions technicians use computers to run diagnostic tests on vehicles. Many of today's vehicles have computerized systems for emissions control.

When servicing vehicles, automotive emissions technicians first enter the vehicle identification number into a networked computer. The computer tells the technician if there are any notices from the manufacturer regarding warranties or recalls. Technicians also use hand-held computers and scanning tools to locate problems. Once problems have been detected, automotive emissions technicians consult service manuals, either printed or on CD-ROM. Service manuals provide directions regarding proper procedures to follow, tools to use, and parts to order. For example, service may involve replacing a catalytic converter, which converts exhaust into less harmful substances.

Government regulations also affect the work of auto emissions technicians. The Clean Air Act of 1990 set forth stringent regulations concerning automotive emissions. These regulations cover new vehicles as well as those already on the road. Following national guidelines issued by the Environmental Protection Agency (EPA), individual states have enacted their own rules and regulations regarding automotive emissions testing.

One of the programs mandated by the EPA is known as Inspection and Maintenance (I/M). An I/M program requires that emissions control systems be tested to make sure they are working properly. When conducting a mandatory auto emissions test, a technician enters the vehicle identification number into a computer and connects the vehicle's exhaust system to a portable testing device. This device measures the content of the vehicle's exhaust emissions. The machine prints out the results of the test and indicates whether or not the vehicle's emissions are within allowable guidelines.

If a vehicle fails its emissions test, a technician makes the necessary repairs. The Environmental Protection Agency has set a $450 limit on the repairs that can be made to bring a vehicle into compliance with current exhaust emissions guidelines. Sometimes only minor repairs are needed, such as replacing spark plugs and adjusting the timing. If a vehicle's catalytic converter has to be replaced, however, the repairs become more complicated.

Working Conditions

Automotive emissions technicians work under conditions similar to those for other automotive service technicians. They typically work standard 40-hour weeks. They work indoors under somewhat noisy conditions typical of auto repair shops. Conditions in repair areas vary but are generally well lighted and ventilated. The work of automotive emissions technicians does not require heavy lifting and is generally not physically demanding.

Employment

Automotive technicians who specialize in exhaust emissions tend to be employed in larger repair shops and service departments of vehicle dealerships. Other employers include service stations and specialty shops, including locations that specialize in tune-ups, oil changes, or muffler replacements.

In the future, automotive emissions technicians may be employed at facilities that specialize solely in testing emissions. Since government regulation of vehicle emissions is most stringent in urban and metropolitan areas, that is where the most automotive emissions technicians are employed. While automotive technicians have traditionally been men, many women are entering this field through formal training programs.

Training, Other Qualifications, and Advancement

Automotive emissions technicians are typically high school graduates who have two to four years of training. Automotive maintenance courses are offered in high schools, vocational-technical schools, colleges, and universities. Many training programs are run on a cooperative basis by vehicle manufacturers and local educational institutions. Specialists in exhaust systems generally have a background in automotive maintenance, then receive additional training in their specialty. Beginning technicians usually start as trainees, working with more experienced technicians for six months to two years.

Automotive service training programs are certified by the National Automotive Technicians Education Foundation (NATEF). NATEF is affiliated with the National Institute for Automotive Service Excellence (ASE), which certifies automotive service technicians in nine specialty areas. The appropriate certification category for automotive emissions technicians is Advanced Engine Performance. Technicians can obtain certification by passing ASE's certification examination after completing two years of relevant automotive experience. Approximately three-fourths of all automotive service technicians were ASE-certified in one or more categories as of 1995.

Because of the high technology that is being incorporated in today's vehicles, automotive emissions technicians must have some advanced training. They must also be computer literate. Since new technologies are being introduced every year, it is necessary for automotive emissions technicians to keep up by taking additional training while working.

Automotive emissions technicians must have the academic ability to learn new applications and technologies. They should have a good academic background in reading, mathematics and geometry, and science, especially chemistry and physics. They must have the ability to read service manuals that are written at the twelfth-grade level.

Like other automotive service technicians, automotive emissions technicians have the ability to apply mechanical principles to practical situations. Some manual dexterity is needed to work with power and hand tools. They must have good vision to work with objects close at hand.

Qualified technicians can advance by learning more skills through additional training. Those with management potential may be promoted to positions such as shop supervisor, service writer, parts manager, or service manager. Technicians may also advance in their careers by teaching courses in automotive service or by opening their own business.

Job Outlook

Employment of all automotive service technicians is projected to increase about as fast as the average for all occupations between 1992 and 2005. Opportunities will be best for those who have graduated from formal, accredited training programs.

Several factors indicate that the demand for qualified automotive emissions technicians will exceed the supply. More stringent government regulations taking effect in 1996 will require trained technicians to conduct increasingly sophisticated emissions tests. By the end of 1995, the EPA will have required nearly 60 counties to have "enhanced" I/M programs in place. By the year 2000, virtually every metropolitan and urban area will have such testing programs in place, affecting some 50 million vehicles. More test-only facilities are expected to open, thus creating employment opportunities.

In addition, many people are also keeping their cars for longer periods of time, with older cars requiring more tests and repairs than new ones.

Earnings

According to the Bureau of Labor Statistics, the average earnings of all automotive service technicians were about $21,000 in 1992. In general, specialists in the more technical aspects of automotive service including exhaust systems can expect to earn more than the average for automotive service technicians.

According to a salary survey conducted by ASE and published in the February 1995 issue of *Brake & Front End*, salaries for automotive service technicians ranged from approximately $19,600 for the least experienced to about $30,000 for the most experienced. Experienced technicians employed in big cities reported higher earnings (about $33,750) than those in medium cities (about $31,600), small cities (about $29,500), and townships (about $24,500). Salaries for the least experienced automotive technicians ranged from about $21,900 in big cities to about $17,200 in townships.

Related Occupations

Other related automotive repair occupations include alternate fuels technicians, collision repair technicians, engine machinists, medium and heavy truck technicians, and automotive counterpersons. Other vehicle repair occupations include diesel truck and bus mechanics, motorcycle mechanics, repair service estimators, and automotive body repairers, painters, customizers.

Sources of Additional Information

- National Institute for Automotive Service Excellence (ASE), 13505 Dulles Technology Dr., Herndon, VA 22071. Phone: (703)713-3800.

- Automotive Service Association, 1901 Airport Fwy., PO Box 929, Bedford, TX 76095. Phone: (817)283-6205 or 800-272-7467.

AVIONICS TECHNICIANS

At a Glance

- **D.O.T.:** 823.261-026

- **Preferred Education:** 1 to 2 years of specific vocational preparation

- **Average Salary:** $35,000 to $45,000 per year

- **Did You Know?** Avionics technicians may specialize in ground station electronic equipment that is used for air navigation.

Nature of the Work

Avionics technicians are electronics technicians who specialize in the installation, repair, and maintenance of a variety of avionics equipment installed in aircraft and space vehicles. An aircraft's avionics includes its weather radar systems, navigation and communication radios, auto pilot, and compass systems. Modern avionics systems are controlled by digital computers rather than mechanical cables and hydraulics. These systems control the aircraft's flight, engine, and other primary functions.

The work of avionics technicians includes preventive maintenance and repair. Following a prescribed maintenance schedule, avionics technicians inspect components of avionics equipment for defects such as loose connections and frayed wire. They also make sure that the equipment has been assembled and installed according to specifications. Avionics technicians conduct periodic tests on avionics equipment under simulated or actual operating conditions, using such testing devices as oscilloscopes, digital meters and counters, and circuit analyzers.

Avionics technicians identify defective components through scheduled tests or because of a pilot's description of a problem. If an avionics problem has been noted during a preflight check, avionics technicians may be under considerable time pressure to check electrical connections, replace a gauge or other component, and use electrical test equipment to identify the precise cause of the problem.

Avionics technicians monitor the performance of the avionics equipment and calibrate installed or repaired equipment according to prescribed specifications. They adjust radio equipment by signalling ground stations and making appropriate adjustments. They may accompany flight crews to perform in-flight tests and adjustments, noting whether any post-flight repair work is needed.

Instead of working on avionics systems in aircraft, avionics technicians may specialize in ground station electronic equipment that is used for air navigation, communications between aircraft and ground services, and control of aircraft movements. These technicians maintain and repair radar, radios, computers, wire communications systems, and other electronic devices located at airports and along the network of federal airways in a variety of locations.

Working Conditions

Avionics technicians generally work under noisy conditions in airplane hangars and repair shops. They generally work indoors but occasionally have to work outdoors and in bad weather. In some cases they must be willing to fly in aircraft and perform tests and maintenance while in flight.

Avionics technicians work in a rapidly changing field due to the impact of new technologies. They must keep up with new technologies and are usually required to continue their training throughout their careers.

They are subject to higher than average levels of stress due to responsibilities associated with maintaining safety standards. They may be under time pressure to identify problems and complete repairs in time for a scheduled flight.

The work of avionics technicians is generally not physically demanding. Like other ground personnel in the air transportation industry, they usually work 40 hours per week on eight hour shifts that may involve afternoons or evenings.

Employment

Avionics technicians who work for regularly scheduled airlines are usually employed at airports, terminals, and overhaul bases located throughout the United States and overseas. Airports are located near major cities. The major overhaul facilities are in New York, Los Angeles, San Francisco, Denver, Atlanta, Kansas City, Tulsa, and Minneapolis. Regularly scheduled airlines usually have line stations located at every airport they serve, and experienced avionics technicians may be able to request employment at the line stations of their choice.

Avionics technicians may also be employed in general aviation by air taxi and fixed base operations, repair stations certified by the Federal Aviation Administration (FAA), aerial applicators, flight training schools, corporations owning fleets of aircraft, and aircraft manufacturers. General aviation offers avionics technicians more local employment opportunities than regularly scheduled airlines.

The federal government also employs avionics technicians to work on military aircraft at military installations in the United States and abroad. The FAA employs avionics technicians at their ground stations throughout the United States. The FAA operates an overhaul base in Oklahoma City, Oklahoma, and an electronic research facility in Atlantic City, New Jersey. Avionics technicians specializing in ground station equipment are employed by the FAA at Airway Facilities Sector Field Offices located throughout the country. These field offices are usually located at airports, but they may be in remote locations as well.

Training, Other Qualifications, and Advancement

Avionics technicians generally have one to two years of specific vocational preparation. Two-year programs leading to an associate degree in avionics are available from public or private universities. Applicants must have a high school diploma or equivalent. Appropriate high school courses include mathematics, physics, computer science, chemistry, English, and aerospace education.

Avionics technicians can also be trained while serving in the military. They may also be eligible for apprenticeship training programs through their employer.

Avionics technicians should have a strong background in technical subjects. They must have an understanding of the physical principles involved in the operation of an aircraft and its systems. As avionics technology has become more advanced, so too have the educational requirements for avionics technicians.

In some case avionics technicians may be required to have a license from the Federal Communications Commission (FCC). A General Radiotelephone Operator License is required to maintain and repair FCC-licensed transmitters used in aviation. The license, which is good for an individual's lifetime, may be obtained by passing a licensing exam covering basic radio law, operating procedures, electronics fundamentals, and repair and maintenance techniques. Individuals who work on transmitters must either be licensed by the FCC or work under the direct supervision of a licensed individual.

Avionics technicians who repair radios and other instruments on an aircraft must have a Repairman Certificate from the FAA. Applicants for certification must have 18 months of practical experience or complete an approved course of formal training. In addition they must be recommended for certification by their employer and can only repair aircraft in connection with their employment.

Avionics technicians generally have an interest in applying mechanical principles to practical situations by building and repairing objects. They need well developed reasoning, mathematical, and language skills as well as a desire to work with their hands.

Avionics technicians can advance in several ways. As they improve their skills and qualifications, they are able to command premium wages and work in locations of their choice. Opportunities for cross-training as aircraft mechanics provide additional means for advancement. Individuals with administrative abilities can be promoted to supervisory and executive positions, especially if they work for a government agency. Avionics technicians with supervisory experience may apply for avionics inspector positions with the FAA.

Job Outlook

Employment in the air transportation industry is expected to increase faster than for all occupations as a whole, according to the Bureau of Labor Statistics. Within the air transportation industry, precision production, craft, and repair occupations, including avionics technicians, are expected to increase by 30 percent between 1990 and 2005.

Employment prospects for avionics technicians appear best in the general aviation sector, where there is a shortage of avionics technicians. Licensed, well-trained individuals with strong technical backgrounds will have the best chance for employment.

Earnings

Earnings of avionics technicians depend on the type of employer as well as experience and qualifications. Major airlines pay around $11 to $16 an hour for entry-level avionics technicians. Within five years, avionics technicians can earn from $35,000 to $45,000 or more. Individuals holding FAA Repairman Certificates in avionics are usually given incentives. Salaries in general aviation are generally lower than for major airlines, starting at $7 to $10 per hour.

Avionics technicians working for the FAA usually start at the GS-5 or GS-7 levels and earn between $16,973 and $21,023. They can advance to G-11 ($31,116 to $40,449) and possibly higher.

According to *American Salaries and Wages Survey*, avionics technicians in New York earned an average wage of $23,000 in 1991.

Most employees in the air transportation industry receive a variety of standard benefits, including paid holidays, vacations, insurance plans, retirement programs, and sick leave. Employees of major airlines may be eligible for free or reduced fare transportation.

Related Occupations

Related occupations in the air transportation industry include airplane repairers, airplane mechanics, and aviation safety inspectors. Electronic equipment repairers may also work in hospitals, marine industries, offices, and factories. Other occupations that involve repairing and maintaining electronic equipment include appliance and powertool repairers, automotive electricians, broadcast technicians, electronic organ technicians, telephone and communications equipment repairers, and vending machine repairers.

Sources of Additional Information

• International Society of Certified Electronics Technicians, 2708 W. Berry St., Fort Worth, TX 76109. Phone: (817)921-9101.

- Electronics Technicians Association, 602 N. Jackson, Greencastle, IN 46135. Phone: (317)653-8262.

- FAPA: Future Aviation Professionals of America, 4959 Massachusetts Blvd., Atlanta, GA 30337. Phone: (404)997-8097.

For lists of potential employers, contact:

- Air Transport Association of America, 1301 Pennsylvania Ave., Ste. 1100, Washington, DC 20004-7017. Phone: (202)626-4000.

- Regional Airline Association, 1200 19th St. NW, Ste. 300, Washington, DC 20036-2401 Phone: (202)857-1170.

- Aircraft Electronics Association, PO Box 1963, Independence, MO 64055-1963. Phone: (816)373-6565.

For information about General Radiotelephone Operator Licenses, contact:

- Federal Communications Commission, 1919 M St. NW, Washington, DC 20554. Phone: (202)632-7240.

For information about FAA Repairman Certificates, educational opportunities, and careers in avionics, contact:

- Federal Aviation Administration, Aviation Education Div., 400 7th St. SW, Washington, DC 20590. Phone: (202)267-3471.

BICYCLE MECHANICS

At a Glance

- **D.O.T.:** 639.681-010
- **Preferred Education:** On-the-job experience
- **Average Salary:** $16,000
- **Did You Know?** In the past 10 years, the number of bicyclists has increased by more than 33 percent, totaling more than 100 million riders.

Nature of the Work

More than 13 million bicycles were sold in 1993, the highest number in a decade. The increasing popularity of bicycling, both on- and off-road, has resulted in a large number of bikes that require regular maintenance and repair. While some bicyclists do their own maintenance, many have their bikes repaired or fine-tuned by trained bicycle mechanics.

Before making repairs, bicycle mechanics generally lift bikes onto stands, making them easier to work on. Routine maintenance typically involves giving the bicycle a tune-up. Bicycle mechanics lubricate the bicycle's moving parts and adjust the brakes. Brake and gear cables are checked and replaced if they are frayed, kinked, or rusted. Using various

hand tools, bicycle mechanics may also check the tightness of all threaded parts, in some cases lubricating the threads. They tighten or loosen spokes to align the wheels. Bearing adjustments may be checked to be sure they are not too tight. Worn components are replaced as needed.

In some cases, bicycles may require minor repairs. Bicycle mechanics may use a bench grinder to shape replacement parts. If the bicycle frame is bent, bicycle mechanics can use a special vise to straighten it. They may also repair or replace accessories and equipment such as handlebars, stands, lights, and seats.

When a customer orders a new bicycle, bicycle mechanics assemble the new bike or make sure it has been correctly assembled. Even new bicycles may require some frame straightening and other adjustments. In some shops, bicycle mechanics build customized bicycles for their customers.

Other jobs done by bicycle mechanics may include welding broken or cracked bicycle frames using a torch and welding rods, and painting bicycle frames using a spray gun or brush. Bicycle mechanics usually provide customers with repair estimates and order parts that are not in stock. They discuss bicycle maintenance and repairs with their customers and may instruct them in basic maintenance procedures.

Race mechanics are bicycle mechanics who specialize in maintaining and repairing bicycles for racing teams. They travel with the racers and work on the bicycles before, during, and after racing. In a multi-stage race, they may spend from three to six hours every evening after racing has been completed to clean and inspect the bicycles. They clean the bicycles using detergents and grease solvents. They service the bicycles by making minor equipment changes. Gearing is usually changed after each stage of a multi-stage race. Special wheels and discs as well as other specialized equipment may have to be installed. Brake arms must be centered and wheels aligned. Tires are inspected for wear and replaced as needed.

Working Conditions

Bicycle mechanics usually work on bikes indoors in a shop area of a bike store. Their work requires average strength, involving frequent lifting of 10 to 25 pounds. Working hours for bike mechanics vary depending on whether they are full- or part-time. However, bike mechanics generally work on weekends when many retail shops are open. In some areas of the country, the work may be somewhat seasonal, becoming busier during the summer months.

Race mechanics work under somewhat different conditions than shop mechanics. Race mechanics are under more time pressure to make repairs. They work in many different settings depending on the race location and often have to travel.

Employment

According to the Bureau of Labor Statistics, there were approximately 14,000 bicycle mechanics employed in 1992. Many of them work for independent bicycle dealers and in the bicycle departments of large sporting goods and department stores. Bicycle dealerships include family-oriented shops that sell a full range of bicycles and accessories, "pro shops" that specialize in the most expensive bicycles, and "multi-specialty stores" that may carry exercise and personal fitness equipment and equipment for other sports in addition to bicycles. Pro shops may also employ race mechanics, who are also employed by racing teams.

Employment opportunities are the best in states with the most bicycle dealers. The largest number of independent bicycle dealers is in California, with more than 1,000 dealerships. Other states with large numbers of dealers are New York and Florida. Dealers tend to be concentrated in population centers, including major cities and towns with large universities.

Training, Other Qualifications, and Advancement

Bicycle mechanics usually learn their skills on the job, often as part-time employees of bicycle shops. They may also learn bicycle repair in high school shop courses and at some vocational-technical schools. There are at least four specialized institutes that provide formal training for bicycle mechanics. Some bicycle manufacturers offer free training for employees of stores that carry their brand. In addition, bicycle mechanics can teach themselves through home instruction courses and by reading books and manuals on bicycle repair.

Bicycle mechanics must have good mechanical skills. Their work requires manual dexterity and the ability to see objects close at hand. Good communication skills are also needed to deal effectively with customers.

Bicycle mechanics can advance to supervisory or management positions in the shop or store where they are employed. Some mechanics become sales representatives for bicycle manufacturers.

Job Outlook

According to the Bureau of Labor Statistics, employment of bicycle mechanics is expected to increase much faster than the average for all occupations. The 14,000 bicycle mechanics employed in 1992 are projected to increase to 20,000 by 2005, an increase of more than 45 percent.

Bicycle ownership is at its highest level. In the past 10 years, the number of bicyclists has increased by more than 33 percent, totaling more than 100 million riders. Together with the continued popularity of bicycling among adults as well as children, these factors indicate demand for bicycle mechanics will increase. However, the number of independent bicycle dealerships has decreased from a high of about 8,000 in the 1980s to about 6,800 in 1994. With more bicycles being sold by large sporting goods and department stores, there may be fewer independent bicycle shops employing bicycle mechanics.

The bicycle industry also tends to be cyclical. Sales of new bicycles fluctuate with the economy. The need to repair and maintain bicycles, however, is not normally affected by economic fluctuations. When people keep their bicycles longer before buying new ones, they are more likely to need them repaired and maintained.

Earnings

According to *American Salaries and Wages Survey*, bicycle mechanics can expect to earn anywhere from minimum wage to approximately $16,000 per year.

Related Occupations

There are numerous occupations for mechanics, installers, and repairers, including aircraft mechanics and engine specialists, automotive body repairers, automotive mechanics, diesel mechanics, electronic equipment repairers, elevator installers and repairers, farm equipment mechanics, heating and cooling technicians, home appliance and power tool repairers, industrial machinery repairers, small-engine mechanics, and vending machine repairers and servicers.

Sources of Additional Information

- Bicycle Federation of America, 1506 21st St., NW, Ste. 200, Washington, DC 20036 Phone: (202)463-4622.

- Bicycle Manufacturers Association of America, 3050 K St. NW, Ste. 400, Washington, DC 20007. Phone: (202)944-9297.

- League of American Bicyclists, 190 W. Ostend St., Ste. 120, Baltimore, MD 21230. Phone: (410)539-3399 or (800)288-BIKE.

- National Bicycle Dealers Association, 2240 University Dr., Ste. 130, Newport Beach, CA 92660. Phone: (714)722-6909.

BIOMEDICAL EQUIPMENT TECHNICIANS

At a Glance

- **D.O.T.:** 019.261-010

- **Preferred Education:** Associate degree

- **Average Salary:** $21,000 to $25,000

- **Did You Know?** Biomedical equipment technicians often work directly with physicians, nurses, and other medical personnel.

Nature of the Work

Hospitals and medical centers across the country now depend heavily on high-technology to treat patients and save lives. Many hospital rooms look more like computer rooms with the large number of heart-lung machines, dialysis machines, magnetic resonance imaging machines, and other medical equipment currently in use. Biomedical equipment technicians make sure these machines are always in top operating condition.

Biomedical equipment technicians repair, calibrate, and maintain medical equipment and instrumentation. They inspect and install machines before they are used by physicians, nurses, scientists, and engineers. While some biomedical equipment technicians specialize in one type of equipment, others work on all types of machines. These can include patient monitors, electrosurgical units, blood analyzers, anesthesia devices, and other technical equipment.

They use special tools and measuring devices, along with their knowledge of the products, to keep the machines working properly. Biomedical equipment technicians perform regularly scheduled maintenance to prevent break-downs. Using special instruments, they check a machine's circuits, meters, and gauges to see if they are working properly. Biomedical equipment technicians must keep detailed and accurate records of equipment repairs and maintenance procedures and deal with equipment manufacturers when necessary.

Biomedical equipment technicians often work directly with physicians, nurses, and other medical personnel. They consult with the medical staff to make sure the equipment is working properly and safely and make modifications as directed. They also demonstrate and explain the proper use of specific machines. Some biomedical equipment technicians assist during surgery and other medical procedures. They may also work with physicians, researchers and scientists in developing new equipment.

Working Conditions

Biomedical equipment technicians generally work a 40-hour week, often in a clinical setting. Biomedical equipment technicians who work for equipment manufacturers may be required to travel to install or repair equipment at customer sites. Their work schedules sometimes include weekends, holidays, and evenings. Some technicians are "on-call" for emergencies, which can be stressful. Biomedical equipment technicians must be able to work calmly and effectively under stressful conditions. They also must follow strict safety guidelines while performing certain tasks. They frequently interact with others, such as medical personnel and equipment manufacturers.

Employment

There were 9,500 electromedical and biomedical equipment repairers employed in 1992. Biomedical equipment technicians work for hospitals, medical research centers, medical equipment manufacturers, medical colleges and schools, research institutes, industrial laboratories, and medical supply companies. Some biomedical equipment technicians serve in the Armed Forces.

Training, Advancement, and Other Qualifications

Employers generally require an associate degree in biomedical equipment technology or a related field such as electronics. Approximately 70 two-year colleges offer degrees in this field. Few four-year colleges offer bachelor degrees in biomedical equipment technology. General coursework includes electronics, mathematics, and science. Biomedical equipment technicians must also have a background medical

terminology. Specialty courses cover biomedical equipment design and construction.

Although certification is not required, biomedical equipment technicians can increase their earnings and advance their careers by completing a certification program. The International Certification Commission for Clinical Engineers and Biomedical Technicians offers candidate certification and full certification. Applicants must pass a six-hour examination. Those with experience may have the examination waived.

Biomedical equipment technicians must keep up with developments in products and technology. Therefore, extensive continuing education is necessary. Many technicians receive this training from equipment manufacturers.

High school students interested in a career in biomedical equipment technology should take courses in electronics, algebra, calculus, trigonometry, physics, biology, English, and computer science.

Biomedical equipment technicians should enjoy electronics and mechanics and working with tools. Good color vision and eye-hand coordination are also necessities. Biomedical equipment technicians need excellent written and oral communication skills to understand and convey detailed technical information.

Some biomedical equipment technicians advance to become biomedical engineers.

Job Outlook

Employment opportunities for biomedical equipment technicians will increase faster than average through the year 2005. One reason for this growth is the increased use of highly technological equipment in hospitals. Another reason is the growing pressure to hold down health care costs. Biomedical equipment technicians help do this by maintaining and repairing expensive machines.

Biomedical equipment technicians work all across the United States, with most jobs located near major cities.

Earnings

In 1990, entry-level biomedical equipment technicians in the Midwest earned an average hourly wage of $10.27. This equals approximately $21,000 per year. The average wage for biomedical equipment technicians in the Midwest was $12.43 per hour, or about $25,800 per year. Average 1991 hourly wages for biomedical equipment technicians in the South ranged from $10.40 to $12.20, which equals about $21,632 and $25,376, respectively.

Related Occupations

Other occupations similar to biomedical equipment technician include bottle-house quality-control technician, laboratory assistant (blood and plasma), laboratory technician (pharmaceutical), biological aide, ophthalmic photographer, biological photographer, and aerospace physiological technician.

Sources of Additional Information

For additional information contact:

• Society of Biomedical Equipment Technicians, 3330 Washington Blvd., Ste. 400, Arlington, VA 22201. Phone: (703)525-4890.

• Association for the Advancement of Medical Instrumentation, 3330 Washington Blvd., Arlington, VA 22201. Phone: (703)525-4890.

• Biomedical Engineering Society, P.O. Box 2399, Culver City, CA 90231. Phone: (213)206-6443.

BUS MAINTENANCE MECHANICS

At a Glance

■ **D.O.T.:** 625.281-010

■ **Preferred Education**: High school diploma or equivalent

■ **Average Salary:** $9.43 to $22.22 per hour

■ **Did You Know?** Bus maintenance mechanics that work on diesel engines must complete a diesel mechanic training program to keep up with technology's increasing electronic sophistication.

Nature of the Work

Every day millions of people depend on buses for transportation, but like all motor vehicles, they need maintenance and repair to keep them running properly. This service is performed by bus maintenance mechanics.

Bus maintenance mechanics maintain, repair, and overhaul buses. They follow job orders and examine buses to diagnose the nature and extent its malfunction. Jobs may be routine or complicated.

Bus maintenance mechanics may disassemble a unit and inspect parts for wear. During routine jobs, bus maintenance mechanics may repair or replace parts such as pistons, rods, gears, valves, and bearings. They may adjust brakes, align front end wheels, repair or replace shock absorbers, recharge and replace batteries, and solder radiator leaks. In addition, they may replace and adjust headlights, and install and repair accessories such as radios, heaters, mirrors, and windshield wipers.

During more complicated jobs, maintenance mechanics may overhaul or replace gas or diesel engines, transmissions, differentials, blowers, carburetors, distributors, generators, pumps, and starters. They may rebuild crankshafts and cylinder blocks. They may rewire ignition systems, lights, and instrument panels. Following an accident, bus maintenance mechanics may mend damaged body and fenders by hammering out or filling in dents and welding broken parts.

Working Conditions

Bus maintenance mechanics typically work 40 hours a week, five days a week. Overtime is sometimes necessary.

Mechanics usually work indoors, although occasional road work may be necessary. Work areas are well-lighted and ventilated; some employers provide locker rooms and shower facilities. Bus maintenance mechanics have to stand, crouch or lie in awkward or cramped spaces to perform their job. They handle dirty, greasy and sometimes heavy parts and equipment. Bus maintenance mechanics are subject to typical shop hazards, such as cuts and bruises.

Employment

According to the U.S. Bureau of Labor Statistics, there were 263,000 bus and truck mechanics and diesel engine specialists in 1992. Bus mechanics are employed by bus lines, public transit companies, and school systems.

Training, Other Qualifications, and Advancement

Most employers prefer bus maintenance mechanics have a high school diploma or equivalent. Applicants should have thorough knowledge, either through work experience or formal training in the standard practices and procedures, materials, and tools of the automotive mechanic trade. Those who work on diesel engines need to complete a diesel mechanic training program due to diesel technology's increasing electronic sophistication.

Training can be achieved at a vocational or trade school; mechanics training programs usually take one or two years. Related high school shop classes are highly recommended. Various skills and training can be learned on-the-job. Beginners usually perform tasks such as fueling, lubricating, driving vehicles out of the shop, and cleaning parts, but as they gain experience and increase their skills, they can advance to mechanic's helpers and perform more complex jobs.

Many mechanics become certified for recognized achievement, although this is often voluntary. Certified mechanics are usually more employable. To retain certification, certain tests must usually be taken every five years.

Experienced bus maintenance mechanics who demonstrate technical and leadership skills may advance to supervisory positions.

Job Outlook

According to the U.S. Bureau of Labor Statistics, job opportunities for bus mechanics are expected to grow 24.4 percent by the year 2005, as fast as average for all occupations. Factors contributing to the increase include a growing population, safer school buses for children, a reduction in air pollution. In addition, the fact that buses are a less expensive mode of transportation also adds to the need for properly maintenanced buses. Employment growth will account for many new jobs, but most openings will come from replacing retiring mechanics.

Earnings

Earnings for bus mechanics varies by employer, geographic location, and the bus mechanic's experience. Sources report that in the early 1990s, bus maintenance mechanics earned a median hourly wage of $14.10. Nationally, they averaged $11.60 to $17.00 per hour. According to *American Salaries & Wages Survey*, bus mechanics in the South earned $9.88 to $22.22 per hour in the early 1990s. Full-time bus mechanics usually receive benefits that include paid vacation and holidays, health and life insurance, and retirement plans. Unionized bus maintenance mechanics must pay union dues.

Related Occupations

Other occupations similar to bus maintenance mechanics include diesel mechanics, automobile mechanics, industrial truck mechanics, and motorcycle mechanics.

Sources of Additional Information

* Automotive Service Industry Association, 25 Northwest Point, Elk Grove Village, IL 60007-1035. Phone: (708)228-1310.

* American Trucking Association, Inc., Maintenance Council, 2200 Mill Rd., Alexandria, VA 22314-4677. Phone: (703)838-1700.

* National Automotive Technicians Education Foundation, 13505 Dulles Technology Dr., Herndon, VA 22071-3415. Phone: (703)713-0100.

* ASE, 13505 Dulles Technology Dr., Herndon, VA 22071-3415. Phone: (703)713-3800.

CABLE TV INSTALLERS/REPAIRERS

At a Glance

* **D.O.T.:** 821.261-010; 821.281-010; 821.361-010
* **Preferred Education:** Specialized training
* **Average Salary:** $26,000 to $40,000 per year
* **Did You Know?** Many cable companies provide on-the-job training for unskilled cable installers.

Nature of the Work

Most Americans no longer receive television programming over the airwaves. Instead, they rely on a vast network of cable and optical fiber to receive everything from around-the-clock news to sports, films, comedy, and music videos. It is

the responsibility of cable TV installers and repairers to maintain this network and bring cable TV to customers.

Cable TV installers prepare the customer's home for cable reception. This generally requires placing wiring in the house, connecting the wire to the customer's television set, and checking the strength of the television signal. Connecting the TV set to the cable may include a special terminal device called a converter. Installers explain the operation of the system to the customer and describe the channels and programming available. In addition to these initial installation functions, installers may also be responsible for disconnecting and removing equipment if a customer decides to cancel their service.

Some installers are responsible for servicing the cable lines that run from the street to the home. Installers also may respond to customer requests for service if problems occur with the converter.

Most service requests, however, are handled by cable repairers. Trunk technicians correct failures in the main cable line. This trunk line is the main artery of a cable system. It is connected to the cable system's plant area and runs along main streets and highways. These lines must be carefully maintained since problems with them could disrupt service to a large number of customers.

Service technicians are another part of the technical staff. These technicians respond to problems with a customer's cable reception. Generally, this requires service calls to the home. Sometimes, however, service technicians work on amplifiers, poles, and lines. They correct electrical malfunctions and repair faulty cable lines. Service technicians also perform preventive maintenance by electronically scanning the system to detect small problems before they become large problems.

Bench technicians work in the cable system's repair facility. They examine and repair broken or malfunctioning equipment, such as cable converters. Bench technicians diagnose the broken piece of equipment, repair it, record the repair, and return the equipment to use if possible.

Working Conditions

Working conditions for cable TV installers and repairers vary with the job. Installers, trunk technicians, and service technicians work part of the time outdoors. This may include exposure to heat, cold, or poor weather. Because television cables are strung from utility poles or are underground, these workers must climb and lift or work in stooped and cramped positions. Most installers or repairers usually work a 40-hour week, but are subject to 24-hour call for service. For example, when severe weather damages lines, they may work long and irregular hours to restore service. There is some danger of electrical shock. Bench technicians work indoors in a repair department or shop.

Employment

The U.S. Bureau of Labor Statistics classifies cable TV and telephone line installers and repairers together. These workers held 165,000 jobs in 1992. Cable TV installers and repairers work for cable television companies across the United States.

Training, Advancement, and Other Qualifications

Many cable companies provide on-the-job training for unskilled cable installers. These employers typically prefer high school graduates. Trainees first learn the various parts of a cable system. Some cable companies use technical education material offered by the National Cable Television Institute. Trainees then work under the supervision of skilled installers. They learn how to climb poles safely, make installations in homes, and troubleshoot equipment. After they learn the job, installers begin working alone.

Some installers and technicians receive training by completing one- or two-year programs at a technical school or community college. These programs cover the basics of electronics, broadcasting theory, blueprint and diagram reading, and physics. Many of these schools have job placement offices to help graduates find employment.

Cable TV installation is considered an entry-level job. Installers can advance to become technicians. Service and trunk technicians can be promoted to technical supervisor or chief technician.

Cable TV installers and repairers should be polite and patient so they can communicate with customers. Because the work can involve a great deal of climbing, installers and repairers should have stamina and must be unafraid of heights. The ability to work as part of a team is also necessary.

Job Outlook

The cable television industry experienced rapid growth in the 1980s and created thousands of new jobs. However, with most of the households in the United States already wired for cable television, future emphasis will be placed on maintaining and upgrading existing systems. This will result in slower growth for installers and repairers. The National Cable Television Association expects employment in the industry to continue to increase as systems are rebuilt and upgraded, and programming becomes even more sophisticated and diverse. Many cable systems are being supplemented or replaced by fiber optics.

Earnings

According to the U.S. Bureau of Labor Statistics, installers and repairers who worked full time earned a median weekly wage of $648. The middle 50 percent earned between $503 and $770. The bottom 10 percent earned less than $350; the top 10 percent earned more than $874 a week.

Related Occupations

Other occupations concerned with erecting and repairing power lines and circuits include electric meter installer, electrical installation supervisor, line supervisor, line maintainer, line repairer, relay technician, and emergency service restorer.

Sources of Additional Information

- Society of Cable Television Engineers, 669 Exton Commons, Exton, PA 19341 Phone: (215)363-6888

- National Cable Television Association, 1724 Massachusetts Ave. NW, Washington, DC 20036 Phone: (202)775-3550

- National Cable Television Institute, 801 W. Mineral Ave., Littleton, CO 80120 Phone: (303)761-8554

CAMERA REPAIRERS AND PHOTOGRAPHIC EQUIPMENT TECHNICIANS

At a Glance

- **D.O.T.:** 714.281-014 and 714.281-022

- **Preferred Education:** On-the-job training

- **Average Salary:** $15,000 to $18,000

- **Did You Know?** Camera repairers and technicians are usually high school graduates who have received additional education and training through classroom instruction, home study courses, or on the job.

Nature of the Work

When cameras and other types of photographic equipment need repairs, they are usually worked on by specially trained technicians. Camera repairers and photographic equipment technicians disassemble, inspect, adjust and test cameras including motion picture cameras and equipment using specialized tools and devices. Technicians follow manufacturers' blueprints and repair manuals when conducting tests and making adjustments.

Technicians may use a jeweler's loupe or magnifying glass to locate defects and examine small parts. They test and align camera parts such as the lens system, lens mount, and film transport using precision gauges. Special instruments are used to adjust and check focus, shutter speed, and operating speed of still and motion picture cameras. Technicians may use electronic or stroboscopic timing instruments to calibrate a camera's shutter and lens system.

The focus of a camera's lens system can be tested using optical measuring equipment. Technicians use small handtools to correct any defects in focusing. Other tests may be conducted on the camera's light meter to correct defective readings.

While most repairs can be made without replacing parts, it is sometimes necessary for camera and photographic equipment repairers to fabricate their own replacement parts. They may use drill presses, small lathes, grinders, milling machines, and other power tools.

Cameras and photographic equipment may not work properly unless it is cleaned and lubricated. Technicians and repairers thoroughly clean and lubricate cameras and photographic equipment after they have completed their repairs. They use special equipment to remove small pieces of dirt and dust. They clean the cameras with special chemicals to dissolve dirt and apply lubricants as needed.

Working Conditions

Camera and photographic equipment repairers usually work indoors seated at a bench or work table. The work is sedentary and does not require much lifting. Repairers spend a lot of time reaching, handling, and fingering small parts and tools and may be subject to some eyestrain from doing precision work close at hand.

Employment

There are several employment situations for camera repairers and photographic equipment technicians. These include working for manufacturers, repair shops, or camera stores, where repairers may also do counter work adjusting cameras for the store's customers. Photographic equipment technicians may work for firms that rent cameras and movie equipment. Technicians that specialize in motion picture equipment may work for motion picture or television studios or for companies that rent photographic equipment to such studios.

According to the Bureau of Labor Statistics, there were approximately 7,600 camera and photographic equipment repairers employed in 1992. Approximately two-thirds of them were self-employed.

Training, Other Qualifications, and Advancement

Most employers require at least one year of training or experience. Camera repairers and technicians are usually high school graduates who have received additional education and training through classroom instruction, home study courses, or on the job. They may have originally taken up photography as a hobby or sold cameras and photographic equipment.

Appropriate courses to take in high school include electricity, electronics, mathematics, basic chemistry, physics, photography, and business accounting and management. More advanced training covers topics such as optics, photographic and darkroom techniques, photographic electricity, and camera repair. Advanced training is available through home study courses, vocational schools, and community colleges. In addition, some repairers acquire the necessary training through apprenticeships or in the armed forces.

Camera repairers and photographic equipment technicians must continue their studies while they are employed. They must keep up with new technologies and expand their knowledge of different makes and models of cameras and other photographic equipment. They may take special training seminars offered by equipment manufacturers and others.

Camera repairers and technicians are individuals who enjoy applying mechanical principles to practical situations. Precision working with small parts and equipment requires a great deal of patience. The work also requires manual dexterity, good vision including the ability to see objects close at hand,

soldering skills, and general mechanical ability. Repairers and technicians should also be able to work without supervision, be neat and organized, and be able to communicate and get along with customers.

Repairers and technicians can advance from entry-level positions to senior technicians and supervisory positions. With experience they may establish their own businesses and work as independent contractors.

Job Outlook

The Bureau of Labor Statistics projects that employment of camera and photographic equipment repairers will increase at about the same rate as the average for all occupations between 1992 and 2005. However, this is a small occupation, and the 7,600 repairers employed in 1992 are expected to increase to only 8,800 by 2005. Many of the openings are due to people leaving the occupation.

Earnings

Earnings for camera and photographic equipment repairers often depend on individual skill and ability as well as on the employment situation. Those who work for manufacturers tend to earn higher salaries than those working for camera stores or other retailers. Self-employed repairers have about the same earning potential as those who work for manufacturers. Some repairers receive commissions in addition to their base salaries.

Limited data indicates that starting salaries range from $10,000 to $12,000 in camera stores and from $13,000 to $15,000 in manufacturing companies. With experience, repairers can expect to earn average salaries of $15,000 to $18,000 working in a camera store and $19,000 to $26,000 working for a manufacturer. Self-employed repairers and technicians can earn between $25,000 and $50,000 depending on their skills and abilities. Management and supervisory repairers and technicians with manufacturers can earn between $30,000 and $50,000.

Related Occupations

Other occupations involving photography and related fields include darkroom technicians, electronics technicians, electronics test technicians, photo lab workers, and photographers.

Occupations in scientific, medical, and technical equipment repair include orthotics and prosthetics technicians and assistants, lens mounters, dental ceramists, dental laboratory managers and technicians, instrument repairers and technicians in any industry, watch repairers, and opticians.

Another related field is that of musical instrument repairers and tuners.

Sources of Additional Information

For additional information contact:

- National Association of Photo Equipment Technicians, 3000 Picture Pl., Jackson, MI 49201. Phone: (517)788-8100.

- Society of Photo-Technologists, 367 Windsor Hwy., Box 404, New Windsor, NY 12553 Phone: (914)782-4248.

COMPUTER SERVICE TECHNICIANS

At a Glance

- **D.O.T.:** 828.261-014

- **Preferred Education:** 1 to 2 years postsecondary education

- **Average Salary:** $32,200

- **Did You Know?** The increasing use of computer technology should cause employment of computer and office machine repairers to grow faster than the average for all occupations through the year 2005.

Nature of the Work

Computers have become an integral part of society. Millions of computers help businesses, organizations, and government agencies efficiently maintain and process information. When computers malfunction or require maintenance, computer service technicians are hired to keep them operating properly.

Computer service technicians install, maintain, and repair computer systems. They work on all types of computers, including mainframes, minicomputers, and microcomputers. They also service computer peripheral equipment such as printers and terminals. After a computer is purchased by a business, computer service technicians help with the installation. They work with the customer to lay out the computer system. They make cable and wiring connections according to the computer manufacturer's specifications. Technicians may also install software into a system and set up programs for the customer. Once the computer is installed, technicians operate the system to demonstrate the equipment and check for malfunctions.

Computer service technicians often perform preventive maintenance on computer systems. They inspect the computer's components, clean and oil the mechanical parts, and advise the customer on more efficient use of the system. But even with preventive maintenance, computer systems do break down. When this happens, the computer is said to "crash" or "go down." Computer service technicians visit the customer site and inspect the computer to look for the cause of the problem. They run diagnostic programs and use testing equipment. Since computer repair is precise work, finding the problem may take hours. Some problems can be fixed at the customer site. For more serious problems, technicians may need to take the computer to a repair facility.

Computer service technicians keep detailed records of their service calls. Some computer technicians specialize in

servicing a particular type of computer or peripheral. Some specialize in a particular repair or installation. Computer service technicians are also called computer maintenance technicians, field engineers, or customer engineers.

Working Conditions

Computer service technicians typically work 40 hours-per-week, with the possibility of overtime and weekend work. Some may be on call 24 hours a day. Technicians may work on rotating shifts. Those with special expertise may travel to different cities to do a specific job, which may take several days. Technicians who visit customer sites generally work in computer rooms, which are well-lighted and air-conditioned. Others work in repair shops. The job is not physically demanding, but involves precision work and manual dexterity. In some cases, computer service technicians are under stress to make repairs quickly. There is also the possibility of small cuts, burns, bruises, and shocks.

Employment

According to the Bureau of Labor Statistics, approximately 83,000 computer and office machine repairers worked mainly on computer equipment in 1992. Most computer technicians work for computer manufacturers. Others work for companies that provide computer maintenance services, for government agencies, and for other companies or organizations that have large computer systems. Computer technicians work throughout the United States. Most work in metropolitan areas where computer systems are numerous.

Training, Advancement, and Other Qualifications

Many computer service technicians develop their skills through community or technical colleges. These programs generally take one to two years to complete. Courses cover subjects such as basic electronics, computer programming, computer troubleshooting, and algebra. Some employers consider basic electronics training from the armed forces excellent preparation. Technicians receive on-the-job training. There is also a significant amount of continuing education.

Computer service technicians must have good communication skills. A pleasant disposition and a neat appearance are also beneficial. Good eyesight and color vision are needed to inspect small parts. Because computer service technicians usually work alone, they must be able to do their jobs with little supervision.

Experienced computer service technicians with advanced training may become specialists who help other technicians with difficult problems. They may also become supervisors or service managers. Some experienced technicians start their own businesses.

Job Outlook

The increasing use of computer technology should cause employment of computer and office machine repairers to grow faster than the average for all occupations through the year 2005. According to the Bureau of Labor Statistics, the number of computer and office machine repairers is expected to grow

30 percent during that time. A survey by William M. Mercer, a New York consulting firm, found that 69 percent of computer-service and software companies planned to add staff in 1995.

Earnings

According to the Bureau of Labor Statistics, the median weekly wage for full-time data processing equipment repairers in 1992 was $619. That equals approximately $32,200 per year.

Related Occupations

Other workers who repair and maintain the circuits and mechanical parts of electronic equipment include appliance and power tool repairers, automotive electricians, broadcast technicians, electronic organ technicians, and vending machine repairers.

Sources of Additional Information

- International Electronics Technicians Association, 602 N. Jackson, Greencastle, IN 46135. Phone: (317)653-8262.

- International Society of Certified Electronics Technicians, 2708 W. Berry, Ste. 3, Ft. Worth, TX 76109. Phone: (817)921-9101.

FLUID POWER TECHNICIANS

At a Glance

- **D.O.T.:** 600.281-010

- **Preferred Education:** High school diploma and graduation from two-year training program

- **Average Salary:** $492 per week

- **Did You Know?** Fluid power technicians review blueprints, schematics, and project instructions.

Nature of the Work

Fluid power equipment is used in industry, agriculture, transportation, defense, and daily life. Jackhammers, automatic door openers, tire inflators, and a car s brake, steering, and transmission system are just some of the hundreds of machines that operate by fluid power. Fluid power technicians build, assemble, service, maintain, repair, and test fluid power equipment.

There are two types of fluid power machines—hydraulic and pneumatic. Hydraulic machines use water, oil, or other liquids in a closed system to transmit or control powered energy. Hydraulic jacks that are used to lift heavy loads are an example of a hydraulic machine. Pneumatic machines are activated by the pressure of air or other gases in a closed system to transmit or control powered energy. Jackhammers

that are used to break pavement are an example of a pneumatic machine.

Fluid power technicians work under the direction of engineers. To perform their job, they review blueprints, schematics, and project instructions.

Using hand tools and power tools, fluid power technicians assemble and repair components of the fluid power system, including pumps, cylinders, valves, reservoirs, motors, filters, and control devices.

Fluid power technicians collect information for development, standardization and quality control by assembling and testing fluid power systems and components under operating conditions. They analyze and record data, such as fluid pressure, flow measure, and power loss due to friction and parts wear. Based on test results, they recommend modifications. Fluid power technicians write technical reports and prepare graphs and schematics to describe the operation and performance of developmental or existing fluid power systems.

Working Conditions

Fluid power technicians typically work 40 hours each week. Evening and weekend shifts are common. Overtime is likely during peak production periods.

Fluid power technicians work indoors in well lighted and ventilated areas. They are, however, exposed to dangerous machinery and must follow safety precautions. They must wear protective safety glasses to protect their eyes and earplugs to protect their ears from loud machine noise. Hard hats, gloves, and a uniform may also be required for protection.

Fluid power technicians do a lot of standing, lifting, and reaching.

Employment

Although there are no specific figures available for fluid power technicians, FPS—The International Organization for Fluid Power and Motion Control Professionals reports that there are 350,000 people working in the industry.

Fluid power technicians work in many different settings, most of which are in factories where fluid power systems are used in manufacturing. Others work for research and development laboratories; companies that produce and sell fluid-power equipment to industrial plants; companies that repair and maintain the fluid power components of heavy machinery used in construction, on farms, and in mining; or for the aircraft industry, of which fluid-power technology is an integral part of the flight controls, landing gear, and brakes of airplanes.

Training, Other Qualifications, and Advancement

Most employers prefer that fluid power technicians have a high school diploma and graduate from a related two-year training program offered by vocational/technical school or community college. A few colleges offer technical programs specifically on fluid power systems, but training in mechanical or electrical technology is usually sufficient. High school courses that are helpful include geometry, algebra, physics, computer science, and shop. Fluid power technicians should also have good oral and written communication skills.

FPS—The International Organization for Fluid Power and Motion Control Professionals offers a Fluid Power Certification to those who pass specific tests. Certifications are valid for five years. Experienced fluid power technicians may advance to supervisory positions.

Job Outlook

According to the U.S. Department of Labor, job opportunities for machinists such as fluid power technicians is expected to decline only slightly through the year 2005. Most job openings will result from the need to replace workers who have retired or transferred to other occupations. The best opportunities will be for those with two years of college or technical training.

Earnings

Earnings for fluid power technicians vary according to employer, geographic location, and experience. According to the U.S. Department of Labor, weekly earnings for machinists such as fluid power technicians averaged $492 in 1992. Earnings usually range from $275 to $750 per week, with most earning between $376 and $623.

Fluid power technicians also receive benefits that include paid vacations and holidays, health and life insurance, and retirement plans.

Related Occupations

Other machinist occupations similar to fluid power technicians include layout inspectors, layout builders, machine builders, machine model makers, metal patternmakers, and automotive machinists.

Sources of Additional Information

For more information on a career as a fluid power technician, contact:

* FPS—The International Organization for Fluid Power and Motion Control Professionals, 2433 N. Mayfair Rd., Ste. 111, Milwaukee, WI 53226. Phone: (414)257-0910.

* The Association for Manufacturing Technology, 7901 Westpark Dr., McLean, VA 22102.

* The National Tooling and Machining Association, 9300 Livingston Rd., Fort Washington, MD 20744.

* The Tooling and Manufacturing Association, 1177 S. Dee Rd., Park Ridge, IL 60068 Phone: (708)825-1120.

* Precision Metalforming Association, 27027 Chardon Rd., Richmond Heights, OH 44143.

LOCKSMITHS

At a Glance

■ **D.O.T.:** 709.281-010

■ **Preferred Education:** Specific vocational preparation

■ **Average Salary:** $11,700 to $26,000 per year

■ **Did You Know?** In addition to installing new locks, locksmiths repair, clean, adjust, and replace parts on mechanical and electronic locks and security systems.

Nature of the Work

Trained locksmiths are called on by businesses and private individuals to install, modify, and repair locks and electronic security devices that are used to protect and safeguard homes, offices, vehicles, garages, and other types of property. They make duplicate keys for their customers as needed. They also answer emergency calls when customers have accidentally locked themselves out of their homes, offices, or vehicles. Some businesses, such as motels, hotels, and apartment complexes, contract with locksmiths to regularly make new master keys, reset combinations, and re-key door locks.

Locksmiths install new or replacement locks based on their customers' needs. They consult with their customers to determine what type of locks would be most appropriate and where they should be located. Using power tools and small hand tools, they cut or drill openings for the locks and fit them in place. Some locksmiths are qualified to install electronic alarm and surveillance systems, burglar alarms, access control systems, and time locks. When such systems have been installed as part of a building's construction, locksmiths are called on to make final adjustments to make sure they work properly.

In addition to installing new locks, locksmiths repair, clean, adjust, and replace parts on mechanical and electronic locks and security systems that are already installed. They completely disassemble the locks and examine the parts to locate defects. They clean and adjust internal mechanisms. If necessary they install replacement parts that are either supplied by the manufacturer or specially made. Locksmiths are able to make replacement parts by using lathes, drills, grinders, and other power and small hand tools. After completing the repairs, they reassemble the locks and check their operation.

Locksmiths also open or release locks for customers who have locked themselves out of their homes, offices, or vehicles. When answering these types of emergency calls, locksmiths start by examining the locks and using lockpicks, listening devices, or other special instruments to release the locks. They first try to open the lock using the least damaging method, such as by using lockpicks or special keys. If these methods fail, then they may try drilling or wrenching the lock until it either opens or is destroyed.

Locksmiths are experts at making duplicate keys. With the key to be duplicated clamped in place, they use a rotary file or milling cutter on a tracing lathe to cut duplicate keys by guiding a tracing bat over the original key. The new keys are examined to make sure they match the originals.

Locksmiths are also responsible for maintaining an inventory of parts, locks, keys, and tools. Those who are self-employed must arrange their own schedules and keep appropriate business records.

Working Conditions

The work of locksmiths is generally not physically demanding, although some work on safes and bank vaults may require strenuous effort. Locksmiths frequently work with their hands and must be able to manipulate small mechanical parts and tools. They should also have good vision to focus on objects close at hand.

Locksmiths work on site and in repair shops. Most repair shops are clean, well lighted, and adequately supplied with tools, parts, and equipment. Locksmiths typically stand or sit at counters or workbenches when making repairs or cutting duplicate keys. When locksmiths go on site to make installations or repairs or answer emergency calls, conditions may vary greatly.

Locksmiths typically work a 40-hour week. Self-employed locksmiths may work from 35 to 60 hours per week. Locksmiths are generally on call to answer emergencies at night or on weekends.

Employment

According to the Bureau of Labor Statistics (BLS), there were approximately 18,000 locksmiths and safe repairers employed in 1992. Many locksmiths are self-employed and run their own businesses. They also work for other locksmiths, burglar and alarm system companies, hardware and department stores, and large manufacturing companies. Some locksmiths are employees of the federal government and service hospitals, military installations, and government buildings. Other employers include hotels, motels, housing developments, and school systems.

Training, Other Qualifications, and Advancement

Locksmiths generally have one to two years of specific vocational preparation that is obtained on the job or through a private locksmith school. Apprenticeship on-the-job training may take from three months to four years. Some on-the-job training programs include classroom demonstrations as well as practical experience. Programs offered through private locksmith schools provide a basic knowledge of the trade and may shorten the length of on-the-job training.

Appropriate background courses to be taken in high school include mathematics, mechanical drawing, metalworking and shop, basic electronics, and physics. Students should generally be interested in applying mechanical principles to practical situations using machines and hand tools.

Some English and business education can help locksmiths improve their communication skills and ability to run their own business. Locksmiths must have reading and language skills sufficient to be able to read and follow detailed operating manuals, lock and key specifications, and other written and oral instructions. Other valuable personal traits include patience, emotional stability, honesty, dependability, accuracy, and the ability to get along with others.

Locksmiths may start out as apprentices and advance to journey positions. They may become supervisors of other locksmiths. Self-employed locksmiths may expand their business and hire others to work for them. With additional training they may be able to install and repair electronic security and alarm systems.

Many city, county, and state governments require locksmiths to be bonded and/or licensed. While requirements vary from place to place, locksmiths usually must be fingerprinted and pay a licensing or registration fee. They may have to post a surety bond if they are self-employed and run their own business.

Job Outlook

The Bureau of Labor Statistics projects that employment of locksmiths will grow at about the same rate as the average for all occupations between 1992 and 2005. Social factors such as population growth and growing public concern over security and crime indicate a continued demand for the services of locksmiths. New construction in residential and office buildings along with the need to replace outdated locks and security systems will also create a continuing demand for locksmiths.

Earnings

Earnings for locksmiths depend upon geographic location, individual skill and experience, and employer. According to *American Salaries and Wages Survey*, the average wage for employed locksmiths was slightly above $18,000 per year in New York during 1991. The Associated Locksmiths of America reports that starting salaries range from $9,360 to $13,000. The average salary range for experienced locksmiths is between $11,700 and $26,000. Highly skilled locksmiths can earn as much as $50,000 annually. Contracts with large businesses can add substantial earnings to a locksmith's business.

Related Occupations

Related occupations for mechanics, installers, and repairers include precision instrument repairers, watchmakers, riggers, medical equipment repairers, meter installers and repairers, camera and photographic equipment repairers, bicycle repairers, automobile or motorcycle mechanics, and air conditioning mechanics.

Other related occupations involving metal fabrication, assembly, and repair include model makers and builders, mold stampers and repairers, patternmakers, and aircraft wireworkers.

Sources of Additional Information

- Associated Locksmiths of America, 3003 Live Oak St., Dallas, TX 75204. Phone: (214)827-1701.

MARINE MECHANICS

At a Glance

- **D.O.T.:** 623.281-038

- **Preferred Education:** High school diploma

- **Average Salary:** $17,000 to $26,000 per year

- **Did You Know?** In some parts of the country, the work of marine mechanics is seasonal, and that during winter they often spend time repairing snowmobiles and snowblowers.

Nature of the Work

Although less complicated than truck or automobile engines, small inboard and outboard boat motors require regular maintenance and periodic servicing to keep them operating efficiently. Boat owners are especially concerned with minimizing the possibility of motor breakdowns while they are using their boats on lakes and other bodies of water. It is the job of marine mechanics to maintain boat engines and diagnose problems when breakdowns occur. They also service other electrical and mechanical equipment on boats.

Marine mechanics work with common handtools, power tools, and testing equipment. When performing routine service maintenance, marine mechanics adjust, clean, and lubricate boat engines. When necessary they replace or adjust worn or defective parts such as spark plugs, valves, gaskets, pumps, distributors, and carburetors. Marine mechanics spend most of their time on routine maintenance.

Some marine mechanics may specialize in one type of engine such as outboard or inboard engines. Outboard engines are smaller than inboard engines and are relatively easy to remove from boats to work on. Inboard engines are usually only removed for major overhauls. Marine mechanics typically work on inboard engines right in the boat itself. The engines may be located in awkward spaces, and they may need operate hoists and other equipment to maneuver large boats into position so they can work on them.

When engine breakdowns occur or engines are not running properly, marine mechanics use their specialized knowledge of small engines to diagnose the problem. With the help of testing equipment such as electric testing meters, engine analyzers, and compression gauges, they compare an engine's performance to the manufacturer's specifications. They may use wrenches, pliers, screwdrivers, and other tools to dismantle motors.

Small engines have many different operating parts that can cause problems when they become worn or defective. Marine mechanics may adjust an engine's generator using handtools and a soldering iron to repair faulty wiring. They may install piston rings, adjust carburetors, or grind valves. Using hand and power tools, including lathes and drill presses, they may repair or replace gears and other parts.

When repairs are completed marine mechanics reassemble the engine, aligning it with the boat's propeller shaft. They run the engine and perform additional tests to make sure it is running properly. They may take the boat for a test drive to check the engine's performance.

Marine mechanics may also work on other electronic and mechanical equipment that is found on boats, such as a power-tilt, bilge pumps, and power take-offs. In small repair shops and marinas, marine mechanics may also spend time painting and patching boat exteriors. In larger shops they may spend time supervising other mechanics.

Working Conditions

Marine mechanics generally work in shops or marinas; occasionally they will work outdoors. In some parts of the country, the work of marine mechanics is seasonal. During winters they may be laid off or spend time repairing snowmobiles and other equipment associated with winter activities. During boating season they may be required to work a lot of overtime. In warmer climates, marine mechanics work year round.

Employment

According to the Bureau of Labor Statistics (BLS), there were approximately 35,000 small engine specialists, including marine mechanics, employed in 1992. Most employment opportunities are near large or small bodies of water. Marine mechanics working near smaller lakes tend to specialize in outboard motors. Those working near large bodies of water tend to work on a greater variety of engines.

Typical employers of marine mechanics include boat dealers, marinas and boat yards, and independent repair shops. Boat manufacturers and boat rental companies also employ marine mechanics.

Training, Other Qualifications, and Advancement

Marine mechanics are usually high school graduates with two to four years of specific vocational preparation. Employers look for individuals with mechanical aptitude and some knowledge of small engines. Appropriate background courses include small engine repair, electronics, mechanical drawing, automobile mechanics, science, and business or shop math. Some marine mechanics receive mechanical training through vocational or technical schools.

Marine mechanics generally start their employment as trainees, first performing routine maintenance on engines and gradually learning to do more complicated repairs. Their on-the-job training may be complemented by special training courses that are conducted by equipment manufacturers or distributors. These courses help marine mechanics upgrade their skills and learn about new developments in the field.

Many marine mechanics own their own tools; they must have well-developed reasoning abilities to be able to identify and diagnose mechanical problems; and they must be able to use shop math to calculate dimensions, material amounts, material costs, and related items.

Marine mechanics can advance in several ways. In larger shops they may be promoted to supervisory positions; they may start their own independent repair shops; or advance to higher paying jobs as automobile, truck, or heavy equipment mechanics.

Job Outlook

According to the BLS, employment of small engine specialists, including marine mechanics, is projected to increase by more than 20 percent between 1992 and 2005, slightly higher than the average for all occupations. Many job openings will occur as a result of the need to replace workers who leave this occupation each year for other occupations or retirement.

Several factors will support an increased demand for marine mechanics, including: a more disposable personal income that can be spent on recreational boating; the increasing popularity of recreational boating itself; and the growing complexity of mechanical and electronic boating equipment and accessories. As the nation's population increases in the South and West, more people will become recreational boaters.

Earnings

According to the BLS, motorcycle and small engine specialists, including marine mechanics, had median earnings of approximately $22,600 in 1992. Half of them earned between $17,000 and $26,000. According to *American Salaries and Wages Survey*, marine mechanics and repairers in Texas earned between $8,500 and $27,000 in 1994-95. Marine mechanics employed in small shops with one to three mechanics tend to receive fewer fringe benefits than those working in larger shops. Larger repair shops typically provide their employees with a benefits package that includes paid vacations, health insurance coverage, and some type of pension plan.

Related Occupations

Related occupations include motorcycle engine mechanics, other small engine specialists, automobile mechanics, diesel mechanics, farm equipment mechanics, and mobile heavy equipment mechanics. Other related marine occupations include deck engineers, marine engine machinists, and marine engineers (also known as marine engine maintenance mechanics).

Sources of Additional Information

• American Boat Builders and Repairers Association, PO Box 1236, Stanford, CT 06904. Phone: (203)967-4745.

• International Association of Machinists and Aerospace Workers, 9000 Machinists Pl., Upper Marlboro, MD 20772.

Phone: (301)967-4500.

• National Marine Electronics Association, PO Box 50040, Mobile, AL 36605. Phone: (205)473-1793.

• National Marine Manufacturers Association, 401 N. Michigan Ave., Ste. 1150, Chicago, IL 60611. Phone: (312)836-4747.

PAPER PRODUCTS TECHNICIANS

At a Glance

■ **D.O.T.:** 638.261-010

■ **Preferred Education:** High school diploma

■ **Average Salary:** $596 per week

■ **Did You Know?** Paper products technicians work in the plants that produce paper products.

Nature of the Work

Paper products technicians, also known as *automated equipment technicians*, install, maintain, repair, and replace the machinery and equipment used to make paper products, especially those used to emboss, die-cut, score, fold, and transfer paper or cardboard stock to form box blanks, knockdown advertising displays, and similar products.

Although paper products technicians are employed by the manufacturers of the machinery and equipment, they work in the plants that produce the paper products.

When installing new machinery, paper products technicians first meet with the customer s engineering staff to discuss the layout of equipment, resolve any problems with machinery design, and avoid construction problems in the plant. Then, they arrange the machine parts according to the sequence of the paper product s assembly, as well as the most effective use of plant floor space.

According to the floor plans and the customers instructions, paper products technicians direct workers in positioning the equipment. Using hand tools, electrical testing instruments, soldering irons, and wiring diagrams, they assemble and install electrical and electromechanical components and systems. They adjust controls and set up the machinery for the particular type, thickness, and size of the paper or cardboard stock to be processed; for the appropriate sequence of operating stages; and to ensure maximum efficiency. To verify that the newly installed equipment is operating properly, paper products technicians perform a trial run.

Paper products technicians instruct the customer's equipment operators and engineering and maintenance staff on the set up, operation, and maintenance of the equipment.

Following a preventive maintenance schedule or upon the customer s request, paper products technicians repair and service the equipment. They modify previously installed equipment to make certain it is compatible with new units. They also install safety devices or attachments to old equipment.

To make certain that equipment continues to operate at peak efficiency and with the customer s desired level of performance, paper products technicians will occasionally meet with customer s engineers to determine the most effective methods of programming the machine for processing.

Working Conditions

Paper products technicians typically work about 40 hours per week, although overtime may be necessary during peak production times. Because they work around machinery, paper products technicians wear protective glasses, hard hats, and gloves as safety precautions. They must also follow safety procedures to avoid factory-related hazards.

Paper products technicians must work quickly and accurately because machines that are not operating will cost a company time and money.

Employment

According to the U.S. Bureau of Labor Statistics, there were about 73,000 millwrights employed in 1992. This figure includes paper products technicians.

Most paper product technicians are employed by manufacturers of paper-making equipment. They perform most of their work at plants where paper products are manufactured. Employment for paper products technicians is concentrated in heavily industrialized areas.

Training, Other Qualifications, and Advancement

Most employers prefer that paper products technicians have a high school diploma and some vocational training or experience. Courses in science, math, mechanical drawing, and shop are helpful.

Paper products technicians receive most of their training on the job or from a apprenticeship. Apprenticeship programs include lessons in erecting, dismantling, moving, and repairing machinery.

Paper products technicians should be able to work independently and as part of a team. Physical strength is also important.

Experienced technicians may advance to supervisory positions.

Job Outlook

According to the U.S. Bureau of Labor Statistics, job openings for paper products technicians will increase 8.7 percent through the year 2005. Most job opportunities will arise from the need to replace those who leave the trade. During hard economic downturns paper products technicians may experience layoffs or shortened workweeks. Paper products technicians do, however, have relatively stable jobs and the trend toward replacing rather than repairing machinery may lead some employers to hire more paper products technicians because they are trained in the installation and alignment of machinery, as well as its repair.

Earnings

Paper products technicians earnings can vary by employer and geographic location. According to the U.S. Department of Labor, median weekly earnings of full-time workers were $596 in 1992. Weekly Earnings usually range from $479 to $724.

Paper products receive benefits that include paid vacations, health and life insurance, and retirement plans.

Related Occupations

Other occupations with duties similar to paper products technicians include industrial machinery repairers, mobile heavy equipment mechanics, aircraft mechanics, diesel mechanics, farm equipment mechanics, and machine assemblers.

Sources of Additional Information

For further information on a career as a paper products technician, contact:

- American Forest and Paper Institute, 1111 19th St. NW, Ste. 800, Washington, DC 20036 Phone: (202)463-2700.

- Associated General Contractors of America, 1957 E St. NW, Washington, DC 20006 Phone: (202)393-2040.

- Association for Manufacturing Technology, 7901 Westpark Dr., McLean, VA 22102 (703)893-2900.

- Center for Packaging Education, PO 020240, Brooklyn Heights, NY 11202-0005 Phone: (718)624-0034.

- Industrial Designers Society of America, 1142-E Walker Rd., Great Falls, VA 22066 Phone: (703)759-0100.

- Institute for Packaging Professionals, 481 Carlisle Dr., Herndon, VA 22070 Phone: (703)318-8970.

- National Institute of Packaging, Handling, and Logistic Engineers, 6902 Lyle St., Lanham, MD 20706.

- Packaging Education Forum, 481 Carlisle Dr., Herndon, VA 22070 Phone: (703)318-7225.

- The United Brotherhood of Carpenters and Joiners of America, 101 Constitution Ave. NW, Washington, DC 20001.

PARTS ORDER AND STOCK CLERKS

At a Glance

- **D.O.T.:** 249.367-058 and 185.167-038

- **Preferred Education:** On the job training

- **Average Salary:** $11,500 to $27,000 per year

- **Did You Know?** Parts order and stock clerks consult manuals, parts lists, and other reference materials to determine correct part numbers and other information.

Nature of the Work

Parts order and stock clerks are responsible for the acquisition, storage, issuance, and sales of parts for motor vehicles or industrial equipment. They purchase parts from suppliers on an as-needed basis or to maintain a specified inventory level in anticipation of future needs. They may work with the purchasing department to obtain appropriate purchase order numbers, or they may assign purchase order numbers themselves. They write up purchase orders for parts that have been requested for specific jobs as well as for inventory. They consult manuals, parts lists, and other reference materials to determine correct part numbers and other information.

When parts orders are received, parts order and stock clerks verify each shipment to make sure it matches their original order. They match invoices to be paid against their original purchase orders and maintain records of orders, receipts, and sales. They check the parts for quantity and quality, making sure that the correct parts were sent. They notify the individuals who originally requested the parts that they have been received, or they put the parts into inventory.

Parts order and stock clerks periodically check the physical inventory of their department. They may follow guidelines from a parts or service manager to determine when the parts inventory should be replenished. In smaller parts departments they may be responsible for monitoring the parts inventory and placing orders when stock levels reach a minimum. They make sure that parts are correctly placed into inventory according to plan so that they can be easily retrieved.

In many cases parts order and stock clerks serve as counter clerks and sell parts to the general public. They use their knowledge of what parts are available to inform customers of the full product line. They may suggest complimentary or alternate parts to customers. They may act as troubleshooters for customers doing their own repairs.

In smaller departments parts order and stock clerks may act as managers of parts departments. Their managerial responsibilities may include controlling inventory, security, and merchandising. They may develop displays and advertising for parts being sold.

Working Conditions

Parts order and stock clerks interact with a variety of people, including service and body shop managers, automotive technicians and mechanics, and the general public. Those who work in motor vehicle dealerships generally work more than 40 hours per week with some evening and weekend hours. Very few are employed on a part-time basis.

Parts order and stock clerks generally work under quiet conditions. If they work in an automotive repair shop they may be subject to drafty and noisy conditions, although such shops are usually well-ventilated and lighted.

Employment

There are approximately 300,000 businesses engaged in the manufacturing, distribution, and sale of parts, accessories, tools, and supplies for motor vehicles in the United States. Parts order and stock clerks are employed by motor vehicle dealerships, repair shops, parts stores, and parts suppliers. An estimated 13,000 stock clerks worked for motor vehicle dealers in 1990, according to the Bureau of Labor Statistics.

Training, Other Qualifications, and Advancement

Parts order and stock clerks generally receive six months to one year of on-the-job training. Most motor vehicle dealers now require a high school diploma. Courses in automotive service, business, electronics, mathematics, and computer science are considered helpful. These may be taken in high school or in a variety of adult education classes, technical institutes, and junior and community colleges.

Individuals may enter the parts field by first being employed in such capacities as a pick-up and delivery person, parts helper, or shipping clerk. Experience helping out in the service department of a motor vehicle dealer can provide a basic knowledge of repairs and parts replacements.

Individuals interested in working with parts should have a sound technical background. They must be able to work well with a variety of people, including service managers, automotive mechanics, and the general public. Good organizational skills and attention to detail are needed to keep a parts department operating efficiently.

Parts order and stock clerks can advance to managerial positions with additional experience and training. They may become parts managers in motor vehicle dealerships or supervisors in auto parts stores.

Job Outlook

Employment growth for stock clerks in general, and automotive parts order and stock clerks in particular, is expected to be much slower than for all occupations as a whole. According to the Bureau of Labor Statistics, the number of stock clerks in general is projected to increase by 8.8 percent between 1992 and 2005. For those employed in motor vehicle dealers, the increase is projected to be approximately 7 percent from 1990 to 2005.

The employment outlook is much stronger for parts managers in motor vehicle dealers, where employment of executive, managerial, and administrative personnel is projected to increase by nearly 26 percent between 1990 and 2005.

Earnings

Stock clerks in general earn lower than average wages. Wages depend on size and type of employer as well as geographic region. According to *American Salaries and Wages Survey*, the average annual wage for stock clerks working in automotive dealers and service stations in Maine was about $11,500 in 1991. The average annual wage for parts managers working in automotive dealers and service stations in Maine was about $27,000 in 1991.

Related Occupations

A wide range of industries employ stock clerks. Other related occupations that have similar duties include shipping and receiving clerks, distributing clerks, routing clerks, stock supervisors, and cargo checkers. With additional training automotive parts order and stock clerks may qualify for other positions within a motor vehicle dealership, such as motor vehicle service technician, service manager, office manager, parts manager, or salesperson.

Sources of Additional Information

* Automotive Service Industry Association, 25 Northwest Point, Elk Grove, IL 60007-1035. Phone: (708)228-1310. Fax: (708)228-1510.

* National Automobile Dealers Association, 8400 Westpark Dr., McLean, VA 22101. Phone: (703)827-7407.

PIANO TUNERS AND TECHNICIANS

At a Glance

■ **D.O.T.:** 730.361-010 and 730.281-038

■ **Preferred Education:** 2 years of training

■ **Average Salary:** $20,000

■ **Did You Know?** Individuals can become registered piano tuners or technicians by passing written and practical tests administered by the Piano Technicians Guild.

Nature of the Work

There are an estimated nine million pianos in American homes and another one million in schools, colleges and universities, concert halls, auditoriums, and theaters. To stay at peak performance, these pianos need regular maintenance and upkeep. Piano tuners and technicians service pianos so they perform properly.

A piano has 230 strings, 88 keys, and approximately 12,000 parts. When a piano player presses a key, a felt-covered hammer strikes a wire, known as a string, which vibrates to make sound. Piano tuners adjust the strings to the proper pitch. A string's pitch is the frequency at which it vibrates--and produces sound--when it is struck. Tuners begin by adjusting either the "A" or "C" string. To test the A or C note, tuners mute the surrounding strings with strips of felt or rubber. They then strike the key and compare the sound with the pitch of a tuning fork or electronic tuner. Tuners use a tuning lever to tighten or loosen the string until its pitch matches that of the tuning fork. All other strings are corrected to this reference tone.

Piano tuners can replace worn parts or broken strings, but more extensive repairs may require the services of a piano technician. Piano technicians find and correct problems with a piano's thousands of parts. They may have to dismantle a piano to inspect the parts. Using common and special hand tools, technicians replace worn or broken parts, such as hammers, strings, shanks, sounding boards, and foot pedals. Technicians align parts and adjust the striking action of the keys. They also may tune pianos. Some technicians rebuild or refinish damaged pianos.

Working Conditions

Many piano tuners and technicians work on pianos in homes, churches, and schools. Therefore, they may spend a significant amount of time traveling. Others work in a shop or store. Those who are self-employed generally have offices and work rooms in their homes. Cold weather months are the busiest time for most tuners and technicians. This is the time most people stay indoors and use their pianos. Some may work overtime during the busy season. They may work evenings and weekends.

Employment

According to the U.S. Department of Labor, musical instrument repairers and tuners held about 12,000 jobs in 1992. Most worked on pianos. About two-thirds were self-employed. Salaried repairers and tuners worked in music stores, repair shops, and musical instrument manufacturers.

Training, Other Qualifications, and Advancement

Piano tuners and technicians typically need a high school education and one or two years of additional training. Several technical schools and colleges offer courses in piano technology. Correspondence courses are also available. Graduates of these courses, which typically cover tuning and minor repairs, can refine their skills by working with an experienced tuner or technician. Music stores, large repair shops, and self-employed tuners and technicians sometimes hire trainees to work under the supervision of experienced workers. Usually two to five years of training and practice are required to learn how to tune and repair pianos.

Piano tuners and technicians need good hearing. They should have a keen sense of pitch. The ability to play the piano is helpful. Knowledge of woodworking is also useful. Students interested in opening their own business should take business and accounting courses.

Individuals can become registered piano tuners or technicians by passing written and practical tests administered by the Piano Technicians Guild. The guild also conducts training programs at local chapter meetings and at regional and national seminars. Tuners and technicians who work for large dealers, repair shops, or manufacturers can advance to supervisory positions.

Job Outlook

Employment of musical instrument repairers and tuners, which includes piano tuners and technicians, is expected to remain stable though the year 2005, reports the U.S. Bureau of Labor Statistics. According to the bureau, the number of people employed as musicians will increase, but the number of students of all ages playing musical instruments will grow only slowly. Since many repairers and tuners are near retirement age, replacement needs will be high.

Earnings

According to limited information from the U.S. Department of Labor, annual earnings for repairers and tuners employed by music stores averaged about $20,000. Self-employed repairers and tuners averaged almost $40,000. It may take self-employed repairers and tuners several years to build up a clientele large enough to earn a good living.

Related Occupations

Other occupations in the fabrication and repair of musical instruments and parts include accordion maker, accordion repairer, electric organ inspector and repairer, harp maker, harpsichord maker, pipe-organ builder, pipe-organ tuner and repairer, violin maker, and violin repairer.

Sources of Additional Information

- Piano Technicians Guild, 3930 Washington St., Kansas City, MO 64111-2963. Phone: (816)753-7747.

SOLAR ENERGY SYSTEM INSTALLERS

At a Glance

- **D.O.T.:** 637.261.030

- **Preferred Education:** Technical education or apprenticeship.

- **Average Salary:** Varies.

- **Did You Know?** Many solar energy system installers begin their careers as plumbers, sheet metal workers, or carpenters before becoming solar energy installers.

Nature of the Work

Advances in technology now make it possible to use the energy of the sun to heat buildings and water. Solar energy system installers repair and install the equipment that makes this energy conversion possible.

Solar energy systems consist of solar energy collectors, or panels, to gather the sun's rays, holding tanks to store the energy, and distribution systems to circulate the power. Using blueprints and other specifications, solar energy system installers locate the proper position for this equipment within a building, which may be a commercial building or private residence. Solar collectors are generally placed on roofs, while holding tanks and distribution systems are installed inside the buildings.

Solar energy system installers need the skills of a carpenter, plumber, and electrician to perform their work properly. Before installing the equipment, they use power saws and drills to cut holes in a building's roof, walls, and ceiling. They use hand tools to install the supports and brackets that hold the equipment in place. They cut, thread, and fit plumbing, and they lay out and connect electrical wiring between the system's controls and pumps. Installation may require adding solar energy collectors to an older building or working in a building still under construction.

Once the system is installed, solar energy system installers check it for malfunctions. They use electrical testing equipment to check circuits and components. They also use pressure gauges to test the plumbing for leaks. If there is defective equipment, they repair and replace it.

Solar energy system installer helpers assist experienced installers. They saw and drill holes, and help install the equipment, plumbing, and wiring as directed. Helpers load and unload materials. They also cut pipe threads and wrap insulation around pipes.

Working Conditions

Installing solar energy systems can be very physical work. Solar energy installers frequently carry heavy materials. Much of their time is spent standing or walking. They must climb stairs, ladders, and ramps. They also stoop, kneel, and crouch to install fixtures and fittings. Although they work mainly indoors, solar energy system installers spend some of their time outside, often high above the ground on roofs and scaffolds. Other risks include sharp tools and hot pipes. Solar energy system installers generally work 40 hours per week.

Employment

According to the Bureau of Labor Statistics, there were 212,000 heat, air conditioning, and refrigeration mechanics and installers in 1992. This figure includes solar energy system installers. Solar energy system installers work throughout the United States. Companies that employ solar energy system installers include manufacturers and distributors of solar equipment. Solar energy system installers also work for building contractors, architectural firms, and heating and air-conditioning contractors. Some installers are self-employed.

Training, Advancement, and Other Qualifications

Energy system installers learn their skills in a variety of

ways. Many began their careers as plumbers, sheet metal workers, or carpenters before applying these skills to solar energy installation. Other installers begin by assisting experienced installers or joining an apprenticeship program. Assistants and apprentices learn their skills on-the-job. They start out by helping with basic tasks and eventually learn to install complete solar systems.

Others take courses in solar energy technology at a community college or vocational school. Students in these programs learn the basics of solar energy system installation and repair. They also take courses in heat and energy transfer, solar design, and solar energy system components. Graduates from these programs can move directly into solar energy installation jobs.

High school students considering a career in solar energy system installation should take courses in shop, mechanical drawing, drafting, algebra, trigonometry, physics, and English. They should like working with their hands.

Some states and local governments require solar energy system installers to be licensed. Most installers do not belong to unions, unless they are union plumbers or electricians.

Job Outlook

The Bureau of Labor Statistics expects job opportunities for air-conditioning, heating, and refrigeration mechanics and installers to grow faster than the average through the year 2005. This group includes solar energy system installers. Some of these jobs will result from growing concern for energy management and conservation. Others will result from employee turnover.

Earnings

In 1992, heating, air-conditioning, and refrigeration mechanics and installers in Minnesota earned between $9.50 and $20.79 per hour. This group includes solar energy system installers. Installers in Alaska earned between $7.50 and $32.27 per hour in 1991. Wages for installers in South Carolina ranged from $6.52 per hour to $13 per hour in 1991. In New Hampshire, installers earned up to $19 per hour in 1991.

Related Occupations

Solar energy systems installers work with equipment and appliances used to supply heat, conditioned air, refrigeration, water, and related utilities. Similar occupations include heating-and-air-conditioning installer and servicer, gas-appliance servicer, refrigeration mechanic, evaporative-cooler installer, air and hydronic balancing technician, and pump erector.

Sources of Additional Information

- American Solar Energy Association, 1518 K St. NW, Ste. 201, Washington, DC 20005. Phone: (202)624-8000.

- American Solar Energy Society, 2400 Central Ave., G-1, Boulder, CO 80301. Phone: (303)443-3130.

- Solar Energy Industries Association, 122 C Street NW, 4th Fl., Washington, DC 20001 Phone: (202)383-2600.

WATCHMAKERS AND REPAIRERS

- **D.O.T.:** 715.281-010

- **Preferred Education:** Four years of specific vocational preparation

- **Average Salary:** Average of $24,188 per year.

- **Did You Know?** About one-third of all watchmakers and repairers are self-employed.

Nature of the Work

The work of watchmakers and repairers, who are also known as horologists, primarily involves repairing watches and clocks rather than actually making or building them. They may be called on to service and repair many different kinds of timepieces, including traditional mechanical clocks and watches as well as newer quartz electronic models. They may also be asked to restore and repair antique clocks and watches. Their work may involve more complicated timing devices, such as electric power system timing equipment and other types of time clocks.

Clocks and watches are small mechanical devices with intricate and often complicated mechanisms or electronics. While many parts have been standardized, qualified horologists may be expected to make a part and finish it to factory specifications. This skill is especially useful when repairing and restoring antique clocks and watches.

Other aspects of watch and clock repair involve cleaning and adjusting timepieces using special tools, measuring instruments, bench machines, and cleaning equipment. As they work with tiny parts, horologists use a loupe, which is a special type of magnifier, to examine the parts for defects and accumulations of foreign matter. Using such tools as pliers, screwdrivers and tweezers, they take the timepiece apart to examine individual parts such as hands, mainspring, escape wheels, and balance wheel. A special machine then cleans, rinses, and washes the parts.

Horologists determine the problem with a specific timepiece by testing the balance wheel using truing calipers and identifying worn or damaged parts. They true the balance wheel assembly, if necessary, and replace any worn or damaged parts. Most parts are standardized, but in some cases horologists may have to make a part to specifications. They then assemble the mechanism and lubricate any moving parts. A demagnetizing machine removes any magnetic properties. After replacing the mechanism in its case, they test the assembled instrument for accuracy using a watch-rate recorder, making any needed final adjustments.

Working Conditions

Individuals who repair clocks and watches usually work in clean, well-lighted workshops. Full-time horologists generally work a standard 40-hour week with some overtime, depending on their workload. They frequently use their hands and fingers to handle delicate parts and manipulate tools. They may also be subject to eyestrain from working with small objects at close range.

Employment

There were approximately 9,400 watchmakers and repairers employed in the United States in 1992, according to the Bureau of Labor Statistics (BLS). Internationally, there are an estimated 12,000 skilled horologists, down from 30,000 just a generation ago.

Retail jewelry stores that offer watch repair services are the primary employers of watchmakers and repairers. More than half of all jewelry stores offer some type of watch repair service. Of those that do, about half employ at least one full-time repairer, slightly less than half employ only part-time repairers, and less than ten percent employ both full- and part-time repairers. Other employment opportunities exist with department stores and watch and clock manufacturers.

About one-third of all watchmakers and repairers are self-employed. They may operate their own shops, obtaining business by contracting with jewelry stores to perform their watch and clock repairs. They may also build a retail clientele and eventually may offer more diversified services and products.

Training, Other Qualifications, and Advancement

Watchmakers and repairers generally have at least four years of specific vocational preparation. They may learn their craft in private schools, public vocational high schools, or technical colleges. Basic schooling programs run from one to two years. New graduates often work with experienced repairers to gain practical experience. In addition, some states offer four-year apprenticeship programs.

There are more than 20 watch and clock making schools in the United States. Most of them do not have specific educational requirements for admission. However, a high school diploma or equivalent is desirable. Students must be able to follow instructions and read manuals and charts. A background in subjects such as mathematics, physics, chemistry, electricity, electronics, mechanical drawing, and machine or metal shop is useful.

Training programs usually emphasize individual instruction. Class sizes are typically small, and students are allowed to progress according to their ability. They learn the complete range of skills necessary to become watchmakers and repairers, including truing hairsprings, removing and replacing balance staffs, adjusting escapements, setting friction jewels, operating a lathe, replacing teeth in wheels, polishing pivots and pinions, and overhauling complete clocks and watches. The assembly and disassembly of watch movements are taught along with the newer electronic quartz technology, where students learn soldering techniques and basic electrical skills.

Watchmakers and repairers are people who enjoy working with small mechanical devices and repairing instruments. They must be able to apply mechanical principles to practical situations. They are often required to interpret a variety of instructions. They need to be inquisitive, analytical, and able to diagnose mechanical failures. Good vision, hand-eye coordination, and manual dexterity are also needed.

Horologists advance in their field by improving their skills and being able to take on more responsibilities. The American Watchmakers Institute offers several levels of certification to its members who pass the required proficiency tests. Self-employed watchmakers and repairers can build their business by taking on more clients, hiring assistants, and offering a variety of products and services.

Job Outlook

The Bureau of Labor Statistics projects that the 9,400 watchmakers and repairers employed in the United States in 1992 will dwindle to 7,000 by 2005. Other factors suggest, however, that the demand for their services will grow. Internationally, the number of skilled horologists may in fact increase over time.

Statistics show that the use of watches and clocks in the United States is increasing at a rapid pace. People of all ages continue to buy watches, and many of them are multiple watch owners. Complex watches, such as those that display the date and other time-related information, are becoming increasingly popular. Electronic quartz watches have resulted in additional business for repairers who are simply asked to replace the energy cells. All of these factors point to a growing demand for the services of watchmakers and repairers. In addition, the international Watchmakers of Switzerland Training and Educational Program (WOSTEP) is committed to programs designed to add 25,000 horologists worldwide in the next decade.

Earnings

According to the 1994 annual survey conducted by *Jewelers' Circular-Keystone* (JCK) magazine, watchmakers and repairers employed in jewelry stores on a full- or part-time basis earned a median salary of $24,188 in 1993, down from $28,620 in 1992. Stores with an annual volume of more than $1 million reported median salaries for horologists of $30,307 in 1993, down from $31,000 in 1992. Top pay for all stores reporting in the survey was $47,400. The trend toward lower reported salaries was accounted for by an increase in part-time employment by jewelry stores of watchmakers and repairers.

The American Watchmakers-Clockmakers Institute reports that beginning technicians can expect to earn between $15,000 and $20,000 annually, depending on geographic location and individual skills. Experienced repairers can earn $35,000 and up if they are employed full-time. Self-employed repairers who own their own shops generally earn more.

As reported in the JCK survey, benefits for watchmakers and repairers working in jewelry stores usually include at least medical insurance, paid sick leave, merchandise discounts, and paid vacations. More than half of all jewelry stores offered some education financial assistance and unpaid maternity leave. Larger stores generally offered more benefits.

Related Occupations

The training that horologists receive often qualifies them for employment in the electronic and instrument repair field, including commercial and industrial electronic equipment repairers, communications equipment mechanics, computer and office machine repairers, electronic home entertainment equipment repairers, precision instrument repairers, and telephone installers and repairers. With additional training they may become involved in jewelry repairing and manufacturing.

Sources of Additional Information

For more information contact:

- American Watchmakers-Clockmakers Institute, PO Box 11011, 3700 Harrison Ave., Cincinnati, OH 45211. Phone: (513)661-3838. Fax: (513)661-3131.

Construction Trades and Extractive Occupations

ASBESTOS REMOVAL WORKERS

At a Glance

- **D.O.T.:** 869.684-082

- **Preferred Education:** High school diploma

- **Average Salary:** $446 per week

- **Did You Know?** Job opportunities in this field are on the rise due to several regulatory requirements, such as many banks requiring that buildings be asbestos-free before a real estate loan is granted, and the 1986 government act requiring all public and private schools to have an asbestos management plan.

Nature of the Work

Nearly every building built before 1976 contains asbestos, a flame-retardant insulation product now known to cause cancer in humans. Asbestos is considered the most pervasive of all environmental hazards and this is demonstrated by several regulations: the U.S. Environmental Protection Agency requires that asbestos be removed from a building before it undergoes major renovation or is demolished; the 1986 Asbestos Hazard Emergency Act requires that all public and private schools have an asbestos management plan; and many banks require that buildings be asbestos-free before a real estate loan is granted. Of course, not just anyone can remove this substance. Precise attention to details is critically important when dealing with asbestos; according to the Occupational Safety and Health Administration, there is "no safe level of exposure" to this substance. Asbestos removal workers are specially trained and equipped to remove hazardous asbestos from ceilings, walls, beams, boilers, floor tiles and other structures.

For every project, asbestos removal workers put on protective suits, masks and respirators. Then, they assemble scaffolding and seal off the work area with plastic sheeting. They position a mobile decontamination unit or portable showers at the entrance of the work area and set up special filtered vacuum cleaners and air-filtration devices inside the work area.

Using a tank with an attached hose and nozzle, asbestos removal workers spray a chemical solution over asbestos-covered surfaces to soften the asbestos. Once the asbestos has softened, the workers scrape and cut it from the surfaces. Workers shovel the asbestos into plastic disposal bags and seal the bags with duct tape. Using vacuums, the asbestos removal workers clean the work area of loose asbestos and deposit it into disposal bags, which are also sealed.

Once all of the asbestos is completely removed, the workers dismantle the scaffolding and places plastic sheeting and disposal bags into transport bags. All materials exposed to or containing asbestos is bagged and sealed, and loaded into a special truck for final disposal.

Asbestos removal workers must then shower and otherwise decontaminate themselves to remove any asbestos particles from their body.

Working Conditions

Asbestos is known to cause cancer in humans and asbestos removal workers are specially trained to protect themselves from the dangers of asbestos and other irritants. Asbestos workers wear protective suits, masks, and respirators, take decontamination showers, keep work areas well-ventilated, and follow strict safety guidelines.

Asbestos removal workers typically have 40-hour workweeks. They work indoors in older buildings, all built prior to 1976. Work areas include basements, attics, and inside walls and ceilings. Besides containing asbestos, these areas are also dusty and dirty. Asbestos removal workers spend most of their time standing, kneeling, bending, and climbing ladders.

Employment

According to the U.S. Bureau of Labor Statistics, there were 57,000 insulation workers, which includes asbestos removal workers, employed in 1992. Most asbestos removal workers are employed by asbestos abatement companies, insulation companies, or construction contractors. Most asbestos removal workers work in urban areas, where the majority of older buildings are located.

Training, Other Qualifications, and Advancement

Asbestos removal workers usually have to be licensed.

License requirements vary, but most states require asbestos removal workers to complete a three-day training program in compliance with the 1986 Asbestos Hazard Emergency Act (AHERA). The National Asbestos Council (NAC) provides this training in over 100 locations throughout the nation. The program emphasizes "hands-on" training in which students build a decontamination unit, handle a respirator and filtered vacuum cleaners, and perform simulated asbestos removal. Students also receive classroom instruction on government regulations, work practices, health effects, worker protection, and testing for asbestos. The NAC also offers a two-day course on complying with Occupational Safety and Health Administration regulations governing industrial asbestos removal in plants and factories, and an annual AHERA recertification program.

Due to the fact that asbestos is a health hazard and removal procedures are carefully governed, asbestos removal workers who commit safety violations are terminated.

Employers prefer that entry-level workers have a high school diploma and be at least 18 years old. Experienced asbestos removal workers may advance to become supervisors, superintendents, contract estimators, or maintain their own asbestos removal business.

Job Outlook

Job opportunities for asbestos removal workers are expected to grow faster than average for all occupations through the year 2005.

There are many federal regulations that require the removal of asbestos from buildings. The U.S. Environmental Protection Agency requires that asbestos be removed from a building before it undergoes major renovation or is demolished. The 1986 Asbestos Hazard Emergency Act requires that all public and private schools have an asbestos management plan. Many banks require that buildings be asbestos-free before a real estate loan is granted. All of these regulatory requirements should elevate asbestos removal and employment growth.

Earnings

According to the U.S. Department of Labor, median weekly earnings for full-time insulation workers (including asbestos removal workers) were $446 in 1992. Most earned between $334 and $608 per week, but the range fell from less than $279 to more than $796 per week. According to *American Salaries & Wages Survey*, asbestos removal workers earned anywhere from $8 to $16.20 per hour, depending upon geographic location and level of experience.

Asbestos removal workers usually receive benefits that include health and life insurance and a retirement plan .

Related Occupations

Other occupations similar to asbestos removal workers include insulation workers, carpenters, carpet installers, drywall applicators, floor layers, roofers, and sheet-metal workers.

Sources of Additional Information

For more information on a career as an asbestos removal worker, contact:

- Insulation Contractors Association of America, 1321 Duke St., Ste. 303, Alexandria, VA 22314 Phone: (703)739-0356.

- International Association of Heat and Frost Insulators and Asbestos Workers, 1776 Massachusetts Ave., N.W., Ste. 301, Washington, DC 20036. Phone: (202)785-2388.

- National Asbestos Council, Environmental Information Association, 1777 NE Expressway, Ste. 150, Atlanta, GA 30329. Phone: (404)633-2622.

- National Insulation and Abatement Contractors Association, 99 Canal Center Plaza, Ste. 222, Alexandria, VA 22314. Phone: (703)683-6422.

BOATBUILDERS

At a Glance

- **D.O.T.:** 860.131-014; 860.131-022; 860.361-010

- **Preferred Education:** Apprenticeship program

- **Average Salary:** $13.24 per hour.

- **Did You Know?** Some technical schools offer programs in boatbuilding and repair. Coursework includes topics such as woodworking tools and machinery, traditional boatbuilding, and small craft design.

Nature of the Work

Every day, boats of all types make their way along the country's rivers, lakes, canals, and coastal waters. Many of these boats are custom-built by highly-skilled boatbuilders.

Boatbuilders use new and traditional methods to make and repair wooden boats. To begin building a boat, boatbuilders lay out a full-scale outline of the boat on a mold loft floor. This outline is used to make pattern pieces, or templates, of the boat's parts. These templates are placed on pieces of wood and lumber. Boatbuilders trace along the templates and then use carpenter handtools and power tools to cut out the parts.

To build the boat's hull, boatbuilders use an overhead hoist to raise large, precut sections of the hull off the ground. Following the dimensions of the layout, they move the sections in place. Then, they secure the pieces with adhesives, nails, screws, and bolts. Boatbuilders may need to bend some pieces, such as the ribs and sidings, to make them fit. These pieces are placed in a steam chamber, softened, and molded. Boatbuilders may fasten molded sidings directly to the keel (the long piece of wood that extends through the center of the bottom of the boat) or secure molded ribs to the keel and cover the ribs with planking. They also may caulk the seams between the plankings.

Once the hull is completed, boatbuilders build and install other structures such as the pilot house, cabin, rudder, and foundations for machinery, shafting, propeller supports. They also install the decking, masts, booms, and ladders.

Boatbuilder supervisors manage and coordinate the activities of boatbuilders. They assign tasks to workers, train new workers and perform other supervisory tasks.

Specialized boatbuilders, called joiners, install and repair wooden furnishings in boats. These furnishings may include doors, paneling, and other woodwork. The wood may be teak, oak, mahogany, or plywood with a special veneer. They fit hardware such as hinges and doorknobs to the furnishings. Joiners also install glass, skylights, tile, and linoleum.

Working Conditions

Most boatbuilders work a standard 40-hour week. They generally receive extra pay for overtime and for work on weekends and holidays. Boatbuilders typically work outdoors in large yards or under sheds. They may bend, stretch, kneel, and stand while performing their tasks. Since boatbuilders work with hand and machine tools, they must take precautions to prevent injury.

Employment

According to the U.S. Department of Labor, approximately 39,500 boatbuilders were employed by about 2,000 boatyards in 1991. Many boatyards are located along the eastern seaboard from Maine down to Florida. States bordering the Great Lakes, such as Michigan, Wisconsin, and Minnesota, also have numerous boatyards. Along the west coast, California, Oregon, and Washington have many boatyards. Boatyards are also located in inland states such as Ohio, Tennessee, and Arkansas.

Training, Other Qualifications, and Advancement

Like other craftsworkers, many boatbuilders learn their skills through apprenticeship programs. Apprenticeships are available through boatyards. They typically last three to four years. Unions also sponsor apprenticeships.

Some technical schools offer programs in boatbuilding and repair. Coursework includes topics such as woodworking tools and machinery, traditional boatbuilding, and small craft design.

Boatbuilders should be able to use handtools and work well with others. As boatbuilders get new skills, they can advance to positions of greater responsibility.

Job Outlook

According to the U.S. Bureau of Labor Statistics, the boatbuilding industry will experience modest growth between the years 1992 and 2005. One reason for the pickup in growth is the cancellation of the luxury tax. The combination of the tax and the economic recession in the early 1990s resulted in a significant downturn in boat sales and many layoffs. The

industry is expected to add jobs as it recovers. The National Marine Manufacturers Association expects about 5,000 boatbuilders nationwide to be hired in 1995 because of the increased demand for boats.

Earnings

According to a 1994 survey by the American Boat Builders & Repairers Association, the average hourly earnings of a boatbuilding carpenter were $13.24. The highest hourly rate was $20.14; the lowest was $8.25. Foremen earned between $9.25 and $28.13 per hour, with an average rate of $16.32. General managers earned up to $34 per hour.

Related Occupations

Other workers who use tools to fabricate, install, and repair structures made of wood include carpenters, maintenance carpenters, acoustical carpenters, mold carpenters, bridge carpenters, railcar carpenters, and carpenters supervisors.

Sources of Additional Information

- American Boat Builders & Repairers Association, PO Box 1236, Stamford, CT 06904 Phone: (203)967-4745.

- Industrial Union of Marine and Shipbuilding Workers of America, 719 E. Fort Ave., No. 23, Baltimore, MD Phone: (410)837-0056.

FLOOR COVERING INSTALLERS

At a Glance

- **D.O.T.:** 864.381-010

- **Preferred Education:** High school diploma

- **Average Salary:** $375 per week

- **Did You Know?** Since most new homes and commercial buildings are built with plywood or concrete subflooring, rather than hardwood flooring, the need for floor covering installers is on the rise.

Nature of the Work

While many older homes have hardwood floors, most floors in modern homes and commercial buildings are built of less attractive materials, such as plywood or concrete, which must be topped with some type of floor covering. Comfort, elegance, and safety have lead manufacturers to create floor coverings in a wide variety of styles, colors, patterns, and qualities. Floor coverings are generally grouped into three categories: carpets, resilient floors, and ceramic tile. Carpet and resilient floors are installed in homes, offices, stores, hotels, and other buildings by floor covering installers.

When an order is ready for installation, floor covering installers are responsible for moving any furniture and for removing any existing carpet or flooring. The floor covering installers then inspect the subfloor to determine its condition and fix any flaws that could be visible through the new floor covering. After repairing the floor and cleaning its surface, the installers can plan the layout of the new floor covering and the actual installation process begins.

Floor covering installers measure the area to be covered. The placement of seams and traffic patterns are major considerations in planning the layout. The floor covering should be placed where it will have the best possible appearance and be able to withstand its intended wear.

With wall-to-wall installations, installers roll out, measure, mark, cut, lay, and tack or tape underlay padding across the floor. Then, they roll out, measure, mark, and cut the carpet, allowing for three to four extra inches of carpet on each side for the final fitting. They install the carpet by stretching it to fit smoothly and evenly on the floor and tightly against each wall and door threshold to remove wrinkles. Special attention is given to the direction and pattern of the carpet before finally attaching it to a tacking strip around the edges of the room. Excess carpet is trimmed. Since most carpet rolls are manufactured in 12-foot widths, wall-to-wall installations require installers to tape or sew sections together for larger rooms. Heat-taping is the method most commonly used for sealing seams. After the flooring job is completed, installers check for imperfections in the layout, correct any flaws, and remove extra carpet scraps. Resilient floor coverings undergo a similar installation process, but it may be glued directly to the floor.

Floor covering installers will inform the customer of how to maintain and care for the floor covering and give the customer any related literature on floor upkeep.

Floor covering installers use special carpet-laying and floor covering tools such as carpet knives, knee knickers, and power stretchers. They also use hand tools such as hammers, drills, staple guns, and rubber mallets.

Working Conditions

Floor covering installers generally work 40 hours per week. To avoid disturbing customers or employees, floor covering installers may work evenings and weekends when carpeting stores or offices.

Carpets and other floor coverings are installed in completed or nearly-completed structures, thus work areas are usually lighted, safe, and fairly clean. Floor covering installers do a lot of kneeling, bending, reaching, and stretching. They also lift heavy rolls of carpet.

Employment

According to the U.S. Bureau of Labor Statistics, there were 62,000 carpet installers employed in the United States in 1992. Many worked for flooring contractors or floor covering retailers. Nearly 65 percent of carpet installers are self-employed. Installers are employed throughout the nation, but are concentrated in urban areas with high levels of construction activity.

Many installers belong to the United Brotherhood of Carpenters and Joiners of America or the International Brotherhood of Painters and Allied Trades.

Training, Other Qualifications, and Advancement

Most floor covering installers learn on the job as helpers to experienced installers. Beginners may work as helpers for up to two years, performing simpler tasks, such as installing stripping and padding, and stretching newly-installed carpet. As beginners gain experience, they perform more difficult duties, such as measuring, cutting, and fitting.

Others learn from apprenticeship programs that include on-the-job training and classroom instruction. Apprenticeship programs provide comprehensive training that usually lasts from three to four years.

Beginning carpet installers and apprentices should be 18 years old and have manual dexterity. A high school education is preferred, although it is not necessary. A driver's license and a criminal background check are usually required. Employers also want individuals who are neat in appearance and are able to work well with customers. Precision and attention to detail are essential. High school level math, especially geometry, is helpful. Floor covering installers must generally supply their own tools.

Carpet installers may advance to supervisors or installation mangers for large installation firms. Some installers become salespersons or estimators. Many installers also go into business for themselves as independent subcontractors.

Job Outlook

Job opportunities for carpet installers are expected to grow 21.6 percent through the year 2005. Today, most new homes and commercial buildings are built with plywood or concrete subflooring, rather than hardwood flooring. This trend will stimulate the need for floor covering installers. In addition, renovating and refurbishing existing structures will continue the need for floor covering installers. Most openings, however, will arise from the need to replace retired floor covering installers.

This occupation is affected by economic downturns. When the economy slows, the demand for new carpet and other floor covering falls. However, since floor covering installers also work in older buildings and homes, employment generally remains more stable than other construction occupations.

Earnings

According to the U.S. Department of Labor, the median weekly earnings of full-time carpet installers in 1992 was $375. Most carpet installers earned between $275 and $510 per week, but some earned as high as $700 per week and as low as $185 per week.

Carpet installers are paid either a flat hourly wage or by the number of yards of carpet installed. Rates vary according to geographic location and whether the installer is affiliated with a union. Unionized carpet installers typically earned more than non-union carpet installers.

U.S. Department of Labor sources estimate that in 1992, experienced unionized carpet installers earned between $16 and $25 per hour. Starting wage rates for apprentices and other trainees were about half of experienced workers' rates. Nonunion carpet installers are usually paid by the number of yards installed. In 1992, they received $1.50 to $2.75 per yard installed.

Carpet installers are often paid extra for moving furniture, upholstering, or carpeting stairs. Full-time and unionized carpet installers usually receive benefits such as paid vacations and holidays, health and life insurance, and a retirement plan.

Related Occupations

Other occupations similar to floor covering installers include carpenters, cement masons, drywall installers, floor layers, lathers, painters, paperhangers, roofers, sheet-metal workers, terrazzo workers, and tile setters.

Sources of Additional Information

For more information on a career as a floor covering installer, contact:

- Floor Covering Installation Contractors Association, PO Box 948, Dalton, GA 30722-0948. Phone: (706)226-5488.

- United Brotherhood of Carpenters and Joiners of America, 101 Constitution Ave. NW, Washington, DC 20001. Phone: (202)546-6206.

- International Brotherhood of Painters and Allied Traders, 1750 New York Ave. NW, Washington, DC 20006. Phone: (202)637-0720.

MUSEUM EXHIBIT TECHNICIANS

At a Glance

- **D.O.T.:** 739.261-010

- **Preferred Education:** High school diploma

- **Average Salary:** $18,394 per year

- **Did You Know?** Museum exhibit technicians are skilled craft workers who interpret the ideas of curators, scientists, and historians to construct various museum displays and exhibits.

Nature of the Work

Every day museum visitors marvel at museum exhibits. To understand the context of an exhibit piece, however, it must be carefully displayed. This may involve adding descriptive text near an object to understand its background,

adding light around a painting so that it can be clearly seen, constructing a replica of a 19th-century kitchen—complete with authentic kitchen tools—to create the feeling of stepping back in time, or mounting assembled skeletal remains so that it resembles its original configuration and is not a jumbled mass of bones. The production of exhibits is the responsibility of museum exhibit technicians. Museum exhibit technicians are skilled craft workers who interpret the ideas of curators, scientists, and historians to construct and set up various museum displays and exhibits.

The first step in a project is to consult with the museum s curatorial and educational staff, who provide the exhibit technicians with designs of how they want the exhibit to appear. These designs may be sketches, blueprints, drawings, photographs, or scale models. The exhibits may be art objects created by people, such as paintings, sculptures, tapestries, pottery, or medieval armor; natural objects, such as fossils or skeletons; or historical objects that were once used everyday, but are now considered antique. Most objects are authentic, but some are carefully detailed reproductions. The exhibits may be permanent, temporary, or circulating—meaning they travel to different museums to be enjoyed by people in a variety of locations.

Once the exhibit plans are determined, exhibit technicians are ready to construct the exhibit. This may entail using a variety of construction materials, such as wood, plywood, fiberglass, electric wiring, plumbing, adhesives, and hand and power tools. Exhibit technicians may perform any number of construction duties. They may cut, assemble, and fasten parts to construct framework, panels, and shelves. They may spray or brushes paint, enamel, varnish, or another finish onto structures. They may mount fittings and fixtures, such as shelves, panel boards, and shadowboxes to framework. They may install electrical wiring, light fixtures, audiovisual equipment, control equipment, or other apparatus in the framework, according to design specifications. They may affix murals, photographs, mounted legend materials, and graphics in the framework. Once the exhibit structure is built, the technicians test all electrical, electronic, and mechanical components to verify that they operate, and make repairs and adjustments as needed. From here, the exhibit technician may assist in cleaning, repairing and arranging the collection pieces or specimens and display accessories in the exhibit.

Museum exhibit technicians are often responsible for maintaining the inventory of building materials, tools, and equipment, and order supplies as needed. They may also supervise the work of carpenters, electricians, and other workers contracted to construct and install the exhibit's components.

Working Conditions

Museum exhibit technicians perform their work indoors. They do moderate lifting and carrying. Their job also requires a fair amount of bending, stretching, climbing and standing on ladders, and working in tight spaces. They must follow safety rules when working with tools to prevent injury.

Employment

Museum exhibit technicians are employed by museums

of all types. Museums are located throughout the country, but the best employment opportunities are found at large museums in big metropolitan areas.

Training, Other Qualifications, and Advancement

Employers prefer museum exhibit technicians to have at least a high school diploma. Most training is received on the job. The ability to perform construction work, such as working with wood, metal or plastics is very helpful. Model making and graphic arts skills is also desirable.

Museum exhibit technicians should be able to conceptualize exhibit designs according the style of the museum, make aesthetic judgments, and follow design blueprints and instructions. They should also be able to work with hand and power tools.

Experienced museum exhibit technicians may advance to a supervisory position, such as a museum exhibit designer.

Job Outlook

Museum exhibit technicians have an occupation that technology can t automate. This fact suggests the employment outlook for museum exhibit technicians is good. Economic downturns, however, can have a negative affect on job openings. During these times, many museums are affected by budget cuts, forcing directors to put a freeze on hiring and cut staff hours.

Earnings

According to the *American Salaries and Wages Survey*, in South Dakota museum exhibit technicians receive an average of $8.85 per hour. This is the equivalent to approximately $18,394 per year.

Related Occupations

Other occupations similar to museum exhibit technicians include display makers, prop makers, model makers, and art conservators.

Sources of Additional Information

For more information contact:

- American Association of Museums, 1225 I St. NW, Washington, DC 20005.

- American Institute for Conservation of Historic and Artistic Works, 1400 16th St. NW, Washington, DC 20036.

- National Trust for Historic Preservation, Office of Personnel Administration, 1785 Massachusetts Ave. NW, Washington, DC 20036.

Heavy Contruction

HIGHWAY MAINTENANCE WORKERS

At a Glance

- **D.O.T.:** 899.684-014

- **Preferred Education:** No minimum educational requirement

- **Average Salary:** $6 to $20 per hour

- **Did You Know?** Deteriorating bridges and poor highway conditions have resulted in increased demand for highway maintenance and repair.

Nature of the Work

The United States has millions of miles of highways and roads—the largest system in the world. The vast majority of all travel and the shipping of domestic goods are by road. Billions of dollars are spent annually on maintenance and repair. Highway maintenance workers are responsible for maintaining the roads and highways that link the nation.

Highway maintenance workers keep local, state, and interstate highways, municipal and rural roads, airport runways, and rights-of-way in safe condition. Working in teams, they perform this duty in several ways.

Tasks vary with the location of the roads they maintain. They travel by truck to the location that needs attention.

Highway maintenance workers patch broken or eroded pavement (potholes) damaged by de-icing salt, ice, rain, and heavy traffic. Highway maintenance workers first clean and prepare the hole. Asphalt is then poured into the hole. The asphalt is spread and smoothed, completely filling the hole. The asphalt is finally sealed and the hole is repaired. Similarly, highway maintenance workers also clean and seal joints and cracks in asphalt and concrete pavement.

Highway maintenance workers erect and repair guard rails, snow fences and other barriers. They also erect and repair highway markers such as stop signs and other traffic signs, as well as signs that direct motorists to major routes. Highway maintenance workers operate machines and trucks that paint dividing lines between traffic lanes, edge lines and pedestrian crossing lines.

It is also the responsibility of highway maintenance workers to maintain the sides of roads and medians, keeping them safe as well as pleasant looking. They mow grass, plant and care for trees and other plantings, pick up litter and debris, clear brush by hand or machine, kill weeds, dig up stumps, fill holes with dirt, cut down overhanging branches that block drivers' views of stoplights and oncoming traffic, and remove trees that are damaged in a storm and fall across a road. They load, haul away, and dispose of all debris.

Highway maintenance workers also respond to roads affected by weather conditions. When it snows, they drive snowplows and blowers to clear major roads. During icy conditions, they drive salt trucks that pour salt to prevent motorists from sliding into accidents. In the autumn, they use trucks that blow away leaves that clog street gutters and surface drains. In the spring and summer they drive machines that sweep pavement. They also clean up and repair road damage caused by storms, floods, and landslides. Aside from weather-related problems, highway maintenance workers repair road and roadside property damage caused by vehicular accidents or vandals.

In addition to roads and highways, highway maintenance workers are responsible for inspecting, maintaining and repairing bridges, tunnels, drainage systems, and other structures that concern road travel. They may also be responsible for maintaining traffic lights, warning signals, highway lighting, historical markers, and rest stops.

Highway maintenance workers upkeep and repair their equipment and the buildings they use. They store materials for snow and ice removal. Highway maintenance workers use many different hand tools and power tools such as pneumatic drills (jackhammers), and operate machinery such as backhoes, bulldozers, cherry pickers, cranes, front-end loaders, paving machines, post-hole diggers, rollers, and tow trucks.

Because highway maintenance workers perform their job so close to traffic, some serve as flaggers who monitor and direct traffic through the section or road under repair. This job plays an important role in avoiding accidents and injuries to both motorists and the workers.

Working Conditions

Highway maintenance workers usually work 40 hours per week, although overtime may be required to complete a project.

Night, evening, and weekend work is sometimes necessary to avoid busy traffic times.

Highway maintenance workers work outdoors in weather conditions of every kind, including very hot and very cold temperatures, rain, snow, sleet, and high winds. Every day they are subjected to dirt, dust, loud machinery noise, and the heat and odor of asphalt. They work extremely close to moving traffic and run the risk of serious injury by motorists, especially those who ignore construction warning signals.

Highway maintenance workers stand most of the day, unless they operate a truck. They sometimes work at tall heights on bridges or in water inside tunnels. They also do a lot of kneeling, climbing, crawling, bending, and stooping. They must wear protective clothing, including steel-toed boots (which they may have to furnish themselves), hard hats, and possibly earplugs to protect their ears from noisy equipment. They must also follow safety rules to avoid injury from dangerous machinery.

Employment

According to the Bureau of Labor Statistics, in 1992 there were 168,000 highway maintenance workers employed in the United States. Most highway maintenance workers are employed by city, county, and state agencies. Private construction companies also contract highway maintenance workers. In most states workers belong to a union.

Training, Other Qualifications, and Advancement

There is no minimum educational requirement to become a highway maintenance worker, although many employers prefer a high school diploma or GED. Prospective highway maintenance workers may be required to pass a physical examination before being hired. Those who wish to work in large cities or on state highways must pass a civil service exam to show competency in reading and basic math. Maintenance truck drivers need a valid driver's license.

Most training is received on the job. Special courses provided by the employer may be needed to learn special skills. Highway workers often begin performing simple tasks, such as clearing brush and picking up litter.

Experienced highway maintenance workers who demonstrate leadership abilities and technical skills may advance to become a highway maintenance supervisor.

Job Outlook

According to the U.S. Bureau of Labor Statistics, job openings for highway maintenance workers will increase 29 percent by the year 2005, somewhat faster than average for all occupations. Growth is expected in highway, bridge, and street construction. Deteriorating bridges and poor highway conditions will result in increased demand for highway maintenance and repair. Most highway maintenance depends on government resources. Budget cuts or increases will also affect the demand for highway maintenance workers.

Earnings

According to *American Salaries and Wages Survey*,

highway maintenance workers' earnings vary from state to state. In 1992 a highway maintenance worker in Minnesota earned an average of $13.46 per hour. Other states had average hourly wages ranging from $6.30 to $10.64. Some states have highway maintenance workers who earn up to $20 per hour.

Wages depend upon the size and wealth of the city, county, or state in which the worker is employed. Wages can also depend upon the highway maintenance worker's experience and the type of work he or she performs.

Most states and municipalities offer full-time highway maintenance workers benefits such as paid vacations and holidays, sick leave, health and life insurance, and retirement plans.

Related Occupations

Other occupations in the construction industry include bricklayers, stone masons, carpenters, concrete finishers, drywall installers, pipelayers, paving, surfacing, and tamping equipment operators.

Sources of Additional Information

- American Federation of State, County and Municipal Employees, 1625 L St. NW, Washington, DC 20036. Phone: (202)452-4800.

- American Road & Transportation Builders Association, 501 School St. SW, Washington, DC 20024.

- Associated General Contractors of America, Inc., 1957 E St. NW, Washington, DC 20005.

- International Brotherhood of Teamsters, Chauffeurs, Warehousemen and Helpers of America, 25 Louisiana Ave. NW, Washington, DC 20001. Phone: (202)624-6800.

PAVING MACHINE OPERATORS

At a Glance

- **D.O.T.:** 853.663-010

- **Preferred Education:** High school diploma

- **Average Salary:** $14 per hour

- **Did You Know?** Although jobs are found throughout the country, temperatures must be over 40 degrees Fahrenheit to pave, so work is seasonal in many climates.

Nature of the Work

Without pavement, modern transportation would be virtually non-existent. Asphalt paving machine operators are responsible for laying the millions of miles of pavement spread across the nation to carry cars, trucks, and buses to their destinations as well as allow airplanes and trains to function.

Asphalt paving machine operators operate equipment used for applying asphalt, concrete, or other materials to make roads and highways, parking lots, airport runways, driveways, water reservoirs, sanitary landfills, and railroad track beds. Most roads are paved with hot mix asphalt, a sticky, black recyclable mixture of asphalt, cement, and aggregate (gravel, sand, crushed stone). Its strength and economical cost make it the best known substance for paving roads.

Asphalt paving machine operators perform a variety of duties. They operate the paving machine, the tractor that powers the paver. The paving machine maintains a constant flow of asphalt into the hopper, the machine that keeps the asphalt warm and easy to spread.

Asphalt paving machine operators control the amount of mix that goes onto the roadway. They make sure that the asphalt is mixed to the proper thickness, and that it is appropriately spread, leveled and smoothed. They handle the screed, the machine that smooths and spreads the mix onto the ground's subsurface. Paving machine operators observe the distribution of paving material along the screed and control its direction to eliminate voids at curbs and joints. They operate the valves that regulate the temperature of the asphalt flowing from the hopper when asphalt begins to harden on the screed.

Asphalt paving machine operators watch for mixing errors that are apparent by the consistency of the asphalt mix or if the asphalt is giving off odd color smoke. They also watch for any debris, such as dirt, rocks, or paper, that may have gotten into the mix.

Asphalt paving machine operators drive rolling machines across the new pavement surface to compact the hot asphalt mix and smooth out any roughness or unevenness. They also use special rakes and straightedge lutes to distribute, spread, and smooth the asphalt. Using special tools and equipment, they are able to control the width of the pavement.

At the end of a job, asphalt paving machine operators thoroughly clean the machines for the next job and make sure that all of their equipment is in proper working condition.

Working Conditions

Asphalt paving machine operators often work 10 to 14 hours per day for six or seven days a week. At times, paving machine operators work in very hot, humid weather. They are subjected to asphalt fumes and loud machinery noise. They also work near traffic and are at risk of injury from careless motorists. They must wear hard hats, steel-toes shoes, safety goggles, long-sleeved uniforms, and gloves to protect themselves from the hot mix asphalt and other construction hazards. Paving machine operators who operate the screed must stand and walk for long periods. Paving machine operators sometimes must travel long distances to a job and may stay at a motel until the job is finished.

Employment

According to the Bureau of Labor Statistics, there were 72,000 paving, surfacing, and tamping equipment operators employed in the United States in 1992. Paving machine operators are employed by city, county, state and federal agencies, and construction companies.

Although jobs are found throughout the country, temperatures must be over 40 degrees Fahrenheit to pave, so work is seasonal in many climates. In colder regions, paving machine operators work from March until October. In southern regions, workers are often able to work all year.

Employers prefer that asphalt paving machine operators have a high school diploma or equivalent, but it is not required. Knowledge of machinery from high school shop classes or vocational school is very helpful.

An apprenticeship is an excellent way to learn the job, but a high school diploma is necessary. Employers provide classroom and on-the-job training. Paving machine operators need to remain alert and be in good physical condition. Paving machine operators who have experience, advanced skills, and leadership abilities may be promoted to supervisory or superintendent positions.

Job Outlook

According to the Bureau of Labor Statistics, job openings for paving machine operators will increase 47.7 percent, much faster than average for all occupations. Employment in heavy construction is projected to increase somewhat faster than the industry average. Growth is expected in highway, bridge, and street construction. Deteriorating bridges and poor highway conditions will result in increased demand for highways maintenance and repair.

Earnings

According to the Bureau of Labor Statistics, highway and street construction workers earned an average of $607 per week, or $14 per hour, in 1993. Workers receive overtime pay for work beyond 40 hours per week. Many employers provide full-time workers with benefits such as paid vacations and holidays, medical and life insurance, and retirement plans.

Related Occupations

Related construction industry occupations include tamping machine operators, tower-crane operators, dredge operators, power-shovel operators, irrigation system installers, pile-drive operators, rock-drill operators, and bulldozer operators.

Sources of Additional Information

For additional information on a career as a paving machine operator, contact:

- Asphalt Institute, Research Park Dr., PO Box 14052, Lexington, KY 40512-4052. Phone: (606)288-4960.

- National Asphalt Pavement Association, NAPA Bldg., 5100 Forbes Blvd. Lanham, MD 20706-4413. Phone: (301)731-4748.

PIPELAYERS

At a Glance

- **D.O.T.:** 869.664-014

- **Preferred Education:** No minimum educational requirement

- **Average Salary:** $5 to $16.61 per hour

- **Did You Know?** Most pipelayers are employed by construction contractors, government agencies, communications companies, and utilities companies.

Nature of the Work

Nearly every commodity modern man has learned to depend on—running water, plumbing, gas, oil, electricity, telephones—are all carried by pipes installed by pipelayers. Pipelayers assemble, lay, and maintain glazed or unglazed clay, concrete, plastic, or cast-iron pipe for water mains, drains, sanitation or storm sewers, gas or oil lines, and electrical, cable and other conduit.

Following blueprints or other instructions, pipelayers plan the route for the pipe to be laid. Using either shovels or trenching machines, they dig trenches to the proper depth. They level or grade the base of the trench with tamping machines or hand tools. Pipelayers then cut the pipe to the appropriate length and position and align the pipes. They signal a tractor driver to properly lay the pipes in the trench. Once the pipes are inside the trench, the pipelayers weld, glue, cement or otherwise connect the pipe sections and seal the joints. After the pipes are properly installed, pipelayers check the slope using a carpenter's level or lasers. Pipes are finally covered with earth or other matter.

Pipelayers also locate existing pipes that need to be repaired or replaced and make the necessary corrections. They may use magnetic or radio indicators to find the pipes.

Working Conditions

Pipelayers work 40 hours per week, five days a week. Overtime is necessary when deadlines must be met. Pipelayers work outdoors in nearly all weather conditions, including hot and cold temperatures, rain, snow, sleet, and high winds. A pipelayer's work area is typically four to 50 feet underground, dirty, sometimes wet, and noisy from construction equipment. Pipelayers work with powerful tools and machines that can be very dangerous if not handled properly. Pipelayers must wear protective clothing, including steel-toed boots and hard hats, that they may have to purchase themselves.

Pipelayers frequently lift and balance very heavy equipment and pipes, climb in out of holes, and stoop, kneel, bend, and crawl.

Employment

According to the U.S. Bureau of Labor Statistics, there were 48,000 pipelayers and pipelaying fitters employed in the United States in 1992. Most pipelayers are employed by construction contractors, government agencies, communications companies, and utilities companies.

Training, Other Qualifications, and Advancement

There are no specific educational requirements for pipelayers. Employers want potential pipelayers to have reading and basic math skills in order to follow written instructions and blueprints, and operate technical equipment. Most pipelayers receive on-the-job training from an experienced pipelayer or manager.

Pipelayers need to be in good physical condition and not mind working in cramped quarters and around loud machinery. Pipelayers must be alert at all times and be aware of the hazards and safety requirements of their job.

A pipelayer with demonstrated leadership and technical skills may advance to become a crewman or supervisor.

Job Outlook

According to the U.S. Bureau of Labor Statistics, job opportunities for pipelayers will increase 26.4 percent by the year 2005, about as fast as average for all occupations. Jobs will come from new openings and the need to replace experienced workers who leave the field.

Earnings

Pipelayers' wages may vary depending on experience, employer, and geographic location. According to *American Salaries and Wages Survey*, pipelayers in the Southeast earned $5 to $9 per hour in 1992; those in the Northeast earned $8.15 to $16.61 per hour; and Midwest pipelayers earned $9.50 to $15.55 per hour.

Many pipelayers typically belong to unions. Unionized pipelayers receive benefits that include paid overtime, paid vacations, health and life insurance, and retirement plans.

Related Occupations

Other occupations in the construction industry include bricklayers, stone masons, carpenters, concrete finishers, drywall installers, highway maintenance workers, insulation installers, paving, surfacing, and tamping equipment operators, plumbers, and structural and reinforcing metal workers.

Sources of Additional Information

For more information on a career as a pipelayer, contact:

- American Federation of State, County and Municipal Employees, 1625 L St. NW, Washington, DC 20036. Phone: (202)429-1000.

- American Road & Transportation Builders Association, The ARTBA Bldg., 1010 Massachusetts Ave., NW, 6th Fl., Washington, DC 20001 Phone: (202)289-4434.

- Associated Builders and Contractors, 1300 N. 17th St., Rosslyn, VA. 22209 Phone: (703)812-2000.

- Associated General Contractors of America, Inc., 1957 E St. NW, Washington, DC 20005 Phone: (202)393-2040.

- International Brotherhood of Teamsters, Chauffeurs, Warehousemen and Helpers of America, 25 Louisiana Ave. NW, Washington, DC 20001. Phone: (202)624-6800.

Production Occupations

Metalworking and Plastics-working Occupations

BLACKSMITHS

At a Glance

- **D.O.T.:** 610.381-010

- **Preferred Education:** 1 to 4 years training.

- **Average Salary:** $24,000

- **Did You Know?** Blacksmiths who produce decorative ironwork pieces of their own design may be known as artist-blacksmiths.

Nature of the Work

Blacksmiths heat and shape iron and other metals to produce practical or decorative metal objects. Blacksmiths work in forge shops in many different industries, including steel, railroad, mining, and manufacturing industries. They forge and repair metal items such as tongs, edged tools, hooks, chains, machine and structural components, and agricultural implements. They may repair large industrial machinery or small handtools.

Blacksmiths generally use hand tools, anvils, presses, and power hammers. They heat metal stock in a forge or furnace, paying careful attention to the metal's changing color as it is heated. Once the metal stock has been heated to the correct temperature, they hammer it into the desired shape and size. They may hammer it by hand on an anvil or use a power hammer. The may use a fly press, which drops the selected tool onto the metal with a great deal of force. If necessary they may forge-weld metal parts by heating and hammering them together. In some cases, blacksmiths must reheat the metal while they are working on it.

Once a piece has been shaped, blacksmiths reheat it and cool it in a bath of water or oil. They may temper the metal piece by heating it and then allowing it to cool to room temperature. They may use hammers and chisels to put the finishing touches on a piece.

Blacksmiths who produce decorative ironwork of their own design may be known as artist-blacksmiths. They often set up their own blacksmith shops or studios and build their own forges. Some artist-blacksmiths use propane-powered forges to create temperatures of 3,000 degrees or more. They produce ironwork that ranges from practical to decorative pieces, often following their own designs and patterns. They may produce commercial guard rails and window bars, for example. Practical yet artistic pieces might include weather vanes, decorative iron gates, and fireplace tools. Decorative pieces may include candlesticks and sculpture. Some blacksmiths specialize in architectural pieces, including stairway railings, garden trellises, and entrance gates. Blacksmiths who specialize in different kinds of blades are known as bladesmiths. Those who specialize in making horseshoes are known as farriers.

Working Conditions

Blacksmiths spend at least part of their time working in the dark, so they can better see the colors of the heated metal in the forge's fire. They are frequently exposed to extreme heat as well as to smoke and fumes from their forge or furnace. In addition to extreme heat they are also subject to loud noise while working. They usually wear protective clothing, including steel-toed boots, a leather apron, gloves, and goggles. However, they are subject to the risk of injuries such as cuts and burns associated with working with hot metals and machinery.

The work of blacksmiths is physically demanding. They frequently have to lift heavy weights of up to 50 pounds and occasionally as much as 100 pounds. They usually remain standing during most of their work shift.

Blacksmiths generally work a standard 40-hour week, with some overtime possible. Those who work in industrial settings may have to join a union.

Employment

The Bureau of Labor Statistics does not publish separate employment statistics for blacksmiths but categorizes them with all other precision metal workers, of which there were 88,000 employed in 1992. The Artist-Blacksmith Association of North America (ABANA) counts approximately 3,000 members worldwide, and there were an estimated 400 artistic blacksmith shops in the United States in 1991.

Blacksmiths who are not self-employed may work in different industries. Typical employers include metal manufacturing firms, especially those that manufacture metal parts, machinery, and transportation equipment. The railroad, mining, and steel industries also employ blacksmiths.

Nearly all blacksmiths are men, but there are some well known artist-blacksmiths who are women.

Training, Other Qualifications, and Advancement

Although blacksmiths are not required to be high school graduates, most employers prefer that they complete high school. Appropriate high school courses include mathematics and geometry, mechanical drawing, blueprint reading, graphics, chemistry, physics, and industrial arts.

Blacksmiths generally need two to four years of training to provide them with a working knowledge of metal characteristics and of the different techniques used in working with hot metals. Industrial employers may provide on-the-job training. Apprenticeship programs generally last from two to four years. Specialized training for blacksmiths is available at some craft centers and through workshops given by blacksmiths who teach. Southern Illinois University in Carbondale offers a well known program that trains artist-blacksmiths.

Blacksmiths must be in good physical condition. They must also have good vision, including the ability to see objects close at hand, good depth perception, and accurate color vision. They must have the manual dexterity to work with hand and power tools.

Blacksmiths can advance to more skilled jobs in industrial settings as well as to supervisory positions. Artist-blacksmiths can become better known and attract more clients by showing their work in galleries and museums. They may become associated with architects and provide custom ironwork for new homes and buildings.

Job Outlook

According to the Bureau of Labor Statistics, employment of all other precision metal workers including blacksmiths is expected to increase only slightly between 1992 and 2005. Some blacksmith positions are being replaced by forge shop workers. Opportunities for artist-blacksmiths tend to be cyclical and somewhat dependent on the general state of the economy.

Earnings

The national average wage for blacksmiths and forge shop workers is approximately $24,000 annually. Earnings vary according to experience, employment situation, and industry.

Related Occupations

Related metal fabrication and repair occupations include welders, patternmakers, automobile body repairers, fitters, sheet metal workers, boilermakers, aircraft body repairers, railroad car repairers, and millwrights. Other related occupations include forge shop workers, forge press operators, roller machine operators, furnace, kiln, and oven operators, mold machine operators, metal refining workers, and foundry workers.

Sources of Additional Information

* Artist-Blacksmith Association of North America (ABANA), PO Box 1181, Nashville, TN 47448. Phone: (812)988-6919.

* Forging Industry Association, Landmark Office Towers, 25 Prospect Ave. W., Ste. 300, Cleveland, OH 44115. Phone: (216)781-6260.

* International Brotherhood of Boilermakers, Iron Ship Builders, Blacksmiths, Forgers and Helpers, 753 State Ave., Ste. 570, Kansas City, KS 66101. Phone: (913)371-2640.

GEMOLOGISTS AND GEM CUTTERS

At a Glance

- **D.O.T.:** 199.281-010 and 770.281-014

- **Preferred Education:** Education and training.

- **Average Salary:** $28,000

- **Did You Know?** Many gemologists and gem cutters gain their first experience as hobbyists, taking short-term courses of instruction and practicing what they have learned.

Nature of the Work

People buy and wear jewelry made from many different materials. Gold, silver, copper, pewter, and bronze are some of the metals most commonly fashioned into jewelry. Diamonds, emeralds, rubies, jade, and amethysts are some of the commonly used stones, but there are thousands of natural and synthetic gemstones to be found in jewelry. When people wish to have their gemstones appraised or identified, they often consult a gemologist.

Gemologists are jewelers who specialize in identifying and appraising diamonds and other gemstones as well as gem materials. They play an essential role in the jewelry trade. Using their skills at identifying and grading gemstones, gemologists determine the most efficient manner in which rough stones can be fashioned into finished gems and ultimately into pieces of jewelry.

They examine gemstones using special optical instruments, such as polariscopes, refractometers, and microscopes, to differentiate between specimens and to detect flaws, defects, or other peculiarities affecting a gem's value. They may use a dichroscope, which consists of an eyepiece at one end and a small square opening at the other. Depending on the stone being examined, the dichroscope allows one or two colors to be visible, from which gemologists can determine the stone's identity. Such examinations are necessary to differentiate between natural, synthetic, treated, assembled, and imitation colored stones.

Gemologists also employ other techniques in gem identification. They may immerse stones in chemical solutions to determine their specific gravities and other key properties. These tests enable gemologists to determine the physical properties of stones and differentiate genuine stones from their substitutes.

Gemologists are able to grade diamonds and other gemstones according to established grading systems. They examine stones for their luster, brilliance, and dispersion, or fire as it is sometimes called. Luster refers to a stone's surface appearance; gemologists recognize eight different types of luster. Brilliance is the relative amount of light reflected by a stone. Fire or dispersion refers to the prismatic separation of light into spectral colors. A diamond that shows the distinct flashing of each color of the spectrum is said to have more fire or dispersion than one that doesn't. When it comes to grading diamonds, gemologists use a system based on the four C's: color, clarity, cut, and carat weight.

Gem cutters generally have the skills of trained gemologists combined with the ability to turn rough stones into finished gems. When they select rough stones, they visualize how the finished gem will look. They look for flaws and use optical instruments to identify the stones.

Gem cutters may specialize in one of two ways to cut gems, cabochon or faceting. A cabochon is a stone that has been cut into a convex shape. A faceted stone is cut with one or more planes. Rose-cut stones can have as many as 12 or 24 facets. Brilliant cuts have 57 facets.

Gem cutters may develop their own designs, cutting as many as 300 facets on a stone. Faceting involves grinding a series of mirrors on a stone. Cutters use a faceting machine, which is similar to an electrical sander. Grinding wheels, called laps, are coated with different grades of abrasives. Gem cutters attach the stone they are working on to a dopstick, which is a small stainless steel rod. They position the dopstick in a mechanical arm at a fixed angle above the grinding wheel, then lower the stone and grind a facet. They grind a series of facets by rotating the dopstick and altering the angle of the mechanical arm as needed. After they have cut a stone, gem cutters polish it using polishing laps, which can be made from tin, wood, ceramics, and other materials.

Working Conditions

Gemologists and gem cutters work under conditions similar to that of other jewelers. The work of gem cutters is very precise and painstaking. Gemologists must be able to sit quietly for long periods of time. They must be able to pace themselves, working quickly enough to be productive but slowly and carefully enough to avoid making mistakes.

The work of gemologists and gem cutters is not physically demanding, although manual dexterity is required. Gemologists spend a lot of time reaching and handling stones, tools, and precision instruments. They may also spend more time interacting with other people, especially if they are employed in sales or appraisals.

Employment

Gemologists often work in the sales departments of retail jewelry stores, where they may appraise gems and other jewelry that is brought into the store. They may offer to purchase jewelry that is brought in for appraisal. Gemologists also buy and sell diamonds and other gemstones at wholesale. They are also employed by jewelry manufacturers. They may specialize in sorting, buying, and grading rough gem material or in diamond grading. There are approximately 300 members of the Accredited Gemologists Association.

There are probably fewer than 100 custom gem cutters in the United States. Most of the gem cutting for the commercial jewelry trade is done overseas in cutting centers located in Germany and Thailand. Gem cutters may work for manufacturers or be self-employed. Self-employed gem cutters may work for gem dealers and collectors on a contract basis, or they may choose to market and sell their work themselves. Trade shows and art fairs provide them with an opportunity to show their work. Some custom gem cutters have an established clientele.

While gemologists and gem cutters are employed throughout the United States, the best employment opportunities are in cities such as New York and Los Angeles and other affluent areas.

Training, Other Qualifications, and Advancement

Gem cutters can learn their occupation in one to two years. Training programs are available through technical schools, community colleges, colleges, and universities. Most technical school and college programs require applicants to be high school graduates. Many gemologists and gem cutters gain their first experience as hobbyists, taking short-term courses of instruction and practicing what they have learned. Some are experienced jewelers who have decided to specialize in gemology or gem cutting.

The Gemological Institute of America offers a six-month program leading to a certificate as a graduate gemologist at its Santa Monica, California, and New York City campuses. There are no prerequisites, except applicants must have a working knowledge of the English language. Students may take the same program as a home study course, which usually takes two or three years to complete. The on-campus course is conducted in a laboratory-like setting and covers a range of topics in gemology.

Gemologists and gem cutters are people with mechanical aptitude and the ability to apply craft technology to the precision work of cutting and examining gemstones. They must have manual dexterity to handle gemstones, a variety of tools, and precision instruments. Good hand-eye coordination, patience, and concentration are also needed. Gem cutters also need a sense of design to create a finished gem from a rough-cut stone.

Opportunities for advancement depend a great deal on individual skills and abilities. Gemologists can sometimes advance in retail jewelry by opening their own stores. Gem cutters can expand their business by attracting new clients and marketing their gems successfully.

Job Outlook

While the Bureau of Labor Statistics does not publish

separate employment projections for gemologists and gem cutters, the occupational category of jewelers is expected to increase at about the same rate as the average for all occupations through 2005. Opportunities in retail jewelry are expected to be better than average.

Earnings

Most gemologists work in retail jewelry stores, where the median salary was approximately $28,000 in 1991 according to a *Jewelers' Circular-Keystone* salary survey. Benefits may include tuition reimbursement for work-related courses and discounts on jewelry purchases. Earnings data for custom gem cutters is not available, but most are able to generate a sufficient return on their investment.

Related Occupations

Related occupations involving precision work and craft technologies include dental laboratory technicians, polishers, engravers, and watchmakers and repairers. There are also other specialized occupations involving the fabrication and repair of jewelry, ornaments, and related products.

Sources of Additional Information

- Gemological Institute of America, 1660 Stewart St., Santa Monica, CA 90404. Phone: (310)829-2991 or 800-421-7250.

- Jewelers of America, 1185 Sixth Ave., 30th Fl., New York, NY 10036. Phone: (212)768-8777 or 800-223-0673.

- Manufacturing Jewelers and Silversmiths of America, 100 India St., Providence, RI 02903-4300. Phone: (401)274-3840 or (800)444-MJSA.

- American Gem Society, 8881 W. Sahara, Las Vegas, NV 89117. Phone: (702)255-6500.

- Accredited Gemologists Association, c/o Leo Schmied, 10820 Kingston Pike, No. 24, Knoxville, TN 37922. Phone: (615)966-0580.

GUNSMITHS

At a Glance

- **D.O.T.:** 632.281-010

- **Preferred Education:** Training and experience.

- **Average Salary:** $19,000 to $33,000

- **Did You Know?** Most gunsmiths are self-employed and operate their own gunsmith shops.

Nature of the Work

Anyone who owns a gun is likely to use the services of a gunsmith. Gunsmiths are precision workers who clean, repair, and modify guns of all kinds using hand and machine tools. They work with wood as well as metal. Their work includes making customized rifles, restoring old guns, converting military guns to sporting guns, adjusting trigger mechanisms, and engraving designs on rifle stocks.

Gunsmiths clean and repair firearms by first taking them apart. They dismantle the gun's moving parts, which collectively are called the gun's "action." They clean each part of the action, examining the parts for signs of wear or damage. They replace worn or damaged parts with new parts that they make or obtain from the manufacturer. They may replace or install other parts such as optical sights, pistol grips, recoil pads, and decorative pieces.

Gunsmiths may have to make replacement parts for different reasons. The gun may be so old that the original manufacturer is out of business or no longer has parts in stock. Gunsmiths fabricate parts using a variety of hand and machine tools, including grinders, planers, and millers. They may grind and polish metal parts, immersing them in a bluing salt bath to make them resistant to rust and add a blue color to the metal. After working on a gun, gunsmiths make certain it was correctly reassembled. They test-fire guns to check their strength characteristics, alignment, and assembly.

Gunsmiths may perform other repairs and modifications, including reboring gun barrels to enlarge the caliber of the bore by using a boring machine. They may operate a broaching machine to cut rifling into the barrel of small arms. They may install choke tubes on shotguns to control shot patterns and make trigger pull adjustments. They may recut a gun's stock, adding decorative work and finishing it to a customer's specifications. Other stock work that gunsmiths do for rifles and shotguns includes refinishing wooden stocks by hand sanding and rubbing them with special finishing oils and quick-drying lacquers.

Gunsmiths also fabricate custom guns for their customers, usually working from a set of blueprints. They may draw their own plans based on their own designs. Using a combination of woodworking and metalworking techniques, they perform procedures such as carving the stock, fitting the stock to a magazine-box and trigger-guard assembly, fitting the barrel and action in the stock, and finishing the stock. Using similar techniques, they also restore antique guns and convert military rifles to sporting ones. Using techniques such as carving, inletting, and engraving, they may add decorative touches to guns.

Working Conditions

Gunsmiths typically work indoors under relatively noisy conditions typical of a machine shop. Additional noise is caused by test-firing guns. They normally work a standard eight-hour day, five days a week.

Their work is not physically demanding, but they may stand for long periods of time. They may face some risk of injury from tools and chemicals. They must follow standard safety procedures when test-firing guns.

Employment

The major employers of gunsmiths are gunsmith shops,

gun manufacturers and distributors, and sporting goods stores. Most gunsmiths are self-employed and operate their own gunsmith shops.

Training, Other Qualifications, and Advancement

Gunsmiths are highly trained precision workers who typically have at least four years of training. Some gunsmiths have previous experience in tool and die work or similar occupations. Individuals can begin preparing for a career as a gunsmith by taking high school courses in subjects such as mechanical drawing and drafting, woodworking, shop, mathematics, blueprint reading, and metalworking. Courses in physics and chemistry can also be helpful.

After high school individuals may choose to enroll in a two-year program leading to an associate degree or certificate in gunsmithing, or sign up for an apprenticeship that typically lasts about four years. There are approximately 13 schools in the United States that currently offer two-year degree programs in gunsmithing. A list of schools is available from the Career College Association. Apprenticeships are available with experienced gunsmiths and through gun manufacturers. Another alternative is to sign up for a home-study course.

Two-year degree programs may range from 1,800 to 2,800 classroom hours. Students receive hands-on instruction from experienced gunsmiths in machine shop settings as well as classroom instruction. Courses typically cover the basic subjects of drill press operation, shop math, blueprint reading, hand tools, and grinding, sanding, and polishing. In the machine shop, students learn how to use lathes, milling machines, grinders, and welding equipment. More advanced courses cover stockmaking, ballistics, gun sights, conversions, and trigger assemblies. Longer programs may include classroom study in subjects such as algebra, drafting, metallurgy, and technical report writing.

Gunsmiths must have mechanical abilities and the desire to apply mechanical principles to practical situations. They must be able to use a variety of machine and hand tools, and they must have the necessary patience to do precision work. Woodworking as well as metalworking skills are needed. They must have well developed reasoning skills to be able to interpret and make schematic drawings. Basic math skills are needed, including a knowledge of geometry and algebra.

Gunsmiths do not have a clear path for advancement. Most gunsmith shops are small. Gunsmiths with capital and experience may choose to open their own shop. Custom gunsmiths can advance by developing a reputation for quality work and craftsmanship and building a client base.

Job Outlook

Gun ownership is widespread, and there is a steady demand for the services of gunsmiths. Since it is a relatively small occupation, demand generally outpaces the supply of qualified gunsmiths. However, certain regions may have an oversupply of gunsmiths. Prospects are better for those gunsmiths who are interested in opening their own shops or are willing to relocate.

Earnings

Gunsmiths who are not self-employed can expect to start at $10,000 to $12,000 per year. Nationally, experienced gunsmiths earned between $19,000 and $33,000 per year, with some gunsmiths earning $40,000. Self-employed gunsmiths can earn up to $50,000 annually.

Self-employed gunsmiths must carry liability insurance. They also have to make a substantial investment in machinery and tools.

Related Occupations

Other occupations involving precision mechanical work include tool and die makers, machinists, photoengravers, and tool designers. Other occupations for mechanics and repairers include locksmiths, musical instrument repairers, watch and jewelry repairers, industrial equipment repairers, HVAC (heating, ventilation, and air conditioning) mechanics and repairers, and electrical and electronics equipment repairers.

Sources of Additional Information

- Career Colleges Association, 950 First St. NE, Ste. 900, Washington, DC 20002. Phone: (202)336-6700.

For more information about gunsmithing, contact:

- American Custom Gunmakers Guild, PO Box 812, Burlington, IA 52601-0812 Phone: (319)752-6114.

- National Rifle Association of America, 11250 Waples Mill Rd., Fairfax, VA 22030.

- National Shooting Sports Foundation, Flintlock Ridge Office Ctr., 11 Mile Hill Rd., Newtown, CT 06470-2359. Phone: (203)426-1320.

Plant and Systems Operators

NUCLEAR REACTOR OPERATORS

At a Glance

- **D.O.T.:** 952.362-022

- **Preferred Education:** Licensing by the Nuclear Regulatory Commission

- **Average Salary:** $960 per week

- **Did You Know?** There are 100 nuclear power plants in the U.S.

Nature of the Work

While coal is still the dominant fuel used to generate electricity, the use of nuclear power continues to rise. Today, nuclear power plants generate about 20 percent of the country's energy. Nuclear reactor operators are highly-trained specialists who control the nuclear reactors in these plants.

Nuclear reactors are large furnaces that generate steam through a process called nuclear fission. Nuclear fission occurs when atoms split and release energy. This energy comes in the form of heat, which is used to boil water and produce steam. The steam drives large turbines, or engines, that produce electricity.

Nuclear reactor operators are responsible for the safe operation of the reactors. Working in a control room, they read and control instruments that manage the power level within the reactor. This is done by controlling such factors as the flux level, reactor period, coolant temperature, and rate of flow.

Operators use an intercom system to dispatch orders and instructions to other plant personnel who operate pumps, compressors, switchgears, and water-treatment systems. They may help prepare, transfer, load, and unload nuclear fuel elements. Also, operators may control the operation of auxiliary equipment such as turbines and generators.

Nuclear reactor operators must be concerned with safety at all times. An accident at a nuclear power plant could release dangerous radiation into the surrounding community. An explosion could destroy everything for miles around the plant.

Working Conditions

Nuclear reactor operators often work in air-conditioned control rooms and either stand or sit at a control station. These control rooms are equipped with modern computer equipment that allows operators to assess the status of the reactors. Typically, the work is not physically strenuous, but it does require constant attention. Nuclear plants operate around the clock, so operators often work nights and weekends, usually on rotating shifts. Each shift generally lasts 8 hours.

Rigid safety procedures help keep the work environment in a nuclear plant safe. When working near nuclear reactors, operators wear dosimeters that register exposure to nuclear radiation. Nuclear power plant operators are subject to random drug and alcohol tests.

Employment

According to the Nuclear Regulatory Commission, there were approximately 5,200 licensed nuclear facility operators in 1995. These operators work for utility companies licensed by the NRC to operate nuclear power plants. There are about 100 nuclear power plants in the United States.

Training, Other Qualifications, and Advancement

Nuclear reactor operators must be licensed by the Nuclear Regulatory Commission. To receive a license, operators must pass a written exam and operating test. Extensive training and experience are necessary to pass the examinations.

Operators usually begin their careers as technicians or trainees. Employers generally prefer to hire high school graduates with strong math and science skills for these positions. College-level courses in nuclear technology or nuclear power plant operations are also helpful. Many two year colleges grant associate degrees in these programs.

On-the-job training in a nuclear plant usually comes from licensed operators. Technicians begin by learning basic plant operation followed by intense instruction on simulators. It can take several years of training to gather the skills, knowledge, and experience needed to pass the licensing examinations.

Licensed nuclear reactor operators must pass annual requalifying examinations to retain their license. With further training and experience, nuclear reactor operators may advance to senior reactor operators, who are qualified to be shift supervisors.

Job Outlook

Few new nuclear power plants are expected to be operational by the year 2005, limiting the demand for nuclear power plant operators. However, the number of operators needed at existing nuclear power plants may increase due to changing NRC regulations. Openings will also occur as workers transfer to other occupations or leave the labor force.

Earnings

According to the Bureau of Labor Statistics, nuclear power plant operators earned weekly wages of about $960 in 1992. Senior reactor operators earn 10 to 15 percent more than licensed reactor operators. In addition, nuclear power plant employees usually receive paid holidays and vacations, health and life insurance, and pension plans.

Related Occupations

Other occupations concerned with operating and maintaining equipment associated with generation and transmission of electricity include power plant operator, motor room controller, turbine operator, switchboard operator, substation operator, and hydroelectric station operator.

Sources of Additional Information

* American Nuclear Society, 555 North Kensington Ave., La Grange Park, IL 60525. Phone: (708)352-6611.

* U.S. Nuclear Regulatory Commission, Washington, DC, 20505 Phone: (301)415-7000.

Printing Occupations

DESKTOP PUBLISHERS

At a Glance

- **D.O.T.:** 979.382-026

- **Preferred Education:** Specialized training.

- **Average Salary:** $23,000

- **Did You Know?** Many desktop publishers are self-employed and work for clients on a freelance basis. Others use desktop publishing software extensively in their work and may be known by alternate job titles.

Nature of the Work

Desktop publishing is the technology that allows individuals to combine text and graphics on a personal computer to produce flyers, newspaper pages, booklets, newsletters, advertisements, and other types of published materials.

A wide range of companies, agencies, and organizations have adopted desktop publishing as a relatively quick, cost effective method to produce a large amount of high-quality material for publication. Desktop publishing brings in-house some of the prepress functions, such as design, typesetting, and paste-up, that formerly had to be done by outside specialists. Consequently desktop publishing gives companies, and individuals within a company, greater control over the publishing process and quality of the final product.

Desktop publishing was made possible by the introduction of desktop publishing software for personal computers in 1984. Desktop publishing (DTP) software integrates text and graphics in a what-you-see-is-what-you-get (WYSIWYG) environment. When creating a document for publication, desktop publishers import text files from word processing software into the DTP software. They create style sheets, which control such design elements as type style and size, leading between lines, number of columns, and column width. In some cases they may add codes to the word processing file that correspond to specific styles, so that when the file is imported into the DTP environment the specific styles are automatically assigned.

If specific styles are not assigned through the use of coding, then desktop publishers use a mouse to highlight areas of text and assign styles to those areas. For example, they may highlight a headline using a mouse and assign a type size and style to the headline.

In addition to working with text files, desktop publishers may also import graphic files. When a published document requires an illustration, for example, they may first create a graphic box on the page and then import an illustration into the box from a graphic file. In more complex documents with many illustrations, especially when more than one color will be used in printing the document, the graphic elements may be kept in separate files.

Once the page or document has been formatted and all of the design elements are in place, desktop publishers then have a range of options for producing their output. They may simply print the file using a high-quality laser printer. They may save the file to a disk and send the disk to a service bureau for high-quality output. Finally, they may send the disk directly to a printer, who may be able to print the final publication directly from the disk. In any event, the desktop publishers' output is used to make multiple copies of the document.

Desktop publishers produce a wide range of materials. Virtually anything that can be printed can be produced using DTP software. These include advertising materials, restaurant menus, posters and flyers, direct mail brochures, newsletters, calendars, magazines, and even packaging, slides, and tickets. Desktop publishers provide printers with the final form of the document to be printed, either on disk or as camera-ready artwork. In some cases documents may be photocopied rather than printed, especially when they are being used internally within a company or organization.

In recent years the position of desktop publisher has become a stand-alone job. Many desktop publishers are self-employed and work for clients on a freelance basis. Individuals who use desktop publishing software extensively in their work may also be known as art directors, graphic designers, editors, electronic publishing specialists, and technical writers.

Working Conditions

Desktop publishing is sedentary work that is done under generally quiet conditions in front of a computer terminal.

Desktop publishers may work standard 40-hour weeks, but deadlines and workloads can result in overtime. They frequently work under time pressure to meet publication schedules.

Employment

It is difficult to estimate the number of desktop publishers because of the many different job titles by which they are known. They are employed throughout the United States at many different types of companies, agencies, and organizations. Many desktop publishers are self-employed, serving the needs of one or more clients. The best opportunities for employment and finding clients are likely to be in printing, publishing, and communications centers such as New York, Chicago, Los Angeles, and other urban areas.

Desktop publishers are employed by advertising agencies, public relations agencies, design studios, and other firms involved in graphic and commercial art. Book and magazine publishers, newspapers, and other companies in traditional publishing fields are major employers of people with desktop publishing skills. A growing number of typesetting businesses are employing individuals with desktop publishing skills to provide support for their clients.

Large corporations in virtually any industry may employ desktop publishers to produce their in-house publications and other printed materials. Desktop publishing positions could exist in virtually any department of a large corporation, including human resources, training, advertising and promotion, and administration. Desktop publishers may also work for government agencies that produce materials for publication.

Training, Other Qualifications, and Advancement

Desktop publishers must have some training in design, some knowledge of printing and publishing procedures, and computer skills sufficient to be able to work with DTP software. Many of these skills can be learned in school or on the job. Many employers provide specialized training.

Educational requirements vary depending on type of employment. Desktop publishers usually have at least a high school diploma. Relevant high school courses include computer studies, graphic design, and commercial art. Two- and four-year degree programs provide additional training in areas such as fine arts, design, typography, commercial art, computer studies, communication, and business administration.

Some colleges offer programs leading to a certificate as a desktop publishing specialist. These programs provide training in using DTP software and cover applications in publishing, printing, advertising, and other fields. Other sources of training include software publishers and vendors, private training companies, and vocational schools.

Perhaps more significant than educational qualifications are the desire and ability to learn new techniques, applications, and software. Desktop publishers have to keep up with new design trends and rapid technological developments in DTP software and computer hardware. They can do this by attending professional seminars, reading books and magazines in the field, and networking with other desktop professionals.

Desktop publishers are people who enjoy applying their sense of design to produce materials for publication. Their eye for design must be complemented by careful attention to detail, a knowledge of grammar and spelling, the ability to proofread, and a willingness to work accurately and quickly.

Learning to use more than one DTP software program may result in better employment opportunities. In some employment settings there is an opportunity to advance to supervisory positions. Experienced desktop publishers can set up their own business and become self-employed.

Job Outlook

Demand for desktop publishers is expected to increase as more and more companies realize the savings that are associated with using inexpensive personal computers with graphics capabilities to produce materials for publication. Many traditional prepress positions, such as typesetters and compositors, will be replaced with desktop publishers. The best opportunities will occur in publishing, advertising agencies, public relations firms, large corporations, and in printing trade services industries. Many companies will create separate desktop publishing departments to handle publications for the entire company.

However, competition is expected to remain keen for desktop publishing positions. There will be many qualified individuals seeking employment as desktop publishers. In addition, companies often train their employees in desktop publishing without advertising a new position.

Earnings

Earnings of desktop publishers vary depending on geographic location, nature of employment, and types of services provided. According to *American Salaries and Wages Survey*, the average earnings for desktop publishers were more than $23,000 in 1991. Self-employed desktop publishers can charge a high hourly fee but must pay for their own equipment and supplies.

Related Occupations

Related careers that require art and design skills include art director, graphic designer, and illustrator. Other careers that may involve desktop publishing and word processing include editor, editorial assistant, reporter, and technical writer. Related occupations in the printing industry include prepress precision workers such as strippers, paste-up workers, electronic pagination systems workers, camera operators, platemakers, compositors and typesetters, and photoengravers.

Sources of Additional Information

- National Association of Desktop Publishers, 462 Old Boston St., Topsfield, MA 01983. Phone: (508)887-7900 or (800)874-4113.

- Graphic Arts Technical Foundation, 4615 Forbes Ave., Pittsburgh, PA 15213. Phone: (412)621-6941.

ELECTRONIC PAGINATION SYSTEM OPERATORS

At a Glance

- **D.O.T.:** 979.282-010

- **Preferred Education:** High school diploma

- **Average Salary:** $7.85 to $20 per hour

- **Did You Know?** Electronic paginator is considered the most advanced method of typesetting, and job openings for operators will increase by nearly 80 percent over the next ten years.

Nature of the Work

Newspapers, catalogs, advertisements, and much of the printed materials we read is designed and arranged by electronic pagination system operators.

Electronic pagination is considered the most advanced method of typesetting. Using a computer with a large video display monitor, electronic pagination system operators design and layout pages as they will appear in final print for newspapers, circulars, catalogs, advertisements, and other printed material.

First, electronic pagination system operators study the layout or other instructions to determine the work to be performed and the sequence of operations. Then, they retrieve from computer system memory the text, graphics, and other information that will be presented on the pages.

Electronic pagination system operators format the text by selecting and entering the size and style of the type, page dimensions, column width, appropriate spacing, background colors and shapes, the coordinates of images, and other options. This information is stored in the computer, but may be easily changed or manipulated. Electronic pagination system operators arrange columns, graphics, artwork, photographs, and other images on the page. They may retouch images and colors to enhance, but not alter, the presentation. They may also create special effects such as vignettes, mosaics, and image combining. Once the text and graphics are arranged and the pages assembled, electronic pagination system operators transmit the completed pages for production into film or directly onto plates. From there the pages are printed on paper and the process is complete.

Working Conditions

Electronic pagination system operators typically work 40 hours per week. Those employed by newspaper agencies may work night shifts, weekends, and holidays.

Electronic pagination system operators work in general office areas. They sit at a desk with a computer terminal and display. If not careful, electronic pagination system operators run the risk of computer eyestrain and carpal tunnel syndrome. Electronic pagination system operators also have the pressure of meeting quick deadlines and tight schedules.

Employment

According to the U.S. Department of Labor, there were 18,000 electronic pagination system operators employed in 1992. The majority are employed by newspaper plants and commercial printing firms that print catalogs, newspaper inserts, and advertisements.

Training, Other Qualifications, and Advancement

Most of the actual work performed by electronic pagination system operators is learned on the job. Employers prefer to hire individuals with a high school diploma. Graphic arts and computer experience is highly recommended and can be learned at vocational/technical school or community college.

Employers want electronic pagination system operators to have good oral and written communication skills and good basic math skills.

Job Outlook

According to the U.S. Bureau of Labor Statistics, job openings for electronic pagination system operators will increase 77.9 percent by the year 2005. This is much faster than the average for all occupations. The increasing proportion of page layout and design that is performed electronically will lead to the need for more electronic pagination system operators.

Earnings

Earnings for electronic pagination system operators depends upon the employer, geographic location, and experience. According to *American Salaries & Wages Survey*, electronic pagination system operators earned $7.85 to $20 per hour in 1994. Average earnings range between $8.35 and $17 per hour.

Full-time electronic pagination system operators usually receive benefits that include paid vacations, health and life insurance, and retirement benefits.

Related Occupations

Related prepress precision occupations include typesetters, printing strippers, paste-up workers, job printers, camera operators, platemakers, compositors, and photoengravers.

Sources of Additional Information

- The Graphic Arts Technical Foundation, 4615 Forbes Ave., Pittsburgh, PA 15213.

- Education Council of the Graphic Arts Industry, 1899 Preston White Dr., Reston, VA 22091.

- Graphic Communications International Union, 1900 L St. NW, Washington, DC 20036.

- The National Association of Printers and Lithographers, 780 Palisade Ave., Teaneck, NJ 07666.

Textile, Apparel, and Furnishing Occupations

CUSTOM TAILORS

At a Glance

- **D.O.T.:** 785.261-014

- **Preferred Education:** On the job training

- **Average Salary:** Varies

- **Did You Know?** There were approximately 113,000 custom tailors and sewers employed in 1992, representing approximately 11 percent of all apparel workers.

Nature of the Work

Although more people are buying factory-made clothes these days, some people prefer to have their clothes made specifically for them. Custom tailors provide customers with clothes that have been designed and fitted to suit their customers' individual tastes. Such custom-made garments are usually dress clothing such as suits, dress shirts, topcoats, and overcoats.

Custom-made garments are completely handmade by custom tailors from fabrics and patterns selected by the customer. The first step in making a custom garment such as a men's suit is for the tailor and client to select a fabric. Custom tailors usually have a wide assortment of fabrics from which clients may choose. They are knowledgeable about different fabrics and can help their clients choose the appropriate fabric for the garment's intended use.

Custom tailors also have a selection of patterns and styles for clients to choose from. Tailors use their knowledge of current styles to help their customers choose an appropriate design. In some cases custom tailors may create original designs and patterns based on their customers' preferences.

Once a fabric and style have been selected by the customer, the tailor takes measurements and designs and cuts the patterns. The patterns are then placed over the material. Custom tailors draw outlines of the patterns on the fabric and then cut the fabric by hand using shears. The individual pieces of fabric are then pinned or basted together. Basting is a type of stitching that can be done by hand with a needle or by using a sewing machine.

Tailors may require several fittings while they are producing a custom-tailored men's suit or other type of garment. Once the suit has been assembled prior to final stitching, custom tailors add padding and stiff fabrics to give it shape. They also press the garment to shape it. Once all the fittings have been completed and alterations made, the tailor then puts the finishing touches on the garment.

Finishing operations include using machines to finish seam edges and make button holes and hems. Custom tailors sew on the buttons and other trim and give the garment a final pressing. Altogether it takes approximately two full days of work for a skilled custom tailor to complete a man's tailor-made suit.

Some custom tailors specialize in certain types of garments. Others specialize in certain tasks, such as fitting or cutting. Custom tailors may also do alterations or make repairs on factory-made clothes for their customers. They may supervise other workers.

Working Conditions

Custom tailors generally work in clean, well-lit conditions. Their work is not physically demanding, although frequent reaching and handling requires some manual dexterity. They spend some time talking and listening to their customers. When they are busy or their customers are in a hurry, custom tailors are under pressure to complete their work on time.

Average working hours vary from part-time to standard 35 to 40 hour weeks for custom tailors employed in retail establishments. Tailors with their own shops tend to work longer hours.

Employment

Custom tailors are employed in a variety of retail establishments from large department and clothing stores to smaller specialty shops. Some own their own shops, and a smaller number of custom tailors work out of their homes. A high percentage of custom tailors work part-time. There were approximately 113,000 custom tailors and sewers employed in 1992, according to the Bureau of Labor Statistics, representing approximately 11 percent of all apparel workers.

Training, Other Qualifications, and Advancement

Custom tailors are usually high school graduates who have learned their trade through an apprenticeship, on the job, or through a specialized course of study. It takes four to 10 years of specific vocational preparation to master the art of custom tailoring. Custom tailors who learn on the job may start as sewers or alterers in a small shop, garment factory, or large clothing or department store. They must gain practical experience in apparel manufacture, design, or alteration.

High school courses that can help prepare someone for a career as a custom tailor include tailoring and sewing, art, design, and business subjects. Some larger cities have special high schools devoted to fashion and design, such as the High School of Fashion in New York. Specialized programs in trade schools provide students with knowledge and practical experience in such areas of the trade as cutting room operations, machine operations, hand sewing, and pressing.

Custom tailors must have a strong sense of design and style along with good eyesight and hand-eye coordination to do precision work. To make accurate calculations and measurements, they must have mathematical ability. It's also important that custom tailors have the patience to successfully deal with customers who are sometimes difficult to please.

Custom tailors may advance in their trade by seeking employment at prestigious shops, supervising other employees, or opening their own business.

Job Outlook

Most employment opportunities over the next decade will result from the need to replace people who leave this occupation. According to the Bureau of Labor Statistics, there will be fewer custom tailors and sewers employed in 2005 than in 1992. There will be approximately 11,000 openings annually for custom tailors and sewers, largely due to replacement needs.

Earnings

Since many custom tailors are self-employed or work part-time, there is only limited earnings data available. Geographic location and type of employment affect the earnings of custom tailors. According to *American Salaries and Wages Survey*, individuals employed as tailors or dressmakers earned anywhere from minimum wage to $20,000 per year. Tailors who work for large establishments can expect to receive good benefits, and most stores allow their employees to take substantial discounts on clothes purchased there. Established tailors with their own shops can earn $40,000 or more.

Related Occupations

There are many related occupations in custom sewing, tailoring, and upholstering, including dressmakers, garment fitters, custom shoemakers, shoe repairers, automobile upholsterers, and furniture upholsterers.

Related occupations in mass produced apparel industries include designers, markers, cutters, sewing machine operators, hand sewers, pressers, and inspectors.

Sources of Additional Information

- American Apparel Manufacturers Association, 2500 Wilson Blvd., Ste. 301, Arlington, VA 22201. Phone: (703)524-1864.

- Custom Tailors and Designers Association of America, 17 E. 45th St., New York, NY 10017. Phone: (212)661-1960.

- National Association of Milliners, Dressmakers, and Tailors, 157 W. 126th St., New York, NY 10027. Phone: (212)666-1320.

Woodworking Occupations

CABINETMAKERS

At a Glance

- **D.O.T.:** 660.280-010

- **Preferred Education:** Apprenticeship training

- **Average Salary:** $4.25 to $7 per hour

- **Did You Know?** Job opportunities for cabinetmakers and bench carpenters are predicted to grow 24.5 percent through the year 2005, which is faster than the average for all occupations.

Nature of the Work

Cabinetmakers are carpenters who specialize in building cabinets, counters, shelves, and other fixtures for homes and businesses. They also make customized furniture such as bookcases and tables. Cabinetmakers are generally responsible for a project from start to finish.

Cabinetmakers begin by studying project blueprints and drawings and deciding upon the best method for completing a piece. They choose the proper lumber for the job, taking care to select wood with the appropriate color, grain, and texture. Cabinetmakers then use a ruler to measure the wood according to specifications.

Cabinetmakers use a variety of handtools and woodworking machines to cut and shape the wood. To cut the wood, they often use jigsaws, circular saws, and power saws or mortising machines to make square or rectangular cuts. To trim and shape wood, cabinetmakers use planes, chisels and wood files. They also use electric drills and other hand-held power tools.

Since furniture is not made from one piece of wood, cabinetmakers must fit many pieces of wood together to form a complete unit. They bore holes into the wood using a boring machine, and then insert screws and dowels into the holes. Cabinetmakers may then use glue, nails, and other fasteners to reinforce the connections.

Once the furniture is built, cabinetmakers use sandpaper to smooth the surfaces and joints. This prepares the furniture for finishing. Cabinetmakers apply stain, varnish, or paint to the furniture. They may also install hinges, catches, drawer pulls, and other pieces of hardware.

Working Conditions

Cabinetmakers generally work 40 hours per week. They work indoors, either in a shop or at the customer location. Self-employed cabinetmakers may work out of their homes. Cabinetmakers must wear safety glasses and ear protection when operating dangerous equipment, as well as masks for protection against harmful vapors and toxic fumes when applying synthetic finishes.

Employment

According to the Bureau of Labor Statistics, there were 114,000 cabinetmakers and bench carpenters employed in 1992. Some are self-employed. Others work for shops that build furniture. Self-employed cabinetmakers operate businesses all across the country, but are primarily located in the South. Some cabinetmakers belong to unions.

Training, Other Qualifications, and Advancement

There are several ways to become a cabinetmaker. One way is to work for an experienced cabinetmaker and learn skills through on-the-job training. Another way is by taking courses through a community college or vocational school. These programs generally last two years. Students can gain on-the-job experience at the same time or after completing the program. Some cabinetmakers begin their careers through union-sponsored apprenticeship programs. Apprentices learn through classroom training and on-the-job experience. A formal apprenticeship program takes about four years to complete.

A high school diploma is not required for a career in cabinetmaking. However, cabinetmakers can enhance their job employment opportunities by earning a high school diploma. High school students interested in cabinetmaking should take courses in mathematics, science, shop, woodworking, and English.

Experienced cabinetmakers working in shops can become inspectors and supervisors. Cabinetmakers should have good eye-hand coordination, enjoy working with their hands, and take pride in their work.

Job Outlook

According to the Bureau of Labor Statistics, opportunities for cabinetmakers should be particularly good. Job opportunities for cabinetmakers and bench carpenters are predicted to grow 24.5 percent through the year 2005, which is faster than the average for all occupations. Employment in woodworking industries is highly sensitive to changes in the economy, so job growth may be affected by economic cycles.

Earnings

According to *American Salaries and Wages Survey*, beginning wages for cabinetmakers in California ranged from $4.25 per hour to $7 per hour in 1992. Skilled cabinetmakers earned up to $10.50 per hour. Cabinetmakers with three years experience earned up to $15 per hour. Cabinetmakers in South Dakota earned an average of $5.10 per hour in 1992, while supervisors averaged $6.70 per hour. Wages for cabinetmakers in Minnesota ranged from $7 per hour to $15.78 per hour in 1992.

Related Occupations

Other occupations similar to cabinetmaking include loft worker, wood patternmaker, wood model maker, hat-block maker, molding sander, multiple-drum sander, stroke-belt-sander operator, and cylinder sander operator.

Sources of Additional Information

- American Furniture Manufacturers Association, P.O. Box HP-7, High Point, NC 27261. Phone: (919)884-5000.

- International Woodworkers of America, U.S. AFL-CIO, 25 Cornell, Gladstone, OR 97027. Phone: (503)656-1475.

FURNITURE FINISHERS

At a Glance

- **D.O.T.:** 763.381-010
- **Preferred Education:** High school diploma
- **Average Salary:** $10,500 to $26,000 per year
- **Did You Know?** Furniture occupations are more prevalent in the East and in furniture manufacturing centers such as High Point, NC and Grand Rapids, MI.

Nature of the Work

Furniture comes in a wide range of styles, sizes, and finishes. Many types of finishes can be applied to give furniture a distinctive look, including stain, varnish, shellac, lacquer, and paint. Furniture finishers are precision woodworkers whose tasks range from preparing furniture surfaces to finishing and graining them. They use their knowledge of wood properties, finishes, and furniture styling to finish or restore wood furniture. Furniture finishers may specialize in specific types of furniture or finishes, including pianos and organs and television cabinets, and antique finishes, powder gilder finishes, and whiteners. They may work on new, damaged, worn, or used furniture.

Many steps are involved in finishing pieces of wood furniture. Furniture finishers may begin working on used or worn furniture by disassembling the piece and masking areas adjacent to those areas to be finished. Using handtools they may remove accessories such as handles, knobs, and hinges. Old finishes are removed using steel wool, sandpaper, other abrasives, or solvent and putty knives. Excess solvent may be removed using cloths that have been dipped in paint thinner or sal soda. They may use bleaching acids and neutralizers to restore wood to its natural color.

Furniture finishers prepare wood surfaces for finishing by first applying plastic putty, wood putty, or lacquer stick to fill nicks, depressions, holes, and cracks using spatulas or knives. Sandpaper or powersanders are used to smooth the wood surfaces for finishing. At this point furniture finishers are ready to select the appropriate finishing ingredients, which may include stains, varnishes, shellacs, lacquers, or paints. They mix the finishing ingredients by hand or machine to obtain the desired color, shade, or finish. In some cases they may have to match existing finishes. Once the finishing ingredients have been selected and mixed, furniture finishers apply them using brushes or spray guns. Several coatings may be applied. Each one must dry completely before another coating can be applied. Some sanding and smoothing may be done between coatings.

The final steps in finishing wood furniture are graining and polishing. Furniture finishers create wood grain effects by using graining rollers, combs, sponges, or brushes. They can also simulate wood grain finishes over metal surfaces by spreading graining ink with cheesecloth. After graining they polish and wax the finished surfaces.

Working Conditions

Furniture finishers work indoors under fairly noisy conditions typical of a workshop. They are occasionally exposed to noxious fumes, odors, and other unpleasant atmospheric conditions. They may wear dust or vapor masks or complete protective safety suits, or they may work in spray booths that remove vapors and particles from the atmosphere.

For the most part the work of furniture finishers is light and not physically demanding, although they often have to stand for long periods of time.

Employment

According to the Bureau of Labor Statistics (BLS), there were approximately 37,000 furniture finishers employed in 1992. They generally work in furniture repair shops, in retail furnishing stores, or in furniture manufacturing plants. Some furniture finishers are self-employed.

Furniture repair shops are generally located in heavily populated areas. Furniture makers are more prevalent in the East and in furniture manufacturing centers such as High Point, NC and Grand Rapids, MI.

Training, Other Qualifications, and Advancement

Furniture finishers generally have two to four years of specific vocational preparation that can be learned on the job or through vocational education programs. Some employers offer formal apprenticeship programs in furniture making. Furniture finishers do not need a high school diploma, but graduating could enable them to take vocational education programs in woodworking and furniture making. These programs may be offered at colleges and universities as well as at technical schools and community colleges. Applicable courses include building trades, carpentry, shop math, wood shop, and upholstering.

Furniture finishers are generally mechanically inclined and detail oriented, and have manual dexterity. They must be able to adhere to specifications and standards in their work. Basic math skills are needed to calculate object dimensions, materials needed, and the costs. They must have well developed reasoning abilities to interpret a variety of instructions in written, oral, diagrammatic, or schedule form.

Furniture finishers may have limited advancement opportunities that are dependent on such factors as availability, seniority, and individual skills and abilities. Those working for furniture manufacturers may become inspectors or supervisors. Others may set up their own furniture repair shops. With additional training and an interest in antiques, furniture finishers may become antique furniture restorers.

Job Outlook

The BLS projects that employment of furniture finishers will increase by 18 percent between 1992 and 2005, somewhat lower than the average for all occupations. Employment in all woodworking occupations is highly sensitive to economic cycles. Other factors that may limit employment opportunities in this industry include environmental measures relating to woodworking processes, technological advances, competition from imports, and the increased use of alternate materials.

Earnings

Earnings vary depending on the size and type of employer, geographic location, and individual experience and training. According to the BLS, median earnings for furniture finishers were approximately $20,000 in 1992. Earnings ranged from a low of $10,500 to a high of $26,000 for most workers. In Grand Rapids, Michigan, furniture finishers earned an average of $18,000 annually in 1992. In North Carolina earnings ranged from $8,400 to $18,000 for furniture finishers in 1990, according to *American Salaries and Wages Survey*.

Furniture finishers generally receive a standard benefits package, including paid vacations and holidays, medical insurance, and a pension plan.

Related Occupations

Related occupations in woodworking include patternmakers and model makers, furniture restorers, cabinetmakers, sawyers, and woodworking machine operators.

Sources of Additional Information

- American Furniture Manufacturers Association, PO Box HP-7, High Point, NC 27261. Phone: (919)884-5000.

- Grand Rapids Area Furniture Manufacturers Association, 1500 E. Beltline SE, Grand Rapids, MI 49506. Phone: (616)942-6225.

- United Furniture Workers Insurance Fund, 1910 Airlane Rd., PO Box 100037, Nashville, TN 37224. Phone: (615)889-8860.

Miscellaneous Production Occupations

AUTOMOTIVE PAINTERS

At a Glance

- **D.O.T.:** 845.381-014 and 845.684-014

- **Preferred Education:** High school diploma is not required, but advised; related courses from vocational and technical schools are suggested.

- **Average Salary:** $12,000-$33,000 per year

- **Did You Know?** One of the most difficult aspects of automotive painting is matching the original paint.

Nature of the Work

Painted surfaces of automobiles and other vehicles enhance the vehicle's visual appearance while also providing essential protection for the underlying metals and plastics of the vehicle's body. When these painted surfaces become damaged through accidents or age, they must be repainted by automotive painters working in auto repair shops or similar facilities. Automotive painters also work as manufacturing painters applying paint to new cars in automobile manufacturing plants.

Repainting a damaged vehicle takes several steps. Automotive painters utilize their knowledge of surface preparation and painting techniques to achieve a perfect match. They begin by cleaning, sanding, and applying chemical solutions to prepare and condition the vehicle's surface prior to painting. They use power sanders and sandpaper to remove the original paint or rust. If necessary they may fill in small dents and scratches with body filler.

One of the most difficult aspects of automotive painting is matching the original paint. Quite often the vehicle to be repainted is several years old, and its paint has faded from its original hue. Automotive painters mix and thin the paint and other coatings. They follow a standard formula or color chart. They may use a viscometer that measures the viscosity of the paint to make sure it is the right consistency. They may use spatulas or mixing equipment when mixing and thinning paint.

Some parts of the vehicle may not need to be repainted,

so automotive painters use masking tape and other materials to cover those surfaces, including stainless steel and chrome trim, lights, mirrors, vinyl roofs, and other accessories on the vehicle.

Once the vehicle is ready to be painted, automotive painters usually use a handheld spray gun to apply successive coats of paint. Depending on the surface being painted, they may first apply a coating of primer. Metal surfaces usually take a lacquer or enamel primer, while the plastic surfaces found on newer vehicles take a flexible primer.

Each successive coating of paint must first be completely dry before subsequent coatings can be applied. Automotive painters speed up the drying process by using heat lamps or, in some cases, a special infrared oven. They may regulate controls on the drying equipment to cure and dry paint. Once a coating is dry they sand the surface using power sanders and sandpaper or steel wool to remove irregularities and provide for better adhesion of the next coating.

Prior to applying the final coating of finished paint, automotive painters may apply a sealer over the undercoatings. After the sealer is allowed to dry the final topcoat of paint is applied. If necessary they polish the finished surface using a power buffer or handcloth.

Automotive painters also use brushes to handpaint some areas of a vehicle. They may lay out and paint insignias, pinstripes, and other markings on painted surfaces. They may follow blueprints or other specifications when painting designs and symbols, using stencils, patterns, measuring instruments, brushes, and spray equipment.

Other aspects of automotive painters' work include setting up portable ventilators, exhaust units, ladders, and scaffolding prior to painting. They may have to operate moving and lifting equipment to move materials and supplies to the painting area. In some cases they remove accessories from vehicles, including mirrors and chrome. Some of the duties involved with automotive painting may be done by helpers working under the direction of automotive painters.

Working Conditions

Automotive painters work indoors in areas that usually have special ventilation and lighting. They may wear masks or respirators since they are constantly exposed to fumes, odors, and other unpleasant atmospheric conditions. They may occasionally be exposed to toxic chemicals as well. Establishments where automotive painters work are subject to regulations concerning the emission of volatile organic compounds under the Clean Air Act of 1990, which has helped reduce their exposure to hazardous chemicals.

In some cases automotive painters belong to a union. Self-employed automotive painters may work longer hours if the work requires.

Employment

According to estimates from the Bureau of Labor Statistics (BLS), there were more than 15,000 automotive painters employed in 1992. Approximately 11,000 painting and coating machine operators were self-employed in 1992, and most of those were automotive painters.

Automotive painters work in privately owned collision repair shops, in franchised or specialty automotive paint shops, in service departments of new and used car dealerships, and in automobile manufacturing plants. Other employers include trucking companies, bus lines, and other organizations that repair their own vehicles. Cities and other densely populated areas offer the most employment opportunities for automotive painters.

Training, Other Qualifications, and Advancement

Automotive painters generally have one to two years of specific vocational preparation that is learned on the job. They often start as helpers and learn by experience. Helpers perform tasks such as removing accessories from vehicles, masking surface areas, and polishing finished work. With experience they progress to more complicated tasks, such as mixing paints and using spray guns to apply primer coats.

While automotive painters do not have to be high school graduates, completion of high school allows them to take additional training in automotive body repair and painting at community colleges and vocational or technical schools. Other training programs are offered by paint and equipment manufacturers.

Automotive painters with at least two years of experience may become certified by the National Institute for Automotive Service Excellence (ASE). They must pass at least one certification exam to become certified. ASE offers four different certification exams in the area of automotive body repair and painting, including a multiple-choice exam on painting and refinishing. Passing all four exams earns an ASE Master Body/Paint Technician rating.

Automotive painters are usually mechanically inclined individuals who enjoy applying mechanical principles to practical situations. They must have good vision, including good color vision and depth perception. They must be able to see clearly to work with objects close at hand. Some manual dexterity is required to operate power tools and work with paints.

Automotive painters have limited opportunities for advancement. Some automotive painters open their own shops and become self-employed. With additional training and experience they may acquire new skills and become automotive body repairers.

Job Outlook

While the BLS does not publish separate employment projections for automotive painters, employment in the occupational category of painting and coating machine operators is projected to increase by only 1.2 percent between 1992 and 2005. However, turnover in the industry is moderately high, and employment opportunities will occur as a result of the need to replace workers leaving the occupation.

Employment of automotive painters will also be affected by the impact of regulations under the Clean Air Act of 1990. The cost of new equipment may have an adverse effect on smaller or less profitable repair shops, thus eliminating some employment opportunities for automotive painters. In spite of fluctuations in the economy, automotive painters can expect fairly steady work from automobiles damaged in accidents.

Earnings

The BLS reported that painting and coating machine operators earned a median annual salary of approximately $19,400 in 1992. According to *American Salaries and Wages Survey*, automotive painters earned anywhere from $12,000 in entry level positions to $33,000 annually. In Michigan automotive painters employed by automobile manufacturers earned between $32,500 and $37,000 annually. Earnings depend on factors such as experience, employer, geographic location, and unionization.

Related Occupations

Related occupations include construction painters, furniture and wood finishers, polishers and buffers, automotive body repairers, building maintenance workers, electrolytic metal platers, and hand painting, coating, and decorating occupations.

Sources of Additional Information

For more information on a careeer as an automotive painters, contact:

- Automotive Service Association, 1901 Airport Fwy., Ste. 100, PO Box 929, Bedford, TX 76095-0929. Phone: (817)283-6205.

- Automotive Service Industry Association, 25 Northwest Point, Elk Grove Village, IL 60007-1035. Phone: (708)228-1310.

- National Institute for Automotive Service Excellence (ASE), 13505 Dulles Technology Dr., Herndon, VA 22071-3415. Phone: (703)713-3800.

LAUNDRY AND DRY CLEANING WORKERS

At a Glance

- **D.O.T.:** 361.362

- **Preferred Education:** High school diploma

- **Average Salary:** $8,000 to $26,000 per year

- **Did You Know?** Population growth and personal increases in income will support a growing demand for laundry and dry cleaning services.

Nature of the Work

A wide range of items are handled by laundry and dry cleaning workers. Families may send out their diapers, clothes, and linens for professional laundering or dry cleaning. Work uniforms, towels, gloves, and similar items are handled by industrial laundries. Laundry and dry cleaning workers in hospitals, nursing homes, and other healthcare facilities wash or dry clean clothes, bedding, drapes, and similar items for their patients.

General duties of laundry and dry cleaning workers include marking, washing, finishing, checking, and wrapping articles. Workers may perform some or all of these duties, depending on the size of the operation and the degree of specialization. When items are dropped off workers may sort and mark them so that they can later be matched with a customer's receipt. They are responsible for adjusting controls for different fabrics. They may operate dry cleaning machines, prespot garments, and then spot them again after dry cleaning. Items are then sorted and the count verified according to a laundry or sales ticket. Pressing and inspecting the items for the finished quality is the next step. Other general duties may include mending items and bagging them for storage.

Laundry workers generally tend one or more machines that wash commercial, industrial, or household articles. They sort articles requiring similar treatment and load them into washing machines or direct other workers to do so. They are responsible for how much soap, detergent, water, bluing, bleach, and starch is used, following standard procedures.

Other duties may include washing some articles by hand. Laundry workers may mix solutions of bleach, bluing, or starch and apply them to articles before or after washing. Laundry workers also spot-clean articles to remove heavy stains and/or sterilize them. They may tend to drying machines and give items such as blankets, pants, curtains, and draperies special handling when drying.

Dry cleaning workers use their knowledge of cleaning processes, fabrics, and colors to operate dry cleaning machines. After sorting articles to be cleaned they place them in the drum of the dry cleaning machines. They control the amount of dry cleaning solvent to be used and add liquid soap or chemicals as needed. After the initial dry cleaning is completed, the items are run through an extractor that removes excess cleaning solvent, unless the dry cleaning machine does it automatically. Then the articles are placed in a tumbler that dries them and removes the odor of solvent.

Workers also have to keep their dry cleaning machines clean. By opening valves they can drain the machines of dirty solvent, which goes into a filter tank. They add chemicals to the solvent to aid filtration and start electric pumps that force the solvent through filters that screen lint, dirt, and other impurities. They may empty sludge boxes from the bottom of the tanks. To reclaim the filtered solvent they may operate electric pumps and valves that are part of a distilling system.

In large operations individuals may specialize as markers, dry cleaners, machine washers, spotters, sewers, finishers, inspectors, folders, assemblers, and baggers. In smaller operations one or two workers may perform all of the tasks of dry cleaning and/or laundering. Some operations may specialize in cleaning rugs, furs, leather, or other types of goods and fabrics.

Working Conditions

The work of laundry and dry cleaning workers is moderately demanding physically. They may have to frequently lift bulky loads of up to 25 pounds and occasionally more. They are frequently exposed to high temperatures and may suffer from skin irritations and burns. They may have contact with wet or humid conditions and be exposed to noxious fumes and gases. To some extent these conditions are mitigated by good ventilation. Most work areas are not air conditioned but use large exhaust fans to recirculate air.

Laundry and dry cleaning workers generally have to stand for long periods of time and are engaged in frequent reaching, lifting, and handling of bulky items. They typically work a standard 40-hour week with occasional overtime during busy periods.

Employment

According to the Bureau of Labor Statistics (BLS), there were approximately 162,000 laundry and dry cleaning machine operators and tenders employed in 1992. This figure does not include many of the people employed at dry cleaning "drop shops", which send out items to dry cleaning plants. Including drop shops there are an estimated 50,000 dry cleaning establishments in the United States. Approximately ten percent of all laundry and dry cleaning workers are self-employed.

Laundry workers are employed by commercial laundries, industrial laundries, family laundries, and diaper suppliers. Hospitals, nursing and personal care facilities, hotels and motels, universities, prisons, and other institutions often have their own laundry facilities and employ laundry workers.

Dry cleaning workers are employed by large dry cleaning plants that also have retail shops, wholesale dry cleaning plants that take work from independent shops, and retail shops with their own dry cleaning facilities. In addition, dry cleaning workers may work for some of the same types of institutions as laundry workers. Many dry cleaning plants employ laundry as well as dry cleaning workers.

Training, Other Qualifications, and Advancement

Laundry and dry cleaning workers do not need a high

school diploma, although some employers may prefer high school graduates. They typically receive anywhere from three months to one year of specific on-the-job training. In addition, intensive three-week training courses for dry cleaning workers are offered by the International Fabricare Institute (IFI) in such areas as cleaning, spotting, finishing, management, plant maintenance, and other operations. Other schools offer courses in dry cleaning and related subjects.

Laundry and dry cleaning workers are individuals who enjoy handling machines and equipment or doing manual work. They must be able to adjust to performing repetitive, uncomplicated tasks. They must be able to follow simple directions, observe safety rules, and use their hands, arms, and fingers to move or lift loads of differing weights.

Advancement opportunities for laundry and dry cleaning workers are limited. Some workers may advance to supervisory positions in larger plants. Workers with a knowledge of dry cleaning operations and a business background may open their own establishment.

Job Outlook

According to the BLS, employment of laundry and dry cleaning machine operators and tenders is expected to increase much faster than the average for all occupations between 1992 and 2005. The 162,000 workers employed in 1992 are expected to increase to 237,000 by 2005, an increase of 75 percent.

Population growth and increases in personal income will support a growing demand for the services of laundry and dry cleaning workers. Dry cleaning services will be used more and more by consumers for convenience and to save time. The use of popular fabrics such as wool and silk in clothes and other items gives dry cleaners a steady source of business.

Earnings

Earnings of laundry and dry cleaning workers depend on factors such as job specialty, type and size of employer, and geographic location. Workers in industrial and metropolitan areas generally receive the highest wages. According to the BLS, the median earnings of all laundry and dry cleaning workers were approximately $11,440 in 1990. Michigan reported that laundry workers in hospitals earned between $6.62 and $8.29 an hour in 1990, or between $13,200 and $16,600 per year.

According to *American Salaries and Wages Survey*, laundry and dry cleaning machine operators in several states earned between $8,000 and $11,000 to start and between $15,000 and $26,000 with experience.

Related Occupations

Other laundry and dry cleaning occupations include dyers, feather renovators, fur cleaners, fur glazers, furniture cleaners, and leather cleaners and finishers. Other related occupations include shoe repairers, baggage repairers, hat blockers, laundromat attendants, custom clothing makers, clothing pressers, paper manufacturing machine operators, and pharmacy technicians.

Sources of Additional Information

For more information contact:

- Amalgamated Clothing and Textile Workers Union, 15 Union Sq. W., New York, NY 10003. Phone: (212)242-0700.

- International Fabricare Institute (IFI), 12251 Tech Rd., Silver Spring, MD 20904. Phone: (301)622-1900.

- Textile Care Allied Trades Association, 200 Broadacres Dr., Bloomfield, NJ 07003 Phone: (201)338-7700.

- Textile Processors, Service Trades, Health Care, Professional and Technical Employees International Union, 303 E. Wacker Dr., Ste. 1109, Chicago, IL 60601. Phone: (312)946-0450.

- Uniform and Textile Service Association, 1730 M St. NW, Ste. 610, Washington, DC 20036. Phone: (202)296-6744.

ORTHOTICS AND PROSTHETICS TECHNICIANS

At a Glance

- **D.O.T.:** 712.381-034 and -038

- **Preferred Education:** 1 to 2 years of training

- **Average Salary:**

- **Did You Know?** Orthotics and prosthetics technicians who meet established education or experience requirements may become certified by the American Board for Certification in Orthotics and Prosthetics.

Nature of the Work

Orthotics and prosthetics technicians provide support to prosthetists and orthotists, who provide health care rehabilitation to individuals with disabling limb or spine conditions. Orthotics technicians make orthoses (braces) to provide support for limbs or a spine affected by lack of control, weakness, or paralysis. Prosthetics technicians make prostheses (artificial limbs and joints) for individuals with partial or total absence of limb, such as an arm, leg, foot or hand. The nature of work for both is similar, and an individual may be certified as a Registered Prosthetic-Orthotic Technician (RTPO).

Technicians fabricate the devices to be used by patients. They follow prescriptions and specifications from their supervising orthotist or prosthetist. They select tools and materials to be used in fabricating the device. Their goal is to create a device that has the best possible fit, function, and workmanship as well as one that has the proper appearance. They also repair and maintain orthotic and prosthetic devices. They may fit the device for the patient and give the patient instructions.

Orthotics and prosthetics technicians work with different types of materials. Orthotics technicians tend to work with metals such as carbon graphite and titanium. They may also make braces using steel. They use hand and power tools to bend, form, weld, and saw structural components. They may use hammers, anvils, welding equipment, and saws. They drill and tap holes for rivets and rivet components together. They may shape plastic and metal around a cast of the patient's torso or limbs. If necessary they cover and pad metal or plastic components using layers of rubber, felt, plastic, or leather.

Prosthetics technicians perform similar tasks and work with materials such as wood, foam, various plastics, steel, aluminum, fiberglass, and leather in addition to carbon graphite and titanium. They fabricate metal components in a manner similar to that of orthotics technicians. They may join component parts together by gluing, welding, bolting, sewing, and riveting.

Prosthetics technicians make a wax or plastic impression of the patient's amputated area. Then they prepare a mold from the impression and pour molten plastic into the mold to form the cosmetic part of the prosthetic device. They may create artificial noses, ears, or hands in this way. They assemble layers of padding over the prosthesis and fit and attach an outer covering using a sewing machine, rivet gun, and hand tools. They mix and apply pigment to match the patient's skin color. Using grinding and buffing wheels they clean and polish the finished device.

Orthotics and prosthetics technicians test the devices they have made. The devices must have freely moving parts. The parts must be aligned properly, and the device must have biomechanical stability. Technicians use precision instruments such as plumblines, goniometers, and alignment fixtures to test their finished devices.

Working Conditions

Orthotics and prosthetics technicians work in laboratories where they are subject to moderate to loud noise levels associated with power tools. They may be exposed occasionally to fumes and dust. They frequently have to lift or move objects weighing up to 25 pounds and occasionally as much as 50 pounds. Their work involves frequent to constant reaching, handling, and fingering.

Technicians work under the guidance and direction of prosthetists and orthotists. They occasionally interact with patients when fitting them with a device.

Employment

Technicians are employed by prosthetists and orthotists who have sizeable practices. Although there are such practices throughout the United States, there is a heavier concentration of prosthetists and orthotists in large cities and near major universities than in the rest of the United States. Other employers include clinics, hospitals, and rehabilitation centers. The federal government employs orthotics and prosthetics technicians through the Veterans Administration.

Training, Other Qualifications, and Advancement

Orthotics and prosthetics technicians generally have one to two years of training that is either learned on the job or through a specialized training program. Learning on the job involves working for a prosthetist or orthotist who provides instruction in making devices. Specialized training programs are accredited by the National Commission on Orthotic and Prosthetic Education (NCOPE) and are offered at selected institutions of higher education.

Orthotics and prosthetics technicians may become certified by the American Board for Certification in Orthotics and Prosthetics, commonly known as ABC. ABC offers the following credentials to individuals who meet the education and/or experience requirements and pass a certification examination: Registered Orthotic Technician (RTO), Registered Prosthetic Technician (RTP), and Registered Prosthetic-Orthotic Technician (RTPO).

Orthotics and prosthetics technicians may meet the education and experience requirements for ABC certification in one of two ways. They may be high school graduates or the equivalent and have at least two years of experience working under the supervision of an ABC certified practitioner. If they are high school graduates or the equivalent and have received a formal technician training certificate from a NCOPE accredited program, then no additional experience is required.

The ABC certification examination consists of two parts, written and practical. The written exam covers topics such as componetry, orthometry form interpretation, terminology and biomechanics, anatomy, safety and procedures, and materials. The practical exam assesses skills and knowledge. For orthotics technicians, the practical exam covers metal work, plastic fabrication and finishing, orthometry form interpretation, leatherwork and sewing, shoework, safety and procedures, and delineation and layout. For prosthetics technicians, the exam covers lamination and finish, static and bench alignment, dynamic alignment duplication, thermoplastic fabrication and finishing, leatherwork and layout, safety and procedures, and measurement form interpretation.

Orthotics and prosthetics technicians must have the mechanical ability to do precision work involving accurate measurements and the skills to work with a range of tools and materials. Manual dexterity and good vision are needed to work with objects close at hand.

Unlike other healthcare occupations, technicians can advance to become prosthetists and orthotists after completing additional training and education.

Job Outlook

Orthotics and prosthetics technicians represent a small part of the rapidly growing health services industry. It is estimated that one out of every six new jobs created between 1990 and 2005 will be in the health services sector. More specifically, employment opportunities in the category of "all other" health professionals, paraprofessionals, and technicians not otherwise classified by the Bureau of Labor Statistics are expected to increase by nearly 44 percent between

1990 and 2005.

Several factors may affect employment of orthotics and prosthetics technicians. Among these are an increasing awareness and sensitivity to individuals with disabilities, larger numbers of older people requiring prostheses and orthoses, and the fact that Medicare makes them affordable for senior citizens. In addition, advances in technology are providing for more applications for prosthetic and orthotic devices.

Earnings

Limited data is available for salaries of orthotics and prosthetics technicians. They typically earn somewhat less that prosthetists and orthotists, whose starting salaries in 1990 ranged from $20,000 to $25,000 a year. Hospitals typically pay prosthetists and orthotists from $30,000 to $36,000, with technicians earning less.

Related Occupations

Related occupations concerned with the fabrication and repair of scientific, medical, and technical equipment include instrument makers, model makers, camera and photographic equipment repairers, watch repairers, dental ceramicists, dental laboratory technicians, and opticians. Other occupations involving medical and health technology include biochemistry technologists, microbiology technologists, cytogenetic technologists, histotechnologists, and other medical technologists.

Sources of Additional Information

- American Board for Certification in Orthotics and Prosthetics, 1650 King St., Ste. 500, Alexandria, VA 22314. Phone: (703)836-7114.

Photographic Process Workers

COLOR PRINTER OPERATORS

At a Glance

- **D.O.T.:** 976.380-010

- **Preferred Education:** High school diploma

- **Average Salary:** $330 per week

- **Did You Know?** Color print operators are responsible for turning rolls of film into picture prints.

Nature of the Work

Whether we use them to snap photos during vacations, holidays and special occasions, for documentation purposes, or just for fun, these days nearly every one of us owns a camera. Each of us does not, however, process our own photos. We drop off our roll of film at a photo stand and in anywhere from an hour to a few days we have color prints to look at. Color printer operators are responsible for turning our rolls of film into picture prints.

Color printer operators operate computerized automatic photofinishing equipment that produces color photographic prints from negatives. First, color printer operators load the machine with a roll of printing paper. Then, they read the customer's photofinishing order to find out the film type, the number of prints desired, and delivery date. With this knowledge, color printer operators are able to determine the appropriate machine settings and lens requirements for printing the photos. They adjust machine controls to regulate frame and paper size. The machines that process and print undeveloped rolls of color film usually come in only two size options, 3x5 and 4x6; enlargements and reprints are handled by separate individuals. For print production and billing purposes, the color printer operators key in film type and the number of exposures to be printed.

To make the prints, color printer operators sit at a console and scan and control the video display. They select the best exposure times by operating controls on the console. During this time, the photofinishing machine produces color prints from the negatives. After the photographic paper has been printed, the operators take it from the machine and put it in the developer.

Color printer operators inspect the finished prints for defects, such as smudges, and remove any defects with a brush, cloth, or cleaning fluid. The operators insert the processed negatives and prints into an envelope to return to the customer. Finally, they remove the customer's sales slip from the photofinishing machine's billing unit and attach the slip to the envelope containing customer's negatives and prints.

In addition, color printer operators measure and mix chemicals and transfer solutions to the photofinishing equipment's reservoirs. They also test prints for conformance to color density values.

Working Conditions

Color printer operators typically work 40 hours each week, including Saturdays. Overtime is sometimes necessary during peak times such as the summer and Christmas holidays.

Work is performed indoors. Color printer operators spend a great deal of time sitting at photofinishing machines. The work is repetitious and operators must work at a rapid pace without sacrificing quality.

Employment

According to the U.S. Bureau of Labor Statistics, there were 49,000 photographic processing machine operators employed in 1992. Most color printer operators work for one-hour photo labs and commercial photo labs.

Training, Other Qualifications, and Advancement

Most color printer operators receive on-the-job training from experienced workers or equipment manufacturers. Operating processing machines requires little technical skills and most color printer operators learn their trade within hours. Employers prefer that applicants have a high school diploma.

Color printer operators need to have manual dexterity and good hand-eye coordination. They must be comfortable working with computers and be able to adapt to technological advances.

Job Outlook

According to the U.S. Bureau of Labor Statistics, job

opportunities for computer printer operators will increase 18.8 percent by the year 2005. Most opportunities will result from replacement needs, as the turnover rate for color printer operators is rather high.

Earnings

According to the U.S. Department of Labor, in 1992, earnings of full-time photographic process workers, which includes color printer operators, averaged $330 per week. Other sources claim that earnings for color printer operators usually start at minimum wage and go up to around $7 per hour.

Related Occupations

Other careers in photofinishing include photo checkers, chemical mixers, custom printers, electronic imagers, quality controllers, slide-mounting specialists, paper processing technicians, spotters, sorters, and strippers.

Sources of Additional Information

For more information on a career as a color printer operator, contact:

- Photo Marketing Association International, 3000 Picture Pl., Jackson, MI 49201. Phone: (517)788-8100.

FILM DEVELOPERS

At a Glance

- **D.O.T.:** 976.681-010
- **Preferred Education:** Specialized training
- **Average Salary:** $330 per week
- **Did You Know?** Most employers prefer high school graduates or those with experience in film processing.

Nature of the Work

While amateur photographers generally rely on one-hour photo labs or the local drug store to process their photographs, professional photographers often depend on the specialized skills of film developers.

Film developers are skilled workers who understand every stage of film development. When developing black and white photographs, film developers begin by mixing the chemical solutions needed to develop the film. This includes the developing and fixing solutions. After taking the film from its container, they submerge the film in the developer solution to bring out the latent image. They then immerse the negative in a series of baths. A stop-bath solution halts the developer action, a hypo-solution fixes the image, and water removes the chemicals. The film developer then dries the prints. Film

developers sometimes use machines to perform these steps.

Film developers who produce color photographs, negatives, and slides follow a similar color reproduction process. These workers may be called color-laboratory technicians.

Working Conditions

Film developers work primarily in darkrooms. They generally work 40-hour week, but overtime is common. Film developers may spend much of their time standing. There is light physical activity, but film developers need the use of their arms, hands, and fingers for reaching, handling, and touching delicate materials.

Film developers are frequently exposed to chemicals and fumes. While most darkrooms are well ventilated, film developers must wear rubber gloves and aprons to protect themselves from chemical hazards.

Employment

Photographic process workers held approximately 63,000 jobs in 1992, according to the Bureau of Labor Statistics. About 30 percent of these workers were employed by portrait studios and commercial laboratories that specialize in processing the work of professional photographers. Other film developers work for manufacturers, newspaper and magazine publishers, advertising agencies, and other organizations.

Training, Advancement, and Other Qualifications

Film developers can receive training in high school, vocational-technical institutes, private trade schools, adult education programs, and colleges and universities. Some film developers receive on-the-job training, taking up to three years to become fully-qualified. Most employers prefer high school graduates or those with experience in film processing. Film developers can attend periodic training seminars to improve their skills.

Film developers need good eye-hand coordination, good manual dexterity, and good vision, including normal color perception. They advance in their careers and increase their incomes by gaining experience and improving their skill levels.

Job Outlook

According to the Bureau of Labor Statistics, employment for photographic process workers is expected to grow about as fast as the average for all occupations through the year 2005. While advances in technology may affect job growth for photo processing machine operators, it is unlikely to affect the demand for film developers and other precision photographic process workers.

Earnings

Earnings of film developers and other photographic process workers vary greatly depending on skill level, employer, and geographic location. In 1992, average earnings for full-time workers were approximately $330 per week, or about $17,160 per year.

Related occupations

Film developers need a specialized knowledge of the photodeveloping process. Other workers who have a knowledge of photodevelopment include film inspectors, quality control technicians, microfiche duplicators, darkroom technicians, microfilm processors, and film laboratory technicians.

Sources of Additional Information

- Photo Marketing Association International, 3000 Picture Pl., Jackson, MI 49201. Phone: (517)788-8100.

PHOTOGRAPH RETOUCHERS

At a Glance

- **D.O.T.:** 970.281-018

- **Preferred Education:** High school diploma and special training

- **Average Salary:** $520 per week

- **Did You Know?** Earnings for photograph retouchers can be as high as $30-$50 per hour.

Nature of the Work

An unexpected facial blemish, a stray hair, a shiny forehead, or food particles between the teeth are particularly embarrassing when permanently captured on a photograph—especially wedding and graduation portraits. Fortunately, these problems can be eliminated by photograph retouchers, who are able to skillfully mask minor photographic imperfections.

Photograph retouchers work with photographs such as portraits, wedding photos, and commercial art. Using retouching pencils, airbrushes, and specially blended chemicals and pigments, photograph retouchers retouch photograph negatives and prints to enhance the subject's desirable features and conceal any flaws. (A photograph's subject may be one or more persons or an inanimate object, such as a car.) Photograph retouchers also remove spots and unwanted background objects.

First, photograph retouchers examine the negative or print to determine which features should be accented or minimized. With portraits, for example, photograph retouchers are able to smooth the subject's skin tones, soften facial contours, accent lips and eyes, conceal any blemishes, wrinkles, stray hairs, and subdue harsh highlights. They retouch negatives by shading and painting with a retouching pencil that is able to mark the surface of the negative. Similarly, photograph retouchers use airbrushes and paints on prints to accentuate

lights and shadows and produce clear and attractive features. Increasingly, photograph retouchers are using computer software programs to perform these same functions for retouching photographs.

Photograph retouchers also carefully retouch and restore damaged and faded photographs to rebuild or recreate the missing portions of the original.

Working Conditions

Photograph retouchers usually work about 40 hours per week. They work indoors in clean, well-lighted, and air conditioned offices. Photograph retouchers perform most of their work sitting at a special desk that allows them to best manipulate photographic negatives. They may experience some eyestrain.

Independent photograph retouchers may work out of their own home.

Employment

According to the U.S. Bureau of Labor Statistics, in 1992 there were 14,000 persons employed as precision photographic process workers; this figure includes photograph retouchers.

Employment opportunities for photograph retouchers exist in professional portrait studios, commercial photography studios, custom photography labs, large commercial photo labs, and industrial or corporate in-house facilities. Skilled photograph retouchers may work as independent freelancers, after establishing relationships with professional photographers and processing labs. Jobs for photograph retouchers are concentrated in larger, urban areas.

Training, Other Qualifications, and Advancement

Photograph retouchers learn their trade through vocational/technical college, specialized training seminars, and years of on-the-job training from experienced retouchers. Employers prefer that photographic retouchers have a high school diploma and some knowledge of the field. Many technical and community colleges across the country offer training programs in photofinishing.

Photograph retouchers should have manual dexterity and a flair for detail. They should be able to handle tasks with precision and have patience.

Job Outlook

According to the U.S. Bureau of Labor Statistics, job openings for precision photographic process workers, which includes photograph retouchers, will increase 26.1 percent by the year 2005. This is as fast as average for all occupations. Most job openings will result from replacement needs.

Earnings

Earnings for photograph retouchers vary depending on skill level, experience, employer, and geographic location. According to one source, the earning potential for a professional retouch artists can be as high as $30 to $50 per hour. According to the U.S. Department of Labor, earnings for full-time photographic process workers, which includes photograph retouchers, range from $210 to more than $520 per week in 1992. Because of their skill level, photograph retouchers are probably on the higher end of this range.

Related Occupations

Other careers in photofinishing include color printer operators, photo checkers, chemical mixers, custom printers, electronic imagers, quality controllers, slide-mounting specialists, paper processing technicians, spotters, sorters, and strippers.

Sources of Additional Information

For more information on a career as a photograph retoucher, contact:

Photo Marketing Association International, 3000 Picture Pl., Jackson, MI 49201. Phone: (517)788-8100.

Transportation and Material Moving Occupations

LOCOMOTIVE ENGINEERS

At a Glance

- **D.O.T.:** 910.363-014

- **Preferred Education:** Related experience and six-month training program

- **Average Salary:** $54,000 to $59,000

- **Did You Know?** Locomotive engineers undergo periodic physical examinations and must pass safety and efficiency tests.

Nature of the Work

Coal, grain, forest products, chemicals, metallic ores, and many other essential commodities move along the country's railroads every day. Thousands of skilled workers make the railroad industry a vital part of the national railroad system. Locomotive engineers are among the most highly skilled workers on the railroad.

Locomotive engineers drive locomotives over railroad tracks between distant stations and yards. Most engineers run diesel locomotives; others run electric locomotives. In addition to knowing how to operate locomotives, engineers must understand the signal systems, speed regulations, and the yards and terminals along their routes.

After receiving a starting signal from the conductor, engineers operate the throttle to start and accelerate the train. Since engineers are responsible for the smooth and safe operation of the train, they must be constantly aware of its condition. They monitor the train's performance by watching dials and meters that measure speed, fuel, temperature, battery charge, and air pressure in the brake lines. Engineers watch for obstructions along the track and make adjustments for changes in weather conditions. They also talk to workers in the traffic control center over a radio to receive information or instructions concerning stops, delays, or oncoming trains.

At the end of the run, locomotive engineers use the airbrakes or dynamic brakes to slow and stop the train. They inspect the locomotive for damaged or defective equipment. Minor repairs are made on the spot. Major problems are reported to the engine shop supervisor.

Working Conditions

Locomotive engineers work in engine cabs that can be confining, noisy, and subject to vibration. They must be alert at all times to react to an emergency. Because trains run 24 hours a day, seven days a week, locomotive engineers often work nights, weekends, and holidays. They may be away from home for several consecutive nights depending on the length of the run.

Employment

According to the Bureau of Labor Statistics, locomotive engineers held 19,000 jobs in 1992. Most are employed by railroad companies. Others work for state and local governments and mining and manufacturing companies that operate their own railroad cars. Almost all locomotive engineers belong to a union.

Training, Other Qualifications, and Advancement

Railroads prefer that applicants for locomotive engineer jobs be at least 21 years old and have a high school education. Many engineers began their careers as brake operators, engineer's helpers, conductors, or other railroad workers. Beginning engineers often complete a six-month training program that includes classroom and hands-on instruction in locomotive operation. At the end of the training program, they must pass a test covering locomotive equipment, airbrake systems, fuel economy, train handling techniques, and operating rules and regulations.

Newly trained engineers are placed on the "extra board." Extra board engineers substitute for regular engineers who are absent due to illness, vacation, or other personal reasons. New engineers may wait years until they collect enough seniority to receive a regular assignment.

Engineers undergo periodic physical examinations. They also must pass safety and efficiency tests. Engineers who fail to meet these physical and conduct standards may be restricted to yard service.

Job Outlook

Employment of locomotive engineers is expected to

increase approximately 8 percent between the years 1992 and 2005. In addition to this growth, many additional job openings will arise as workers retire.

According to the U.S. Department of Labor, demand for railroad freight service will grow as the population and economy expand. Opportunities for many railroad workers will be limited, however, because of ongoing reductions in the size of operating crews and improvements in the efficiency of railroad operations. Employment opportunities for locomotive engineers should be slightly better than other rail occupations, because they are less affected by technological changes and reductions in crew size.

Earnings

Earnings of locomotive engineers depend on the size of the train and the type of service. According to 1991 figures from the Brotherhood of Locomotive Engineers, through-freight engineers averaged about $59,600 a year; passenger engineers earned $57,900; and way freight engineers averaged about $54,100.

Related Occupations

Other occupations concerned with transporting passengers and freight by controlling the movement of trains, trolleys, and other railway vehicles include yard engineer, locomotive operator helper, and locomotive firer.

Sources of Additional Information

- Association of American Railroad Information & Public Affairs, 50 F St., N.W., Washington, DC 20001 Phone: (202)639-2100.

- United Transportation Union, 14600 Detroit Ave., Lakewood, OH 44107-4250.

- International Brotherhood of Locomotive Engineers, 1370 Ontario St., Mezzanine Level, Cleveland, OH 44114.

OPERATING ENGINEERS

At A Glance

D.O.T.: 859.683-010

Preferred Education: 1 to 2 years on-the-job training

Average Salary: $26,700

Did You Know? The construction industry together with state and local governments employ approximately 75 percent of all operating engineers.

Nature of the Work

Operating engineers play an important role in the construction industry by operating power-driven equipment needed to build, maintain, and repair roads, bridges, dams, airports, large commercial buildings, sewer lines, and other major projects. The power equipment that they control ranges from relatively simple to very complex. Operating engineers may specialize in one category of equipment, or they may be qualified to operate several different types of equipment. They are often classified according to the machines they operate and are also called heavy equipment operators or construction equipment operators.

Lightweight equipment is the easiest to operate. Lightweight equipment includes air compressors, which are used to run special power tools. Operators keep the compressors supplied with fuel and water. They monitor the pressure level and make minor repairs as needed.

Operating engineers also operate more complex medium-size construction equipment, such as road graders, bulldozers, trench excavators, and scrapers. These machines are used in maintenance and repair work by state and local governments for roads and highways and other projects. They are also used in different types of construction projects to move rocks, trees, earth, and other obstacles.

Operating engineers may work in loading operations as hoist and winch operators. They lift and pull loads using power equipment and may work in manufacturing, logging, transportation, public utilities, and mining in addition to construction.

They also operate excavation and loading machines. These power-driven machines are usually equipped with scoops, shovels, or buckets. They are used to excavate earth and remove loose materials from construction sites. They are used in mining as well as in construction.

Among the heaviest and most complex machinery that operating engineers control are cranes. These machines are used in construction and manufacturing to lift materials, demolish buildings, and drive piles into the ground. Cranes may have different attachments to their booms, including buckets, wrecking balls, and pile drivers, depending on the nature of the project.

Operating engineers typically control their heavy equipment from a cab in the machine itself. They operate the equipment using a combination of pedals, buttons, dials, and levers in the cab. They often need to judge distances, including heights and distances from the ground. In some cases they are guided by hand or flag signals from co-workers.

Other duties and responsibilities of operating engineers include performing routine maintenance on their machinery and equipment. They may also have to make minor repairs.

Working Conditions

Operating engineers generally work outdoors and are subject to extreme weather conditions, including heat, cold, rain, and even snow. They often work long hours during good weather and are laid off during winters. They may be frequently moved from one work site to another. Some construction sites, such as for highways and dams, may be located in remote sites.

The work of operating engineers can be hazardous. Work

often takes place near collapsing excavations, and operating engineers are at risk due to falling objects, snapped cables, and damaged power lines. Operating engineers must follow standard operating and safety procedures to avoid rollovers, collisions, and other accidents while operating bulldozers, scrapers, and other equipment. The heavy equipment they operate also poses additional hazards. In addition to being extremely loud, their machines may emit noxious fumes.

The work of operating engineers is physically demanding. Operating engineers are frequently required to lift objects weighing up to 25 pounds and occasionally as much as 50 pounds.

Employment

According to the Bureau of Labor Statistics, there were 136,000 operating engineers employed in 1992. They are classified as an occupational category within material moving equipment operators, of which there were nearly 1 million in 1992.

The construction industry together with state and local governments employ approximately 75 percent of all operating engineers. These are industries associated with the construction, repair, and maintenance of highways, bridges, dams, harbors, airports, subways, water and sewage systems, and electric power plant and transmission lines. Other industries that employ operating engineers include manufacturing and mining.

Training, Other Qualifications, and Advancement

Operating engineers are usually high school graduates with one to two years of training that may be learned on the job. Recommended high school courses include auto mechanics, mechanical drawing, English, algebra, geometry, and general sciences.

Operating engineers may also learn their trade by enrolling in an apprenticeship program. These programs are three years in length, divided into six-month periods of reasonably continuous employment. In some cases the length of the apprenticeship is performance-based and depends on the ability of the apprentice. The programs are administered by local committees of the International Union of Operating Engineers and the Associated General Contractors of America. Other programs are conducted by the armed forces.

Applicants must be at least 18 years of age and generally not older than 30, although maximum age requirements can be waived. They must be physically able to perform the work of operating engineers and also meet other requirements of the local committee concerning education, aptitude, and ability. In addition they must be high school graduates.

Apprenticeship programs include 144 hours of classroom instruction in addition to three years of trade experience. Classes cover such topics as hydraulics, engine operation and repair, cable splicing, welding, safety, and first aid. Programs are available for crane equipment operators, grading and paving equipment operators, and plant equipment operators.

Training in the operation of some types of equipment is

also available through private vocational schools. The quality of these schools varies considerably, so most experts recommend contacting local employers for their opinions concerning a specific school.

Operating engineers are interested in and have the ability to operate heavy machinery and equipment. They must be able to follow work orders, signals, and oral instructions. Some mechanical aptitude may be needed to perform basic maintenance and repair on their equipment.

In addition they must have better-than-average hand-eye coordination to operate the controls of their machinery. Good vision is also needed, including the ability to judge distances and spatial relationships, the ability to observe a field of vision while the eyes are fixed on one point, and clarity of vision at 20 feet or more. Other characteristics necessary to perform well include alertness, good judgment, and the ability to work with other trades without extensive supervision.

Operating engineers have a clear path of career advancement. After completing an apprenticeship program they become journeymen. If they have exceptional knowledge and ability they may become foremen, directing the work of several journeymen. Foremen can advance to become superintendents, who are in charge of completing projects on time. Superintendents, foremen, and even journeymen with extensive experience can become contractors and establish their own businesses.

Job Outlook

The Bureau of Labor Statistics projects that the 136,000 operating engineers employed in 1992 will increase by more than 17 percent to 159,000 by 2005. This is somewhat lower than the average growth rate for all occupations. Among material moving equipment operators, the highest growth rates are projected for excavation and loading machine operators and grader, bulldozer, and scraper operators. Many employment opportunities will arise from the need to replace experienced workers who leave for other occupations.

Earnings

According to the Bureau of Labor Statistics, the median weekly earnings were $514 for operating engineers in 1992, or approximately $26,700 annually assuming full employment for the year. Entry-level earnings reported in *American Salaries and Wages Survey* ranged from minimum wage in Colorado to $22,000 in Minnesota to $34,000 in Alaska. Experienced operating engineers earned approximately $36,000 in Colorado and Minnesota and more than $70,000 in Alaska.

Earnings depend to some extent on the type of machinery operated as well as geographic location. Work in metropolitan areas tends to pay more than work in rural areas. Apprentices generally start at about half the wages paid to journeymen and progress to where they earn 95 percent of journeymen's wages at the end of three years.

Related Occupations

There are many types of equipment operators in such industries as construction, mining and quarrying, manufacturing, logging, and transportation. Other occupations that involve operating mechanical equipment include industrial truck and tractor operators, bus drivers, manufacturing equipment operators, and farmers.

Sources of Additional Information

- Associated Builders and Contractors, 1300 N. 17th St., Rosslyn, VA 22209. Phone: (703)812-2000.

- Associated General Contractors of America, 1957 E St. NW, Washington, DC 20006. Phone: (202)393-2040.

- International Union of Operating Engineers, 1125 17th St. NW, Washington, DC 20036. Phone: (202)429-9100.

SUBWAY AND STREETCAR OPERATORS

At a Glance

- **D.O.T.:** 910.683-014, 913.463-014

- **Preferred Education:** High school diploma or equivalent

- **Average Salary:** $18.46 per hour

- **Did You Know?** Job opportunities for subway and streetcar operators are expected to grow 57.2 percent through the year 2005.

Nature of the Work

Many American cities have subways and streetcars to transport passengers to their various destinations. Speedy subways and elegant streetcars are guided along their tracks by subway operators and streetcar operators.

Subway operators drive subway trains. Observing the rail signal system, they start, slow, or stop the subway train. They open and close the doors and try to ensure that passengers get on and off the subway train safely. Subway operators make necessary announcements to riders over a public address system. To meet predetermined schedules, subway operators control the amount of time spent at each station. Subway operators recognize common equipment problems. When breakdowns or emergencies occur, subway operators contact their dispatcher or supervisor. During an emergency or breakdown, subway operators evacuate passengers off subway cars.

Streetcar operators drive electric-powered streetcars that transport passengers. They start and stop the streetcar and open and close doors to allow passengers to board or disembark. As passengers board, the collect fares and issue transfers. They give schedule, route, fare, and related information to passengers who request it. They drive streetcars in accordance with traffic regulations, observing traffic lights, pedestrians, and other vehicles on the street to avoid accidents. They record coin receptor readings at the beginning and end of each shift to determine the amount of money received during their shift.

Working Conditions

Subways and streetcars may operate 24 hours a day, seven days a week, thus, subway and street car operators often work night shifts, weekend shifts, and holiday shifts. At times, subway and streetcar operators work multiple shifts. The more undesirable shifts are usually assigned to operators who have the least seniority. Operators may have to contend with disruptive passengers.

Employment

According to the U.S. Bureau of Labor Statistics, there were 22,000 subway and streetcar operators employed in the United States in 1992. Subway and streetcar systems are located in urban areas. Subway and streetcar operators are employed by local public transit authorities.

Training, Other Qualifications, and Advancement

Employers prefer that subway and streetcar operators have a high school diploma. They also usually require operators to be over 18 years of age, have a valid drivers' or chauffeurs' license, and a good driving record without violations.

Some employers require subway and streetcar operators to work as bus drivers for a specified period of time prior to working as a commuter rail operator. New operators receive classroom and on-the-job training that lasts from a few weeks to 6 months. After training, operators usually must pass qualifying examinations covering the operating system. They must demonstrate the ability to troubleshoot problems and handle evacuation and emergency procedures.

Subway and streetcar operators need to be in good health, be able to communicate clearly, and be capable of making quick and responsible judgments.

Experienced subway and streetcar operators can advance to station managers.

Job Outlook

Job opportunities for subway and streetcar operators are expected to grow 57.2 percent, much faster than average for all occupations, through the year 2005. Job growth reflects the installation of new subway systems and the addition of new lines to existing systems. Because subway and streetcar operators receive relatively high earnings and the jobs do not require education beyond high school, applicants face substantial competition for available positions.

Earnings

According to the American Public Transportation Association, in 1992, subway and streetcar operators earned on average $18.46 per hour. Full-time workers usually receive paid vacations, health and life insurance, and retirement plans.

Related Occupations

Other occupations similar to subway and streetcar operators include locomotive engineers, railroad yard engineers, hostlers, locomotive firers, and car barn laborers.

Sources of Additional Information

- American Public Transit Association, 1201 New York Ave. NW, Ste. 400, Washington, DC 20005 Phone: (202)898-4000.

Handlers, Equipment Cleaners, Helpers, and Laborers

AIRPORT UTILITY WORKERS

At a Glance

- **D.O.T.:** 912.663-010

- **Preferred Education:** High school diploma

- **Average Salary:** $11,500 to $22,000

- **Did You Know?** The expected growth in air travel will support the demand for more airport utility workers.

Nature of the Work

Crews of airport utility workers are responsible for all ground servicing of aircraft from the time they land until they take off again. Also known as ramp service personnel or ramp agents, these individuals perform tasks that are largely unnoticed by most airline passengers. Their duties include preparing for the arrival of airplanes, directing airplanes to their gates, loading and unloading baggage and mail, cleaning the aircraft and restocking it with provisions, and preparing aircraft for takeoff. Larger airlines employ specialized ramp agents to handle each function while smaller airlines require workers to perform a combination of duties.

Airport utility workers generally work as part of a crew. Teamwork and communication are essential to the efficient functioning of these crews. Since they often work under very noisy conditions that require ear plugs, workers usually communicate using hand signals or two-way radios. They must follow established procedures and are often guided in their work by lines and letters painted on the ground, or tarmac.

One crew of airport utility workers may prepare for the arrival of an aircraft by getting all of the necessary equipment into position. They place wheel chocks on the ground following painted lines, and prepare the ground power unit (GPU) if necessary, by switching on the power and lowering the ground power cord. Beltloaders and tugs are positioned to be on the right side of the airplane, where the cargo doors are located. Beltloaders are driveable conveyor belts that are used to load and unload baggage and cargo. A tug is a vehicle used to pull baggage and cargo carts. Other tasks that may be performed by airport utility workers fueling, meal provisioning, and deicing.

Once an airplane has landed, a ramp agent known as a marshaler directs the pilot using two orange wands for hand signals. The aircraft follows directional lines that are painted on the tarmac, but the pilot is guided by the marshaler's orange wands. Once the aircraft is parked at the gate, airport utility workers chock the wheels of the nose gear. Other workers watch for foreign objects on the tarmac that could be sucked into one of the plane's engines.

When the aircraft has come to a complete stop, an airport utility worker known as a gate agent drives the jetbridge up to the aircraft door. The jetbridge, or jetway, is a mobile bridge used for deplaning that connects the airplane to the airport gate. The jetbridge must line up with the aircraft door. Once the jetbridge is in position, other airport utility workers hook up the GPU from the jetbridge to the nose section of the airplane. Once the ground power is turned on, the marshaler signals the pilot to turn off the airplane's auxiliary power unit.

The aircraft is now ready for offloading. Airport utility workers drive the beltloaders up to the plane's cargo bins without actually touching the aircraft. All of the cargo, baggage, and mail is then offloaded from the aircraft onto the beltloader.

Airport utility workers who offload baggage must pay careful attention to destination codes on luggage tags. Some baggage on through-flights will stay on the aircraft while others will be transferred to other aircraft to reach its final destination. Baggage that has reached their final destination and need only be delivered to passengers inside the terminal.

In some cases outgoing baggage is loaded immediately onto the aircraft. Airport utility workers keep track of the number of bags going on each flight by marking a baggage stroke sheet. Baggage is put onto the aircraft from gate carts that have been placed at the proper gate by runners. If there is a last-minute gate change, all of the baggage should be in the gate cart so that the gate cart can be transported to the new departure gate.

When an aircraft is ready for departure, airport utility workers use a push tug to push the plane back; at least three workers are needed for pushback. These include a headset agent, who stays in contact with the pilot through two-way radio communication, and one or two wing walkers. Wing walkers carry a set of orange wands for hand signals and check each side of the aircraft for area traffic.

The headset agent directs other workers and gives hand signals to perform different tasks after receiving approval from the pilot. The wheel chocks and ground power unit are removed approximately five minutes before departure. At departure time the gate agent pulls the jetway away from the aircraft and the pilot indicates when the brakes are off and pushback can begin. The headset agent signals the pushtug operator to slowly begin pushing the aircraft. The pushtug operator watches the headset agent and wing walkers for any signs of danger.

Once the departing aircraft is in position to move forward under its own power, the pilot starts the engines. The headset agent requests the pilot to set the brakes, allowing the towbar to be removed by other workers. The pushtug operator tows the disconnected towbar back to the gate area. At this point the headset is disconnected and the ramp agent uses hand signals to guide the pilot away from the gate area. The pilot then takes control of the aircraft.

Additional tasks that may be handled by airport utility workers include fueling, cleaning and deicing, and provisioning and catering. Some of these tasks may be contracted out by airports to outside vendors. Fuelers operate fueling equipment, drive fuel trucks, and deliver fuel to the aircraft. Cleaning may involve dumping lavatories using a lav cart or truck. Airport utility workers attach a hose to the aircraft underneath the lavatories from the lav truck and release the waste to be dumped. Provisioning may require workers to pick up meals from caterers and load them onto aircraft. Workers may also stock beverage carts, clean galley trash cans, and replenish other supplies.

Working Conditions

The work of airport utility workers is usually physically demanding, and quite noisy. They are frequently exposed to weather extremes and are often exposed to the possibility of injury from moving mechanical parts.

Airport utility workers work under constant time pressure to accomplish their tasks according to schedule. Conditions can become very hectic when there are delays due to weather or mechanical problems and several airplanes arrive at the same time. Many airport operations are on 24-hour schedules, requiring airport utility professionals to often work in shifts.

Airport utility workers are regulated by the Federal Aviation Administration and must follow its rules. All ramp agents must wear a uniform.

Employment

According to the Bureau of Labor Statistics (BLS), there were approximately 73,000 helpers, laborers, and hand material movers employed in the air transportation industry in 1992, an occupational category that includes airport utility workers. Most employment opportunities are at major airports located near large cities such as Dallas and Fort Worth, Chicago, Atlanta, Los Angeles, San Francisco, Detroit, Denver, Miami, New York, and Boston.

Training, Other Qualifications, and Advancement

Airport utility workers are generally in entry level positions and do not need to meet any specific educational requirements. They can learn the basics of their job within a week and can become proficient with three to six months of on-the-job training. Most newly hired workers are trained under the guidance of an experienced employee or manager.

Airport utility workers who drive airport vehicles must obtain an airport driver's license in addition to a regular driver's license. Vehicle operators must pass a test on safety restrictions and equipment requirements in order to obtain their airport driver's license.

Workers must be in good physical condition and able to perform routine duties while adhering to standard operating procedures. They must be able to work well with others and communicate by voice or hand signals with their fellow crew members.

Opportunities for advancement are limited. In some cases airport utility workers may advance to supervisory positions.

Job Outlook

According to the BLS, employment of helpers, laborers, and hand material movers in the air transportation industry is projected to increase by nearly 32 percent between 1992 and 2005, faster than the average for all occupations. Overall employment in the air transportation industry is projected to increase by approximately 33 percent between 1992 and 2005.

The expected growth in air travel will support the demand for more airport utility workers. Increases in population, income, and business activity will result in more passenger and cargo traffic. In addition, more aircraft are being purchased for business, agricultural, and recreational purposes.

Earnings

Limited earnings data is available for airport utility workers. According to the BLS, the occupational category of handlers, equipment cleaners, helpers, and laborers earned a median income of about $15,500 in 1992. About half earned between $11,500 and $22,000. In the air transportation industry, aircraft and interior cleaners earned an average of $22,000 in 1994.

Related Occupations

Other air transportation occupations include dispatchers, airport attendants, transportation agents, parachute riggers, and line-service attendants. Other related occupations include boat-loader helpers, boat loaders, water tenders, pond tenders, and gas-and-oil servicers.

Sources of Additional Information

- FAPA: Future Aviation Professionals of America, 4959 Massachusetts Blvd., Altanta, GA 30337. Phone: (404)997-8097.

- Federal Aviation Administration, Public Affairs Office, 800 Independence Ave. SW, Washington, DC 20591. Phone: (202)267-8521.

- Laborers' International Union of North America, 905 16th St. NW, Washington, DC 20006. Phone: (202)737-8320.

AUTOMOBILE DETAILERS

At a Glance

- **D.O.T.:** 915.687-034

- **Preferred Education:** On-the-job training.

- **Average Salary:** $4.50 per hour

- **Did You Know?** The Entrepreneur Group rated automobile detailing one of its *25 Hot Businesses for the Nineties* in 1992.

Nature of the Work

Working as an automobile detailer involves much more than washing cars. Automobile detailing encompasses all aspects of exterior as well as interior car maintenance. Automobile detailers do their work by hand, which involves everything from washing and waxing vehicles to using Q-Tips to clean brake pedals. Detailing does more than keep a car looking brand new; it preserves its value.

Automobile detailers use cleaning solutions, water, cloths, and brushes to wash a vehicle's exterior. They apply wax to the body and use a cloth or buffing machine to create a shine. If they find chipped paint on a car's surface, automobile detailers use touch-up paint to cover the spot. They vacuum the interior to remove loose dirt and debris. To remove tough stains from the interior, automobile detailers use special cleaning agents, applicators, and other cleaning devices. They also apply spot and stain resistant chemicals to preserve and protect upholstery, rugs, and other surfaces. Leather and vinyl surfaces receive special treatment with revitalizers and preservatives.

Under the hood, automobile detailers remove grease and grime from a vehicle's engine with steam cleaning equipment and various cleaning agents. Occasionally, automobile detailers will come across dirt, grease, or grime that does not respond to normal cleaning procedures. When this happens, automobile detailers use their experience and special purpose cleaners to make the engine spotless. Automobile detailers use a spray gun or aerosol can to paint an engine's components.

Automobile detailers sometimes provide additional services, such as installing cellular phones, audio equipment, vehicle alarms, and auxiliary lighting.

Working Conditions

Automobile detailing can be described as "hands-on and on-the-knees work." Automobile detailers use their hands all day long and spend many hours standing, kneeling and climbing in and out of cars. Since the job requires meticulous attention to detail, automobile detailers need good vision. Automobile detailers often work in a loud environment. They may be exposed to harmful chemicals, fumes, odors, or dangerous machinery, so they may need to wear safety clothing, such as gloves and hearing protection.

Employment

According to the Bureau of Labor Statistics, there were 219,000 people employed as vehicle washers and equipment cleaners in the United States in 1992. In addition, there were an estimated 10,000 to 12,000 detailing shops operating in the United States during 1991. Automobile detailers work for automobile detailing shops all across the country. New and used car dealerships also employ automobile detailers. Many automobile detailers own their own businesses.

Training, Advancement, and Other Qualifications

There are no special educational requirements for automobile detailers. Most receive on-the-job training where they learn the occupation's many skills, such as operating a high speed buffer and applying chemical compounds. Automobile detailers should be conscientious, meticulous, precise, and thorough.

Job Outlook

Changes in the automotive industry are creating a boom for automobile detailers. As vehicle prices rise, owners are more interested in keeping their cars longer and extending the value of their original investment. In addition, the use of new materials by auto manufacturers has created a demand for care beyond the scope of typical do-it-yourself car washes.

According to the Bureau of Labor Statistics, the number of vehicle washers and equipment cleaners is expected to grow faster than the average for all occupations by the year 2005. The bureau estimates there will be 52,000 new vehicle washer and equipment cleaner jobs created during that time.

Automobile detailing is an excellent opportunity for individuals wishing to be self-employed. The Entrepreneur Group rated automobile detailing one of its *25 Hot Businesses for the Nineties* in 1992. One option to starting an independent business is an automobile detailing franchise. Franchisers generally cover a percentage of the total start-up expenses.

Earnings

Base wages for automobile detailers can be low. For example, the average wage offered to automobile detailers in South Dakota in 1992 was $4.50 per hour. But like many in the car washing business, automobile detailers can increase their incomes through tips. Wages are better for self-employed automobile detailers. In 1992, the average price for a thorough interior and exterior detailing job averaged $150 per vehicle. Some deluxe jobs cost up to $550.

Related Occupations

Other occupations concerned with parking, cleaning, polishing, lubricating, and servicing vehicles include parking lot attendants, automobile-service-station attendants, automatic car wash attendants, tire repairers, used-car lot porters, steam cleaners, and taxi servicers.

Sources of Additional Information

International Carwash Association, 401 N. Michigan Ave.,

Chicago, IL 60611-4267 Phone: (312)321-5199.

AUTOMOBILE LUBRICATION TECHNICIANS

At a Glance

- **D.O.T.:** 915.687-018

- **Preferred Education:** High school diploma

- **Average Salary:** $4.25 to $13.43 per hour

- **Did You Know?** The auto lubrication business has become so successful that it is dominated by major franchise operations with franchises located throughout the country.

Nature of the Work

Businesses that offer fast, low-cost oil changes are a growing segment of the automobile maintenance industry. With the decline of full-service gasoline stations, oil change specialists have stepped in to serve the needs of consumers who don't have the time, means, or desire to do it themselves. The business has become so successful that it is dominated by major franchise operations with franchisees located throughout the country.

Individuals who perform oil changes and provide other maintenance services are known as auto lubrication technicians. Their primary task is to drain the old oil out of the crankcase, replace the filter, and add new oil. Technicians typically work in bays located below the garage floor. In some cases the car may be raised on a hoist to allow access to the oil filter and crankcase.

There is often more than one auto lubrication technician working on each car. One technician may be assigned to handle the paperwork and greet customers. Other routine services that are performed include checking other fluid levels, such as manual or power transmission, power steering, radiator, and windshield washer fluids. Additional responsibilities may include checking tire pressure, cleaning and/or vacuuming a car's interior, checking the wiper blades, and providing other checks and services on the automobile.

Auto lubrication technicians need to communicate with each other to make sure that the correct oil and filter are used.

Auto lubrication technicians also work for automobile dealers and gas stations. On cars that do not have sealed lubricating systems, technicians may use grease guns to inject grease into the automobile's springs, universal joints, and steering knuckles. They may also lubricate other moving parts using specified lubricants.

Working Conditions

Auto lubrication technicians typically work in shops or garages. The work is moderately heavy and requires frequent reaching and handling. Technicians generally work a standard 40-hour week. Most shops are open during normal business hours and occasionally on weekends.

Employment

There were approximately 6,000 shops specializing in quick oil changes in the early 1990s. They accounted for approximately one-third of the oil change industry. Most retail oil changes are handled by automobile dealers and some gas stations.

Although the Bureau of Labor Statistics (BLS) does not publish separate employment statistics for auto lubrication technicians, there were approximately 190,000 service station attendants including auto lubrication technicians employed in 1992.

Training, Other Qualifications, and Advancement

Auto lubrication technicians do not have to meet any educational or experience requirements. They typically receive on-the-job training that can last from three to six months. They must learn about different car models and the correct lubricating fluids to use.

Auto lubrication technicians are individuals who can perform routine work and have some mechanical aptitude and manual dexterity.

Job Outlook

Although the BLS does not publish separate employment projections for auto lubrication technicians, several factors suggest that the outlook is good. According to an article in the *Washington Post*, January 31, 1995, the average number of cars serviced per day at quick-lube centers has increased from about 40 in 1990 to more than 45 in 1994. The growth of quick-lube centers can be accounted for not only by the convenience it provides, but also by its role in recycling oil. Many oil change shops have begun accepting old oil as a community service, then turning it over to a licensed recycler.

Earnings

According to a 1993 survey by *National Oil and Lube News*, auto lubrication technicians were paid an average of $5.85 per hour, or approximately $11,700 annually. *American Salaries and Wages Survey* reported that lubrication servicers earned between $4.25 and $13.43 per hour in 1994.

Related Occupations

Other automotive service occupations include tire repairers, automobile seatcover installers, industrial garage servicers, and automobile detailers.

Sources of Additional Information

- Automotive Oil Change Association, 12810 Hillcrest, Ste. 213, Dallas, TX 75230. Phone: (214)458-9468.

- Automotive Service Association, 1901 Airport Fwy., Ste. 100, PO Box 929, Bedford, TX 76095-0929. Phone: (817)283-6205.

- Automotive Service Industry Association, 25 Northwest Point, Elk Grove Village, IL 60007-1035. Phone: (708)228-1310.

- Convenience Automobile Services Institute, PO Box 34595, Bethesda, MD 20827. Phone: (301)897-3191.

FURNITURE MOVERS

At a Glance

- **D.O.T.:** 905.663-018, 905.687-014

- **Preferred Education:** High school diploma or GED

- **Average Salary:** Approx. $12.92 per hour in 1992

- **Did You Know?** Furniture movers can advance their careers by becoming estimators or supervisors; some go on to form their own moving companies.

Nature of the Work

The average person will move several times in his or her lifetime, and as stressful as this task can be, most find the simplest way to move is to hire professional furniture movers.

Furniture movers are most often hired by individuals to move furniture and other household goods, such as sofas, tables, book shelves, lamps, dishes, and major appliances. They are also hired by businesses to move office equipment and furniture such as desks, chairs, copying machines, and filing cabinets, as well as sensitive equipment and machinery for industrial plants.

Furniture movers typically work in teams of two to six, depending on the size of the job. At least two movers, a van driver and one or more helpers usually travel per moving van.

In a typical moving job, the head mover or supervisor will come to the customer's home to assess the moving job—the amount of objects (or number of rooms) to be moved, what kind of packing needs to be done, the amount of time the move should take, and the location of the final destination. At this time the mover calculates an estimate and informs the customer how much the move should cost.

Furniture movers must be careful not to break, scratch, or otherwise damage the furniture that they are moving. They make a written inventory of goods moved onto the van to have a record in case something is lost or damaged. Fragile objects such as dishes and lamps and sensitive items such as televisions and VCRs must be carefully wrapped and boxed. They also dismantle items such as beds and tables and lift the heaviest of household goods, such as pianos, sofas, and refrigerators. All boxes and containers are usually labeled with the name of the owner, contents, and where boxes should be placed in new home. Furniture is carefully loaded onto the van, protected with blankets and pads, and secured with fasteners and ropes. Movers must make the most efficient use of space on the van without risking damage to the furniture during the move.

After packing the truck, furniture movers must transport the customer's goods to their final location. They must be careful while driving to avoid damage to the furniture. Interstate travel may involve having the truck weighed at a weigh station.

Once the furniture arrives at the destination, one of the movers may collect the fee from the customer, if the bill has not already been paid. The movers must interact with the customer to determine where furniture is to be placed. Furniture movers may also assemble or reassemble furniture and hook-up appliances.

Drivers often read road maps, calculate mileage, and use hand tools to disassemble and assemble goods. Movers may have more than one customer to move per day.

Some furniture movers are employed by retail stores to deliver furniture and major appliances to customers who have ordered these items. These movers visit several customers daily. They may load the furniture or appliance onto the van the night before delivery. They plan their delivery routes daily. They contact the customer the morning of delivery to give the customer an approximate time of arrival, make certain that the customer will be at home, and verify directions to the customer's home. Once at the customer's home, the mover may assemble the furniture or hook-up appliances. They may also give the customer brief instructions on proper use and care of the item delivered. Before leaving, they get the customer's signature as proof of delivery.

Working Conditions

Movers usually work 40 to 48 hours per week. Federal regulations enforced by the Bureau of Motor Carrier Safety of the U.S. Department of Transportation limit the number of hours truck drivers may drive. Drivers can work no more than 10 hours without being off duty for at least 8 consecutive hours; drivers cannot drive more than 60 hours in any consecutive 7-day period.

The work is rather seasonal because many people move during the summer. The last week of each month is also a very busy time for furniture movers because many people need to move before their leases expire to avoid additional rental payments.

Furniture movers must have enough physical strength and stamina to lift, balance, and carry very heavy objects—including pianos, sofas, and refrigerators—which can weigh hundreds of pounds. They also climb stairs while carrying these things.

Movers handle trucks and vans of various sizes. They spend a lot of time in their moving van, where they often experience heavy traffic, stormy weather, snow, and icy roads. Sometimes night driving is required. There is also the possibility that a moving van will break down and the driver must see that it is repaired as soon as possible. Technology has made the cab of trucks more comfortable, with air conditioning, improved cab design, and comfortable seats.

Employment

According to the Bureau of Labor and Statistics, there were 2,391,000 drivers of light and heavy trucks employed in the United States in 1992; furniture movers are a segment of this group.

Furniture movers are employed by moving companies that provide packing, transporting, and delivery service for individuals and business, and by retail stores that sell furniture and other large household goods. Employers may provide service for only a local region, or may provide interstate or international service.

Training, Other Qualifications, and Advancement

There is no minimum educational requirement to become a furniture mover, although most employers prefer a high school diploma or GED. A valid driver's license is necessary and truck driving experience is desirable. Employers want movers that have good driving records. There are vocational schools that offer training in truck driving courses and many employers provide training in proper packing methods. Good oral and written communication skills and the ability to do basic math is also necessary. Most experience is gained through on-the-job training.

State and federal regulations establish qualifications and standards that furniture movers, especially van drivers, must meet. Drivers of trucks may need a special commercial driver's license issued by their state motor vehicles administration. The U.S. Department of Transportation requires that truck drivers involved in interstate commerce be at least 21 years old; some companies require drivers to be at least 25 years old. Those who have epilepsy or must take insulin for diabetes are not permitted to be interstate drivers. Furniture movers typically need to pass an annual physical exam and have good vision with or without corrective lenses. Federal regulations require employers to perform random periodic drug and alcohol tests. Controlled substances are prohibited unless prescribed by a licensed physician.

Furniture movers may advance by becoming estimators or supervisors for moving companies; some movers form their own moving companies or work as independent contractors for existing firms.

Job Outlook

Jobs in the trucking industry are expected to grow 26 percent through the year 2005. Truck driving occupations have among the largest number of job openings each year. Many openings are the result of increased demand, but most come from natural attrition—experienced workers transferring from the field, retirement, etc. Furniture movers, specifically, can expect a steady demand growth as the population increases and people continue to move.

Earnings

Furniture movers are generally paid an hourly wage. In the early 1990s, furniture movers reportedly earned anywhere between $6 and $22 per hour. Full-time van drivers earned between $18,000 and $30,000 annually, while van helpers earned between $18,000 and $21,000 per year. According to the U.S. Bureau of Labor Statistics, in 1992, truck drivers as a whole earned an average wage of $12.92 per hour.

Wages vary by employer, geographic location, experience, and size of job. Long-distance drivers may be paid by the mile. Work beyond 40 hours per week is typically considered overtime. Full-time furniture movers usually receive paid vacations and holidays, sick leave, health and life insurance, and retirement plans.

Related Occupations

Other occupations that involve transporting and delivering include truck drivers, tow-truck operators, food-service drivers, newspaper delivers, and garbage collectors.

Sources of Additional Information

For more information on a career as a furniture mover, contact:

- National Council of Moving Associations, 11150 Main St., Ste. 402, Fairfax, VA 22030 Phone: (703)934-9111.
- National Moving and Storage Association, 11150 Main St., Ste. 402, Fairfax, VA 22030-5066. Phone: (703)934-9111.
- American Trucking Associations, Inc., 2200 Mill Rd., Alexandria, VA 22314 Phone: (703)838-1700.
- Professional Truck Driver Institute of America, 8788 Elk Grove Blvd., Ste. 20, Elk Grove, CA 95624.

PACKAGE DELIVERY WORKERS

At a Glance

- **D.O.T.:** 230.663-010
- **Preferred Education:** High school diploma
- **Average Salary:** Varies.
- **Did You Know?** Package delivery drivers receive extensive on-the-job training from their employers. They must learn the exact procedures required for making deliveries and pickups.

Nature of the Work

Many companies today compete with the United States Postal Service (USPS) in the package delivery business. Two of the largest are United Parcel Service (UPS) and Federal Express (FedEx). These and other package delivery services offer overnight delivery, second-day air, and other special services in addition to standard delivery. Thanks to package delivery workers, these packages almost always reach their destinations on time.

Drivers who work for package delivery services play a critical role in the overall system of package delivery. Most package delivery services operate on a hub and spoke system whereby packages are routed through different locations until they are delivered to their final destination by a route driver. Hubs are large sorting and distribution centers that are strategically located in different regions of the country.

Before packages reach route drivers, they are sorted at a distribution center. Route drivers pick up packages for their route at local distribution centers and deliver them to businesses or individuals. They collect charges, fill out delivery forms, and issue receipts for deliveries. They also pick up packages from businesses or individuals to be sent out. They may review the sender's paperwork to make sure it is in order. They keep a log of all pickups and deliveries. They may use a hand-held computer scanner to keep track of pickups, deliveries, and other transactions.

Package delivery workers who stick to an established route and drive a car, van, or small truck are also known as route delivery workers or route drivers. This category of delivery workers also includes route drivers who deliver goods to retail outlets or directly to consumers. Goods might include such items as groceries, produce, beer, milk, and laundry. Like other package delivery workers, these kinds of route drivers stick to an established route and service a regular list of customers. However, they are also responsible for making sales and usually work for the company whose goods and packages they deliver.

Other types of package delivery workers serve as messengers and couriers within a specific geographic or metropolitan area. They delivery documents and packages from one business to another within a city or other geographic region. Their main competition comes from facsimile, or fax, machines. However, there are some business transactions that require original documents. Businesses rely on messenger and courier services to deliver such documents and packages in a timely fashion.

Messengers and couriers have duties similar to those of route delivery workers. However, they usually work for courier services that limit deliveries and pickups to a single city, metropolitan area, or geographic region. Unlike most route workers, they usually have to supply their own vehicles and are responsible for their upkeep and maintenance.

Messengers and couriers often start their delivery days from home, receiving instructions over the telephone regarding their first pickups and deliveries. They do not drive an established route and often have to remain on call or in touch with their central office. After making a pickup and delivery, they contact their main office by phone or two-way radio to receive instructions for the next pickup and delivery. Depending on their geographic location, they may use small trucks, vans, automobiles, motorcycles, or bicycles to make pickups and deliveries.

Some messengers and couriers work for specialty courier services or specialize in certain kinds of deliveries. Typical areas of specialty include medical samples, legal documents,

entertainment-related items, and securities. In some cases, specialty couriers must have a background in the field in which they specialize.

Working Conditions

Drivers for package delivery services usually drive a vehicle supplied by their employer. They may wear uniforms. Messengers and couriers, on the other hand, usually supply their own vehicles and are responsible for expenses associated with driving them.

Package delivery workers spend a lot of time outdoors and are subject to all kinds of weather conditions. Their work is not physically demanding, and there are usually weight limits to packages they can deliver. They may use carts or dollies to move packages from buildings to their vehicles.

It is not uncommon for couriers and other package delivery workers to work long hours. However, during the day their work is not always continuous, and they may have down times when they can rest or take a break. Some route workers can stop working early if they have finished their assigned deliveries. Messengers and couriers usually have the option of working full- or part-time, mornings, days, evenings, or weekends. Route workers generally have standard working hours.

Employment

Package delivery drivers are employed by numerous public and private package delivery services. The two largest package delivery services are United Parcel Service (UPS) and Federal Express (FedEx). Most employment opportunities for package delivery drivers are in major metropolitan areas.

According to the Bureau of Labor Statistics, there were approximately 140,000 messengers and couriers employed in 1992. Approximately 16,800 worked for messenger and courier services, and an equal number worked for law firms. Hospitals and medical and dental laboratories also employed about 16,800 couriers in 1992. Other employers include financial institutions and other types of businesses.

These figures do not account for part-time and other employees of courier services. Other data from the Bureau of Labor Statistics indicates there were approximately 6,000 courier services employing some 235,000 individuals in 1992. It was one of the fastest growing segments of the trucking and warehousing industry in the 1980s.

Training, Other Qualifications, and Advancement

Couriers and package delivery drivers do not need a high school diploma, but many employers prefer high school graduates. Package delivery drivers receive extensive on-the-job training from their employers. They must learn the exact procedures that are required for making deliveries and pickups. Keeping accurate records becomes quite important when it is necessary to track misdelivered or lost packages. Since drivers receive extensive training, prior experience is not usually required.

Employers look for package delivery drivers who are

familiar with the geographic area in which they will be working. Drivers must have a current valid driver's license, usually a commercial driver's license or one in a category required by the state in which they are working. Couriers are often required to supply their own vehicles, which must be fully insured. Specialty couriers may have to have some experience or training in the field in which they will be working. For example, couriers who specialize in delivering medical samples and supplies may be required to have experience as lab technicians or medical assistants.

Couriers and package delivery drivers are individuals who enjoy working with business details and performing well-defined tasks. Since they spend a lot of time interacting with customers, they must be able to get along well with others and have good communication skills. Employers look for individuals who are service-oriented and have a lot of energy. The work requires attention to detail, and good handwriting is a plus.

Opportunities for advancement are limited without additional education and training in business management. Good performers are usually rewarded with regular pay raises. In some cases, it may be possible to advance to a supervisory position. Management and administrative positions with package delivery services usually require a college degree as well as experience with package delivery.

Job Outlook

According to the Bureau of Labor Statistics, employment of messengers will remain at almost the same level between 1992 and 2005, increasing by less than 2 percent. Many messengers work in this occupation for only a short time, so most employment opportunities will result from the need to replace other workers.

Earnings

Limited salary data is available for couriers and package delivery drivers. According to figures cited in the April/June 1993 issue of *Courier Magazine*, couriers can earn anywhere from $125 to $975 per week. Some firms pay couriers a straight salary ranging from $7 to $10 per hour including benefits. Other employers pay couriers a commission based on their volume of deliveries. Couriers who are paid on a commission basis earned an average of $400 per week and more than $20,000 per year. Some couriers can make as much as $35,000 to $45,000 per year. However, they are also responsible for expenses associated with their own vehicles, including maintenance, insurance, and fuel.

Package delivery drivers usually receive a straight salary. They are given a company vehicle to drive, so they don't have the same expenses that couriers do with respect to their vehicles. They also receive a standard benefits package that usually includes medical insurance and paid vacations.

Related Occupations

Other sorting and distribution occupations include advertising material distributors, sorters, process servers, mailroom supervisors, library pages, and telephone directory deliverers. Other occupations involving trucking include dispatchers, material movement equipment operators, manufacturers' and wholesale sales representatives, truckdrivers, and traffic, shipping, and receiving clerks.

Sources of Additional Information

- American Trucking Association, 2200 Mill Rd., Alexandria, VA 22314. Phone: (703)838-1700.

- Express Carriers Association, 2200 Mill Rd., Alexandria, VA 22314. Phone: (703)838-1887.

- Messenger Courier Association of the Americas, 9418 Battle St., Ste. 201, Manassas, VA 22110. Phone: (703)330-5600.

SWIMMING POOL SERVICERS

At a Glance

- **D.O.T.:** 891.684-018

- **Preferred Education:** High school diploma

- **Average Salary:** $5 to $8 per hour

- **Did You Know?** Swimming pool services clean and repair swimming pools, hot tubs, and whirlpools.

Nature of the Work

Swimming is a popular activity and, these days, it's not difficult to locate a swimming pool. Swimming pools are found at private residences, apartment complexes, schools, hotels, motels, resorts, health clubs, sport clubs, recreation centers, and retirement communities. Whether public or private, a swimming pool must be cared for on a regular basis. Pools that are not cleaned are not only uninviting but are also unsanitary because microscopic bacteria will contaminate a pool that is not routinely cleaned. Swimming pool servicers clean, adjust, and perform minor repairs to swimming pools and their supplementary equipment.

Cleaning is a routine part of a swimming pool servicer's work day. Servicers remove leaves and other debris from the water's surface by scooping it up with a net on a long pole. The floor and walls of the pool are cleaned using a special underwater vacuum cleaner. Swimming pool servicers scrub off scum and dirt from the pool's tiles and gutters using a stiff brush and detergent. They also clean and unclog the drain strainers and hose down the pool deck.

A very important duty that swimming pool servicers perform is to test the pool water for chlorine level, residual bacteria, and proper pH balance (a measure of acidity and alkalinity in the water.) Public pools may need to be tested hourly, while private pools may need to be tested only two or three times a week. Swimming pool servicers collect a sample of a pool's water in a jar and add a few drops of a special chemical. The chemical causes the water to turn a certain color. This color is compared to colors on a chart to determine the quality of the water. Depending on the water's quality, swimming pool servicers decide the amount of chlorine and other chemicals to add to the pool's water to purify it, making it safe and clean for swimming.

Chlorine and other chemicals are usually added to a pool by pouring them into a feeder in the pool's circulation system. Swimming pool servicers are careful to add the right amount of chemicals because too little will allow bacteria and algae to grow and too much can irritate the eyes and skin. When adding chemicals, servicers wear protective gloves and follow strict procedures for applying the chemicals.

Swimming pool servicers also perform minor maintenance and troubleshooting jobs. They inspect, clean, adjust, and make necessary repairs to the pool's circulation system, pumping equipment, filter system, heating system, pipes, drains, tanks, and gaskets. They check and adjust pressure and vacuum gauges, thermostats, and other instruments. They also replace loose or damaged tile.

Pool openings and closings are another segment of a swimming pool servicer's job. In colder climates, outdoor pools must be closed for the winter. To prepare an outdoor pool for the winter, swimming pool servicers drain a pool's filters and tanks and plug drains and other openings. They remove and store the pump, diving boards, slides, ladders and other pool accessories and equipment. They clean all surfaces and inspect parts. They cover the pool with a heavy, weather-resistant tarp to prevent weather-related damage and to obstruct anything from entering the pool.

In the late spring, when outdoor pools are opened, swimming pool servicers will remove the pool cover, hose down the deck, uncover any drain plugs, and check for cracks, leaks, or otherwise damaged or faulty parts and equipment, and make necessary repairs.

Swimming pool servicers inform the pool's owner or manager of any procedures that will be performed before they are worked on. Servicers also prepare service reports of all chemicals and materials used and work performed.

Swimming pool servicers carry out similar tasks on hot tubs and whirlpools.

Working Conditions

Swimming pool servicers typically work 40 hours each week. During busy times overtime may be necessary. Public pools are usually serviced when they are closed, which means many swimming pool servicers work late evening or night shifts, or early morning shifts. Weekend hours are also common.

Swimming pool servicers work both indoors and outdoors. They do a lot of standing, reaching, bending, and kneeling. They are exposed to chemicals, dirt, scum, algae, and bacteria. They must wear protective clothing, such as gloves, uniforms, and goggles. They do a lot of traveling from pool site to pool site. Most work alone, but some larger jobs may require two servicers. Depending on the size of a pool and the amount of work necessary, servicers may work on only one pool or more than three pools each day.

Employment

Swimming pool servicers are part of the 1.6 million equipment cleaners, handlers, helpers, and laborers employed in the United States in 1992. There were no specific figures available for swimming pool servicers.

Because many swimming pools are located outdoors, swimming pool servicers are most busy in summer months, especially in northern climates where outdoor pools are only open during warm weather.

Most swimming pool servicers are employed by swimming pool service and installation firms. These firms are located throughout the country, but are concentrated in urban areas.

Training, Other Qualifications, and Advancement

Swimming pool servicing requires no formal education, although employers prefer to hire individuals with a high school diploma. Servicers must have a valid driver's license. Beginners receive two to eight weeks of on-the-job training under the supervision of an experienced swimming pool servicer. Servicers may choose to take the Certified Pool/Spa Operators Training Program offered by the National Spa and Pool Institute.

Experienced and highly motivated swimming pool servicers may advance to supervisory positions or open their own swimming pool servicing business.

Job Outlook

According to the U.S. Bureau of Labor Statistics, job opportunities for workers such as swimming pool servicers will increase 26.1 percent through the year 2005. Emphasis on health and physical fitness will increase swimming pool use. Accordingly, there will be a growing number of private and public swimming pools, hot tubs, and whirlpools. Some health departments are concerned about bacterial growth in residential swimming pools and may enforce inspections and regulations.

Earnings

According to *American Salaries & Wages Survey*, in 1994, swimming pool servicers earned $5 to $8 per hour. This would average about $200 to $320 per week. Earnings for swimming pool servicers largely depend upon the employer, geographic location, and the servicer's experience and job efficiency.

Related Occupations

Other structural maintenance occupations similar to swimming pool servicers include pipe changers, dock hands, building cleaners, steam-cleaning machine operators, and chimney sweeps.

Sources of Additional Information

- National Swimming Pool Foundation, 10803 Gulfdale, Ste. 300, San Antonio, TX 78216. Phone: (210)525-1227.

- National Spa and Pool Institute, 2111 Eisenhower Ave., Alexandria, VA 22314. Phone: (703)838-0083.

Dictionary of Occupational Titles Index

The following index lists D.O.T. numbers for each occupation covered in *Speciality Occupational Outlook: Trade and Technical.* These numbers correspond to entries in the Fourth Edition, Revised 1991 *Dictionary of Occupational Titles*, which contains brief descriptions of over 12,000 federally-recognized job titles. Also listed are S.O.C. codes corresponding to the job categories cited in the 1980 S*tandard Occupational Classification Manual.*

Job Title Index

Jobs covered in this edition of *Speciality Occuaptional Outlook: Trade and Technical* appear in **bold**. Jobs covered in the first edition of *Speciality Occupational Outlook: Professions* appear in *italix*. All other occupations are covered in the 1994-95 edition of the *Occuapitonal Outlook Handbook.* Page numbers for each occupation are listed.

M

Y

Z